EU Criminal Law and Policy

Values, Principles and Methods

The EU now possesses a clear legal basis for taking action on criminal law matters and steering the policy and practice of Member States in relation to crime and criminal law. However, for what is now an important area of law, there remains a striking absence or uncertainty regarding its theoretical basis, its legitimacy and its conceptual vocabulary.

This book offers a review of the significance of EU criminal law and crime policy as a rapidly emerging phenomenon in European law and governance. Bringing together an international set of contributors, the book questions the nature, role and objectives of such 'criminal law', its relationship with other areas of EU policy and law, and the established rules of criminal law and criminal justice at the Member State level.

Taking up such subjects as the application of criminal law across national boundaries and in the broader European context, effective enforcement, and the working out of a new European policy, the book helps to structure an increasingly significant subject in law which is still finding its direction. The book will be of great use and interest to researchers and students of EU law, criminal justice, and criminology.

Joanna Beata Banach-Gutierrez is Associate Professor at the Faculty of Law and Administration, University of Warmia and Mazury in Olsztyn. Her research interests are focused especially on international criminal law and procedure, European criminal justice, comparative criminology and crime policy.

Christopher Harding is Professor at the Department of Law and Criminology at Aberystwyth University. His research spans European and international law, criminal jurisprudence, penal theory, the history of crime and the penal system, and the protection of human rights.

Routledge Research in EU Law

Available titles in this series include:

Towards a System of European Criminal Justice
The Problem of Admissibility of Evidence
Andrea Ryan

The Legal Order of the European Union
The Institutional Role of the European Court of Justice
Timothy Moorhead

The Greening of European Business under EU Law
Taking Article 11 TFEU Seriously
Beate Sjåfjell & Anja Wiesbrock

The Habitats Directive in its EU Environmental Context
European Nature's Best Hope?
Charles-Hubert Born, An Cliquet, Hendrik Schoukens, Delphine Misonne, and Geert Van Hoorick

Global Data Protection in the Field of Law Enforcement
An EU Perspective
Cristina Blasi Casagran

Kadi on Trial
A Multifaceted Analysis of the Kadi Trial
Matej Avbelj, Filippo Fontanelli and Giuseppe Martinico

The Judge and the Proportionate Use of Discretion
A Comparative Administrative Law Study
Sofia Ranchordás & Boudewijn de Waard

European Agencies and Risk Governance in EU Financial Market Law
Paul Weismann

EU Health Systems and Distributive Justice
Towards New Paradigms for the Provision of Health Care Services?
Danielle Da Costa Leite Borges

EU Criminal Law and Policy

Values, Principles and Methods

Edited by
Joanna Beata Banach-Gutierrez
and Christopher Harding

Routledge
Taylor & Francis Group
LONDON AND NEW YORK

First published 2017
by Routledge

2 Park Square, Milton Park, Abingdon, Oxfordshire OX14 4RN
711 Third Avenue, New York, NY 10017

Routledge is an imprint of the Taylor & Francis Group, an informa business

First issued in paperback 2018

British Library Cataloguing in Publication Data
A catalogue record for this book is available from the British Library

Library of Congress Cataloging in Publication Data
Names: Banach-Gutierrez, Joanna Beata, editor, author. | Harding, Christopher, 1951- editor, author.
Title: EU criminal law and policy : values, principles, and methods / edited by Joanna Beata Banach-Gutierrez and Christopher Harding.
Other titles: European Union criminal law and policy
Description: Milton Park, Abingdon, Oxon ; New York, NY : Routledge, 2016. | Series: Routledge research in EU law | Includes bibliographical references and index.
Identifiers: LCCN 2016009836| ISBN 9781138914889 (hbk) | ISBN 9781315690605 (ebk)
Subjects: LCSH: Criminal law--European Union countries. | Criminal justice, Administration of--European Union countries. | International and municipal law--Europe Union countries.
Classification: LCC KJE7975 .E965 2016 | DDC 345.24--dc23
LC record available at http://lccn.loc.gov/2016009836

ISBN: 978-1-138-91488-9 (hbk)
ISBN: 978-1-138-61404-8 (pbk)

Typeset in ITC Galliard by
Servis Filmsetting Ltd, Stockport, Cheshire

Contents

Notes on contributors

Joanna Beata Banach-Gutierrez is an Associate Professor at the Faculty of Law and Administration, University of Warmia and Mazury in Olsztyn. She obtained her LL.M. Diploma with a major in Comparative and International Criminal Law and Criminal Justice and a minor in Comparative and European Law at the Faculty of Law, University of Helsinki. She received the degree of Dr.jur. from University of Wrocław. Her research interests are focused especially on international criminal law and procedure, European criminal justice, comparative criminology and crime policy.

Anna Błachnio-Parzych is Assistant Professor at the Institute of Law Studies of the Polish Academy of Science, Warsaw, Poland. She also works at the Research and Analysis Office of the Polish Supreme Court. She has received scholarships from Max-Planck-Institut für ausländisches und internationales Strafrecht in Freiburg. She was also a Herbert Smith Freehills Visitor at the University of Cambridge. Her research interests mainly concern criminalisation, economic criminal law, human rights, quasi-criminal measures and comparative criminal law.

Jennifer Edwards is a post-doctoral researcher in the field of criminal law, criminal justice, medico-legal issues and EU criminal law. She was researcher on the project *Explaining and Understanding Cartel Collusion* at Aberystwyth University (2012–14) and co-author with Christopher Harding of *Cartel Criminality* (Ashgate, 2015).

Vanessa Franssen is Assistant Professor in the Faculty of Law at the University of Liège, Affiliated Senior Researcher at the Institute of Criminal Law at KU Leuven, and a member of the Brussels Bar. She is a graduate in both law and Romance languages (KU Leuven and Paris 1) and was a Fulbright Fellow at the University of Michigan. Her research interests embrace EU criminal law, economic and financial criminal law, the interplay between criminal law and administrative law in Europe, and EU competition law.

Artur Gruszczak is an Associate Professor at the Faculty of International and Political Studies, Jagiellonian University in Krakow. His principal research areas include EU internal security, cross-border police and customs cooperation and

EU intelligence cooperation. Recently he has published *European Intelligence Community: Law – Procedures – Mechanisms* (in Polish). His forthcoming work is *Intelligence Security in the European Union: Building a Strategic Intelligence Community* (Palgrave Macmillan).

Patrick S. Günsberg practises law in Helsinki and holds a doctorate in law from the University of Helsinki. His special area of research relates to the criminalisation of business cartels and the study of economic crime and criminal justice in that field.

Christopher Harding is Professor of Law at the Department of Law and Criminology, Aberystwyth University, Wales, UK. His research spans European and international law, criminal jurisprudence, penal theory, the history of crime and the penal system, and the protection of human rights. His recent research and publications have focused on the criminalisation of business cartels and the development of EU criminal law.

Hendrik Kaptein is Associate Professor of Jurisprudence at Leiden University. He obtained his doctorate at the University of Amsterdam. His special fields of interest are: legal and general argumentation, criminal law and criminal procedure, and legal ethics.

Raimo Lahti is Professor of Law in the Faculty of Law at the University of Helsinki. He was a member of the Task Force on Finnish Criminal Law Reform between 1980 and 1999. His publications have been predominantly in the fields of criminal science (criminal law, criminology and criminal policy), and his recent research interests focus especially on Europeanised and internationalised criminal justice.

Constantina Sampani is a Lecturer in Law at Aberystwyth University. A graduate of Athens University, the University of Kent and Queen Mary University of London, she has also been in legal practice in Athens and London. Her research interests combine commercial law, criminal justice and criminology and in those fields she has also carried out professional training for Lloyds Maritime Academy.

Jarosław Utrat-Milecki is Professor of Criminal Law and Penology at the Faculty of Applied Social Sciences and Resocialisation at the University of Warsaw, founder and Director of the Division of Culturally Integrated Legal and Social Studies at Institute of Social Prevention and Resocialization and founder and Director of the Prof. G. Rejman European Centre for Penological Studies. His research interests mainly concern penal theory and penology. His principal recent monographs, published in Polish, are *Principles of Penology. Theory of Punishment* (Warsaw University Press, 2006) and *Punishment, Theory and Penal Culture: A Culturally Integrated Perspective* (Warsaw University Press, 2010). Recently, he has combined his academic career with work in the Polish justice system.

Begoña Vidal Fernández is Titular Professor of Procedural Law at the University of Valladolid and a full member of the Institute of European Studies (of the University of Valladolid). She has developed her line of research in the field of EU procedural law and judicial civil and criminal co-operation in the European Union, including judicial protection of fundamental Rights.

Harmen van der Wilt is Professor of International Criminal Law at the University of Amsterdam and has served as a judge *ad litem* in the Netherlands. A graduate of the Free University of Amsterdam and of Maastricht University, his fields of research, in which he has published extensively, are international criminal law, criminal law, human rights and criminal law, and criminal law in Europe.

Preface

The main purpose of the discussion contained in this collection is to alert a wide readership to the significance of EU criminal law and crime policy as a rapidly emerging but still little noticed and imperfectly understood phenomenon in European law and governance. As the two editors noted in a recent joint presentation:

> For many, the term 'EU criminal law' will appear as a novel and contestable term, prompting fundamental questions regarding its meaning and legitimacy. But, moving further into the second decade of the twenty first century, its reality cannot be doubted, as a perusal of a number of new textbook titles, reflection on an increasing body of legislation and case law within the EU legal order, and a closer reading of the competence of the EU institutions in the post-Lisbon Treaty on the Functioning of the European Union should quickly demonstrate. Linked to the Area of Freedom, Security and Justice, the EU now possesses a clear legal basis for taking action on criminal law matters and steering the policy and practice of Member States in relation to crime and criminal law issues. The nature and direction of this body of policy and law remains a matter for discussion and analysis, and in particular the relationship between EU and national rules in the criminal law field will remain a matter of on-going development for some time to come.'[1]

These developments have prompted a certain amount of (mainly legal) commentary and scholarship, tending to focus on the more technical aspects of some new measures (for instance, the European Arrest Warrant) or the mechanics the EU legal process (for instance, the working of mutual recognition),[2] and in this way much of the critical discussion to date has been an examination of some of the trees rather than the wood or forest as a whole. Part of the explanation lies in the

1 Harding, C. and Banach-Gutierrez, J. B., 2013, 'EU Criminal Law and the Protection of Human Rights: the Emerging Interface', *Conference Proceedings: 13th International Conference on Human Rights, Elk, Poland, 2013*, Faculty of Law and Administration, University of Warmia and Mazury in Olsztyn, at 101.

2 For instance, Mitsilegas, V., 2009, *EU Criminal Law*, Oxford: Hart Publishing; Peers, S., 2011, *EU Justice and Home Affairs Law* (3rd ed).

way in which this body of policy and law has been developed and appeared as a legal product: incrementally, haphazardly, in a reactive and opportunistic fashion, quietly and obscurely, almost by stealth. Moreover, this has happened via a complex and poorly understood route, especially during the post-Maastricht 'pillars' phase of the EU.[3] For what is now an important area of law, there remains a striking absence or at least uncertainty regarding its theoretical basis, its legitimacy and its conceptual vocabulary. Fundamental questions have not been widely or prominently debated and await clarification – regarding the nature, role and objectives of this body of rules as 'criminal law', and its relationship with other areas of EU policy and law and the established rules of criminal law and criminal justice at the Member State level.[4] These important questions are constitutional, political and jurisprudential rather than technically legal and provide an opportunity to assess the role of criminal law in a contemporary society which is increasingly supranational and international in its policy making and application of law.

The discussion here, collected together in a group of papers, is the first product of a network of researchers in this field who have started to address some of these fundamental issues. The contributors are based in or from a number of European countries (the UK, Netherlands, Belgium, Poland, Finland, Spain, Greece) and so offer perspectives that to some extent may derive from diverse national traditions (for instance, common law, Nordic, central or southern European) but with a consciousness of what may also be held in common across Europe and what has emerged more recently through processes of integration. The network has had the opportunity to exchange and test ideas, and comment on individual drafts, especially through meetings which have now been established as a series at the Natolin European Centre in Warsaw (drafts of a number of the papers collected here were considered at such a meeting in September 2013).

Following that discussion, it appeared that the collection as a whole could be grouped under two main headings for purposes of dissemination. Some of the discussion is very much centred on basic issues of constitutional location, legitimacy and criminal jurisprudence. Conversely there was also discussion of more specific developments as current snapshots of progress or the lack thereof in this field, critical stocktaking rather than theoretical enquiry. It seemed sensible to propose, therefore, a collection in two main parts.

The first part of the volume, under the heading 'The search for principle, direction and coherence', addresses in a critical fashion fundamental questions regarding the nature, role and method of this body of policy and rules. The dominant issues in this debate include the search for legitimacy, on the basis of ideas of subsidiarity, proportionality (Kaptein, Chapter 6), and necessity (in particular, *ultima ratio* or the principle of last resort, Lahti, Chapter 5); the longer-term

3 Baker, E. and Harding, C., 2009, 'From Past Imperfect to Future Perfect? A Longitudinal Study of the Third Pillar', 34 *European Law Review*, 25–54.

4 Harding, C. and Banach-Gutierrez, J. B., 2012, 'The Emergent EU Criminal Policy: Identifying the Species', 37 *European Law Review*, 758.

impact of European and national culture (Utrat-Milecki, Chapter 3) and the issue of addressing existing and deeply embedded national diversity (Harding and Banach-Gutierrez, Chapter 4); and the contest between the normative and instrumental roles of criminal law in a European context (Franssen, Chapter 7). This discussion is set within the context of a momentum generated by the process of supranational integration (Banach-Gutierrez, Chapter 2) but as a process that is not well self-informed as a policy and legal development (Harding, Chapter 8).

The second section, headed 'Stocktaking progress, achievements and prospects', examines particular topics and problems within the field of action, to illustrate some of the challenges and problems that have emerged so far within this legal and political activity. The chapters in this section deal with a range of topical substantive and procedural issues which exemplify European criminal law and criminal justice at its present stage: the handling of intelligence in the criminal law context (Gruszczak, Chapter 11); policy towards victims of crime (Vidal Fernández, Chapter 12); the role of a European Prosecutor and the potential for restorative justice in this context (Sampani, Chapter 13); the idea of a regional criminal jurisdiction (van der Wilt, Chapter 9); the negotiation of criminal justice (Günsberg, Chapter 10); the regulation of economic and business activities through criminal law (Günsberg, Chapter 14, and Błachnio-Parzych, Chapter 15); and tracing and monitoring national implementation of European rules (Edwards, Chapter 16).

The working hypothesis was initially to expect diversity rather than consensus, and uncertainty rather than coherence, as the result of such an exercise and, as work has progressed, that sense of the subject has indeed been confirmed – in itself, both an interesting and problematical outcome. Indeed, such a provisional conclusion is an argument for closer attention to and wider appreciation of the subject, at a stage when its significance is not in doubt, yet direction and purpose remain ambivalent and unpredictable.

1. EU criminal law as an emergent regime: editorial introduction

Joanna Beata Banach-Gutierrez and Christopher Harding

EU criminal law as a contrapuntal entity

Approaching a subject (or subjects, depending on how inter-related we may see them) such as EU criminal law and crime policy, we may be reminded of the lines: 'something is happening here, but you don't know what it is, do you?'[1] and address that comment to the EU and assorted policy-makers and legal experts when they now talk and write about that subject. Over the past thirty years, and perhaps even longer, something has happened in the context of the European Community and Union, taking shape incrementally and in various forms as EU crime policy and criminal law, but without any explicit statement in a Treaty provision or other constitutional instrument of a plan, purpose, or clear delineation of its scope and reach.[2] There is, sure enough, an increasing sense of something significant bubbling away and ready to burst out into the open, especially at such moments when the European Arrest Warrant became a reality, or the idea of a European Public Prosecutor threatened to do so. But basic questions remain without a clear answer: what does it mean more precisely to talk about an EU crime policy and criminal law? In what sense is this matter 'European', in what sense are we talking about 'crime', and in what sense and in which forms can we talk about either 'policy' or 'law'?[3] In more practical terms, in what way may this new, emergent entity be mapped onto the existing space of national, Member State criminal law, criminal justice and penal orders, with their deep legal and

1 Bob Dylan, 'Ballad of a Thin Man', 1965.

2 For a close and penetrating examination of the constitutional basis of EU criminal law, see: Herlin-Karnell, E. (2012), *The Constitutional Dimension of European Criminal Law*, Oxford: Hart Publishing. That account locates the development of EU criminal law very much within a framework of 'constitutional effectiveness'. For a convenient overview of the scope and development of the body of rules comprising EU criminal law, see: Harding, C. (2015), 'EU Criminal Law under the Area of Freedom, Security and Justice', Chapter 32 in: Arnull, A. and Chalmers, D. (eds), *The Oxford Handbook of European Law*, Oxford: Oxford University Press, 837.

3 For some first attempts to answer this kind of question, see: Daems, T., van Zyl Smit, D. and Snacken, S. (2013), *European Penology?*, Oxford: Hart Publishing, in particular, van Zyl Smit and Snacken's first chapter, 'Distinctive Features of European Penology and Penal Policy-Making', posing the question – 'combining human rights and penological evidence: a distinctive feature of European penology?' (at 6).

cultural heritage? And prospectively, what are the direction, purpose and goals of this process? Whereas the European Single Market has a long-standing constitutional statement and treaty foundation, EU criminal law seems to reside in a conceptually amorphous territory of 'justice and home affairs' and 'freedom, security and justice'. The student new to the subject might justifiably feel that it was an enterprise set up to tease and obfuscate – 'yes, this is all very important, but we cannot tell you very well how it is happening, or where it is going.'

The papers brought together in this collection are part of an attempt to inform our understanding of this uncertain and haphazard process. They do so, it may be argued, by largely drawing upon what is there first of all at the national level – concepts, principles and strategies of criminal law and criminal justice – and then what may have emerged therefrom as a wider European heritage and culture of criminal law, as a more immediate basis for an integrated EU project of crime policy and criminal law: thus, from the national, to the more broadly European, to the more specifically European Union. As such, the following contributions may be read in one way as an exercise in Comparative European Criminal Law, since the prevailing methodology of the discussion is comparative, then deductive. That kind of reading of criminal law history and development is clear enough for example in the case of the *ultima ratio* principle[4] – as an urging of parsimony in the use of criminal law and criminal law sanctions, using the latter as a last resort, as traced through the preferred policy option of a number of continental European legal systems, through to a collection of twentieth-century 'European' principles and legal instruments, to emerge then, as a recent example, in an EU policy statement of 2011.[5] As another example, in a way that overlaps with *ultima ratio* as a theme of discussion, there has also over the last fifty years or more been a more substantive debate about the appropriate use of criminal law in relation to business and financial activity[6] and this has been especially relevant to some of the main lines of European integration. Again, it is possible to see the beginnings of such discussion at a national level as a debate on matters often described in criminological terms as 'white collar crime'. A comparison of national approaches to this question then fed into a broader European dialogue, with consequences at that level, whether in the form for instance of transnational co-operation to deal with money laundering[7] or, rather differently, the forging of a supranational non-criminal law but still repressive system of regulation to deal with competition infringements.[8] In terms of policy development and

4 See discussion by Lahti, Chapter 5.

5 European Commission, 'Towards an EU Criminal Policy: Ensuring the effective implementation of EU policies through criminal law', COM (2011) 573 final.

6 See, for example, the discussion by Günsberg, Chapter 15, and by Błachnio-Parzych, Chapter 16.

7 See, for example, the fourth EU money-laundering directive: Directive 2015/849, on the prevention of the use of the financial system for the purpose of money laundering and terrorist financing) O 2015, L 141/73.

8 Most significantly, in relation to the regulation of anticompetitive business cartels (see Günsberg, Chapter 15).

legal history, this is a natural progression, from a national to a supranational, transnational or international level. The methodology is one of extrapolation of supranational (European) solutions from the experience and models of national criminal law by means of comparative evaluation and theoretical testing. The outcome then is something that is worked out from but still usually operating on two tiers, rather like a musical fugue, as something which is polyphonic or contrapuntal in nature.

To use the metaphor of a fugue may be illuminating, in both its senses, musical and psychiatric. A closer examination of much that now counts as EU criminal law may suggest something like a number of themes or melodies being played independently but at the same time, and brought together by a common harmony. This is a complex notion, but may serve to demonstrate and understand the actual complexity of a normative ordering, involving different levels of activity (national and European, at least), some commonality of principle and substance and underlying inspiration, appearing in different forms at those levels, but brought and held together in a single normative framework. In this way, we can appreciate then the 'contrapuntal' character of an instrument such as an EU directive, with both an EU and a national application and differently formulated in those contexts, but representing overall a single and harmonised normative entity. How well it works as such, like the fugue as a musical arrangement, will depend in the end on the harmonious impact of the piece as a whole. In its (now less used) psychiatric sense, the fugue is literally a mental flight into another realm of perception and experience, with some amnesia about how that has happened. That, in a more critical way, may serve as a description of the evolution of EU criminal law – arriving in a different place, but with an imperfect memory or knowledge of the route to that destination. Thus in dictionary definition terms the subject of EU criminal law may first be metaphorically described as 'a melody or phrase introduced by one part, successively taken up by others, and developed by interweaving the parts, gradually built into a complex form, having distinct stages of development and a marked climax at the end'; and, in more critical terms, as 'a loss of awareness of identity, coupled with a flight from one's usual environment, beginning a new life with a loss of memory of the former life.' In this way the metaphor may serve to illuminate both the more positive and some of the negative characteristics of EU criminal law.

The positive dimension of EU criminal law: harmonious melodies

An important aspect of the subject, which needs constantly to be borne in mind, is that EU criminal law and crime policy take form and operate necessarily at two levels (in some ways, but not entirely, like a federal criminal law).[9] Within

9 Perhaps the time is ripe for some more comparative evaluation of the 'federal' (e.g. the US) and the 'supranational' (e.g. European) in this context. There are similarities and dissimilarities, and much springs from culture and political history. But there is an important common antinomy – the tension between the more local and wider communities of experience and interest.

this perception, it is doubtful whether there is much that is very new about EU criminal law. Has the EU policy-making and legal order formulated much in the way of novel concepts and ideas about criminal liability, types of procedure or substantive offences? Little comes to mind, apart from the work on relational processes, necessary in the context of a two-tier and collective enterprise of establishing and applying norms. There may be some novelty in the principles and procedures of harmonisation and norm application – the emergence of the strategies of subsidiarity and mutual recognition, for instance – but this of course is true of much of the project of European integration. A good part of the essential constitutional and legal business of the latter has been working out the relationship between the European and the national. In that way, much of the history to date of EU criminal law has been the evolution of form and method, from 'conventions', to 'framework decisions', to 'directives', from the intergovernmental to the supranational. Recognising that fact helps to explain the difficulty in bringing together the different epistemological communities of national criminal lawyers and European lawyers. The former have struggled to grasp the technicalities of a new relational and constitutional law ('direct effect', 'indirect effect', 'subsidiarity', 'mutual recognition'? *Je ne comprends pas*).[10] The latter, on the other hand, have not, in terms of provenance and experience, been so familiar with the culture and mindset of criminal law. And when 'EU criminal lawyers' (a fair description of the contributors to this work) appear on the scene, what kind of species are these experts?[11] Or, taking a view of this question inside looking out, as EU criminal lawyers, where have we come from and where are we going?

But there is much that is positive and progressive in this sometimes challenging and difficult experience and learning process. Most evidently there are the benefits of comparative analysis, arising from a discourse based on an exchange of experiences and notes, aimed at the evolution of a good common approach to policy development and methods of regulation. This has for long been an important legal goal within the ongoing project of European integration,[12] based on an instinctive understanding of the value and richness of a diverse cross-European heritage. In this way, much of what now counts as European law, whether intergovernmental in its normative character (such as Council of Europe instruments) or supranational (as in the case of the European Community and now the Union), derives from an itinerary of comparative evaluation, and consideration of the respective merits of maintaining diversity or achieving a common position and method. This reading of the evolution and character of 'EU criminal law' is the theme in a number of the contributions in this collection, examining for

10 There are anecdotal accounts, for instance, of the difficulty of securing publication of papers dealing with EU criminal law in national criminal law journals ('too much European law for our readers').

11 One of the present editors (CH), when asked about his specialism and replying, 'the international and European dimensions of crime control, criminal law and criminal justice', has often then encountered blank looks of incomprehension.

12 For instance, in relation to judicial review on the part of the EU Courts, and the development of the EU basic rights protection regime.

instance the longer history of European criminal law and penal heritage (Utrat-Milecki, Chapter 3, and Banach-Gutierrez, Chapter 2) or the resilience of diversity in approach (the 'penal rainbow') as a characteristic of European criminal law and crime policy (Banach-Gutierrez and Harding, Chapter 4).

Looking at the subject through this kind of lens also enables some reflection on what may be distinctively European in this field, and whether it is justifiable to attribute that extra layer of meaning to the vocabulary of European or EU criminal law. Although it was not part of this project to directly compare European and non-European responses to crime, inevitably some such broader comparisons emerged from the discussion in some of the contributions, or at least may be teased from some reading between the lines. One such implied comparison involves the acceptance or otherwise of 'negotiated' criminal justice through processes such as plea bargaining, strongly characteristic of US practice, or alternatively resistance to that approach, as may be found in some continental European legal orders (as discussed by Günsberg, Chapter 10). Comparisons between more aggressive prosecutorial practices and a greater readiness to employ catch-all conspiracy offences and use a harsh system of imprisonment in the US system, and a more dogmatic assertion of defence rights and the importance of the trial and appeal process in Europe have become more frequent.[13] Such discussion lies to a large extent beyond the brief of an examination of EU criminal law, but the latter does inevitably draw upon the impact of common European well-springs of principle and policy: *ultima ratio* (Lahti, Chapter 5), proportionality, subsidiarity and a rights-based moderation of criminal law sanctioning (Kaptein, Chapter 6), reservation regarding an instrumental use of criminal law (Franssen, Chapter 7), the assertion of victims' interests and rights (Vidal Fernández, Chapter 12), and penal moderation in the form of restorative justice (Sampani, Chapter 13). There is some sense at the present moment that EU criminal law, whilst having predominantly pragmatic and instrumental origins (Franssen, Chapter 7), now stands at a kind of crossroads, with some opportunity and choice to build upon the above listed European sensibilities and preferences and use the political and legal authority of the Union to assert a more definitely rights-based, moderated and variegated approach to criminal law. If opportunities for a specialised European criminal jurisdiction (van der Wilt, Chapter 9) and better-informed policy-making (Harding, Chapter 8) are realised, then a more distinctively principled rather than pragmatic EU system of criminal law may emerge.

The above speculation is one kind of fugue, as a work in progress. Its success, as in musical terms, would depend on a harmonious interweaving of contrapuntal melodies. More exactly, that will depend on both a canny extrapolation from

13 For a graphic recent comparison, see the account of the case of Romano Pisciotti as an illustration of the different legal and enforcement cultures in the US and in Europe, in relation an extradited white-collar offender: MLex interview with Roman Pisciotti, *A Cautionary Tale for White-Collar Criminals*, December 2015. See, more generally, the conclusions in the study by Harding and Edwards: Harding, C. and Edwards, J. (2015), *Cartel Criminality: The Mythology and Pathology of Business Collusion*, Farnham: Ashgate Publishing.

existing sources, as described in the list just above, and then a strategically effective return of principle to application at the national level in disparate contexts (Gruszczak, Chapter 11, Günsberg, Chapter 14, and Błachnio-Parzych, Chapter 15). But that kind of return of distilled principle and policy to the national level may not be easily transparent or readable (Edwards, Chapter 16, and Harding, Chapter 8), Thus, analysing the dynamic of EU criminal law is likely to remain a matter of debate, and assessing its impact also a matter of some speculation – and this observation returns our discussion to the more negative dimension of the subject, its uncertain identity.

Negative impressions: an uncertain role and future

It would be fair to forewarn the reader of this collection that there will emerge from its reading a certain degree of consensus and shared vision from the contributions – a sense of a moment of opportunity for a bold new world of criminal law and crime policy. To some extent that may be read as an ideological preference and optimistic gloss. But the more negative metaphor of fugue, embodying a process of flight, associated with unstable identity and memory, could provide another line of analysis and interpretation. Lurking in some of the discussion here is also a more doomy appreciation of unresolved tension, antinomy and argument. For all its talk of *ultima ratio* and alternatives to criminal liability and sanctions and informed policy-making, is the European Commission's 2011 Communication[14] really as much or more about the instrumental – the implementation and enforcement of certain cherished economic and crime control imperatives, as embodied in the competence setting Article 83 of the Treaty on the Functioning of the European Union (TFEU)? The strong fear among many commentators in the earlier years of this century was that the EU criminal law and crime policy agenda was mainly a vehicle of crime control, as in Jonathan Simon's argument of 'governing through crime'.[15] That perception returns our discussion to an analysis of EU criminal law as reactive (especially to perceived transnational terrorist and organised crime threats via uncontrollable person and information flows) and traumatic, rather than an ordered, considered and principled development of a greenfield site. The pessimistic muse in this line of analysis transfers a long-standing apprehension regarding the sinister aspect of State power to the potentially more alarming exercise of collective State power via the European Union, as a larger and more remote agency of authority and legal control. In that way, we should admit that the subject is at a crossroads and both the short- and middle-term future (without idly speculating on a long-term future) remain unpredictable.

14 See note 4 above.

15 Simon, J. (2007), *Governing Through Crime: How the War on Crime Transformed American Democracy and Created a Culture of Fear*, Oxford: Oxford University Press. See also Estella Baker's reflection on the extent to which that argument may be applicable to the situation in Europe: Baker, E. (2010), 'Governing Through Crime – the Case of the European Union', *European Journal of Criminology*, 7, 187.

To an extent it may be argued that some of this tension is naturally at the heart of the subject. As Herbert Packer sagely asserted[16] half a century ago, criminal law will always represent a balancing act between crime control and the protection of rights, and that may be for the most part a healthy tension. The other kind of contest identified here may be less healthy – that between an instrumental inspiration for criminal law and its expressive role in the guarantee of society's core values (Franssen, Chapter 7). Within that contest, EU criminal law may show some origins in contestable instrumental values. A recovery, validation and empowerment of the expressive function of criminal law (what John Langbein once referred to as the 'rehabilitation of the criminal sanction')[17] may provide a bolder and more exciting – and in an early twenty-first-century context – more significant project for EU criminal law as we all ponder its future direction.

16 Packer, H. L. (1968), *The Limits of the Criminal Sanction,* Stanford, CA: Stanford University Press.

17 Langbein, J. H. (1973), 'Controlling Prosecutorial Discretion in Germany', *University of Chicago Law Review*, 41, 439, at 451–5.

Part I

The search for principle, direction and coherence

2 Supranational integration in criminal matters within the European Union: what could the future bring?

Joanna Beata Banach-Gutierrez

Introduction

This chapter will briefly illustrate the evolution of judicial co-operation in criminal matters within the framework of the European Union (EU). Within the perspective of *communitarisation*, there is a visible trend aiming at a supranational integration in criminal matters. This long-term process concerns both normative and institutional questions at the EU level. In other words, there is a growing European (EU) system of criminal justice as a kind of supranational system *sui generis* that goes beyond national sovereignty and national borders. Such an approach has an impact on the domestic legal orders of the EU Member States. Even though such a system may express the elements of a supremacy doctrine (primacy), still there is some room left for the European identity and legal pluralism of the domestic laws.[1]

Generally, in developments of European (EU) criminal justice, one may distinguish three main phases. The first phase is a period before the Maastricht Treaty entered into force in 1992. Then, one may indicate the time after the Maastricht Treaty entered into force, and further the changes introduced into its provisions through the Treaty of Amsterdam (1997/1999) and the Treaty of Nice (2001). The third phase of this process then started with the later provisions of the Treaty of Lisbon (2009). In a way, this last phase was characterised by the intensification of action, tending towards the establishment of a more consistent and coherent criminal justice system for an integrated Europe:[2] EU criminal policy is taking its gradual steps towards the Area of Freedom, Security and Justice (AFSJ) for all 'citizens of Europe'.

1 Alter, K. J. (2006), *Establishing the Supremacy of European Law: The Making of an International Rule of Law in Europe*, Oxford: Oxford University Press.

2 Fletcher, M., Lööf, R. and Gilmore, B. (2008), *EU Criminal Law and Justice*, Cheltenham: Edward Elgar Publishing.

The Maastricht Treaty and its effects on the development of European (EU) criminal justice

The area of judicial co-operation in criminal matters within the EU has been considerably institutionalised under the Maastricht Treaty. Actually, the Maastricht Treaty may be truly recognised as a kind of 'transition' phase in constructing the stadium of co-operation among EU Member States within a structural organisation, which is characterised by its own autonomous legal order, *sui generis*. The development of European (EU) criminal justice has been started along with the integration process with the aim of removing barriers to the free movement of goods, services, capital and persons. In time, the principles of the Single (Common) Market have gradually required adoption of some regulations or provisions in criminal matters as well. In general, the EU criminal legal norms *per se* are deeply rooted in the commercial law of the EC regime. As a result, the changes that have been introduced by the Maastricht Treaty not only combined the earlier achieved experiences of the Union Member States in the economic sphere, but also they opened the long-term path towards supranational integration in criminal matters, at the European level.[3] Just to recall, during its Maastricht Meeting in December 1991 the European Council decided to complement the EU policy by adding two new fields: the intergovernmental pillars under the Title V, Common Foreign and Security Policy, and Title VI, Justice and Home Affairs (JHA) co-operation. These amendments laid the foundations for the so-called pillar model of the Union, in which the first (supranational) pillar of the EU, that is the institutional structure including the Community institutions, had to co-exist with the two other intergovernmental pillars.[4]

In accordance with the old regime of the Third Pillar, the Member States were obliged to consult, collaborate and co-ordinate their action in the fields of justice and home matters identified as of 'common interest'. Its policy was characterised by a compromise and a heterogeneous construction. In fact, the Maastricht Treaty established a purposeful and coherent inter-state co-operation system in the area of JHA within the framework of the EU. Factually, this has then made possible further steps in the development of a common judicial space in criminal matters within the EU.[5] However, a rapidly developing domain of criminal law created hitherto by the EU Member States acquired a new institutional place within the formal framework and legal instruments of the EU for its closer and more efficient co-operation. One may agree that its first aim was achieved

3 Klip, A. (2009), *European Criminal Law: Ius Communitatis II*. Antwerp-Oxford-Portland: Intersentia; Mitsilegas, V. (2009), *EU Criminal Law*, Oxford: Hart Publishing.

4 den Boer, M. (1996), 'Justice and Home Affairs: Cooperation without Integration', in: Wallace H. and Wallace, W. (eds), *Policy-Making in the European Union*, Oxford: Oxford University Press, 394–401.

5 Klip, note 3 above, 383–400; Fijnaut, C. (2006), 'Police Co-operation and the Area of Freedom, Security and Justice', in Walker N. (ed.), *Europe's Area of Freedom, Security and Justice*, Oxford: Oxford University Press, 241–82.

through introducing the pillar model of the EU by the Treaty of Maastricht (1992), while the second aim was realised for the most part under the changes of the Amsterdam regime (1999) and finally that of the Treaty of Lisbon (2009).[6]

The amendments introduced in the domain of criminal law by the Treaty of Amsterdam and the Treaty of Nice

At the initial stage of the EU functioning as an organisation of *sui generis*, there were slow movements aimed at establishing a closer co-operation in criminal matters. Such a situation was, however, much improved thanks to some amendments introduced by the Treaty of Amsterdam. The new Treaty had a great impact on the process of harmonising the criminal law in the Member States, enhancing at the same time their co-operation in criminal matters. The Treaty of Maastricht provided for an intergovernmental conference to negotiate its revisions. The prescribed conference began in Turin in 1996 and ended in Amsterdam in 1997. On 18 June 1997 the Dutch Prime Minister announced that the conference had agreed upon the text of a new treaty by which the TEU and the EC treaty would be respectively amended. This Treaty, named the Treaty of Amsterdam, entered into force on 1 May 1999. It amended the general provisions of the EU, and a considerable number of provisions of the Treaties belonging to the First Pillar (EC, ECSC and EAEC), as well as those of the second and Third Pillar. The most important factors that had influenced the Amsterdam Treaty were the accession to the EU of Central and East European countries, the institutional structure of the Union, the introduction of the single currency, the Schengen *acquis* (the Schengen law: Schengen Agreement, 1985 (Schengen I) and Schengen Implementation Convention, 1990 (Schengen II)) and the flexibility issue.[7] It was stressed that the EU should be based on the principles of freedom, democracy, respect for human and fundamental rights, and the rule of law. This listing might be actually called the *acquis politique* of the EU, in the perspective of its continuous development, tending to further integration.

As to the institutional structure of the Union, it was decided to retain the five main Community institutions. In the Third Pillar, JHA, the Council was left as major decision-making body, supported by the Coordinating Committee established on the basis of Article 36 TEU (CATS – the '36 Committee'). Furthermore, the function of the intergovernmental Schengen Committee, having certain law-making competences, was taken over by the JHA Council and the Council's General Secretariat. From the legal point of view, the next changes seem to be quite important. What is also noteworthy, is that some provisions of the Schengen *acquis* were transferred *en bloc* from the Third Pillar to

6 E.g. Mitsilegas, note 3 above, 5–57; Perron, W. (2005), 'Perspectives of the Harmonization of Criminal Law and Criminal Procedure in the European Union', in: Husabø, E. and Strandbakken, A. (2005), *Harmonization of Criminal Law in Europe,* Antwerpen-Oxford: Intersentia, 5–21.

7 Barents, R. (1997), 'Some Observations on the Treaty of Amsterdam'. *Maastricht Journal of European and Comparative Law*, 4, 333.

the EC Treaty. In this way, a certain part of the Schengen *acquis* has become a Community law. Consequently, the transfer of the Schengen *acquis* to the First Pillar established a new Title in the EC Treaty: on visas, asylum, immigration and other policies related to free movement of persons (IV EC). Therefore, in this context it is said that the Treaty of Amsterdam formally introduced some 'communitarisation', also colloquially named as 'amsterdamisation'. But the provisions concerning police and judicial co-operation in criminal matters as well the Schengen Information System (SIS) were incorporated into the Third Pillar of the EU.[8]

Title VI of the TEU relating to the 'provisions on co-operation in the fields of justice and home affairs' was amended to 'police and judicial co-operation in criminal matters'. Also then under the Third Pillar were two new legal instruments, decisions and framework decisions, which were binding upon the Member States, whereas the joint actions were eliminated altogether. Specifically, the framework decisions provided the possibility for harmonising criminal law, in the sense of adopting similar or identical norms under national legal orders. Here, the term 'harmonising' is understood as a mirror of 'approximation', the term that is applied in most of the EU official documents. So, the classical instruments of inter-state co-operation, that is to say conventions, started to be effectively replaced by the EU framework decisions.

In fact, initiatives that under the old legal regime might be accepted as the Union conventions, then took the form of the framework decisions. The trend in the EU towards creating a common AFSJ was further confirmed in the Treaty of Nice (2000) and the Treaty of Lisbon (2009). The Treaty of Nice allowed for enhancing the Union policy on judicial co-operation in criminal matters, especially through the role played by Eurojust.[9] And, finally, the Treaty of Lisbon became a crucial instrument on the path of integration in the domain of EU criminal law. It should also be noted with reference to the old legal regime under the Third Pillar of the EU that the Court of Justice implemented in the domain of criminal law some constitutive components of a Community nature. Here, some fundamental judgements should be listed, such as *Maria Pupino*[10] and *Advocaten voor de Wereld VZW*.[11] Furthermore, the general approach towards a 'communitarsation' of criminal law within the EU has been widely reflected in the Court's jurisprudence, namely in the cases of *Ireland v. Parliament and Council*,[12] *Commission v. Council* (Case C-176/03),[13] *Commission v. Council*

8 For further discussion of the SIS, see Mitsilegas, note 3 above, 237–49.

9 *Ibid.*, 187–209.

10 *Criminal proceedings against Maria Pupino*, Case C-105/03 [2005] ECR I-05285.

11 *Advocaten voor de Wereld VZW v. Leden van de Ministerraad*, Case C-303/05 [2007] ECR I-03633.

12 *Ireland v. European Parliament and Council of the European Union*, Case C-301/06 [2009] ECR I-00593.

13 *Commission v. Council of the European Union*, Case C-176/03 [2005] ECR I-07879.

(Case C-440/05)[14] and *Intertanko and others v. Secretary of State for Transport* (Case C- 308/06).[15]

So, in view of these developments, the next logical step seems to be the Treaty of Lisbon, establishing a formal framework for closer inter-state co-operation in criminal matters, characterised by its supranational and transnational character.

New challenges under the supranational legal regime of the Treaty of Lisbon

It is commonly recognised that the Treaty of Lisbon opens a 'new era' in the domain of European criminal law, prescribing an institutional framework for closer co-operation in criminal matters among the EU Member States.[16] First of all, it abolished the pillar structure of EU legislation. As a result, all matters previously dealt with under the Third Pillar (police and judicial co-operation in criminal matters) have been incorporated into the new legal regime for creating an AJSF, based on the general rules and principles of the former Community.[17] The Treaty of Lisbon introduced two treaties as a legal basis for the EU further developments, an international organisation *sui generis*: the Treaty on European Union (TEU) and the Treaty on the Functioning of the European Union (TFEU). The latter replaced the Treaty establishing the European Community.

Matters concerning police and judicial co-operation have been integrated into the TFEU under Title V and the heading 'Area of Freedom, Security and Justice'. The first chapter of this Title lays down general provisions (Articles 67–76), and four other chapters include respectively: policies on border checks, asylum and immigration (Articles 77–80); judicial co-operation in civil matters (Article 81); judicial co-operation in criminal matters (Articles 82–6); and police co-operation (Articles 87–9). The traditional legal instruments of the Community law (regulations, directives and decisions) became officially secondary Union law (Article 288 TFEU). In this way, the old legal instruments under previous the Third Pillar of the EU (common positions, framework decisions and decisions – ex-Article 34(2) TEU) were replaced by the traditional Community legal instruments. According to the TFEU, a fundamental role in judicial co-operation in criminal matters would be played by the principles of mutual recognition

14 *Commission v. Council of the European Union*, Case C-440/05 [2007] ECR I-09097.

15 *R, on the application of International Association of Independent Tanker Owners (Intertanko) and Others v. Secretary of State for Transport*, Case C- 308/06 [2008] ECR I-04057.

16 Herlin-Karnell, E. (2010), *The Lisbon Treaty, A Critical Analysis of its Impact on EU Criminal Law*, eucrim-the European criminal law association's forum, No 2. Freiburg im Breisgau: The Max Planck Institute for Foreign and International Criminal Law, 59–64, available at https://eucrim.mpicc.de/archiv/eucrim_10-02.pdf; Peers, S., 2008, 'EU Criminal Law and the Treaty of Lisbon', *European Law Review*, 33, 50; Baker, E. and Harding, C. (2009), 'From Past Imperfect to Future Perfect? A Longitudinal Study of the Third Pillar', *European Law Review*, 34, 25.

17 *The Lisbon Treaty's Impact on the Justice and Home Affairs (JHA) Council: More Co-decision and New Working Structures*, available at: www.consilium.europa.eu/uedocs/cms_data/docs/pressdata/en/ec/111615.pdf.

and approximation of national criminal law in the prescribed fields of common interests (Article 67(1)).

The strategic guidelines for legislative and operational planning within the AFSJ are within the competence of the European Council (Article 68 TFEU). A significant role for mutual recognition and approximation of criminal procedural norms is directly expressed in Article 82 TFEU. Accordingly, EU directives adopted pursuant to the ordinary legislative procedure may establish minimum rules. Such rules shall take into account the differences between the legal traditions and national systems of the EU Member States. The EU directives shall then concern the following issues:

a) mutual admissibility of evidence between Member States;
b) the rights of individuals in criminal procedure;
c) the rights of victims of crime;
d) any other specific aspects of criminal procedure which the Council has identified in advance by a decision.

With reference to substantive criminal norms under Article 83(1) TFEU, directives may be used to establish minimum rules concerning the definition of criminal offences and sanctions in the areas of particularly serious crime with a cross-border dimension resulting from the nature or impact of such offences or from a special need to combat them on a common basis. These areas of serious crime may cover acts of terrorism, trafficking in human beings and sexual exploitation of women and children, illicit drug trafficking, illicit arms trafficking, money laundering, corruption, counterfeiting of means of payment, computer crime and organised crime. This catalogue may be, however, expanded to include other areas of crime following any Council decision identifying such crimes that meet the criteria specified in this paragraph.

Also, one should notice that the provisions of the TFEU may regulate some institutional questions concerning supranational integration in criminal matters, particularly Eurojust[18] and the European Public Prosecutor's Office.[19] Article 86 TFEU provides: 'in order to combat crimes affecting the financial interests of the Union, the Council, by means of regulations adopted in accordance with a special legislative procedure, may establish a European Public Prosecutor's Office from Eurojust.' The European Public Prosecutor's Office shall be generally responsible for investigating, prosecuting and bringing to judgment, where appropriate in liaison with Europol, the perpetrators of, and accomplices in, offences against the Union's financial interests. It shall exercise the functions of prosecutor in the competent courts of the Member States in relation to such offences. Moreover, the powers of the European Public Prosecutor's Office may be extended to include serious crime having a cross-border dimension that is affecting more than

18 Mitsilegas, note 3 above, 187–209.
19 Klip, note 3 above, 410, at 431.

one Member State. Such provisions reflect the EU tendency towards integrated criminal justice, both normative and institutional.

A significant change introduced by the Treaty of Lisbon is that both EU and national measures in the field of criminal matters can be subject to the judicial review of the Court of Justice. So, the Court of Justice (CJEU) became the competent judicial body to decide on the matters covered in the former Third Pillar of the EU (Article 267 TFEU). Following the coming into force of the Treaty of Lisbon, the CJEU was afforded jurisdiction for matters concerning the AFSJ, which has been fully integrated into TFEU. Since 1 December 2014 the CJEU has full competence for the legal instruments adopted in the area of police and judicial co-operation in criminal matters. In particular, the CJEU may hand down preliminary rulings, independently from the formal declaration by the Member States in accordance with the Protocol on Transitional Provisions for a period of five years (1 December 2009 to 1 December 2014). This full jurisdiction of the CJEU will enable a more consistent and uniform application of EU law in the area of criminal justice.[20] It is also worth mentioning that under the new legal regime the principles of subsidiarity and proportionality are more visible. Specifically, it is said that 'National Parliaments ensure that the proposals and legislative initiatives submitted under Chapters 4 and 5 comply with the principle of subsidiarity, in accordance with the arrangements laid down by the Protocol on the application of the principles of subsidiarity and proportionality' (Article 69 TFEU). In addition, the principle of mutual recognition is officially proclaimed to be a 'cornerstone' for judicial co-operation in criminal matters.

In summary, then, the emerging supranational legal regime in criminal matters is characterised on the one hand by the principle of mutual recognition, but on the other by the approximation of the national legal orders in some specific fields of common interest. These changes may allow then for a closer co-operation in the establishment and application of the criminal law norms at the Union level. Such an approach may directly lead to the Europeanisation of national criminal justice systems in the EU Member States.

Without any doubt, the Treaty of Amsterdam made criminal law a central point in institutional development, and the Treaty of Lisbon may be called a kind of landmark, for further enhancing the European (EU) criminal justice, as a supranational system *sui generis*. Actually, the Treaty of Lisbon officially presupposed a continuity of the supranational integration in criminal matters through abolishing the three-pillar structure of the EU and further *communitarisation* of the areas which traditionally were rooted in the intergovernmental co-operation of the Union Member States. Thus, such an approach opens a 'new era' of the

20 See, for instance, Summers, S., Schwarzenegger, C., Ege, G. and Young, F., (2014), *The Emergence of EU Criminal Law: Cybercrime and the Regulation of the Information Society*, Oxford: Hart Publishing, 53–4; Mitsilegas, V., Carrera, S. and Eisele, K., *The End of the Transitional Period for Police and Criminal Justice Measures Adopted before the Lisbon Treaty. Who Monitors Trust in the European Justice Area?* (PE 509.998), European Parliament, Directorate General for Internal Policies, Policy Deparment C: Citizens' Rights and Constitutional Affairs, Civil Liberties, Justice and Home Affairs, European Union, Brussels 2014.

European (EU) criminal law, both substantive and procedural.[21] In this sense, one may also legitimately speak about a gradually emerging European (EU) field of criminal justice, as a supranational system *sui generis.*

What could the future bring in the domain of criminal law?

EU criminal law at the present stage of its development should be categorised as an emerging legal regime with considerable impact on the domestic laws and regulations of the Member States (see the discussion in Chapter 1). Research findings may allow for some present reflection on the vision of a future EU criminal law.

First, EU criminal law can be considered in the perspective of two key questions, namely (1) the move from the traditional intergovernmental or international co-operation of States in criminal matters to the level of supranational integration, and (2) unification (harmonisation/approximation) of criminal law in the AFSJ versus maintaining the variety of domestic laws and regulations.

Second, special attention should be paid to the phenomenon of the progressive globalisation of law, which is also logically associated with the domain of criminal justice. In this context, the principle of *globality* is replacing the well-known classical principle of *territoriality*, so much the characteristic for national criminal justice systems and the idea of criminal law as a last bastion of national sovereignty. Here, it is worthwhile remembering that global law is commonly regarded as the third phase in the development of international law. Such a long-term process may consequently lead to the adoption of universal norms at the global level, having a supranational nature. But, at the same time, there is still observable a parallel, co-existing transnational criminal law. Speaking then about EU criminal law as a system still characterised by international, supranational and transnational elements, one has to stress an important role of the mutual recognition principle and harmonising the national legal orders of the Member States. What is more, in the creation of EU criminal law as a relatively new legal regime, one should also take account of the axiological values within the process of European integration, and on the trans-European criminal law processes.

Third, the vision for the future EU criminal law can be illustrated in the light of reflections made by André Klip. According to him, in the future one may expect to see the European Public Prosecutor's Office, the introduction of a European Penal Code, a Code of European Criminal Procedure, and even the establishment of a European Criminal Court, as a special chamber of ECJ (see also the discussion by van der Wilt, Chapter 9). So, the core message conveyed by his thinking is 'that national criminal law increasingly loses it position of primacy, giving way to more and more criminal law and institutions that

21 For example, Nuotio, K. (2011), 'European Criminal Law under the Developing Constitutional Setting of the European Union', in: Walker, N., Shaw J. and Tierney S. (eds), *Europe's Constitutional Mosaic*, Oxford: Hart Publishing, 311–38.

transcend national borders'.[22] In the process of integration, EU competence has expanded even to cover such a sensitive domain as criminal law. The integrative approach has its impact not only on the shape of substantive criminal law, but also on the procedural norms. In consequence, there is a more and more visible trans-European criminal law process.[23]

Fourth, one may share the opinion of André Klip that, looking back at the developments of the last twenty years, it is unbelievable what changes took place between 1990 and 2010: 'in Europe during this period there has been seen the evolution of European integration from a 10 Member State European Community to a 27 Member State European Union that has been able to extend its competencies dramatically, which now also includes criminal law.'[24] He also points out that after the entry into force of the Treaty of Lisbon in December 2009, the integration of Europe has acquired new and important dimensions. Specifically, the emphasis is now placed on the full implementation of the principle of mutual recognition in all areas of co-operation in criminal matters between the Union Member States. This trend leads to the establishment of some relevant standards in criminal law and procedure in order to achieve mutual trust in the national criminal justice systems of the Union Member States. In particular, the full implementation of the mutual recognition principle in all spheres of criminal law has resulted in the significant situation in which Member States are executing foreign decisions under the European Arrest Warrant as issued in another Member State. The strategies adopted within the EU indicate that a common fight against criminality should be treated as a priority of a coherent criminal policy.

Fifth, one may distinguish some key elements of EU criminal law as a newly emerging legal regime, which are as follows:

1 Two main methods of legal development and enactment of formal measures, reflecting the essentially supranational role of the EU in managing rather than operating criminal law and criminal justice (mutual recognition, approximation or harmonisation).
2 Two principal bases or justifications for legal action at the European level: accordingly, in Article 83(1) TFEU there is the need to deal with serious crime of a cross-border dimension, and then in Article 83(2) there is the need to ensure effective implementation of EU policies. So, there is still an approach towards more harmonisation of law for more effective co-operation in criminal matters. One may speculate that on the basis of Articles 82 and 83 TFEU, the EU will have gradually its own legislation in all areas of substantive criminal law and criminal procedure.

22 Klip, A. (2011). 'The Future of International and European Criminal Law', in: Muller, S., Zouridis, S., Frishman, M. and Kistemaker, L. (eds), *The Law of the Future and the Future of Law*, FICHL Publications Series No. 11, Oslo: Torkel Opsahal Academic EPublisher, 673.

23 *Ibid.*, 675–7.

24 *Ibid.*, 673–4.

It seems, using the words of André Klip, that actually the EU has entered 'a process of finding its own way in developing the European criminal justice system. . . . Some elements are drawn from common law, others from civil law, but most of it is a wonderful new model of its own'[25] (again, see the discussion in Chapter 1 above). In this respect, the question arises from the very optimistic view of Klip, whether we may accept such a model without criticism, and also in which direction the European criminal justice system should be developed? It seems that there is factually an emergent European criminal justice as a supranational system *sui generis.* But, still there is also room left for national legislation that allows for some diversity. The visible development of the EU criminal law at the present stage has a tendency towards more diversity than unity (see the discussion in Chapter 4).

In resuming the ongoing debate about the future of EU criminal law, we may generally speak about an epoch that is characterised by the decline of the primacy of national criminal law. The principle of territoriality, so characteristic for national criminal justice systems, is gradually being replaced by a principle of European territoriality. Such an approach is a logical step in the progressive globalisation of the present century, influencing the domestic legal orders and in relation to criminal law rendering the principle of territoriality less and less important. Although the EU criminal law project lacks so far a clear presentation, it does, reading between the lines, possess some vision and ambition regarding the role of criminal law in the evolving European polity.

25 *Ibid.*, 677.

3 The effects of the civilising process on penal developments in the European Union[1]

Jarosław Utrat-Milecki

Introduction

The public policy of the European Union is based on knowledge. Knowledge, especially in the field of social sciences, is, however, always a social phenomenon, and it has its own intellectual and institutional history. In a sense one can argue that the most important aspect of modern social sciences is their critical attitude towards their own foundations. From this perspective the meta study of the foundations of any knowledge in social and legal sciences is necessary. Social and legal sciences concern not only matters of fact, but also matters of values. In respect of legal studies, one of the expressions of that value-oriented aspect of legal studies is the principle of proportionality in the application of different legal means to achieve legitimate purposes of law. The debate about the law and the legitimate social purposes of its application concern both knowledge about facts and the evaluation of potentially conflicting values and interests.

A critical approach to established knowledge is one of the main attributes of modern sciences and it is also an important part of European intellectual tradition. It has historically distinguished the European intellectual tradition from the traditional way of thinking in other cultures and civilisations. The first stage of European critical theoretical thinking is related to the very beginning of European secular thought in the philosophy of ancient Greece and it was reinforced again in the modern era in the most systematic way in the Enlightenment.

In respect of legal practice and theory, a lot of modern notions and ways of legal reasoning are directly or indirectly related to the European pragmatic way of reasoning typical of ancient Roman Law. It is not the case that the revival of the importance of Roman Law jurisprudence and especially legal scholarship concerning the principles and institutions of Roman Law started from the late Middle Ages and that this influence has even been strengthened (especially in

1 The article was written on the basis of the research in the framework of the grant of the National Scientific Council of Republic of Poland (Narodowe Centrum Nauki): *Penal Cultures. Cultural Context of the Reforms of Criminal Policy and Criminal Law. The Legal, Penological, Historical, Sociological and Anthropological (Cultural) Analyses of Reforms of Criminal Law in Poland in the Light of European and International Tendencies* (DEC-2011/01/B/HS5/03206).

the German sphere of influence in Europe) since the Renaissance. The pattern of institutions of Roman Law and the way of reasoning developed in ancient Roman jurisprudence was well fitted to the development of the modern way of capitalist production and the pragmatic, practically oriented, attitude of modern society to the regulations of interhuman relations. The question of language was also important in the proliferation of Roman Law and scholarship. Modern legal studies were at the academic level related to studies in Latin, which was from the late Middle Ages the common European language in education – *toutes proportions gardées*, like English for contemporary European and international relations. The concept of *ius commune* to describe the emerging system of law of the European Union directly refers to that tradition of common heritage of ancient Roman (and Canonic) laws, the tradition which had contributed to the development of modern legal studies in Europe since at least the twelfth century.[2]

The emergence of modern criminal law standards

The birth of contemporary modern criminal law is related to the rising importance of central political government and the growing role of the State in providing a safe and rational environment for the life and work of its citizens. The division into private and public law (the development of that concept in jurisprudence is attributed to Ulpian, an ancient Roman legal adviser), after losing its importance for legal theory and practice in the Middle Ages, grew in its importance from the Renaissance. From that time on, the growing role of the division into public and private laws has been related to the growing role of the State in constructing social order which had to secure modern, capitalistic ways of trade and production. The *ius puniendi* (the right to punish) became one of the main aspects of state sovereignty. Criminal law was from that time on strongly associated with the attribute of power of the sovereign state, which was responsible for public peace and security, and in consequence it was responsible for the freedom and ownership of all employers and workers and the rest of society. The criminal law played from that time on an important role in the whole civilising process which led to the modernisation and especially to the emergence of a mostly utilitarian way of thinking about law and order in society.[3]

The idea of state sovereignty was from the eighteenth century on more and more often blended with the idea of the sovereignty of the nation and the idea of the rights of individuals. That new intellectual tendency was quite often expressed through the concept of the State as a product and guardian of the social contract

2 Lessaffer, R. (2012), *European Legal History. A Cultural and Political Perspective*, Cambridge-New York: Cambridge University Press; Berman, H. J. (1983), *Law and Revolution: Formation of the Western Legal Tradition*, Cambridge, MA: Harvard University Press; Debuyst, Ch., Digneffe F. and Pires A. P. (2005), *Histoire des savoirs sur le crime et la peine. 2. La rationalité pénale et la naissance de la criminologie*, Montréal-Paris-Bruxelles: Les Presses de l'Université de Montréal, Presses de l'Université d'Ottawa, De Boeck Université, p. 17–51; Jeanclos, Y. (2009), *Droit Pénal Européen. Dimension Historique*, Paris: Economica.

3 Debuyst *et al.*, note 2 above, 83–143.

of its citizens. That concept was very important for the development of modern criminal law at the time of the Enlightenment. It was the time of the development in legal writings of the concept of the protective function of criminal law in respect of the basic rights of suspects, and this function of criminal law was associated with and expressed by the development of many institutions as well in criminal proceedings as in criminal substantive law, by the way the theoretical and legal division into the criminal procedure and substantive criminal law had been just developing in that time. From that new perspective of the protection of rights of individuals, the criminal law was seen as a way of powerful intervention in the rights of individuals in order to protect public goods. The criminal law started to be regarded as a set of institutions, standards, and rules which should protect innocent individuals from the unjustified intrusion of the State in their rights and even as a legal guardian of the humanitarian treatment of criminals who should be dealt with rationally in order to protect society and not in order to avenge the crime or to provide a spectacle of power. From that time on, the punishment to be justified must be both: for the past crime, which should limit the punishment only to those who committed crime, and it should be used only for the preservation of legal order in the future, which should limit the quantity and quality of punishment to make of it a rational tool of social and criminal law policy. Ideas that were developed in that respect concerned the basic questions of political regime (like the principle of division of powers and the independence of judiciary and judges). They also concerned, however, dogmatic concepts of crime and principles of criminal liability and the question of humanitarian, but effective, punishments. In both cases, political and legal concepts, they were supposed to help to find a balance between the role of criminal law in combating criminality, and the need for protection of individuals from the too extensive intervention of the State into the life of citizens and their welfare under the label of criminal law. That was the time of the origin of the systematic development of so-called classical principles of criminal law based on the idea of justice, utilitarianism, liability based both on the committed act and the established guilt, and criminalisation based on the rational and empirical criteria. The concept of human free will, *homo eligens*, which was the basis for the concept of guilt *(mens rea)*, was also part of the broader concept elaborated in continental doctrines in general terms as the principle of *nullum crimen sine lege poenali anteriori*, which provided the stronger foundation for the principle of protection of the rights of an innocent. In respect of convicted criminals, the principle of humanitarianism and rationality, it means a productive treatment of criminals was broadly developed, thanks especially to the report of John Howard. According to this principle, criminals should be as far as possible reintegrated into the class of good workers for the benefit of society.[4] All the above-mentioned modern tendencies in criminal law and criminal policy had a European and, in practice, also an international character

4 Morris, N. and Rothman, J. D. (eds) (1998), *The Oxford History of Prison. The Practice of Punishment in Western Society*, New York-Oxford: Oxford University Press; Perrot, M. (2001), *Les ombres de l'histoire. Crime et châtiment au XIX siècle*. Paris: Flamarion.

and were not limited to one state. The works of Charles de Montesquieu and especially of Cesare Beccaria and John Howard, and later on of Jeremy Bentham, had been translated into different European languages, and they expressed ideas which in the eighteenth and at the beginning of the nineteenth centuries formed a basis for criminal law principles and general criminal justice reforms in different countries and jurisdictions. Moreover, at the beginning of the nineteenth century many practitioners, politicians and writers went to the newly created United States of America to learn about the modern penitentiary systems. From the first Penitentiary Congress in Frankfurt in 1846, many international conferences in respect of reforms of the prison system, criminal policy and reforms of criminal law were carried on through the nineteenth and twentieth centuries, up to our present times.[5] It means that at least from the nineteenth century we can talk about certain principles and standards worked out in respect of criminal law as well as substantive criminal law, as criminal law proceedings and the law and practice concerning the carrying out of sentences.[6] It should be remembered that some of these standards did not pass the test of time: they were influenced by the historical circumstances and scientific tendencies of their times, and they have been changing, in some respects quite considerably. Probably, the same could be said about the historically biased nature of contemporary standards in respect of criminal policy, working which may only be verified empirically by today's young academics in the future.

Indeed, the further development of criminal law in the second half of the nineteenth century was more and more related to the growing role of the newborn social sciences and so-called scientifically based social policy. The new social sciences strongly influenced the debate on the criminal law, especially from the end of the nineteenth century, and the study of criminal problems again focused more on the question of combating criminality than on protection of individual rights against too extensive intrusion of the State. The classical criminal law treated criminal behavior (committed crime) as a point of departure and the only justification for legal intervention through painful penal sanction. In the positivist school, attention was focused on the criminal and his or her personality, and the crime committed started to be only one (even if a very important) symptom of the criminal character of the perpetrator. The free will concept *(mens rea)* was undermined by the scientific study of 'objective factors' influencing tendencies to criminal behaviour. The penal sanction was justified more and more in relation to the character of a criminal and not that of criminal deed, and penal intervention was more and more considered as a kind of forceful treatment or incapacitative security measure. The guilt of the criminal was not the most important aspect for the defining of criminal policy, but the question of his or her maladjustment and

5 Perrot, M., op. cit; Pratt, J. (2002), *Punishment and Civilization. Penal Tolerance and Intolerance in Modern Society*, London-Thousand Oaks-New Delhi: Sage; Wayne, M. (2007), *Criminology and the New World Order,* Abington-New York: Routledge Cavendish.

6 Melossi, D. (2008), *Controlling Crime. Controlling Society. Thinking about Crime in Europe and America,* Cambridge: Polity, 15–38.

dangerous character. The macro approach of criminology to criminal policy based on scientifically discerned aetiological factors determining criminal behaviour tended to influence also the micro perspective of the principles of application of criminal law in individual cases. The end of the nineteenth century, with its stress on the positive, empirically based, and objective knowledge, brought not only progress, but also a profound crisis into the criminal law field. The concentration on the question of effectiveness in combating criminality led to the development of the above-mentioned positive school in criminology, which, in practice, questioned the classic notions of criminal law. This approach led to the diminishing role of standards that were supposed to guarantee the rule of law in sentencing.

Most criminals (except for so-called incidental criminals, like bad drivers who caused an accident) started to be treated as a quite different class of people from the 'good citizens'. Harsh treatment of criminals had not so often been considered in relation to the question of the rights of (good and careful) citizens.[7] To some extent, it seems to be like that in the contemporary treatment of terrorists.

The extremely positivist direction in criminal law was seriously questioned in the second half of the twentieth century in Europe, especially because of the experiences of the abuses of fascist criminal policy and Second World War atrocities, and later on, owing to the development of new European and mostly American sociological schools in criminology, especially related to interactionism. From the second half of the twentieth century, the necessity of combining both the empirical basis of criminal policy and respect for the standards of criminal proceedings and a humanitarian and just way of sentencing and carrying out sentences again became more and more important. The International Declaration of Human Rights, followed by the adoption of the European Convention on Human Rights and the developing standards in the judicial practice dealing with individual cases, brought to the establishing of common standards in respect of the rule of law in criminal matters: the principle of due process of law, the principle of presumption of innocence, the principle of proportionality (including sentencing), the principle of protection against torture and other inhuman and degrading treatment and punishment, the principle of *ultima ratio* (criminal law as a last resort both in criminalisation and in the choice of penalty, especially the deprivation of liberty in prison) and so on. The development of criminological and penological knowledge led to questioning the modern myth of the nineteenth and the first half of the twentieth century concerning the role of prison in combating criminality and resocialisation of prisoners. It strengthened tendencies for looking into sentences alternative to prison, which would have less negative collateral effects on the criminal, his or her family and on society, and meant sentences that would be less costly and more effective in preventing crime. The development of those tendencies was related to the need for both the developing of effective criminal policy based on up-to-date knowledge, as well as on the need for the protection of basic human rights against

7 Debuyst *et al.*, note 2 above, 221–481; Mucchielli, L. (ed.) (1994), *L'Histoire de la criminologie française*, Paris: L'Harmattan.

too extensive use of criminal law instruments.[8] Tendencies like that were reflected in many international and even more intensively European resolutions and conventions concerning the criminal law and the practice of criminal justice systems. One of the biggest achievements of the critical approach to the criminal law in the last decades of the twentieth century was the emergence of the victim as an actor in the criminal justice system and the working out of standards for protection of rights of victims. The standards for protection of society, standards for the rights of accused persons and the rights of prisoners and other convicts were completed by the standards for the protection of rights of different kinds of victim. From the 1950s, and especially intensively from the 1970s, successive resolutions concerning the criminal justice system (prison rules, treatment of juveniles, alternative sanctions, probation, community services, treatment of foreigners, women, victims of different kind of crime, restorative justice and so on) have been adopted in the framework of the Council of Europe and the United Nations as well.[9]

The emergence of international and European cooperation in criminal justice

The development of international cooperation in different fields, including mainly economy and labour, which was possible due to the rise of technological opportunities, as a consequence brought about also the process of intensification of internationalisation of criminality. The free movement of capital and labour was accompanied by the international cooperation of criminals. Indeed, to distinguish a criminal from a trader or even a hero was not a very easy task, especially from an international perspective; for instance, in the case of the English explorer, adventurer and national hero, Francis Drake.

For this reason, states and slowly emerging international agencies had to provide the legal and institutional basis for cooperation in respect of dealing with criminality on an international level. That aspect of criminal law was especially developed from the eighteenth century in the procedural way by the development of provisions concerning the institution of extradition. From the end of the nineteenth century, cooperation in criminal matters concerned also more and more provisions related to terrorism (in that time mostly crimes committed by anarchists), and, for instance, questions of slavery or prostitution and later on pornography and drugs and question of crimes of war. The acceleration of that trend towards more international cooperation in criminal matters occurred after the Second World War, with the symbolic meaning of the Nuremberg Trials. Europe in that period became the leader of the development of international–regional cooperation in criminal matters. Today we can also observe the international,

8 Utrat-Milecki, J. (2006), *Podstawy penologii. Teoria kary* [*Principles of Penology. Theory of Punishment*]. Warsaw: Warsaw University Press, 98–294.

9 Melossi, note 6 above, 83–228; Armstrong, S. and McAra, L. (2006), *Perspectives on Punishment. The Contours of Control*, Oxford-New York: Oxford University Press; McConville, S. (2003), *The Use of Punishment*, Cullompton: Willan Publishing.

global development of standards for cooperation in criminal matters often related to different agencies under the auspices of the UN as regional cooperation. The most advanced regional cooperation in criminal matters has appeared recently in Europe, which created in the framework of the European Union the common space of freedom, justice and security.[10] The effective protection of free space for the free movement of citizens (labour, capital) required more regulations in terms of standards and institutional cooperation in the application of criminal laws. One of the consequences of that development was also the change from the old principle of reciprocity in criminal cooperation typical for extradition treaties into the principle of trust and recognition of the decisions of the criminal justice agencies (courts) of other members of the European Community in cooperation in criminal matters.[11] Closer cooperation in many fields of economy and social issues in the framework of the European Union led also to much closer cooperation in security and criminal justice matters, which brought about the creation of many European agencies, like Europol or Eurojust, etc. The growing role since the 1990s of the European Community led also to the absorption by the new European Union of the legal heritage of the former European cooperation in the framework of the European Council related to the European Convention on Human Rights.[12] The outline of the tendencies that contributed to the development of modern questions of criminal law and criminal law policy in the framework of the European Union make it possible to formulate some general remarks.

International cooperation in criminal matters is organised, especially in the European context, on the basis of a common legal heritage, the long-lasting cooperation in respect of research and academic teaching, and the exchange of information on the practical work of institutions of the criminal justice system. There are different legal sub-traditions, the most important of which is the split over the continental, more systematic (synthetic) approach to criminal law questions and the Anglo-Saxon common law tradition, which is by the way in a certain sense closer to the way of dealing with law questions by the praetors in the ancient Roman legal tradition. Moreover, in addition, the continental approach may vary from country to country, with differences especially visible between the German and French (Roman) traditions; but also important differences, for instance, in the Scandinavian approach to criminal matters. The differences may concern the dogmatic legal questions related sometimes to certain well-established traditions, but also different approaches to current problems, such as, for instance, the scope of use of electronic monitoring or the acceptance of institutions based on idea of plea bargaining and so on.[13] Those differences in law and legal traditions and

10 Utrat-Milecki, J. (2007 [1997]), *Polityczność przestępstwa* [*Political Aspects of Crime*], Warsaw: Warsaw University Press, 147–231.

11 Banach-Gutierrez, J. (2011), *Europejski Wymiar Sprawiedliwości w sprawach karnych. W kierunku ponadnarodowego systemu sui generis?* Warsaw: EuroPrawo.

12 Bradley, A. W., Janis, M. W. and Kay, R. S. (2008), *European Human Rights Law. Text and Materials.* Oxford-New York, Oxford University Press.

13 Fraser, R. S. and Tonry, M. (eds) (2001), *Sentencing and Sanctions in Western Countries,* Oxford-New York: Oxford University Press.

concepts play quite an important role in developing new ideas, in a similar way to the positive impact of the discussions of different concepts of law and criminal policy at a national level. There are different fundamental questions of criminal law, like the question of the theory of guilt or punishment, which are still being discussed, and which may be the proof of the vital character of penological and criminological studies.[14] The comparative and international (European) level of debate may be a very positive way of influencing national debate, as it was to some extent in the above-mentioned history of congresses, resolutions and conventions. The more institutionalised character of that cooperation in the more dense legal framework of the European Union may be a new and stimulating challenge for the further development of European criminal law doctrines in its umbrella regional dimension, as well as in the different national jurisdictions. If one looks at the tendencies in respect of the developing European criminal law from the international perspective, one can focus on questions related to institutional cooperation and on the different political challenges that influence that cooperation. However, it can be argued that some problematic features related to that cooperation in criminal matters are just present in national criminal law and policy debates and the European debate on criminal law reflects also hot questions important for the different jurisdictions. We can see here a kind of reciprocity. The European cooperation in criminal matters strongly influences in different ways the development of national legal standards and debates, but also national debates and problems faced in national contexts are reflected in debates and projects of criminal law at the international level.[15]

Some questions concerning the tendencies of European criminal law and policy debate

The question of model of crime policy: due process of law or crime control?

In the Anglo-Saxon literature concerning criminal policy, two main traditional approaches to criminal policy are distinguished. The first one is the model of due process of law, which is related to the classical tradition of the Enlightenment. The main concern in that approach to criminal policy is put on the guarantees of due process of law, and the providing of safeguards in legal provisions that make it certain that an innocent person will never be found guilty. The development of many international and European standards dealing with human rights concerns exactly that problem. However, the recent development of the European criminal law seems to be even more concerned with the model of criminal policy called crime control. In that second model, the emphasis is laid on the

14 Duff, R. A. and Green, S. P. (2011), 'Introduction: Searching for Foundations', in: Duff, R. A. and Green, S. P. (eds), *The Philosophical Foundations of Criminal Law*, New York: Routledge; Hart, L. A. (2008 [1968]), *Punishment and Responsibility. Essays in the Philosophy of Law. Second Edition with Introduction by John Gardner*, Oxford-New York: Oxford University Press.

15 Banach-Gutierrez, note 11 above.

effectiveness of criminal justice laws and agencies in combatting criminality. Of course, criminal law has no sense if it is not effective in preventing criminality, and all models of criminal justice have to follow certain minimum standards of human rights protection as well. However, when we compare different models of criminal policy, we can find different approaches towards effectiveness and safeguards and nevertheless the tension between these two approaches to the question of criminality, due process of law and crime control are well documented in the literature and practice of criminal justice systems.[16] This is an issue of the values that have to be dealt with on the basis of the proportionality principle. In the European cooperation, it is visible that this problem tends to be treated differently in respect of more serious crimes like offences of a terrorist nature. In these serious cases, the model of crime control strongly dominates the model of due process of law.[17] However, the question of proportionality between the values of the individual rights of citizens and the effectiveness of criminal policy may concern all sorts of criminal justice activities, for instance in respect of data protection in cooperation of police and other agencies in the framework of the European Union.

The question of the language, culture and law

Another issue important for the study of law is the question of language. It means the very pragmatic issue of providing interpreters in criminal proceedings with foreigners, but also the more sophisticated issue of translating criminal law provisions and criminal doctrine notions into national languages. The European Union respects its own diversity, including the diversity of its national languages. The law is not only a pragmatic instrument of communication, but also a general expression of the social life and culture of society. If European societies decide to respect their identities and in consequence their national languages, the question of translation will persist and it will concern also legal studies, legal practice and legal documents, including the provisions of statutory law and judicial decisions. Language is the crucial aspect in any legal reasoning, and the question of translation of international standards into the legal practice of different jurisdictions with different languages is very important. The same results concerning certain prohibitions or safeguards may be achieved in different ways. In the theory of law, one distinguishes the notion of rule of conduct and written provision. The different legal ways of formulating certain legal questions and different ways of putting rules of conduct into provisions of statutory law may, however, lead to similar practical consequences. Nevertheless, the comparison of different provisions of law written in different languages and belonging to different systems of national

16 Burton, M., Sanders, A. and Young, R. (2010), *Criminal Justice*, Oxford-New York: Oxford University Press, 1–59; Gross, H. (2012), *Crime and Punishment. A Concise Moral Critique*, Oxford-New York: Oxford University Press.

17 Utrat-Milecki, note 10 above (2007), 195–231.

law is in itself a very difficult task.[18] There is a visible tendency in European regulations to more casuistic formulations of provisions of the criminal law, than was developed in many continental national laws. It may probably be related just to the problem of translation. The more casuistic approach makes it possible to define the issue by pointing to very precisely empirically discerned designates. In more abstract formulas, the content of the provision could in translation be interpreted differently in different languages and different legal traditions and different broader legal contexts for interpretation. However, the casuistic law typical for the simple underdeveloped medieval tribal criminal law was duly criticised in modern continental doctrines. The law (statutory provisions of law) is always referring to general and abstract descriptions of certain patterns of action. If a given pattern (for instance a normative, statutory concept of an offence) is too casuistic, the risk of creating different lacunae and inconsistences in the provisions of law increases. From that perspective, the casuistic language of some European resolutions and recommendations may be justified as guidance for national provisions, but it may be quite rational to translate those provisions into national languages and doctrines in a more abstract and general way, covering the same patterns of action but in a way more consistent with modern legal language and continental doctrines of criminal law in respect of the way of normative criminalisation. Otherwise the casuistic language of law may provide a lot of problems, especially if we accept that in continental criminal law there is a tendency to avoid interpretation *per analogiam* (it might be against the principle of *nullum crimen sine lege* and it might lead to greater arbitrariness in application of criminal law and, in consequence, to less certainty in protection of individual rights).

The question of limits to criminalisation and principle of ultima ratio *in penal law (in more sociological terms, the question concerning punitiveness of contemporary European societies)*

During the 1970s, in European criminal law doctrine, and especially in sociological interactionist criminology and conflict criminology, the hypothesis of decriminalisation developed. This argued that the progress of society will lead to decriminalisation and to the broad replacement of criminal law by the regulation of conflicts in society with civil and administrative sanctions or by other less formal social rules. Furthermore, this kind of hypothesis was also quite popular in criminal law doctrine even at the beginning of the twentieth century.[19] At that time, it referred to studies in evolutionary anthropology and it used concepts of the development of punishment close to the theory of Emile Durkheim and, in another version, to concepts of society inspired by the writings of Karl

18 Nelken, D. (2010), *Comparative Criminal Justice, Making Sense of Difference*, Los Angeles-London: Sage; Newburn, T. and Sparks, R. (eds) (2011), *Criminal Justice and Political Cultures. National and International Dimensions of Crime Control*, London-New York, Routledge.

19 Makarewicz, J. (2009), *Wstęp do filozofii prawa karnego w oparciu o podstawy historyczno rozwojowe*, Lublin: Wyd. KU [first edition: *Einführung in die Philosophie des Strafrechts auf Entwicklungsgeschichtlicher Grundlage* (1906), Stuttgart: Ferdinand von Enke].

Marx. However, one can hardly talk about such a general tendency towards decriminalisation any more. Even in the sphere of sexual behaviours, which started to be strongly decriminalised in the 1960s and 1970s (decriminalisation of homosexual intercourse or of adultery in many European countries; in Poland, decriminalisation of those behaviours had already occurred in the penal code of 1932), we now see a new wave of criminalisation of different sexual behaviours. More and more human behaviours in different aspects of activities, from economy, finance, sex, employment, justice system, ecology, etc., are being criminalised.[20] It is not always certain what the principles of those criminalisations are.[21] The doctrines of countries and preferences of scholars in that respect may differ.[22] The important role is played here by the principle of proportionality, the harm principle (quite popular in the Anglo-Saxon world), or the concept of the protection of legal goods (popular in the German *Schutz der Rechtsgüter* doctrine). One of the old principles of European doctrine in respect of criminalisation is the principle of *ultima ratio* (criminal sanction as the last resort). Do we really respect that principle? In Polish doctrine, when we discuss the problem of over-criminalisation and punitiveness, among the factors playing a role in criminalisation one mentions the requirement by European standards and rules. Otherwise, certain types of offence and criminal sanction probably would not have been introduced. When one talks about the problem of governing through crime[23] in the Anglo-American literature, what one means is the easy resort to criminal law sanctions to deal with different social problems. It is argued that, in the United States, the use of criminal sanctions becomes the *prima ratio* and not *ultima ratio*, what makes a considerable practical and theoretical difference. It seems that the European debate concerning the place of criminal policy among other public policies would be quite refreshing and could help to redefine the meaning of the principle of *ultima ratio*, and to work out a more balanced approach to the possible principles of criminalisation and the European standards in that respect.[24]

The question of the criminalisation of migrants

A very important question for the European debate in respect of the criminal justice system is the issue of the treatment of migrants, especially persons from

20 Husak, D. (2009), *Overcriminalization. The Limits of the Criminal Law*. Oxford-New York: Oxford University Press.

21 Lauterwein, C. C. (2010), *The Limits of Criminal Law. A Comparative Analysis of Approaches to Legal Theorizing*. Surrey-Burlington: Ashgate.

22 Von Hirsh, A. and Simester, A. P. (2012), *Crimes, Harms and Wrongs. On the Principles of Criminalisation*, Oxford-Portland, OR: Hart Publishing; Gardocki, L. (1990), *Zagadnienia teorii kryminalizacji*, Warsaw: PWN.

23 Simon, J. (2007), *Governing Through Crime. How the War on Crime Transformed American Democracy and Created a Culture of Fear*, Oxford-New York: Oxford University Press.

24 Dumortier, E. and Snacken, S. (eds) (2012), *Resisting Punitiveness in Europe. Welfare, Human Rights and Democracy*. New York: Routledge.

outside Europe. In Western countries it is very obvious that in different jurisdictions Europe faces the overrepresentation of migrants (and their adult children) in the criminal justice system and especially in prisons. Moreover, we can see that in dealing with migrants, very punitive measures are used (like detention centres, which are placed outside the criminal justice system), but in practice it means that there is even less protection of the rights of individuals in dealing with those foreigners who are mainly accused of illegally staying and working in the European space of justice, security and freedom (is this only for legal Europeans, therefore?). There is a tendency to criminalise the question of migration in many ways, which is one of the aspects of the above-mentioned uncertain nature of separation of criminal policy from other public policies relating to social problems. The problem of migration raises again the question related to the theoretical conceptualisation of meaning and the notion of punishment and of the criminal justice system itself, as some punitive measures are used outside that system in dealing with some migrants. It means that those punitive measures are used also outside principles worked out in criminal justice to protect the rights of individuals.[25]

The human rights question as the only limiting principle in crime policy

The European Union is treated as a rational means of civilising process in respect of social policy, including criminal policy, at least from the perspective of central Europe. One of the symbolic dimensions of that civilising process is the abolition of the death penalty in European countries (including all countries of the Council of Europe). The abolition of the death penalty is treated as a symbol of a new European approach towards criminal policy.[26] For this reason, in 2007 the European Union adopted officially a special day for a symbolic protest against the death penalty (10 October). The European standards in criminal policy concern provisions that should guarantee the humane treatment of all persons in the criminal justice system. The European standards (adopted by the Council of Europe) concern minimum prison rules (rec 2, 2006) and recommendations towards non-custodial sanctions, and the Council of Europe tries to promote best practices in resolving social conflicts, including also so-called restorative justice or different policies of diversion from criminal justice. They are supposed to be respected by all members of the European Union. That important civilising role of the European Council and the European Union may sometimes not be fully consistent with the above-mentioned tendency to overcriminalisation, inspired also by European agencies, and by those agencies and different documents of the European Union stressing the effectiveness in crime control which may lead

25 Becket, K. and Murakawa, N. (May 2012), 'Mapping the Shadow State. Toward an Institutionally Capacious Approach to Punishment', in: Moffut, K. H and Lynch, M. (eds), *Theorizing Punishment's Boundaries. Theoretical Criminology. An International Journal*, special issue, Vol. 16.

26 Girling, E. (2006), 'European Identity. Penal Sensibilities, and Communities of Sentiment', in: McAra, note 9 above.

to underestimation of the question of the due process of law. In the American literature, it is emphasised that general human rights provisions may exclude certain extreme cases from practice and legislation, but they are not enough to define criminal policy. Two countries may well respect or disrespect human rights, although one may have a much larger field of criminalisation and more punitive sanctions then the other.[27] In the framework of the Council of Europe, and especially the European Union, the standards of human rights and criminal policy are more detailed and developed than at the international level (limiting for instance the opportunity of the 'three strikes and you are out' policy towards recidivism),[28] but nevertheless the scope for debate over rational criminal policy stays quite large. To refer, in debate about that question, only to the general interpretation of the provisions of human rights standards is not enough for the development of humanitarian standards of effective criminal policy.

The question of the European penal code

The general unification and harmonisation of laws in the European Union relatively, to a lesser extent, concern criminal law policy. In that respect, the European Arrest Warrant has a symbolic character. It has replaced the mechanism of extradition and is a new institution based more on trust and recognition rather than on the traditional principle of reciprocity, typical of cooperation in criminal matters within the extradition law.[29] The criminal law is related traditionally very strongly to the attributes of the power of State (right to punish) and its internationalisation is more complicated than in respect of civil or administrative law. However, even in that respect, one can observe important changes. First of all, the changes concern the character of the European Union itself, the creation of a kind of European citizenship and the strengthening of the authorities of the European Union and of their democratic legitimacy. The growing freedom of movement without border control has also contributed to the need for developing different kinds of cooperation and coordination of work in the field of criminal justice and police matters. In the framework of the European Union there is a growing need for the recognition of offences against European institutions and those that are committed together by different persons in different countries, as in the case of organised crime. The combating of international (inter-European) organised crime requires the close cooperation of European and national agencies, the exchange of information and the harmonisation of laws. It is important to remark that the general tendency in national jurisdictions today is to strengthen in criminal matters the role of proceedings in comparison to substantive law.[30]

27 Petersilia, J. and Wilson, J. Q. (2011), 'Introduction', in: Petersilia, J. and Wilson, J. Q., *Crime and Public Policy*, Oxford-New York: Oxford University Press, 4.

28 'The severity of penalties must not be disproporionate to the criminal offence' (art. 49 [3] of the EU Charter of Fundamental Rights [2000/C 364/01]).

29 Banach-Gutierrez, note 11 above.

30 Dripps, D. A. (2011), 'The Substance–Procedure Relationship in Criminal Law', in: Duff and Green, note 14 above.

That tendency well fits the needs of cooperation between national and European agencies, which is based mostly on proceedings. For this reason it is probable and desirable that certain offences important for the European Union as a whole, and proceedings concerning cooperation in all criminal matters will be codified. However, for many reasons, including national sovereignty and the question of national languages, it is much less probable that the European criminal code(s) will replace national provisions. One can rather expect a kind of federal structure in which the general European offences and European proceedings will be codified, but the great part of offences and proceedings will stay in national jurisdictions with some different traditions, but respecting certain general standards set in European documents. It is also possible to see something like the American model penal code, which would summarise the main criminal principles as a guidance and recommendation for different national jurisdictions.

European unity and national diversity in respect of criminal law and criminal policy

It has been stressed here that European criminal law is also a still-changing modern instrument of public policy, as it is well rooted in the long legal tradition of European nations. The criminal laws and criminal law doctrines are aspects of European civilisation. The criminal law, although on the institutional level strongly related in modern times to the national state, in its doctrine and theory belonged to academia and in that respect criminal law has many universal aspects. That universal dimension of criminal law finds its expression in modern times in the reception of similar criminal law institutions over many jurisdictions, but also in different congresses, conferences, works of different international associations concerning criminal and penological matters, which prepare a lot of recommendations and resolutions and the cooperation of academics and exchange of students in that respect. Last but not least it led to the reception of main criminal law standards more or less all over the world, so they became in practice more international than simply a European heritage that has been still developing further in the global context.[31]

From that perspective, the close interrelation of criminal law doctrines and the reception of different legal institutions from different jurisdictions is a quite normal, well-established practice; it is *'Nihil novi sub sole'* (nothing new under the sun). We can therefore see that excessively strong opposition between the criminal law of the European Union and national penal codes seems to be not so well justified. The new aspect now brought into the question the relations of national penal law and universal doctrine is probably the much greater institutionalisation of cooperation and exchange of ideas.[32] Nevertheless, it should be emphasised that interactions between doctrines, laws and practices in respect of criminal

31 Cavadino, M. and Dignan, J. (2006), *Penal Systems*, London-Thousand Oaks-New Delhi: Sage, 3–49; Newburn and Sparks, note 18 above, 1–29.

32 Banach-Gutierrez, note 11 above.

justice matters are much more the rule than the exception in the European tradition, going back to antiquity as well as to modern times, from the nineteenth century to the present day. It means also that the development of the criminal law and criminal policy of the European Union does not necessarily question or threaten the development and very existence of different national legal cultures and different national traditions in respect of criminal law. One can even argue that the main controversies concerning criminal policy are not related to the differences between jurisdictions, but to the differences among scholars and their interpretations of data and differences in stressing certain values. It means that the development of European criminal law may be probably more controversial from the point of view of politics and because of the technical linguistic problems of some representatives of criminal justice systems, rather than because of real problems of doctrines of criminal law. The differences in doctrines may be identified, as far as the main categories of criminal law are concerned – like construction of types of offence and their forms, different approaches to principles of criminal liability and its limits, ideas and rationalisation of punishment and the principles of sentencing and execution of penalties – as the more detailed questions of forms of alternative punishments and probation, electronic monitoring, etc. There are important differences in approaches to different questions and institutions in different jurisdictions, but nevertheless, sometimes there are even greater differences among scholars from the same jurisdiction, concerning the most fundamental questions of criminal law like punishment and guilt, as well as many quite detailed legal and criminological questions. The exchange of ideas and concepts of institutions of law on a European level in a more institutionalised way related to the administration of the EU, may well even help to develop different concepts and the choice of the best practices and solutions. One of the problems that can be discussed is whether there is too much administrative influence into the academic debate about the concepts and institutions of criminal law. Unfortunately, an excessively casuistic approach to criminal law provisions may provoke such tendencies. There are some cases in which the academic debate is in a way frozen through too detailed regulation of positive law (to some extent it even happened in Poland in relation to the general concept of guilt and the question of *mens rea*). All the same, such problems are possible to overcome and they are not limited to international cooperation. In opposition, some harmonisation may be a natural effect of discussing and sharing ideas, concepts and of course empirical data concerning criminal policy: that effect has already been with us for a long time, and its strengthening should be welcomed. The possible codification of the criminal law of the European Union would certainly have a strong effect on national doctrines of national states and would help to modify national legislation in a more harmonious way, which would make cooperation in criminal matters easier. However, as far as the European project is respecting the diversity and independence of Member States, it is not desirable to deprive these societies of their national criminal laws and national legal traditions. From the general point of view, a kind of richness of approaches and concepts from different European legal cultures may be regarded as a very positive stimulating factor, helping in developing new solutions, and not only as a kind of old-fashioned tradition which should be overcome in due time.[33] The unity of European nations in the framework of European values should not replace the cultures and traditions of Member States and their societies, and their laws are one of the main cultural and political expressions of the existence of cultural richness and diversity of Europe. It is also good to remember that even in much more culturally and politically homogenous societies, like the United States of America, the differences between the penal codes of Member States may be in some respect even greater than typical differences between the doctrines and legal provisions of criminal laws of different members of the European Union. It would be false to define the target of the development of European criminal law doctrine as the whole unification of criminal law and criminal policy on the continent. There is not only the question of whether it is feasible, but also if it is desirable. It is argued here, that at least in the politically important future it is not desirable. From this point of view the peaceful co-existence of national criminal law and criminal policy with the development of European Union criminal law and criminal policy should not be put in doubt. Both tendencies, the developing of European Union criminal law and criminal policy and the development of criminal law and criminal policy in different national jurisdictions of its Member States, may influence each other with reciprocally beneficial effect.

33 Henham, R. (2012), *Sentencing and the Legitimacy of Trial Justice*. London-New York: Routledge.

4 EU criminal law: national boundaries and the European penal rainbow

Joanna Beata Banach-Gutierrez and Christopher Harding

Introduction

In recent years, and more especially since the 'mainstreaming' of EU crime policy and criminal law following the changes brought about by the Treaty of Lisbon, EU criminal law and criminal justice measures have intruded more significantly into the EU Member State legal orders. In this sense the jurisdictional boundaries of the Member States have become less of a barrier to supranational legal activity, as processes of legal harmonisation and mutual recognition have gained pace. It may then be asked whether the national criminal law spaces (originally viewed in the European context as cherished domains of national sovereignty) are now being supplanted by a genuinely supranational European criminal law space. But at the same time, there is an observable resilience of some distinct national or European sub-regional legal and penal traditions and cultures, which may counteract the formal legal dismantling of boundaries by preserving different *de facto* spaces of policy and practice. Thus for example the apparent supranational gains of mutual recognition under the European Arrest Warrant provisions may be compromised by the endurance of differing philosophies, policies and practices (what may be described as a 'penal rainbow') in relation to the implementation of sentences. The discussion here first of all brings forward evidence of a 'penal rainbow'[1] across the EU countries and national jurisdictions, and then poses questions regarding the impact of such a rainbow on the realisation of a supranational EU criminal law space. This discussion should be set in the broader context of understanding the role and meaning of criminal law in the contemporary world and its expressive significance for societies and their governance:

1 In the words of Advocate General Mazák: 'There is, however, no uniform concept of the notion of criminal law and the Member States may have different ideas when it comes to identifying in closer detail the purposes which it should serve and the effects it may have. It is thus difficult to talk about criminal law in general terms and without specific national connotations.' Opinion in Case C-440/05, *Commission v. Council* ('Ship Source Pollution'), (2007) ECR 1-9100, at 9112. This may serve as a convenient definition of the term 'European penal rainbow' as it is used in this discussion.

> More so than other fields of law, criminal law largely mirrors the particular cultural, moral, financial and other attitudes of a community and is especially sensitive to societal developments.[2]

Context (1): the emergence of EU criminal law and a European criminal law space – from co-operation to integration

The significance of this exercise, as a survey and critical probing of diversity in criminal law and penal systems across contemporary Europe, arises very much from the recent move into the criminal law domain on the part of the EU and the appearance of the phenomenon now going under the shorthand term of 'EU criminal law'. This development, which gained some unsteady momentum within the framework of the former EU Third Pillar,[3] has now been formally ratified by the Treaty of Lisbon and legally 'mainstreamed' within the Treaty on the Functioning of the European Union (TFEU). As such, it is a subject that has moved upwards on the EU agenda, as a matter of crime policy and both substantive and procedural law, with important implications for Member State criminal law and penal systems. However, the nature and role of this emergent corpus of legal activity remains somewhat uncertain, a subject of slippery identity.[4] Is this 'criminal law' and 'penal system' in the same sense, with the same objectives, as those familiar categories at the national level? Is EU criminal law driven by the same concerns and interests and informed and inspired by the same values as national criminal law? And perhaps, most fundamentally, from where, and why has EU criminal law appeared at this particular moment? It is necessary to pose such questions, since the possible answers will inform any critical discussion of the issue (and problem?) of criminal law and penal diversity across the EU as a whole.

An appreciation of this context is also important since it signals a move into another phase of comparative evaluation. Comparative criminal law and comparative penal theory had hitherto been a scientific and academic enquiry which could serve rather tentative intergovernmental projects of criminal justice co-operation, particularly for example under the umbrella of the Council of Europe. Now such study and critical assessment can be called to the service of the more supranational enterprise of the EU, inspired by its core mission of integration and the powerful legal method that it can employ towards that end. It is therefore necessary at the outset of this discussion to stress the difference between intergovernmental and EU legal action. Leaving aside for one moment the possibility for some opt-out in relation to EU criminal law integration, the latter has a more

2 Again, Advocate General Mazák, from his opinion in 'Ship Source Pollution', note 1 above, at 9112. See also the opinion of Advocate General Ruiz-Jarabo Colomer, in Case C-176/03, *Commission v. Council* (2005) ECR I-7907, at 7881.

3 For an overview and historical analysis, see Baker, E. and Harding, C. (2009), 'From Past Imperfect to Future Perfect? A Longitudinal Study of the Third Pillar', *European Law Review*, 34, 25.

4 See Harding, C. and Banach-Gutierrez, J. B. (2012), 'The Emergent EU Criminal Policy: Identifying the Species', *European Law Review*, 37, 758.

energetic and productive dynamic compared to the intergovernmental method, based largely upon optional and broadly drafted treaty arrangements. Especially post-Lisbon, and the EU use of the directive as the default legislative mechanism in this context, there is at least the intention to integrate matters in a more full-blooded way. Treaties, framework decisions and directives are situated along a spectrum of transnational alignment, but the directive is located at the sharper end of that spectrum, in terms of legal force, obligation and timing, and as a trigger for judicial development on the part of the Union Courts. Once agreed and formally adopted, directives require uniform Member State action across the board by a certain deadline, and as instruments for removing or ironing out diversity represent a quantum jump beyond the intergovernmental approach. Indeed, within the former EU context, this could be an issue underlying competence disputes: whether a matter should be dealt with under the First or Third Pillar could make considerable difference in relation to the legal outcome, both in substance and in time. If it is noted that a significant amount of criminal law and penal co-operation and process in Europe has been moved to this supranational domain, then the consequences for transnational action and legal development are that much more significant than hitherto. In so far as directives seek to bring about common and minimum legal positions, the associated tasks of comparative research and evaluation of diversity become more urgent, but also possibly more influential in their contribution to the process of policy formation and legislative change.

The EU and its institutions have therefore inaugurated a new phase, more urgent and purposeful, in the examination and analysis of diversity. This is evident, for example, from the Commission's pondering of the subject in its Communication of September 2011, *Towards an EU Criminal Policy*,[5] and the emphasis there on the need for impact assessment in relation to proposed criminal law and penal measures, and in the sponsoring of expert discussion at the European level in this field (and see the discussion by Lahti, Chapter 5 of this volume).[6] At the same time, respect for diversity, as a broad principle, has achieved stronger political support and formal legal recognition, in both basic treaty provisions (for instance, Article 67(1) TFEU) and in institutional practice. Uniformity, consistency, standard positions and approximation as a *sine qua non* of the integration project have lost a degree of dogmatic force, in favour of a more careful balancing of harmonisation and diversity. To some extent this may be a product of political necessity and of recognition of the political sensitivity and the scale and complexity of undertaking such a project in an expanded Union. But it is also perhaps a consequence of ideological historical shift, a growing sense that, just as biodiversity may be valuable in the environmental natural

5 European Commission, 'Towards an EU Criminal Policy: Ensuring the effective implementation of EU policies through criminal law', COM(2011) 573 final.

6 See the Commission Decision on the setting up of an Expert Group on EU Criminal Policy (Decision 20/2/C 53/05, 21 December 2011). This was on the basis of Article 67 of the TFEU. The decision provides for two meetings a year of the group, the first taking place on 19 June 2012. See also the discussion by Harding (Chapter 8 of this volume).

world context, so lexodiversity may be of value in this domain. In this sense, this is also a moment of historical irony: as the legal opportunity for integration has matured, so also the countervailing appeal of diversity has gained in ideological, political and cultural support.

Context (2): uniformity versus diversity

A second point of context to emphasise – and this is a point about global legal development at the present time – is the general tension between the movement towards uniformity (very characteristic of the 'modernity' in legal systems) and the resistance to that movement, now being expressed through the vocabulary of diversity. In very broad terms this may also be viewed as a contest between 'globalisation' and 'anti-globalisation'. In a more specifically legal context, there is a typical vocabulary and body of concepts associated with each: on the one hand, the *lexicon of uniformity* – harmonisation, approximation, common and minimum standards, integration and homogeneity; on the other hand, the *lexicon of diversity* – exceptionalism, derogation, subsidiarity, relativism, margin of appreciation, heterogeneity and self-determination (with the attendant problem of identifying and agreeing upon the unit of distinction, the 'self' claiming diverse treatment). A major project within legal modernity has been the search for uniformity, especially at transnational and international levels, culminating in major globalising enterprises of integration such as the EU and the WTO. In ideological terms, the enterprise of integration has during the second half of the twentieth century achieved the status of godhead, embodying a legal and political presumption in its favour, and a high burden of justification and proof for exception and derogation. The more recent and stronger counter-claims of diversity need to be viewed in this context. The question to be addressed in this discussion in particular is whether the largely successful and convincing claims for uniformity and integration in the economic and trading sphere may be put forward and sustained with equal force and success in the sphere of criminal and penal matters. A working hypothesis may be suggested: that integration in relation to criminal and penal matters is likely to prove a more complex and troubled process compared to other areas of policy and regulation, predominantly in the economic sector, in the past. Regulating markets is a different matter from controlling crime, and a simple transfer of the earlier instruments and methods of integration from one context to the other is unlikely to prove easily feasible or seen as so readily desirable.

It may be helpful at this point just to summarise what appear to be the main lines of argument regarding both uniformity on the one hand, and diversity on the other, in the context of crime policy, criminal law and penal systems.

The need for uniformity

In relation to crime and penal matters, two main justifications have emerged in favour of uniformity of legal provision, but these pull in different directions.

First, it is claimed that in a transnational and international context the *effectiveness* of criminal law regulation and sanctions depends upon the removal of differences, manifesting themselves for instance as frontier obstacles, varying definitions and procedures, distinct penal philosophies, and diverse standards of treatment. Effective legal control of transnational criminality requires international coordination and co-operation, and then self-evidently the removal or minimisation of differences. In the EU context, these arguments underpin the field of competence now laid down in Article 83(1) and (2) of the TFEU, essentially an instrumental role for criminal law harmonisation in support of an effective control of transnational crime and of the implementation of EU policies. Second, and somewhat consequentially, it is then claimed that the protection of more general integration interests, whether these comprise the free movement of persons as opportunity or the protection of society against crime flows, should not compromise *fundamental ideas of justice, and fair treatment and respect for individual interests*, as embodied in human rights protection. Thus for example rights of defence, access to justice, proportionality in the choice and application of sanctions, and the interest of victims should also receive attention and respect, and this may require a more effective and uniform guarantee at the supranational and international levels. Herein lies the antinomy of the EU's Area of Freedom, Security and Justice (AFSJ), containing a potential contest between security needs (effective crime control) and the requirements of justice and rights protection, and hence two main strands of legislative development in EU criminal law (for instance, European Arrest Warrant versus defence rights).[7]

The need for diversity

In opposition, what are the underlying reasons for urging respect for the principle of legal and penal diversity and restraint regarding a headlong rush towards harmonisation and full integration? Two principal sites of resistance may be identified, one arising from theory and principle, the other an outcome of more pragmatic considerations.

The point of theory and principle is related to what may be seen as inherent qualities in criminal and penal law. Certainly in the European legal and political tradition the control of crime and the use of particular sanctions for that purpose has a constitutional role and explanatory function that serves to identify the society in question. There is a strong sense that criminal law (at least in its 'core' content) expresses and confirms the principal and enduring social and cultural values of that polity, so fulfilling an important expressive and symbolic mission for the society in question.[8] As Mitsilegas (2009) has argued:

7 This also replays the tension identified some time ago in Herbert Packer's classic work, *The Limits of the Criminal Sanction* (Stanford University Press, 1968), presenting different models of 'crime control' and 'due process'. Packer's book remains highly recommended as a key reference point in any discussion of the rationale of criminal sanction

8 See, for instance: Turner, J. I. (2012), 'The Expressive Dimension of EU Criminal Law', *American Journal of Comparative Law*, 60, 555, at 578; Weigend, T., 1993, *Strafrecht durch internationale Vereinbarungen – Verlust an nationale Strafrechtkultur?* ZStW 105, 774, 789; BVerfG, 2BvE

> criminal law is fundamental in a society governed by the rule of law, as it contains rules delineating the relationship between the individual and the State and thus providing guarantees and safeguards for the individual regarding the extent and limits of acceptable behaviour and the reach of State power and force.[9]

The same argument had been expressed in a judicial context by Advocate General Mazák in his opinion in the European Court of Justice in the 'Ship Source Pollution' case:

> In many respects, criminal law stands out from other areas of law. Availing itself of the most severe and most dissuasive tool of social control – punishments – it delineates the outer limits of acceptable behaviour and in that way protects the values held dearest by the community at large. As an expression essentially of the common will, criminal penalties reflect particular social disapproval and are in that respect of a qualitatively different nature as compared with other punishments such as administrative sanctions.[10]

This expressive role for criminal law, coupled then with its more immediately instrumental role in providing security, helps to explain the longstanding and politically cherished idea that, within both an international and a European context, criminal law should remain a special and last sovereign preserve, immune from outside claims and interference. Seen in such terms, preservation of national criminal and penal law is translated into arguments of political sovereignty and national self-determination, and in relation to an increasingly incursive interest on the part of the EU may help in understanding some arguments of legal resistance. In particular, this perception of the role of criminal law can inform debate on the subject in such a way as to add a political and even emotional gloss to a consideration of more technical and functional aspects of the operation of criminal law.

Neither should the resilience of this appeal to the expressive and identity-forming role of criminal law be underestimated – it is interesting to note for instance that at a time of strong European convergence on criminal and penal law matters, a project should be established to work out a distinctively Norwegian and Nordic approach to dealing with crime.[11] Nordic 'exceptionalism', which has a strong grounding in both theory and practice,[12] may be taken as an instructive example of a regional site of resistance in relation to wider European convergence.

2/08 vom 30/6/2009, para 355 (case concerning the review of the compatibility of the Treaty of Lisbon with the German Basic Law).

9 Mitsilegas, V. (2009), *EU Criminal Law*, Oxford: Hart Publishing, at 123.

10 Opinion of Advocate General Mazák, note 1 above.

11 University of Bergen, Faculty of Law, research project: *Criminal Law Theory: A New Norwegian Approach.*

12 See: Pratt, J. and Eriksson, A. (2013), *Contrasts in Punishment: Anglophone Excess and Nordic Exceptionalism*, London: Routledge.

During the 1970s there was a strong Nordic consensus regarding criminal law as *ultima ratio* and even as a declining method of dealing with social delinquency. Subsequently, as policy and argument became more critical of rehabilitative approaches, the Nordic consensus shifted towards a limitation of imprisonment based on ideas of social justice, equality, proportionality and respect for human dignity. Moreover, the expressive role of criminal law was closely linked to a need for popular legitimacy. As Melander commented:

> if the criminal justice system is used to influence the formation and the maintenance of the morals in the society and influence the morality of its citizens, the criminal justice system must at the same time be generally considered as just and legitimate.[13]

To the extent that such Nordic exceptionalism has been modified in more recent years, this may be seen more in the domain of investigation and enforcement and in the context of increasing international and European pressures for more active transnational co-operation. For instance, there has been some expansion of police powers of investigation, especially in relation to organised crime, and drawing upon new technologies. For example, as Husabo reports in relation to Norway,[14] legislation of 1999 allowed wiretapping in the investigation of certain serious crime and computer crime, and police were given access to data stored by telecommunication providers for commercial purposes and empowered to carry out some secret searches. A similar expansion of police powers may be noted in relation to other Nordic countries.[15]

The second, more pragmatic point is linked to some extent. As the ambition and intensity of the European criminal law integration project has gained pace and momentum, via Council of Europe intergovernmental action to EU supranational action, so the scale and complexity of the task has become more evident. In relation to the present membership of the EU, taking into account its geographical and cultural spread, and diversity of legal tradition and historical and political experience, the enterprise of integration has encountered a situation that may aptly be described by metaphors such as 'patchwork', 'rainbow' or even 'kaleidoscope'. In relation to key questions of substantive offence definition, prosecution practice, procedure, sentencing principle and philosophy of sanctions, there is across the Member States a daunting diversity confronting the would-be harmoniser. Recognition of this fact will help to explain the shift

13 Melander, S. (2007), 'Nordic Criminal Justice Policy – Single Path or Separate Ways?' in: Husa, J., Nuotio, K. and Pihlajamäki, H. (eds), *Nordic Law: Between Tradition and Dynamism*. Antwerp-Oxford-Portland: Intersentia, 109, at 119.

14 Husabo, E. J. (2010), 'History and Tendencies in the Development of Criminal Procedure Law in the Scandinavian Countries, and in Norway in Particular', *Law and Justice Review*, 1, 19; and (2013) 'Counterterrorism and the Expansion of Proactive Police Powers in the Nordic States', *Journal of Scandinavian Studies in Criminology and Crime Prevention*, 14, 3.

15 A more specific example of moderation of the more traditional Nordic approach is the move towards harsher penalties in relation to drug offences under the Finnish system.

within EU policy away from harmonisation, which was proving slow and difficult to agree upon, to the strategy of mutual recognition (accepting and living with a certain level of difference), as a more feasible (although after all not unproblematic) way forward.[16] Again, a resort to mutual recognition may be linked to another strand of penal policy in the Nordic exceptionalism referred to above. This was sometimes termed 'soft harmonisation': co-operation in the form of mutual trust rather than formal legal instruments, and eschewing institutions for monitoring the implementation and operation of inter-State co-operation. That, however, may be viewed as mutual trust in its ideal state, where there is a strong existing consensus. Across the whole of Europe now, the strategy of mutual recognition has to confront a greater and more complex diversity of penal tradition. It may be argued then that the resilience of existing diversity is an important issue for comparative criminal and penal law at this stage, and that the main site for confronting and working out the antinomies in this context will be the judicial consideration of mutual recognition issues rather than pre-legislative consideration of harmonisation proposals.

Sites of antinomy in EU criminal law: balancing uniformity and diversity

It would be useful first to recall something of the present character and role of what now goes under the heading of EU criminal law, as background to the presentation of the examples of antinomy below. While the present areas of EU competence in criminal matters now have a relatively specific delineation under the TFEU, especially that laid down in Article 83, it is illuminating to reflect more informally on the matters and concerns which underlie and have driven the emergence of this competence. Arguably, the important phenomenon that has supplied the motor of EU criminal law has been human mobility, the increasingly free movement of persons across the European geographical and legal space. If it is asked what the EU norms of criminal law, criminal justice and penal disposition have been set up to deal with, the answer would seem to be not so much crime as an issue in itself, but rather the facilitation of an increased mobility of persons across the area of Europe, and addressing the consequences of such person flows. As such, criminal law has been used as a mechanism both to support free movement and to control more sinister human mobility.

The first role of EU criminal law may therefore be seen as facilitative in character, a means of ensuring the free movement of both persons and economic activities across the European space comprising the Single Market. This is a well-established role, with some longstanding legal examples of the impact of

16 Commission of the European Communities, *Green Paper on the approximation, mutual recognition and enforcement of criminal sanctions in the European Union*, 30 April 2004, COM(2004) 334 final. See also Lahti, R. (2010), 'Towards internationalization and Europeanization of criminal policy and criminal justice: challenges to comparative research', IMTA Conference, *Criminal Justice: The Connection of Times*, St Petersburg, 8–10 October 2010.

the free movement principle on national criminal law and criminal justice, either negatively to moderate the use of criminal law in so far as that may act as an obstruction to free movement (as for instance in *Casati* in 1981)[17] or positively to promote the effectiveness of EU policy and rules (as for instance in *Amsterdam Bulb* in 1977).[18] It should be noted that this is an *instrumental* role for criminal law: using criminal law as a means to end (ensuring EU law and policy) rather than expressively to embody in itself distinct values and objectives. The objections to such criminal law competence are that it may demote, in a qualitative sense, the value-setting and constitutional role of criminal law and similarly devalue its juridical currency through an over-extensive resort to the rules and procedures of criminal law (see also the contributions by Lahti[19] and Franssen[20] to this volume). This is the domain of EU criminal law now formally based upon Article 83(2) of the TFEU and arguably relating to the 'freedom' component of the AFSJ.

The second role of EU criminal law, addressing sinister person flows across the Union, has more of an association with security as a value of the AFSJ, and is thus *protective* rather than facilitative of citizen interests, by guarding against significant types of transnational criminality (typically terrorist threats, organised cross-border criminal activity, and xenophobia), now encapsulated in the list of 'Euro crimes' contained in Article 83(1) of the TFEU. In this regard, Article 67(3) of the TFEU stipulates: 'the Union shall endeavour to achieve a high level of security through measures to prevent and combat crime, racism and xenophobia.' This, then, is the matter of *criminalité* and *droit criminel sans frontières*. Of this body of policy and law it may be speculated whether it comprises a new domain of criminal law and criminal justice, or is alternatively just a further development of international and regional co-operation. Or, to put that question somewhat differently: are the particular examples of organised crime, racism and xenophobia new areas of European interest, and representative of a move beyond traditional Single Market concerns and consequences towards an expression of distinctively pan-European values, such as individual security, open-mindedness and non-discrimination, democratic governance, non-coercive dispute resolution, and cultural tolerance?

Whether viewed in its facilitative or protective role, EU criminal law relies on certain necessary strategies for its realisation: a common provision of policy and law, legal integration, leading in practical terms to the creation of a single European criminal law space. Within that space there should be a directed use or non-use of some criminal law, complemented by commonly agreed external security measures, and dependent upon measures of co-operation and coordination as between the still distinct national jurisdictions. In legal terms, and more specifically as a practical matter, much of the above also requires commonly agreed, matching and complementary legal definitions, procedures

17 Case 203/80, *Casati* (1981) ECR 2595.
18 Case 50/76, *Amsterdam Bulb BV Produktschap voor Siergewassen* (1977) ECR 137.
19 Chapter 5.
20 Chapter 7.

and sanctions, and so a general need for uniformity across the Member States. Thus, there is a widespread provision for harmonisation (or approximation) at a legislative and regulatory level, and consistency in judicial and administrative practice. But, while harmonisation may be broadly agreed as a necessary strategy, agreement on its specific aspects in relation to criminal law and penal issues may be more difficult to achieve (as will be illustrated further on in this chapter). That has become one of the main sites for antinomy, when resistance to harmonisation emerges as an insistence on maintaining difference in order to preserve crucial national interests or values. Following from this, mutual recognition was taken up as an alternative strategy – to accept ('recognise') the different legal position of another national system, but to live with that difference in the sense that it will not be used to obstruct co-operation (for instance, refuse a requested extradition) between Member States.[21] At first sight, mutual recognition might appear as a feasible solution, by bringing about a *de facto* alignment without the lengthy and inconclusive debate that may be sometimes inherent in attempts to fully harmonise. Yet even mutual recognition may be pushed only so far and its automaticity not easily agreed – the initial agreement to recognise may be possible only by providing in advance for exceptions (and so opt-out) in cases where acceptance of the other approach is strongly resisted. In this way, testing the exceptions to mutual recognition has become another main site of antinomy, where claims for diversity may be (most often judicially) tested against the need for uniformity and co-operation.

Thus, two main routes for testing antinomy have emerged in the EU legal context. First, there has been some discussion in a legislative context, typically for instance in the preparation and negotiation of framework decisions or directives which seek to lay down some common provisions relating to such matters as offence definition or agreed procedures of co-operation at the Member State level. In the second place, some issues have been tested through litigation and left to judicial resolution by either the EU or national courts. In turn, within this last category, two main contexts have emerged, within which such questions have been explored – first, conflicts between application of the free movement principle and national criminal law (as for instance in the *Bonsignore*, *Bouchereau* and *Josemans* cases forwarded to the European Court of Justice for a preliminary ruling, as discussed further on); and then constitutional and human rights-based contestations, typically dealt with by senior national courts. In so far as the outcome of such argument has been the preservation of national diversity over European uniformity, this may be explained through the recognition of the values underlying diversity, or the 'rainbow', expressed for instance in the Commission's Green Paper on approximation, mutual recognition and enforcement of criminal sanctions in 2004:

21 See generally on the role and development of the principle of mutual recognition in EU law: Janssens, C. (2013), *The Principle of Mutual Recognition in EU Law*, Oxford: Oxford University Press.

The differences between the Member States' legislation on penalties are still quite sharp. There are historical, cultural and legal reasons for this, deeply rooted in their legal systems, which have evolved over time and the expression of the way in which Member States have faced and answered fundamental questions about criminal law. These systems have their own internal coherence.[22]

Pre-legislative argument

Attempts to produce new EU legislation, whether in the form of Third Pillar framework decisions or old First Pillar or TFEU directives, have provided the trigger for some of the argument based on national diversity and preferences.

One early example of such argument related to the attempt to define in legal terms the concept of organised crime and participation in such activity. The discussion evolved through the formulation of EU Action Plans of 1997 and 2000, a Joint Action in 1998 and finally a Framework Decision of 2008.[23] One particular point of contestation was the more precise conceptualisation and definition of participation in organised criminal activity and whether the concept of conspiracy should be used as one way of expressing the element of participation. The concept of criminal conspiracy is very much favoured in US criminal law (witness the large number of federal US offences based on conspiracy), and established within UK criminal law, but the subject of much greater reservation and suspicion in many continental European systems.[24] British insistence on retaining the concept of conspiracy led to a complex and protracted negotiation in relation to the Framework Decision, eventually accommodating the British position by retaining conspiracy as a possible basis for criminal liability in this context. The strength of dissension is revealed, however, in the attachment of a 'dissenting opinion' on the part of the Commission, France and Italy to the Framework Decision on this point. The strongly worded opinion insists that, in its eventual form, the Framework Decision did not achieve the minimum degree of necessary approximation, with the implication that this would jeopardise the effective co-operation between Member States which was envisaged in this context.[25]

A similar issue arose in relation to the definition of xenophobia and incitement to racial hatred, again in connection with the drafting of a Joint Action in 1996, and subsequently a Framework Decision in 2008.[26] At the first attempt at

22 Green Paper, note 16 above, at 8.

23 Council Joint Action 98/733/JHA, making it a criminal offence to participate in a criminal organisation, OJ 1998, L 351/1; Council Framework Decision 2008/841/JHA, on the fight against organised crime, OJ 2008, L300/42.

24 On the American enthusiasm for the concept of conspiracy in criminal law (and also the use of vicarious and strict liability) as contrasted with a European insistence on personal individual responsibility as a basis for criminal liability, see: Fletcher, G. P. (1998), *Basic Concepts of Criminal Law*, Oxford: Oxford University Press, at 190–94.

25 For further and more detailed discussion, see Mitsilegas, note 9 above, at 93 *et seq*.

26 Council Joint Action 96/443/JHA, concerning action to combat racism and xenophobia, OJ 1986, L 185; Council Framework Decision 2008/913/JHA, on combating certain forms and expressions of racism and xenophobia by means of criminal law, OJ 2008, L 328/55.

definition for purposes of the Joint Action, the UK entered a national reservation that the measure should apply only to behaviour which is threatening, abusive or insulting and intended to stir up racial hatred (a similar reservation was entered by Denmark). This restrictive position was again adopted by the UK in relation to the Framework Decision, when it secured the insertion of an exception within that measure, to the effect that States may choose to punish only conduct that is likely to disturb public order, or is threatening, abusive or insulting, and where reference to religion is a pretext for discriminatory acts.[27] This provides another example of pre-legislative negotiation which addresses national sensitivities. But in this kind of case, it might also be asked to what extent this is a matter of deeply entrenched national preference, or pragmatic political bargaining. On this particular issue, the UK internal legal position was already broadly comparable with the Framework Decision's objective and it seemed that the UK was mainly concerned to avoid any need for further amendment to its own law. Thus the aim of the negotiation was to ensure that the EU measure would be compliant with existing UK law, to save further legislative action at the national level (see also the contribution by Edwards to this volume).[28] This illustrates the complexity of interpretation in these cases, attempting to judge the national position as principled resistance or political opportunism (when the short-term gains may be, for example, apparent compliance with EU requirements, while at the same time mollifying national Euro-scepticism, although at the (European) cost of protracted EU level negotiation).

A final example that may be taken of such pre-legislative negotiation concerns a measure that emerged as a Framework Decision in 2005, on the mutual recognition of the confiscation of crime-related proceeds, instrumentalities and property.[29] The Framework Decision sought to establish some measure of harmonisation in the form of a minimum set of alternative bases for confiscation of criminal gains. The narrow view was that confiscation should be limited to situations where there was proof that the gain arose from the commission of specific offences. The negotiation in this case eventually accommodated an arguably more punitive, wider position on the part of the UK, under which confiscation could be extended to cover gains evidenced in a 'criminal lifestyle'. This emerged in the wording of the Decision as one of the minimum alternatives – where 'the value of the property is disproportionate to the lawful income' of the property holder, a basis for confiscation already laid down in the UK Proceeds of Crime Act in 2002.[30] Since the criminal lifestyle provision may have proven unconstitutional in some other Member States,[31] the Framework Decision compromised through a set of alternative bases for confiscation.

27 Mitsilegas, note 9 above at 98.

28 Chapter 16.

29 Council Framework Decision 2005/212/JHA, on confiscation of crime-related proceeds, instrumentalities and properties, OJ 2005, L 68/40.

30 Mitsilegas, note 9 above, 102–3.

31 See discussion in the UK House of Lords European Union Committee's 19th Report for Session

Judicial resolution: free movement contestations

Unsurprisingly, over time the use or non-use of national criminal or penal law in a certain way has collided with the application or exercise of the Single Market freedom of movement for persons and economic activity, and this has provided the opportunity to test the resort to or insistence by national systems of particular policies and approaches. Two earlier cases illustrated the way in which Member State policies regarding the application of penal measures and other sanctions could run counter to the free movement of persons as required by the EC Single Market principles. In *Bonsignore* (1975),[32] an Italian worker in Germany had been prosecuted and convicted in relation to an 'accidental' homicide involving the careless use of a firearm, and the German court had ordered his deportation as a measure of general deterrence. This latter measure was contested as contrary to his freedom of movement as a worker, and following a reference to the European Court of Justice, the latter handed down a ruling to the effect that deportation could only be justified as an exception to freedom of movement if necessary on grounds of the particular individual's continuing threat to the safety of others, and not on the basis of general dissuasion. In effect, this resulted in a restriction on the national resort to measures of general deterrence, although not, it should be noted, as a principled objection to such a penal strategy or its effectiveness, but as a practical disallowance of such practice because of its conflict with Single Market imperatives.

There was a similar outcome in the case of Bouchereau in 1977.[33] This concerned the situation of a French worker in the UK, convicted there of drug offences and then subject to a deportation order. The British court ordering the deportation justified its decision on the evidence of the offender's past criminal record, and this, in the subsequent view of the European Court of Justice, again violated free movement rules, since deportation could only be justified on the basis of a present risk to others in society, and previous convictions in themselves would not provide sufficient evidence of such a risk. In this situation there was again a practical limit imposed on the way in which a criminal court was using certain evidence to justify a penal outcome, but again, as in *Bonsignore*, the driving consideration was the prioritisation of the economic Single Market imperative over national penal policy or practice.

More recently, the antinomy between Single Market interests and national penal policy has emerged in a different form, regarding the Dutch tolerance, as a matter of crime and penal policy, of the use of cannabis and its legal consumption in the Netherlands in coffee shops. This policy of Dutch exceptionalism became viewed as encouraging a kind of 'drug tourism', whereby other EU nationals would travel freely to the Netherlands to take advantage there of opportunity

2008–9, *Money Laundering and the Financing of Terrorism, Volume II – Evidence,* HL Paper 132-II, at 163.

32 Case 67/74, *Bonsignore v. Oberstadtdirektor der Stadt Köln* (1975) ECR 297.

33 Case 30/77, *R v. Pierre Bouchereau* (1977) ECR 1999.

to use the coffee shops. To counter this tendency, the local authority in the city of Maastricht introduced in 2005 a city regulation which laid down a residence requirement for using the coffee shops to consume cannabis. This discrimination between Dutch residents and other EU nationals was legally tested in *Josemans v. Burgemeester van Maastricht*[34] as an infringement of EU free movement rights. On reference to the ECJ, on this occasion the Single Market imperative did not prevail, since the Court considered that the Dutch objective of combating drug tourism should take priority. What may be noted here is the crime policy context: this was a strategy of general crime prevention, not a matter of applying individual sanctions on the basis of a particular approach to predicting the risk of crime.

Judicial resolution: constitutional protection and fair trial rights

The other set of examples in which positions of national preference have been judicially tested concerns a more genuine weighing of competing criminal law, justice and penal argument rather than Single Market issues. These examples also focus on some currently significant questions of criminal and penal policy and principle in a European context: extradition, *ne bis in idem*, victim and defendant rights, and the operation of prison terms.

The operation of the European Arrest Warrant (EAW), as laid down in the Framework Decision of 2002,[35] has resulted in a now considerable case law across European jurisdictions, as a fertile site of legal argument where a tension between security and justice interests is presented for resolution in a judicial context. As Mitsilegas commented in 2009, such cases:

> cast light on the different tensions caused by mutual recognition when applied in the national constitutional framework and signify the resurfacing of the debate regarding primacy of European law . . . over national constitutions.[36]

Put another way, the operation of the EAW has emerged as a new EU constitutional flashpoint.

One objective of the EAW was to expedite and enable the rendition of alleged offenders from one jurisdiction to another, and this included a limitation on the historical double criminality condition and a requirement for Member States to extradite their own nationals under the EAW procedure.[37] An occasion arose to test the automaticity of this process in 2005 when Spain requested the extradition of a suspected Al-Qaeda terrorist with joint German and Syrian nationality,

34 Case C-137/09, *Marc Michel Josemans v. Burgemeester van Maastricht* (2010) ECR 1-774.

35 Council Framework Decision 2002/584/JHA, on the European Arrest Warrant and the surrender procedures between Member States, OJ 2002, L 190/1.

36 Mitsilegas, note 9 above, at 135.

37 The requirement of double criminality is (to some extent) listed as a ground for optional non-execution of a warrant under Article 4 of the Framework Decision, and the nationality of the alleged offender is not listed as either a mandatory or an optional ground for refusal to surrender a person.

and this was legally challenged as a violation of fundamental rights guaranteed under the German Constitution. The German *Bundesverfassungsgericht* accepted this argument,[38] reasoning that the principle of fundamental rights protection under both EU and German law could not be compromised by an absolute presumption of trust in other national systems such as appeared to underlie the EAW provisions. Article 16(2) of the German Constitution allowed the extradition of German nationals 'to a Member State of the European Union or to an international court of justice as long as constitutional provisions are upheld'. The Court stressed the expectation of German citizens to be protected within the framework of the German legal system, and ruled that the German legislature, by not transposing the 'territoriality' ground for refusing extradition listed in Article 4(7) of the Framework Decision into the EAW implementing legislation, had thereby breached Article 16(2) of the Constitution.[39]

Similar challenges have arisen in other EU Member States. Again in 2005 the Polish Constitutional Tribunal held that the Polish EAW implementing legislation was contrary to the 'absolute' guarantee under Article 55(1) of the Polish Constitution that Polish citizens be held criminally accountable before a Polish court.[40] In the same year the Supreme Court of Cyprus ruled that the Cypriot implementing legislation was contrary to Article 11(2) of the Constitution, which prohibited the extradition by Cyprus of its own nationals,[41] but in 2007 the Czech Constitutional Court found that implementation of the EAW provision was not contrary to Article 14(4) of the Czech Charter of Fundamental Rights and Basic Freedoms, which stated that Czech citizens could not be forced to leave the country.[42] Although in such cases the more precise legal arguments and constitutional outcomes have been framed in different ways, in a number of these cases there is a strongly principled affirmation of the special and pre-eminent link between individual and State based on citizenship, and the constitutional assertion of the latter over the countervailing value of trans-European criminal law co-operation.[43]

The separate issue of balancing defendant and victim entitlements in criminal proceedings was tested via a different route in the *Pupino* case, well known for the

38 Judgment of the BVerfG of 18 July 2005, 2 *BvR* 2236/04; also reported in English in (2006) 1 CMLR 16.

39 *Ibid.* See also: Geyer, F. (2006), 'The European Arrest Warrant in Germany: Constitutional Mistrust towards the Concept of Mutual Trust', Chapter 5 in: Guild, E. (ed.), *Constitutional Challenges to the European Arrest Warrant*, Oisterwijk: Wolf Legal Publishers.

40 Judgment of the Polish Constitutional Tribunal of 27 April 2005, P 1/05; see Statewatch Press Release of April 2005. See also: Pollicino, O. (2008), 'European Arrest Warrant and Constitutional Principles of the Member States: A Case Law-based Outline in the Attempt to Strike the Right Balance between Intersecting Legal Systems', *German Law Journal*, 9, 1313.

41 Judgment of the Supreme Court of Cyprus of 7 November 2005 (294/2005). See Pollicino, note 40 above, at 1314. See also: Kapardis, A. (2006), 'The Cypriot Constitutional Court's Rejection of the European Arrest Warrant', Chapter 3 in Guild, E. (ed.), *Constitutional Challenges*, note 39 above.

42 Judgment of the Czech Constitutional Court of 3 May 2006 (Pl. US 66/04).

43 For a wider survey and commentary on this kind of case law, see Guild, E., 2006, *Constitutional Challenges*, note 39 above.

European Court of Justice's application of the doctrine of indirect effect in the context of framework decisions.[44] The 2001 Framework Decision on the standing of victims in criminal proceedings enabled children who were alleged to have suffered abuse from teachers to testify under a special procedure, as a measure of victim protection. The Italian Code of Criminal Procedure restricted such victim protection to cases involving alleged sexual offences or a sexual background. On a reference for a preliminary ruling to the European Court of Justice, the latter stated that effect should be given in such cases to the wider provision in the Framework Decision by virtue of its indirect effect, subject only to the protection of defence rights under Article 6 of the ECHR. Although the clash in this case involved 'ordinary' national legislation (the Code of Criminal Procedure) rather than a constitutional provision, there was nonetheless a suggestive difference of emphasis in the Court of Justice's reasoning. In *Pupino*, the European Court of Justice (ECJ) stressed the EU principle of loyal co-operation in order to affirm the prevalence of the EU measure, whereas in the EAW cases referred to above, national constitutional courts had stressed the need for basic rights protection.

The antinomy may also be based on differences as between national criminal law regimes, as distinct from a tension between national and European interests and values. Another case arising from the application of EAW provisions involved a clash between British and Polish penal values as expressed through the imposition of terms of imprisonment. The example involved the transfer of a Polish national (the *Jakub T* case),[45] convicted of rape in the UK, to serve the term of imprisonment in Poland, under the transfer of sentenced persons provision in the EAW Framework Decision. Following trial and conviction by the British court, the offender had been sentenced to concurrent prison terms in respect of the offences committed, but such concurrent terms are contrary to Polish law. There followed a revealing legal saga within the Polish system: first an appeal to the Polish Supreme Court and Constitutional Tribunal,[46] upholding the prohibition on concurrent terms being served, followed by a legislative change, which could then accommodate under Polish law such different approaches to sentencing emanating from other systems.[47]

A final example may suffice here, relating to a discussion of the *ne bis in idem* principle, and again illustrating another route of legal argument. As in the case of the EAW, *ne bis in idem*, or double jeopardy, has proved to be an increasingly significant site of legal argument in the context of trans-European criminal law process. A case of cigarette smuggling across a number of EU Member State boundaries demonstrates well the legal complexity that may arise from the prosecution of such offences. The *Kretzinger* case in 2007[48] involved cigarette smuggling across the borders of Greece, Italy and the UK, so enabling a number

44 Case C-105/03, *Criminal Proceedings against Maria Pupino* (2005) ECR 1-5285.

45 See Banach-Gutierrez, J. B. (2013), 'Globalised Criminal Justice in the EU Context: How Theory Meets Practice', *New Journal of European Criminal Law*, 4, 154, at 159 *et seq.*

46 *Ibid.*, at 160–1.

47 *Ibid.*, at 161.

48 Case C-288/05, *Criminal Proceedings against Jurgen Kretzinger* (2007) ECR 1-6441.

of countries to exercise jurisdiction over the cross-border offending. Jurisdiction had been exercised by Italy, resulting in a trial and convictions, but the latter and the subsequent sentences (actual and suspended prison terms) were handed down *in absentia*, so that the sanctions were not enforced against the offenders as such. Subsequently, jurisdiction was also exercised by German courts, which were able to apply prison terms to the offenders, although on the basis of conviction for elements of the offending transaction carried out in the territory of Greece. On appeal, and reference to the Court of Justice, it was argued that the German sentences were contrary to the *ne bis in idem* provision as laid down in Article 54 of the Schengen Convention. The ECJ agreed in its ruling that there was an infringement of the double jeopardy principle, since the transportation of the smuggled goods across successive internal borders was the same continuing act, and enforcement had already taken place in Italy, albeit via a suspended term of imprisonment *in absentia*. Although the specific legal outcome appears clear enough in this case, the underlying motivation within the legal process is interesting and somewhat obscure: an 'activist' German distrust regarding the seriousness of enforcement in Italy and Greece, perhaps in such a case revealing differing enforcement cultures across Member States?

Antinomies: a summary

The competing values and interests at issue in this illustrative case law are summarised in Table 4.1.

Table 4.1 The criminal law and penal rainbow: a table of antinomy

National preference	*Countervailing argument*
Conspiracy as a component of organised crime (UK)	Less wide-ranging concept of participation in organised crime (Commission, France, Italy)
Narrow definition of xenophobia (UK)	Wider definition (other States)
Evidence of criminal lifestyle as a basis for confiscation of proceeds of crime (UK)	More restrictive view (other States)
Measures of general deterrence (Germany)	Free movement of persons (EC)
Use of previous criminal record (UK)	Free movement of persons (EC)
Restricted access to cannabis consumption/ restriction on drug tourism (Netherlands)	Free movement of persons (EU)
Limits on extradition of own nationals (Germany, Poland, Cyprus)	Enhanced transfer arrangements under EAW (EU, Czech Republic)
Restricted provision for victim protection (Italy)	More extensive victim protection (EU)
Concurrent prison terms (UK)	No concurrent prison terms (Poland)
Active assertion of criminal jurisdiction (Germany)	*Ne bis in idem*: limits on exercise of jurisdiction (EU)

The resilience of diversity: consequences for the supranational order

The above discussion confirms the longstanding awareness and lessons of comparative criminal law and criminal justice: that across national legal systems there is a widespread diversity of philosophy, policy, law and practice in relation to substantive, procedural and penal matters in the criminal law field. Moreover, and significantly for the present discussion, that is a resilient diversity, even in the face of the stronger supranational method and its impulse towards harmonisation and common standards. Indeed, this is so much the case that this domain could provide the new site for contest on matters of legal primacy, as between the integration imperative and national constitutional protection. The present question concerns the more precise implications and consequences of this state of affairs for the emergent project of EU criminal law.

What the brief survey carried out here reveals more specifically is a complicated alignment of argument, and not simply a matter of national interest versus EC or EU interest. Rather, the debate (perhaps unsurprisingly in a criminal justice context) is more a matter of effective crime control versus rights protection. Sometimes the national position may favour crime control objectives, and at other times rights protection. Similarly, the European position may sometimes be an assertion of effectiveness (as in the case of the EAW) and at other times an espousal of rights protection, and the latter may be inspired in some instances by the promotion of Single Market opportunities (especially the free movement of persons), and at other times by pure or 'classic' basic rights doctrine (for instance, regarding victim protection or defence rights). It is not possible to say, therefore, that either national or European positions equate with either more security and crime control or more justice and rights protection. The substantive battle lines are very fluid in this respect.

This is likely to remain an area of vigorous debate, and perhaps increasingly so. As such, resolutions will not prove easy, with the result that the pan-European outcome may be either an agreed (and perhaps rather meaningless) minimal uniformity, or agreed acceptance of diversity, but as a mutual recognition riddled with complexity. The near future may then comprise, on such a reading, a common EU criminal law which is little more than a pale ghost, or on another reading, a more explicit and sharp and lively comparative and constitutional debate regarding the values and direction of criminal law, criminal justice and the penal system.

That last observation leads to a final reflection on what might be termed the 'virtue of diversity' (or more colourfully the pot of gold at the end of the rainbow).[49] It is a matter of perspective. For anybody who is convinced by a globalisation or common or single regime agenda, diversity will appear as problematic,

49 The pot of gold at the end of a rainbow derives from an old European myth, but has been enthusiastically adopted, in Irish folklore in particular, to convey the idea of a buried treasure. However, a physicist would point out that the end of the rainbow is a fiction: a rainbow as an

as an obstacle to common provision, as achieved by standardisation, harmonisation or even the more qualified mutual recognition. But that position assumes an almost Utopian end result in the common policy, as something perfected and final. However, a more sceptical reading of such a vision may fear therein the possibility of stagnation and fossilised dogmatism, and urge instead that history is always a matter of change, requiring a constant source of new solutions, so that contestation and argument regarding alternative approaches is a valuable end in itself. A vital polity and system of governance is one that is continually willing to question itself. In that sense, the richness and achievement of the characteristically European approach lies in its natural diversity rather than its strength in convergence. While recognising the clear value of the 'Union' endeavour, paradoxically almost, that enterprise derives much of its vitality from an ability to draw critically from its own diversity and construct more informed and richer solutions from such an exercise. On such a reading of the subject, the diversity of the 'penal rainbow' should be seen as a rich resource and not as a problematical obstacle to integration.

optical phenomenon is circular, but the surface of the earth obstructs the full human vision of the rainbow. It is indeed a worthy metaphor for this discussion.

5 Towards a principled European criminal policy: some lessons from the Nordic countries

Raimo Lahti

Introduction

Before the entry into force on 1 January 2009 of the Treaty of Lisbon,[1] there was not space for a comprehensive and coherent European criminal policy within the European Union (EU). The Treaty of Lisbon changed the legal framework for such policy planning, because the Treaty grants the EU a limited competence in the fields of both criminal and substantive criminal procedure. In particular, the EU can adopt under Article 83 of the Treaty on the Functioning of the European Union (TFEU) directives with minimum rules of EU criminal law for certain crimes. In addition, Article 325 (4) of the Treaty provides for the possibility to take measures in the prevention of and fight against fraud affecting the financial interests of the EU.

The new legislative framework gives a stronger role to the European Parliament through the co-decision process and a full judicial control to the European Court of Justice. The Charter of Fundamental Rights is legally binding by the Treaty of Lisbon. Therefore, a better balance for human rights considerations in respect of the efficiency criteria has been established.

The Communication 'Towards an EU Criminal Policy', issued by the European Commission on 20 September 2011, aims at presenting a principled framework for ensuring the effective implementation of EU policies through criminal law. According to the Communication, the Treaty of Lisbon considerably enhances the progress with the development of a coherent EU criminal policy which should be based on both the effective enforcement and a solid protection of fundamental rights. The Communication calls for a careful consideration of, for example, whether to include types of sanction other than imprisonment and fines to ensure a maximum level of effectiveness, proportionality and dissuasiveness, as well as the need for additional measures, such as confiscation.[2]

1 *Official Journal of the European Union* (OJ), 9 May 2008, 2008/C 115; the newest consolidated version, 26 October 2012/C326.

2 European Commission, 'Towards an EU Criminal Policy: Ensuring the Effective Implementation of EU Policies through Criminal Law', COM(2011) 573 final, 20 September 2011, especially 7–8, 12.

European Parliament Resolution of 22 May 2012, on an EU approach to criminal law, encourages the Commission to put forward measures that facilitate more consistent and coherent enforcement at national level of existing provisions of substantive EU criminal law, without prejudice to the principles of necessity and subsidiarity. It also encourages the Commission to continue to include in its impact assessments the necessity and proportionality test, to draw on the best practices of those Member States with a high level of procedural rights guarantees, to include an evaluation based on its fundamental rights checklist and to introduce a test specifying how its proposals reflect the general principles governing criminal law.[3] It is noteworthy that the resolution lists separately the principles which govern criminalisation on one hand and criminal law on the other: the first-mentioned include the *ultima ratio* principles of necessity and proportionality (criminal law as a means of last resort) and the last-mentioned include the principles of individual guilt *(nulla poena sine culpa)*, of legal certainty *(lex certa)*, of non-retroactivity and of *lex mitior* as well as the principles of *ne bis in idem* and of the presumption of innocence.[4]

The positive influence of the 'Manifesto on European Criminal Policy' (2009), prepared by fourteen university professors from the Member States of the EU,[5] is discernible in those EU documents. According to the Manifesto, the fundamental principles of criminal policy consist of the requirement of a legitimate purpose, the *ultima ratio* principle, the principle of guilt (*mens rea),* the principle of legality (the *lex certa* requirement, the requirements of non-retroactivity and *lex mitior, nulla poena sine lege parlamentaria*), the principle of subsidiarity, and the principle of coherence.

The first legislative instrument, which is based on Article 83(2) TFEU, is Directive 2014/57/EU of 16 April 2014 on criminal sanctions for market abuse.[6] Therefore, the grounds for this market abuse directive are particularly interesting in assessing whether this kind of approximation of criminal laws of the Member States 'proves essential to ensure the effective implementation of a Union policy' and whether the newly emphasised criminalisation principles are *de facto* applied.

The objective of the Directive 2014/57/EU is, according to the preamble, to ensure effective implementation of the European policy for ensuring the integrity of the financial markets set out in Regulation (EU) No 596/2014 on

3 European Parliament Resolution of 22 May 2012 on an EU approach to criminal law (2010/2310(INI)), OJ 2013/C 264 E/02, points 6 and 8.

4 *Ibid*., points 3 and 4.

5 The Manifesto was originally published in December 2009 in the German online journal *Zeitschrift für Internationale Strafrechtsdogmatik* (www.zis-online.com) in seven languages. The Manifesto is also printed in the *European Criminal Law Review* in 2011, at 86–103. Within the project on a European Criminal Policy Initiative also a 'Manifesto on European Criminal Procedure Law' has been published in 2013 (see *ZIS* 2013, at 430 *et seq.*). See also discussion by Harding in Chapter 8 of this volume.

6 Market abuse directive, OJ L 173/179, 12 June 2014.

market abuse:[7] 'It is essential that compliance with the rules on market abuse be strengthened by availability of criminal sanctions which demonstrate a stronger form of social disapproval compared to administrative sanctions.' Minimum rules should be established with regard to the definition of criminal offences by natural persons, liability of legal persons and the relevant sanctions.[8]

The aim here is to critically analyse the values, interests and guiding principles for a regional (European) criminal policy from a perspective of its sub-region (Finland and other Nordic countries). The above-mentioned documents and legal instruments of the EU illustrate the recent approach of EU institutions to criminal law. In Scandinavia, there is much criticism of the approximation of criminal laws of the Member States.[9] Therefore it is useful to highlight some characteristics of the 'Nordic model'.[10] Three issues will be elaborated in more detail, namely tensions and priorities in criminal policy, defensive versus offensive criminal law policy and the *ultima ratio* principle, as well as the role of punitive administrative sanctions.

Tensions and priorities in criminal policy

Harding and Banach-Gutierrez have analysed the Communication 'Towards an EU criminal policy' and framed it around three major tensions in contemporary criminal law development: criminalisation versus soft compliance, security versus justice and rights protection, and globalisation versus local diversity.[11] Their list of these tensions is illustrative. For instance, in penal theories a basic tension is often described by the contradiction of utility versus justice. Security and utility are comparable concepts.

According to utilitarian theories, the justification of punishment is dependent on how efficient the deterrent, rehabilitating or incapacitating effects of the punishment are, whereas the concept of justice is more connected with the retribution theories. The theory on the expressive function of punishment – demonstration of social disapproval – lies in the borderline, because its justification has been based both on the principle of utility (efficiency) and that of justice.[12] The mechanism through which the general preventive effect of punishment should be reached is not deterrence in the first place but the social-ethical disapproval which

7 Market abuse regulation, OJ L 173/1, 12 June 2014.

8 Market abuse directive, note 6 above, preamble, points 6, 7 and 18.

9 See e.g. Greve, V. (1995), 'The European Union and National Criminal Law', *Scandinavian Studies in Criminology*, 14, 185–203.

10 Cf. generally Suominen, A. (2011), 'The Characteristics of Nordic Criminal Law in the Setting of EU Criminal Law', *European Criminal Law Review*, 1, 170–187.

11 Harding, C. and Banach-Gutierrez, J. B. (2012), 'The Emergent EU Criminal Policy: Identifying the Species', *European Law Revue*, 37, 758–770.

12 See e.g. Raimo Lahti, R. (1985), 'Punishment and Justice – A Finnish Approach', Beiheft 24, *Archiv für Rechts- und Sozialphilosophie* (ARSP), 257–61 (260–61).

affects the sense of morals and justice – general prevention instead of general deterrence, without calling for a severe penal system.[13]

This theory has much support in the Nordic legal thinking when the preconditions for the legitimacy of the penal system are also emphasised. The public must have trust that the criminal justice system operates in an acceptable manner, and it is important to follow such principles as equality, fairness and proportionality in its structure and operation. The emphasis on non-utilitarian values of the criminal justice system – fairness and humaneness – leads to the decrease in the repressive features (punitiveness) of the system, for example through the reduction of prison rate and the introduction of alternatives to imprisonment.[14]

An important effect of the new criminal and sanction policy can been seen in the reduced use of custodial sentences in Finland. Since the mid-1970s, the relative number of offenders sentenced to unconditional imprisonment was on the decrease until 1999: from 118 in 1976 to 65 in 1999 per 100,000 of population and compared to the level in the other Nordic countries. At the same time, the development on registered criminality signalled a similar trend in all of the Nordic countries so that a dramatic cut in the prisoner rate in Finland did not result in a proportionate increase in the incidence of crime compared with other Nordic countries where the prisoner rate stayed quite stable.[15] In 2000–2005 the size increased, to 90 in 2005, but in the most recent years the level seems to be normalised to 65–70 per 100,000 population.

This effect should be assessed with a view to the general objectives and values of the criminal policy that was adopted in Finland. Cost-benefit thinking in policy-making – as it was originally formulated in the late 1960s[16] – suggests that we should aim at the reduction and distribution of the suffering and other social costs caused by crime and by the control of crime. In addition to crime prevention, a strong emphasis should be put on the arguments of justice and humaneness. For instance, the argument of justice requires a just allocation of social costs of crime and crime control among different parties, such as society, offenders

13 See especially Andenaes, J. (1974), *Punishment and Deterrence,* Ann Arbor: University of Michigan Press, especially Chapter 4 ('The Moral or Educative Influence of Criminal Law'). See also Mäkelä, K. (1974), 'The Societal Tasks of the System of Penal Law', *Scandinavian Studies in Criminology,* 5, 47–67.

14 For more detail, see Lahti, R. (1985), 'Current Trends in Criminal Policy in the Scandinavian Countries', in: Bishop, N. (ed.), *Scandinavian Criminal Policy and Criminology,* Copenhagen: Scandinavian Research Council for Criminology, 59–72 (66–9); Lahti, R. (2000), 'Towards a Rational and Humane Criminal Policy – Scandinavian Penal Thinking', *Journal of Scandinavian Studies in Criminology and Crime Prevention,* 1, 141–55 (145–9).

15 For more detail, see Törnudd, P. (1993), *Fifteen Years of Decreasing Prisoner Rates in Finland,* Helsinki: National Research Institute of Legal Policy (NRILP); Lappi-Seppälä, T. (1998), *Regulating the Prison Population,* Helsinki: NRILP,

16 See originally Törnudd, P. (1969), 'The Futility of Searching for Causes of Crime', *Scandinavian Studies in Criminology,* 3, 23–33; Törnudd, P. (1995), 'Setting Realistic Policy Goals', *Scandinavian Studies in Criminology,* 14, 37–50. See also Lahti, R., (1972), 'On the Reduction and Distribution of the Costs of Crime', *Oikeustiede-Jurisprudentia* (Helsinki), 2, 298–313.

and victims, and the argument of humaneness speaks in favour of parsimony and leniency of penal sanctions and the respect of human dignity in crime control.

The reduced prisoner rate should be assessed in relation to the preventive effects of the system of criminal sanctions. The above-described Nordic observation, in addition to other criminological data, is an argument against the fear that a cut in the inmate count will result in a proportionate increase in the incidence of crime. Accordingly, the variations in the prisoner rate should not be looked at as phenomena separate from other events, neither should the criminal policy changes since the late 1960s be seen merely as the results of some ideological agenda pursued by a group of penal experts.

Tapio Lappi-Seppälä has studied the relationship between the penal policy and the prisoner rate extensively. His conclusions include the following contentions: penal severity is closely associated with the extent of welfare provision, differences in income equality, trust and political and legal cultures. So the Nordic penal model has its roots in consensual and corporatist political culture, a high level of social trust and political legitimacy, as well as a strong welfare state. These different factors have both indirect and direct influences on the contents of penal policy.[17]

The results of Lappi-Seppälä's studies suggest that the developments of criminal policy must be assessed in the light of simultaneous structural (social, political and economic) and cultural changes. The criminal policy decisions must be examined with a discerning eye. These decisions should be based on research and rational reasoning. At the same time, structural and cultural circumstances of the society and the increased interdependence of states should be taken into account. The strengthened interaction between different criminal policy models (such as a Scandinavian type) on the European and global level is to be recognised. It is a major challenge, in this respect, to be able to react to, and to influence, the development of criminal law and criminal policy in the European Union and in other international organisations (especially the United Nations).

Defensive versus offensive criminal law policy and the *ultima ratio* principle[18]

In a notable Scandinavian anthology, in which the main message throughout is a warning against increased penal repression, Nils Jareborg distinguishes defensive penal law policy and offensive penal law policy as two different ideal models for decision-making on the criminal justice system. Jareborg argues for the defensive model, whose principles for criminalisation and procedural safeguards correspond

17 For more detail, see Lappi-Seppälä, T. (2008), 'Trust, Welfare, and Political Culture: Explaining Differences in National Penal Policies', *Crime and Justice*, 37, 313–87; and the same author, (2011), 'Explaining Imprisonment in Europe', *European Journal of Criminology*, 8, 303–328; and (2012), 'Penal Policies in the Nordic Countries', *Journal of Scandinavian Studies in Criminology and Crime Prevention*, 13, 1, 85–111.

18 See also generally Lahti, R. (2010), 'Das moderne Strafrecht und das ultima-ratio-Prinzip', in: *Festschrift für Winfried Hassemer*, Heidelberg: C. F. Müller Verlag, 439–48.

to the penal law ideology of a *Rechtsstaat* (a state governed by the rule of law), whereas the offensive approach aims at solving emerging social problems and its legitimacy lies in its efficiency of crime prevention. In the defensive model, criminalisation should be used only as a last resort or for the most reprehensible types of wrongdoing, whereas in the offensive approach the threat of penal sanctions is used not as a last resort, but often in the first place and even for minor transgressions.[19]

In a later article, Jareborg[20] deals in more detail with the *ultima ratio* principle. According to him, it should be perceived as a meta principle, which summarises the criminalisation principles and is of some normative importance. Criminalisation as last resort can hardly be distinguished from the principle of subsidiarity,[21] and it may then encompass the whole of the arguments restricting criminalisation in the sense of *in dubio pro libertate*. There are three sub-principles when deciding whether to punish and with what severity: a) the penal value principle (including the requirements of blameworthiness and retrospective proportionality); b) the utility principle (covering arguments concerning criminalisation needs, control costs and inefficiency); and c) the humanity principle (including the requirement of prospective proportionality and arguments concerning the victim's interests and some sorts of control costs).

For Nils Jareborg the *ultima ratio* principle has only some normative significance, and it is more a question of criminal justice ethics. Panu Minkkinen has compared a continental (German) and an Anglo-American approach to the last resort principle with the conclusion that while the Anglo-American approach understands the last resort principle more in terms of a moral restraint in the use of criminal legislation, the German approach is more inclined to infer the principle from the constitutional framework of the State under the rule of law. For criminal law doctrine, the last resort principle is first and foremost a critical mode of reasoning.[22] In his later article, Minkkinen claims that *ultima ratio* is a politico-moral principle with constitutional significance. At the same time, this last resort principle has always been fuzzy: 'The "last resort" is the human rights fluff that the constitutional culture of "good governance" requires to justify its cultural apparatuses, and not more.'[23]

In the modern criminal law doctrine in Finland, criminalisation principles are derived from the fundamental rights doctrine – the *ultima ratio* principle

19 Jareborg, N. (1995), 'What Kind of Criminal Law Do We Want?', *Scandinavian Studies in Criminology*, 14, 17–36.

20 Jareborg, N. (2005), 'Criminalization as Last Resort *(Ultima Ratio)*', *Ohio State Journal of Criminal Law*, 2, 521–34.

21 See also European Committee on Crime Problems, (1980), *Report on Decriminalisation*, Strasbourg, 29: 'we endorse the principle of the subsidiarity and minimalisation (ultima ratio principle) of penal sanctions.'

22 Minkkinen, P. (2006), '"If Taken in Earnest": Criminal Law Doctrine and the Last Resort', *Howard Journal*, 45, 521–536 (533).

23 Minkkinen, P. (2013), 'The "Last Resort": A Moral and/or Legal Principle?', *Oñati Socio-Legal Series*, 3, 21–9 (28–9).

primarily from the principle of (prospective) proportionality (necessity): fundamental rights may be restricted by means of criminal law only when the aim of protecting a legitimate legal interest *(Rechtsgut)* cannot be achieved by any means less invasive. The same applies to criminalisation principles in a more general sense as well.[24] The effect of criminalisation principles serving to restrict the scope of criminal legislation has by some commentators been expanded to the level of application of law, yet the application of such an interpretative effect remains unclear. In my view, the values underlying human rights and fundamental rights often serve as a counterweight to the utilitarian criminal policy aspects underlying a teleological interpretation, which gives rise to balancing the argumentation between restrictive and expansive interpretation. No common standard may be given for the order of priority or weight of such conflicting arguments, however.

A heightened focus on human rights and fundamental rights has had a positive effect on the debate concerning criminalisation principles, as it has allowed an increasingly differentiated examination of the weight of human rights and fundamental rights and their merits, and has thus added to criminal law theory. In earlier Finnish criminal law thinking, the argumentation concerning criminalisation principles was based on moral philosophy and/or criminal policy arguments only. However, it must be noted that an approach of legal positivism relying on human rights and fundamental rights will not even in future suffice as a foundation for criminal law theory.

The basic values and principles and values guiding the criminal justice system – such as utility, justice and humanity – cannot be reduced into considerations of fundamental rights or human rights without any remainder. Accordingly, criminal legislation aiming at rationality must be rational with regard to both goals and values, whether such justifying grounds are based on research or rational deliberation. The grounds giving legitimacy to the system have an effect at the various steps of the justification chain at the level of both legislation and application of the law. This kind of reasoning can be characterised as pragmatic-rational criminal law thinking. It is in a certain kind of conflict with the critical criminal law theory or critical legal positivism.[25]

What gives rise to tension between the emphases of pragmatic-rational and critical criminal law theory is their attitude towards the *(neo)* criminalisations that are characteristic of the welfare state, concerning the regulation of issues such as economic activity, environmental protection and industrial safety. In Nils Jareborg's terms, there is tension between the defensive and offensive penal law policy. The criminal law reform in Finland was started with those new forms of criminality. The total reform of Penal Code aimed at regulating new types of wrong, which on the basis of an assessment of their harmfulness and

24 For more detail, see Melander, S. (2008), *Kriminalisointiteoria – rangaistavaksi säätämisen oikeudelliset rajoitukset [A Theory of Criminalization – Legal Constraints to Criminal Legislation]*, Helsinki: Suomalainen Lakimisyhdistys.

25 See Minkkinen, 'If Taken in Earnest', note 22 above, at 533; Tuori, K. (2002), *Critical Legal Positivism*, Aldershot: Ashgate. See also Tuori, K. (2013), 'Ultima Ratio as a Constitutional Principle', *Oñati Socio-Legal Series*, 3, 6–20.

blameworthiness should be incorporated into the recodified Criminal Code. The new Criminal Code should handle various types of illegal activity in a more equal and fair way and thus increase its legitimacy among citizens. Thus the penal law policy was inclined towards an offensive one.[26]

There is also a strengthening tendency in the practice of the European Court of Human Rights (ECtHR) to infer positive obligations from the provisions of the European Convention of Human Rights (ECHR),[27] especially in respect to vulnerable people.[28] See, for instance, in *K.U. v. Finland*,[29] where a minor of twelve years old was the subject of an advertisement of a sexual nature on an Internet dating site. Finnish law at that time did not provide for the means to identify the person who placed the advertisement. The Court found there was of violation of Article 8 of the ECHR, because the gravity of the act at stake required efficient criminal law provisions.[30]

In consequence, criminal law is influenced by aims and values pulling in different directions, and criminal law is consequently developing in a more differentiated way. The significance of the *ultima ratio* principle in legislation and application of the law varies depending on the type of wrong, i.e. crime, when account in the consideration is also taken of the principle of fairness and/or positive obligations of criminal law which steer the criminal justice system. This presents a challenge to criminal law research, which must be able to identify the effects of such differentiation and become involved in the elaboration of somewhat differentiating general doctrines. With that in mind, I have personally brought up the general doctrines of economic criminal law. The aim within the European Union should be maximum coherence in economic criminal law, yet at the same time certain differentiation concerning the totality of criminal law can be accepted. Correspondingly, one might refer to international and transnational criminal law as sectors of the subject containing particular characteristics.

The role of punitive administrative sanctions

Traditionally, the theories of criminal policy and criminalisation principles are usually elaborated with an eye to such unwanted forms of behaviour that are already defined as crimes under law, or the criminalisation of which is under consideration. Correspondingly, the word 'punitive' in such a context is perceived

26 Cf. the criticism by Winfried Hassemer: 'Kennzeichen und Krisen des modernen Strafrechts', (1992), in: Lahti, R. and Nuotio, K. (eds), *Criminal Law Theory in Transition: Finnish and Comparative Perspectives,* Helsinki: Finnish Lawyers' Publishing Company, 113–25.

27 Convention for the Protection of Human Rights and Fundamental Freedoms, 4 November 1950, as amended by the provisions of Protocol No. 14 (CETS no. 194) as from its entry into force on 1 June 2010.

28 See generally Ashworth, A. (2013), *Positive Obligations in Criminal Law*, Oxford: Hart Publishing, especially Chapter 8.

29 ECrHR 2 December 2008, *K.U. v. Finland,* Appl. No. 2872/02.

30 For more detail, see Ouwerkerk, J. W. (2012), 'Criminalisation as a Last Resort: A National Principle under the Pressure of Europeanisation?', *New Journal of European Criminal Law*, 3, 228–41 (238).

as referring to punishment under criminal law. During the last decades, it has been increasingly recognised that, in addition to criminal punishments, punitive (penal) sanctions are more and more introduced within the regimes of administrative law for transgressions outside the scope of criminal law.

Nowadays, the Europeanisation of criminal law through the influence of the ECHR and EU law makes it justifiable to use the term 'European criminal law' in a wide sense. Thus it comprises the norms governing behaviour and sanctions that originate in European law, regardless of whether the sanctions that the Member States may impose are in the nature of criminal law or administrative criminal law.[31]

Punitive administrative sanctions (typically punitive fees) have not been introduced in Finland or other Nordic countries, in keeping with a cohesive and consistent approach, and these sanctions have been governed under different laws, making up a disparate group. This starting point can be explained by a legal tradition in which the scope of criminalised behaviour is maintained extensively without any clear distinction between crime and other transgression of law *(Übertretung)*. There has not been place for such a consistent system of administrative criminal law as developed in German *(Ordnungswidrigkeiten)*, parallel to the criminal justice system proper. The aims of expediency and efficiency of the criminal proceedings were the objectives of simplified procedures within the penal justice system only.

In three Nordic countries (Finland, Norway and Sweden), legislative reforms have been recently prepared and partly implemented towards a more principled administrative penal law system.[32] In all of these countries, the legislative materials express the objective to create a consistent system for punitive administrative sanctions, but in none of these cases has such a unified system yet been created. There are numerous types of such sanction already in use, but a systematic review and rethinking of them is still under investigation. Depenalisation relates to primarily petty offences of a low penal value, with the consequence that the sanction to be imposed is a punitive fee instead of a fine.

The most severe punitive administrative fee that has been introduced applies to sanctioning cartels in the competition legislation, as modelled by the EU regulation. The reasoning behind that reform in Finland in the 1990s was (while harmonised legislation in the EU was pending) that the administrative process would provide greater flexibility and effectiveness. Competition law matters also call for specialised expertise. More important than the subjective culpability of the offender's actions is the harm caused by the illegal act on business in general.

In the Swedish legislative work (2013), it was argued that not only petty offences but also transgressions in the economic and financial sectors and

31 See, e.g., Klip, A. (2012), *European Criminal Law*, 2nd ed., Antwerp: Intersentia.

32 See *Rikosoikeuskomitean mietintö* [*Report of the Criminal Law Committee*] 1976:72 (Helsinki 1977); *Norges offentlige utredninger (NOU)* [*Norway's Official Investigations*] 2003:13 (Oslo 2003): Fra bot til bedring [From fine to remedy]; *Statens offentliga utredningar* (SOU) [*State's Official Investigations*] 2013:38 (Stockholm 2013): Vad bör straffas? [What should be punished?]

corporate activities in general could be suitable for depenalisation, and then the severe financial sanctions could serve the function of forfeiture, to take away the illegal profit. At the same time, it was recognised that the application of Article 6 of the ECHR concerning fair trial has not been limited only to sanctions defined as criminal punishments in national legislation, and the case law of the ECtHR concerning this provision thus set legal boundaries on the imposition of both types of punitive sanction.[33]

What kind of interplay exists between criminal sanctions (punishments) and punitive administrative sanctions? To what extent is it a proper legislative response for the systems of criminal sanctions and punitive administrative sanctions to co-exist in parallel? When the answer to the last mentioned question is affirmative, how can the appropriate and fair coordination of the systems and their compliance with the principles of *ne bis in idem* (double jeopardy) and of protection against self-incrimination – in line with the recent case law of the ECtHR and the Court of Justice of the EU – be ensured?

These questions are of considerable current interest at the European and global level when discussing the legal frameworks concerning market abuse, on one hand, and cartels on the other. The market abuse directive of 2014 prescribes criminalisation obligations to Member States but does not exempt them from the obligation to provide in national law for administrative sanctions and other measures for breaches provided in the market abuse regulation (596/2014/EU) 'unless Member States have decided . . . to provide only for criminal sanctions for breaches in their national law'.[34]

In a recent report on criminalising cartels in Finland, the main issue was formulated as to whether individual criminal responsibility of the heads of business should be introduced in addition to the existing administrative sanctioning of corporations.[35] Among the Nordic penal systems, Norway and Denmark recognise such individual criminal responsibility for cartel infringements, but in Sweden, personal responsibility has been enforced by applying a ban from participation in business activities.

The answer in the Finnish report was affirmative, with the reference to the aims and values of the recodified Criminal Code: criminalisation, which may involve the deprivation of liberty of the individual, communicates the social and ethical disapproval of the offence and would probably have a significant preventative effect; the fairness in allocating criminal responsibility would also be in support of such a solution. There would, however, arise problems in consolidating the administrative procedure against the corporation and the criminal process against

33 See especially the 'Engel criteria' worked out by the ECtHR when interpreting autonomously the concept of a 'criminal' [charge] under Article 6 of the ECHR: *Engel and others v. The Netherlands*, Appl. No. 5100/71, 5101/71, 5102/71, 5354/72 and 5370/72, 8 June 1976.

34 Market abuse directive, 2014/57/EU, 2014 OJ L 173, preamble, point 22.

35 The report *Kartellien kriminalisointi Suomessa* [*Criminalising Cartels in Finland*] (Helsinki 2014) was prepared at the Faculty of Law, University of Helsinki (authors: Ville Hiltunen and Raimo Lahti) by order of the Finnish Competition and Consumer Authority. See also the discussion by Günsberg in Chapter 14.

the individual(s). In the report, these problems are dealt with under the following sub-questions: right to a fair trial (protection from self-incrimination, *ne bis in idem*); the chronological relationship between the proceedings; exchange of data between the authorities; and the effects of criminalisation on the leniency system.[36]

The following tentative conclusions can be drawn from the reasoning in the Finnish legislative drafting. In the prevention of crime and other illegal activities in business and financial sectors, the significance and impact of various kinds of preventive tool and reactive enforcement systems on the achievement of the goals and value aims to be set shall be assessed from a comprehensive criminal policy and sanction policy perspective. Thus the examination of enforcement systems shall not be limited only to criminal justice policy or criminalisation principles; the approach to be adopted should instead be one of extensive enforcement policy and sanction policy assessment wherein the various forms of enforcement, such as punishments under criminal law and pecuniary administrative sanctions of a punitive nature, are subjected to a cost–benefit analysis.

The experiences gained from the Finnish legal reforms reinforce the view that the effective prevention of illegal activities in the business and financial sectors calls for the coordination of the regulation under criminal law and administrative law with the simultaneous comprehensive implementation of substantive law and other preventive and reactive tools. The socio-ethical disapproval demonstrated by the threat of punishment and sentencing – with imprisonment, when necessary – can have general preventive effects when the structure of criminalisation and the functioning of the criminal justice system are perceived to be fair and legitimate. The preventive role of criminal law alone is still very limited.

Conclusions

EU criminal policy is emerging. The recent EU documents of the Commission,[37] and the European Parliament,[38] as well as the Manifesto on European Criminal Policy in 2009[39] of the academic community, include good guidelines for further legislative drafting within EU to achieve a more consistent and coherent criminal policy, and they are good starting points for deeper analyses and research. These documents also include a promise to continue the development of the EU criminal policy by resorting to a thorough evaluation of existing EU criminal law measures and to continuous consultation of Member States and independent experts.

Best practices in the Member States and characteristics of their legal cultures should be systematically studied and information about the results disseminated.

36 Cf. generally: Harding, C. (2015), 'The Interplay of Criminal and Administrative Law in the Context of Market Regulation: The Case of Serious Competition Infringements', in: Mitsilegas, V. *et al.* (eds), *Globalisation, Criminal Law and Criminal Justice. Theoretical, Comparative and Transnational Perspectives*, Oxford: Hart Publishing, 199–217.

37 Communication, note 2 above.

38 Resolution, note 3 above.

39 Note 5 above.

This would facilitate interaction and coordination between national criminal policies and the emerging EU criminal policy. The discussion here has illustrated some dimensions of the Nordic legal cultures and their penal policies with the purpose that these experiences could be utilised in assessing the prospects for common European criminal policy. On the basis of this review, I shall now shortly comment on some details of these recent EU documents.

According to the Commission's Communication, an EU criminal policy is particularly warranted in respect of Article 83 (2) TFEU. This is true, but in order to enhance a more coherent criminal policy within the EU, good governance would require that the fundamental principles should guide the whole EU criminal legislation as much as possible. The main objective behind the ancillary competence regulated in Article 83 (2) TFEU is effectiveness (efficiency), and the same objective characterised the EU policy on sanctioning.[40] This objective is in collision with the traditional restraining principles of criminalisation, such as *ultima ratio* principle.[41]

There should be available convincing criminological research as clear factual evidence for assessing the effectiveness of difference sanctions or other measures in the enforcement of EU legislation.[42] The demand for measures that are effective, proportionate and dissuasive seems to reflect a belief in deterrence and severe punishment in relation to which there is much scepticism in the Nordic countries.[43] There is a concern that EU criminal law may lead to increased repression in the Nordic countries.[44] In Scandinavia, crime prevention instead of repression, the legitimacy of criminal justice system, a relatively low level of punitiveness, and humaneness in sanctioning are important values.[45]

In the Commission's Communication, among the fundamental principles guiding EU criminal legislation are the principles of subsidiarity, the protection of fundamental rights, necessity and proportionality *(ultima ratio)* at the level of enacting criminal law measures, and necessity and proportionality at the level of specifying criminal measures. In addition, the legality principle (legal certainty) is mentioned as a principle guiding 'minimum rules' regarding the definition of criminal offences and sanctions.

40 See e.g. Melander, S. (2014), 'Effectiveness in EU Criminal Law and Its Effects on the General Part of Criminal Law', *New Journal of European Criminal Law*, 5, 274–300 (285).

41 See e.g. Huomo-Kettunen, M. (2014), 'EU Criminal Policy at a Crossroad between Effectiveness and Traditional Restraints for the Use of Criminal Law', *New Journal of European Criminal Law*, 5, 301–26.

42 See also the discussion by Harding in Chapter 8 of this volume.

43 Rapporteur Cornelis de Jong in his *Report on an EU approach on criminal law* (2010/2310(INI)) at the Committee on Civil Liberties, Justice and Home Affairs (24.4.2012, A7-0144/2012, European Parliament) took the view that 'all too easily criminal law provisions are proposed for their supposedly symbolic and dissuasive effects'.

44 See e.g. Elholm, T. (2009): 'Does EU Criminal Cooperation Necessarily Mean Increased Repression?', *European Journal of Crime, Criminal Law and Criminal Justice*, 17, 191–226.

45 As to the propensities towards punitiveness in four Nordic countries (Denmark, Iceland, Sweden and Finland), see e.g. Balvig, F. *et al.* (2015), 'The Public Sense of Justice in Scandinavia: A Study of Attitudes towards Punishments', *European Journal of Criminology*, 12, 342–61.

When comparing the Communication and the Manifesto on European Criminal Policy, differences can be seen, in particular, to what extent the requirement of a legitimate purpose is emphasised. The Manifesto rightly requires that the following criteria should be fulfilled: that the interests to be protected should be derived from a) the primary legislation of the EU, and b) the Constitutions of the Member States; that the fundamental principles of the EU Charter of Fundamental Rights are not violated; and that the activities being regulated could cause significant damage to society or individuals. As the Parliament's Resolution points out, the damage can be either pecuniary or non-pecuniary.

But in none of these documents is the relationship between the principles of *ultima ratio,* subsidiarity and proportionality elaborated very much. There is much academic discussion on the principle of *ultima ratio,* but its content is still quite vague from a pan-European perspective.[46] In any case, the principles of *ultima ratio*, subsidiarity and proportionality are keenly connected with one another, especially in respect of EU criminal law. Their legal basis lies in the EU legislation.

Both the Communication and the Manifesto point to the general principle of proportionality in Article 5(4) Treaty on European Union (TEU) and in the EU Charter of Fundamental Rights (especially Article 49(3)) as the legal (constitutional) basis for the *ultima ratio* principle. Criminalisation and criminal sanctions entail social stigmatisation (moral condemnation) and, when resorting to imprisonment as penalty, the most intrusive measure. The national criminal justice systems are traditionally closely linked to the State's power and its value system, and in democratic Member States, reasonable legitimacy of State institutions and trust to their operation is normally attained.[47]

The democratic legitimacy of (and trust of) the EU institutions and its criminal legislation is much more difficult to attain. If we wish to cultivate a similar trust in the activities and institutions of the EU, we must increase the familiarity with common European values among the public, improve openness of the decision-making process and reinforce the status and rights of individuals. The legitimacy argument also strongly supports the demand of developing criminalisation principles and other general principles governing criminal law at the level of EU, as pointed out in Resolution 2010/2310 (INI).

As to the principles of subsidiarity and proportionality and their interaction, the legal (constitutional) basis for them is provided in Article 5 (3)-(4) TEU.[48] These provisions imply that the principles of subsidiarity and proportionality are legally binding, increasingly important principles of EU criminal law and the

46 See especially the papers presented at the workshop '*Ultima ratio*, a Principle at Risk. European Perspective', in 2012 in Oñati, Spain: 3 *Oñati Socio-Legal Series* 2013 (1); also, the special issue on the Effectiveness of EU Criminal Law (eds Melander, M. and Suominen, A.), *New Journal of European Criminal Law*, 5, third issue of 2014.

47 See generally Tankebe, J. and Liebling, A. (eds) (2013), *Legitimacy and Criminal Justice. An International Exploration*, Oxford: Oxford University Press.

48 See also Protocol (No. 2) on the application of the principles of subsidiarity and proportionality and the so-called 'emergency brake' in Article 83 (3) TFEU.

criteria for their assessment and the procedures for their implementation should be developed. The case law of the European Court of Justice will be significant in this respect.[49]

Normally, a distinction is made between the principles of subsidiarity and proportionality by their different scope of application and legal effects. The principle of subsidiarity is applicable in assessing whether the EU should exercise its powers; the proportionality test answers the question of how the EU should exercise its powers. Nevertheless, these principles are keenly interrelated. Proportionality is a principle applied to (alleged) conflicts between two kinds of interest: the individual's interest for autonomy, and public interests. The proportionality principle is traditionally further divided into three tests: a) suitability, b) necessity (cf. *ultima ratio*) and c) proportionality *stricto sensu*.[50]

The principle of proportionality has in the field of criminal law not only the dimension of *prospective* proportionality. It has also the dimension of *retrospective* proportionality according to Article 49(3) of the EU Charter of Fundamental Rights on the severity of penalties. As indicated in the Commission's Communication, in the assessment of proportionality (necessity), the legislator needs to analyse whether measures other than those of formal criminal law, in particular punitive administrative sanctions, could address the problems more effectively, and to what extent various types of sanction should be introduced in *parallel*. For example, punitive administrative sanctions could be reserved for minor transgressions, and criminal liability and sanctions could be preserved for more serious offences; or administrative sanctions could be imposed on corporations, but it would not exclude individual criminal responsibility of the heads of these corporations.

When taking the principles of subsidiarity and proportionality seriously and requiring thorough analyses from the impact assessments preceding legislative proposals, we need much more comparative research on criminal law, criminology and criminal justice.[51] We also need much more evidence-based criminological research to be utilised in criminal policy planning and as a foundation for rational criminal policy. This is particularly true in relation to the decision-making and actors within the EU, where criminal policy has not so far been made on the basis of coherent conceptions and by utilising relevant criminological research. Collection of statistical data is not a sufficient basis for the analyses. There is also need for increased inter-institutional co-operation and coordination within EU organs.[52]

49 For more detail, see Melander (2013), 'Ultima Ratio in European Criminal Law', 3 *Oñati Socio-Legal Series*, note 46 above, at 42–61, with references to the case law.

50 See the conceptual analysis of Asp, P. (2007), 'The Notions of Proportionality', in: Nuotio, K. (ed.), *Festschrift in Honour of Raimo Lahti*, Helsinki: Faculty of Law, University of Helsinki, 207–19.

51 Again, see also the discussion by Harding, in Chapter 8.

52 See European Parliament Resolution 2010/2310 (INI), points 11–20.

6 Toward marginalisation of European criminal law: proportionality, subsidiarity and principled public policy priorities in protecting human life and rights

Hendrik Kaptein

Introduction

So there we were, nicely assembled in the safety of the impressive Natolin Conference Centre, surrounded by colleagues as friendly as they are competent, trying to learn something more about European criminal law. It was so safe and agreeable in the middle of this serenely beautiful park, far away from any real dangers. In fact, and not just during the conference, human safety and welfare have probably never been so marginally threatened, at least in large parts of Europe and in other parts of the more or less developed or even civilised world.

What happened and what has been done to ensure this? There has been lasting general peace in Western Europe since 1945, longer than ever before: the social and economic emancipation of large parts of populations were realised, healthcare and road traffic safety were much improved, food and drinks became ever healthier as a consequence of improved public policies, more and more effective preventive measures against many other hazards were effected, and so on and so on. European organisations may well have contributed to this, and after 1989, great parts of Central and Eastern Europe benefited from this as well.

What are the goals of Europe or even of mankind, at least in public realms? Realisation of human rights in the first place, of course, as a precondition for living a good life, however differently interpreted by different people entitled to enjoy the same basic human rights. Indeed this is one of the very essences of the European integration and general enlightenment project, promising basic equality for all its citizens at least in terms of human rights. Or freedom, security and justice for all Europeans, and not just according to Article 67(1) TFEU.

Still, such human rights are violated at times, just as so many other rightful human interests are not always respected all over Europe. Officially, the administration of criminal justice is the essential *ultimum remedium* against such violations. At least this explains and justifies European attention to the administration of criminal justice, certainly since the Lisbon Treaty.[1] And of course there are

1 This is expressed in European criminal law codifications such as Article 3(2) of the Treaty on European Union (TEU) on 'appropriate measures with respect to preventing and combating

European institutions like Europol, Eurojust and perhaps the future European Public Prosecution Office. It would appear that European criminal law in a wide sense is becoming increasingly popular, in apparently more repressive and punitive times.

Mitigating tones may be found in a Communication from the European Commission.[2] This elaboration of the Treaty of Lisbon for the administration of criminal justice touches upon the basic issue of subsidiarity concerning any administration of criminal justice, European or otherwise:

> While EU criminal law measures can play an important role as a complement to the national criminal law systems, it is clear that criminal law reflects the basic values, customs and choices of any given society. The Lisbon Treaty accepts this diversity . . .
>
> Criminal investigations and sanctions may have a significant impact on citizens' rights and include a stigmatising effect. Therefore, criminal law must always remain a measure of last resort. This is reflected in the general principle of proportionality (as embodied in the Treaty on European Union and, specifically for criminal penalties, in the EU Charter of Fundamental Rights). For criminal law measures supporting the enforcement of EU policies, the Treaty explicitly requires a test of whether criminal law measures are 'essential' to achieve the goal of an effective policy implementation.
>
> Therefore, the legislator needs to analyse whether measures other than criminal law measures, e.g. sanction regimes of administrative or civil nature, could not sufficiently ensure the policy implementation and whether criminal law could address the problems more effectively. This will require a thorough analysis in the Impact Assessments preceding any legislative proposal, including for instance and depending on the specificities of the policy area concerned, an assessment of whether Member States' sanction regimes achieve the desired result and difficulties faced by national authorities implementing EU law on the ground.

This states 'federal' subsidiarity first, as implied by Article 5 TEU: Member States are to administer criminal justice themselves, unless there are overriding reasons for European organisations to step in. Next, 'liberal' subsidiarity implies that other and less costly measures against human rights violations and other wrongs are to be preferred over criminal law and punishment wherever possible. To the

crime', Article 82(2) of the Treaty on the Functioning of the European Union (TFEU) on harmonisation of defendants' and crime victims' rights, and Article 83 TFEU on common minimum standards of material criminal law. European attention to criminal law is also to be found in measures such as Directive 2012/29/EU on crime victims' rights (Directive establishing minimum standards on the rights, support and protection of victims of crime, and replacing Council Framework Decision 2001/220/JHA; OJ 2012, L 315).

2 European Commission, 'Towards an EU Criminal Policy: Ensuring the Effective Implementation of EU Policies through Criminal Law', COM(2011) 573 final.

extent that such means are available, the administration of criminal justice may be less important indeed.

Still, this and other European documents are rather less explicit on wider contexts needed for any sensible determination of subsidiarity of and in the administration of criminal justice. Thus more road safety, better public healthcare, and so much else, may spare rather more lives and limbs than further administration of criminal justice as infliction of pain, at rather lower social and financial costs. Protecting such lives and limbs of course is an important precondition or even part of securing freedom, security and justice.

Indeed human, social and financial costs of any administration of criminal justice by infliction of pain is to be determined first if there is to be some or other sensible determination of subsidiarity of and in administration of criminal justice. No subsidiarity, and in fact no proportionality, may be determined without cost–benefit analysis also in terms of alternative sanctions. This second issue is not really officially addressed in Europe either.

Thus, determining the rightful role of the administration of criminal justice is not just an issue of balancing effective prevention of crime on the one hand and adequate protection of defendants' and crime victims' rights on the other.

So what is the importance of the administration of criminal justice, to what ultimately important ends and in comparison to other means to the same ends? These issues of 'liberal' subsidiarity and also of proportionality are to be clarified before any real progress may be made in sensible determination of 'federal' subsidiarity or in fact of whatever issues of the administration of criminal justice, European or otherwise.

Up to now, Europe has indeed been more or less silent on these background, or in fact not so background, issues, and Member States have been able to more or less freely decide themselves on means and ends of the administration of criminal justice in wider contexts of public policy at large. But given the ongoing reduction of federal subsidiarity, these issues become more pressing on European levels. So it is high time to do something about it, if only on paper.

The second section of the discussion in this chapter explains what this all ought to be about: uncontested and incontestably basic human rights and values, and different means to realise and further them. The priority of several non-criminal varieties of public administration serving and furthering the enjoyment of such rights and values is demonstrated one more time. If preventive sanctions are needed, non-criminal measures like administrative fines and civil damages may often be more cost-effective than criminal punishment (third part of the discussion). Criminal punishment as infliction of pain still seems indispensable as retribution for really wrongful harm caused by crimes like murder (fourth part). The next part discusses retribution as reparation and compensation as less costly, more just and more effective retribution than infliction of pain. Realisation of this may need some more reform of European criminal law and legal practice (sixth part). Finally, there is some discussion of principled priorities in European reform not just of criminal law and punishment.

Ends and means: the general importance of proportionality and subsidiarity

What ought public authorities, European and otherwise, do for their citizens and for other people within their jurisdictions? They should ward off inside and outside threats and dangers, maintain the peace, offer protection for persons, properties and promises (the three 'p's), as presupposition for any decent human existence and society. These basics are further codified and extended in terms of human rights to life, different kinds of freedom, family life, due process and so much more. Indeed the Charter of Fundamental Rights (made binding by the Treaty of Lisbon in 2009) is the most recent statement of such rights in Europe. Subordinate ends may be pursued by more or less democratic and discretionary politics and public administration, but within limits set by such fundamental rights and values and respecting them in the first place. This at least is uncontested legal and political theory in contemporary constitutional and democratic jurisdictions.

Why this restatement or even dreary repetition of these all too well-known basics? Because it may be less well observed, both in theory and in practice, that criminal law and the administration of criminal justice, like all law and all public administration, primarily ought to respect and further these basic values and rights as well. Human rights are worth nothing if not adequately protected and furthered, at least by some or other effective public administration. Protection of human life of course comes first.

Also, all public administration ought to heed one basic principle of subsidiarity: given ends, the least costly – in terms of violation of human and other rights and values – but still effective means are to be used. Sure enough, the administration of criminal justice may spare human lives and protect other human rights and rightful interests. But what exactly are preventive effects of punishment against capital crimes like murder? At what price? Better healthcare may spare and improve still more human lives at the same or even lesser human and financial costs.

The list is well nigh endless. Road safety measures may be much improved as well, and encouraging public transport will spare still more lives and limbs. Or, compare the costs of fighting terrorism by administration of criminal justice and other means, with the costs of forestalling lightning impacts. In the Netherlands and elsewhere, many more people are killed or maimed by lightning than by terrorist attacks even in recent years.

Still, the fight against terrorism by means of ever more extended and intrusive investigation, administration of criminal justice and other repressive measures, devours billions, at the expense of human rights, while, for that matter, almost nothing is done about lightning and so many more potentially deadly dangers and annoyances that could be dealt with at small cost.

Even crime itself as a threat against violation of human life and rights may be better prevented by non-criminal means. Better standards of living, more social justice, better education, better mental healthcare and so on may seriously curb crime. Thus, trafficking in human beings may be more effectively forestalled by weakening motives for economic migration than by any administration of criminal justice, at rather less human and financial cost. Less serious crime, like shop robbery, may be forestalled by doing away with cash payment. The list is almost endless.

Legal means to forestall human rights violations and other offences may include simplifying or even abolishing parts of criminal law. Trafficking in human beings (a main issue in European criminal law) is facilitated by money earned from financial fraud (another main issue), in part a consequence of drugs dealing (also a European crime). Removing all drugs from criminal law and thus ending illegal cash flows may solve part of the problem, trafficking in human beings included. Financial fraud in general may be more effectively forestalled by simplification of the rules than – again – by any administration of criminal justice. This holds good not just for financial crime, of course: 'every criminal law creates its own crime' (one of Beccaria's lessons in *On Crimes and Punishments* not really learned yet, it seems).

This is all about subsidiarity in the field of criminal law and punishment: less expensive measures may lead to the same or even better results. Proportionality is at stake here as well of course. Thus, spending billions of euros on rewiring overhead power lines in order to save one or two lives a year (as recently effected in the Netherlands) is disproportional too, both given attendant benefits and given other spending options with better results in terms of saving human lives. So subsidiarity and proportionality are fundamental in a much wider sense than as simply standards in the administration of criminal justice.

One consequence may be the relative unimportance of the administration of criminal justice, as just one way to protect and further human rights and other values. Many less costly and more effective ways to improve the quality of human life and society are much more viable than any administration of criminal justice. Or, really furthering freedom, security and justice may indeed lead to marginalisation of criminal law.

This wider perspective is conspicuously absent in European documents concerning the administration of criminal justice. Is this a reflection of an almost ineradicable populist penchant to 'crack down' on publicly visible crime in the first place? Too many people and too many politicians attach too much importance to punishment of others, instead of caring for freedom, security and justice by so many sensible other means in the first place.

But then without this wider perspective – that is, proportionality and subsidiarity in public administration at large – nothing much sensible may be stated indeed on proportionality and subsidiarity specifically concerning criminal law and punishment.

Non-criminal sanctions

No public administration, however rational, coherent and practically effective, may really forestall all loss of life and limb, all human rights violations and all criminal offences.

Something must be done against such offences – that is, if they attract any official attention at all. But then adequate reaction to criminal offences need not be criminal. Several other kinds of censure may be effective, or even more effective, both in forestalling crime and in handling its consequences.

Varieties of informal censure may be helpful even against serious crime in some circumstances. Thus peer group and other social pressure is not without its risks of injustice but may still do something against crime. If this works, official sanctioning in whatever form may be superfluous, or: subsidiarity again.

Offender–victim mediation may be one more way to forestall further crime. Such mediation may even be officially backed and regulated, in order to more or less undo the consequences of crime. Such confrontational mediation may be more dissuasive for offenders concerned than (long-time) imprisonment. Mediation may also lead to some or other reparation and/or compensation by offenders for victims. All well known of course, but still not sufficiently practised, it seems.

Reparation and/or compensation may also be effected by civil law damages. Again, prospects of it may be rather dissuasive, certainly so in cases not covered by any kind of (public) insurance. Take the case of somebody pulling an emergency train brake for no reason (as happens at times in the Netherlands, not just before and after football matches). Administrative and/or criminal sanctions against this may not be very discouraging. What about making such offenders pay for harm done to railroad companies and others harmed? No need for any legal reform here, European or otherwise. Indeed one aspect of subsidiarity implies letting the parties involved solve the problem, out of, and if need arises in, court. Nothing like punitive damages is needed for this, as standard damages not paid for by insurance or other third parties may be sufficiently punitive by themselves.

Offenders may also be members of more or less official organisations, such as magistrates, police officers, lawyers, accountants and medical professionals. Their misconduct may lead to grave violations of human rights and other rightful human interest, as is still witnessed not just in Central and Eastern Europe. Curbing this is of prime importance. More social control and more effective disciplinary law ousting offenders from their offices may be rather more effective against (semi-) official misconduct than any administration of criminal justice.

Subsidiarity may also be heeded in public law. Thus administrative sanctions may be effective against road traffic and many more kinds of offence, without recourse to administration of criminal justice and its attendant higher costs and other burdens, both in terms of public money and for offenders concerned.

Substantial chances of being caught are presuppositions of preventive effects of any such non-criminal sanctions. Means to improve such changes are themselves subject to standards of proportionality and subsidiarity of course. Still, improvements may be effected without costing too much money better spent elsewhere and without curbing too many civil liberties. Why not enforce speed limits by checking each and every motor vehicle on public roads, and so on and so on? Countless lives and limbs and so much more might be spared by such (undoubtedly unpopular) measures.

So human life and rights, or freedom, security and justice for all may be furthered by non-criminal sanctions against many offences as well. Again, both proportionality and subsidiarity may imply more or less marginal roles for the administration of criminal justice as a part of public administration in general. European documents like the 2011 Commission Communication indeed do address this important issue of non-criminal preventive sanctions, albeit rather marginally so.

Criminal law and punishment: marginal but still indispensable?

So subsidiarity seems to relegate the administration of criminal justice to subordinate roles in securing freedom, security and justice. But this seems deeply at odds with proportionality. Crime deserves punishment, right? Or rather, the administration of criminal justice and punishment is generally thought to serve more than just prevention of crime. Criminal justice is more than just a part of preventive public policy in principle, then, if it is to realise punitive justice 'in its own right'. If criminals really deserve punishment as infliction of pain, then issues of subsidiarity no longer count, by want of other and lesser 'expensive' means to realise such just deserts. This may be just as self-evident at first sight as deeply questionable in the end.

To illustrate this in terms of life and death issues: what is the difference between murder and other causes of death? Several scenarios are conceivable here – sometimes all too real of course. First, death may be the beneficent finale of a long and more or less happy life lived to the end. This is an end of life itself, death being the inevitable consequence sooner or later. Second, life may be interrupted earlier, as a consequence of internal or even external factors not related to specific human conduct. Think here of fates like incurable illnesses, accidents caused by natural disasters and so on. Third, people may intentionally kill themselves, or have themselves killed, by suicide or euthanasia. Fourth, deadly accidents and other deaths can be caused by others who may be held liable for them. Thus doctors may be negligent or worse, and public administration officials may be lax in safety measures. Fifth, people may decide to end other people's lives by murdering or otherwise wrongfully killing them, or subjecting them to capital punishment.

If the right to life is really fundamental, or even the precondition for enjoyment of whatever rights and so much more, why not try to prevent all avoidable death on equal footing, impartially sparing lives? What makes murder and manslaughter so outstanding? Why not apply the best means to the end of saving lives first, subject to rational standards of proportionality and subsidiarity? Even circumstances leading to suicide and euthanasia may be improved so as to make them as rare as possible, through for example better mental and other healthcare.

Against this it may be put that the experience of harm caused by crime is stronger and causes more resentment, to the degree that such crime is perceived as unjust and avoidable. Thus a death by natural causes may lead to relatives' sadness, mourning and gloom, whereas murder and manslaughter may deeply incite relatives' and others' resentment and even rage against offenders. There may be a public policy reason for acting more against murder than against other avoidable deaths. Still it remains doubtful whether any administration of criminal justice, however intensified, may be really effective against – so often more or less impulsive – murder.

So again the conclusion seems to be that administration of criminal justice still does not rank high on any rational public policy priorities listing aimed at saving human lives. This is not just related to murder and other kinds of killing, of course. It also holds good for many other kinds of crime thwarting human rights in a wide sense.

Highly apposite here are the high costs of the administration of criminal justice and of punishment by incarceration in particular. Long-term detention is not just expensive, it also generates high human and social costs in terms of criminalisation, mental illness and frustration of sociability, both for inmates and their relatives and for society in general. So however serious harm caused by crime may be, criteria of subsidiarity may still lead to desirable marginalisation of criminal law and punishment compared to other means of protecting human life and rights.

However, this is deeply at odds with specific proportionality of crime and punishment as a basic demand of justice. This is, of course, the issue of retribution at large. Such retribution seems to be the only fitting answer to pain and resentment caused by crime. *Fiat justitia.* Then retribution is a kind of right 'on its own', the costs of which are to be balanced against other public policy objectives in terms of human rights and otherwise. How to do this? Sometimes rather punitive public opinion seems to value 'crackdown on crime' rather higher than cheaper and more effective prevention of wrongful harm by public means. This may not be the one right answer, however.

Small consolation is the retributive simplification of balancing costs and benefits of punishment as infliction of pain. If serious offenders really deserve their long-time detention, then whatever harm done to them by this regime is irrelevant in any balancing of interests and rights. Or: just punishment is deserved infliction of pain, at whatever cost.

But what is retribution by infliction of pain really good for? Metaphors like 'restoring the balance' are not helpful here. There is no convincing justification of retribution for crime by infliction of pain.[3] Still this 'tit for tat' mentality is so deep seated in humankind that it seems senseless to plead for abolition of criminal justice by retribution.

European documents like the 2011 Commission Communication are silent on issues of retribution, indeed justifying punishment in terms of 'effectiveness, proportionality and dissuasiveness' only. So, is the EU already convinced that retribution by infliction of pain is meaningless? But then the rest of Europe and the world sticks to retribution as a basic requirement for justice. Again, from a

3 See for example Kaptein, H. J. R. (2004), 'Against the Pain of Punishment: On Penal Servitude and Procedural Justice for All', in: Kaptein, H. J. R. and Malsch. M. (eds), *Crime, Victims and Justice: Essays on Principles and Practice*, Aldershot: Ashgate Publishing, 80–111.

preventive point of view, any administration of criminal justice by infliction of pain may not rank highly in protection of human life and rights. But then retribution, however senseless, from a principled point of view restores such infliction of pain to the public scene. How to reconcile this?

The *ultima ratio* of retribution: making offenders do what they ought to have done

How to escape from this stall, this strange balancing of unquantifiable or even irrational resentment leading to retributive punishment as infliction of pain and its high costs against other and probably rather cheaper measures protecting human life and rights? Such balancing seems an issue of more or less punitively political and administrative discretion at best. But there is a principled way out, suggested already by Beccaria, Bentham and others before and after them: make offenders pay for what they did wrong, including payment for the costs of criminal investigation and procedure.

This is retribution in its original sense indeed: payback. Harm caused by crime is to be fully compensated for by offenders themselves. Ideally, offenders restore original and rightful positions of everybody and every body wrongfully harmed, including the State representing wrongfully harmed public interests, 'as if nothing happened'. So undoing harmful consequences ought to be equivalent to doing the right thing from the start, at least in principle. Thus theft of a pushbike ought to be compensated by return of the bike as it was or an equivalent bike plus full compensation for harm caused by temporary loss of the bike. Then the bike owner may ride and live on as if nothing wrong and harmful ever happened. Why not make offenders work in order to effect this? Retribution as payback is not limited to stolen pushbikes, of course. It holds good for all crime, in principle.

This reinterpretation of retribution also implies, in as far as still to be demonstrated, that offenders are to make up for what they did wrong and nobody else: 'you did wrong, now you got a second and last opportunity to do the right thing, however much harder this may be for you now that it was then.'[4] This 'do it yourself' may preclude simple payment by offenders and/or insurance payment, and prescribe penal servitude benefiting both crime victims and wrongfully harmed public interests. Additional payment may still be necessary in order to further compensate for wrongful harm done.

In fact, such retribution by reparation may even be regarded as a variety of prevention itself. As retribution as restoration of rightful original positions ought to be equivalent to consequences of doing the right thing from the start, such retribution is equivalent to prevention of wrongful harm *ex post facto* in principle.

4 See more extensively on concepts of wrongful harm, liability and compensation, Kaptein, H. J. R. (2013), 'No Human Rights without Retribution: Plights and Promises of Redress as if Nothing Happened', in: Menuge, A. (ed), *Legitimizing Human Rights: Secular and Religious Perspectives*, Farnharm and Burlington: Ashgate Publishing, 159–78.

Also, prices to be paid for such 'super-prevention' by offenders may have special and general preventive effects as well.

Offenders' pain caused by paying such higher prices may also satisfy personal and public resentment. Society cannot do without retribution. At least in this sense, more or less punitive public opinion is right. But then retribution as reparation is a much better 'cement of society' than any punishment as mere infliction of pain may ever be.

What makes this reinterpretation of retribution so relevant concerning proportionality and subsidiarity? First, proportionality consists in the principled equivalence of doing the right thing from the start and 'doing it afterwards' by restoring rightful positions 'as if nothing happened'. Proportionality may also be more specifically ensured by making penal servitude fit the nature of the crime. Littering? Go sweep the streets. Drunken driving? Clean up emergency rooms at night, and so on. Such confrontational community service may be more effective than mere infliction of pain in terms of special and general prevention as well.

Still, penal servitude may be mitigated by lesser degrees of criminal intent and guilt. On the other hand, there is of course no humanly feasible compensation for murder and many more serious crimes. May this lead to life-long forced labour as the best available approximation of retribution for murder? Such vexing problems may well make reparative proportionality rather complex and ever more difficult to realise.

Next, subsidiarity is served because penal servitude is both much cheaper, financial and otherwise, and much more amenable to balancing against other rights and interests. Why should the costs of crime be paid for by public means? 'Clean up your own mess': offenders are to pay for the full cost of wrongful harm done themselves. Thus more public means may be spent on life-saving and other important issues. Also, public costs of making offenders pay the full price of their crimes must be somewhat lower than the costs of any punishment as mere infliction of pain by incarceration or otherwise.

Adding to this, varieties of more or less confrontational penal servitude adapted to different kinds of crime may do offenders less senseless harm, let alone undeserved harm, than idle incarceration so often leading to still more crime and suffering.[5]

Detention of dangerous offenders may still be necessary at times, just as detention may be offered as an unattractive alternative for penal servitude against unwilling offenders.[6] If retribution may really be reparation and compensation by offenders themselves in principle, then punishment as mere infliction of pain by detention or otherwise really is – hopefully rather exclusive – *ultimum remedium*

5 See more extensively on this again, Kaptein (2004), note 2 above.

6 This option also precludes equation of penal servitude with illegal slavery and forced labour. As long as there is an alternative in the form of detention, offenders may still 'escape' from penal servitude if they so wish, although of course alternative detention regimes ought not to be too attractive, at least in this respect.

indeed. This and nothing more ought to be the sense of officially inflicted pain, determining its rightful roles in terms of proportionality and subsidiarity.

So retribution as reparation may both satisfy resentment against crime as a cement of society and lead to better positioning of retributive and painful criminal sanctions in terms of proportionality and subsidiarity, compared to other public policy measures protecting human life and rights.

(European) reform towards reparative criminal law

Retribution as reparation may be more than just a noble dream, as witnessed by more than a few non-criminal reactions to crime as already outlined in the third part of this chapter. Recapitulating in terms of retribution as reparation may be effected between offenders and victims without official intervention, or with the help of some or other public administration incentive against offenders. Civil law damages partly or wholly paid for by offenders themselves, ordered by criminal courts or otherwise, may offer retributive reparation as well. Community service in emergency wards and elsewhere may be dissuasive, reparative and confrontational.

All European member jurisdictions already offer alternatives for punishment as infliction of pain in such terms in principle, not just serving prevention but some or other kind of retribution as reparation as well. This ought to furthered, not just in legislation and in other paperwork. Retribution as prevention *ex post facto* by restoring rightful original positions in principle ought to be a major goal of a Europe really taking seriously protection and furtherance of human life and rights for all. It would be nothing much more indeed than the elaboration of earlier and incomplete statements on proportionality and subsidiarity in the administration of criminal justice.

If the essence of rightful punishment is not pain but penal servitude, crime victims acquire more 'logical' positions in criminal legal practice suitably reinterpreted in terms of retribution as reparation. Crime victims' rights and interests are high on the European agenda, and rightly so. Such rights and interests may only be really served by any administration of criminal justice if 'destructive' infliction of pain is replaced by constructive penal servitude, indeed integrating crime victims' rights and interests into the administration of criminal justice.

Not just wrongful harm done against individual victims, but wrongful harm in general ought to be the primary target of any sensible administration of criminal justice. So it ought to be established beforehand what is really harmful and what is not. The 2011 Commission Communication expresses this need for clear factual evidence as follows:

> To establish the necessity for minimum rules on criminal law, the EU institutions need to be able to rely on clear factual evidence about the nature or effects of the crime in question and about a diverging legal situation in all Member States which could jeopardise the effective enforcement of an EU policy subject to harmonisation.

'Euro crimes' as related to Article 83(1) TFEU comprise ten explicitly listed serious offences with cross-border dimensions: terrorism, trafficking in human beings, sexual exploitation of women and children, illicit drug trafficking, illicit arms trafficking, money laundering, corruption, counterfeiting of means of payment, computer crime and organised crime.

Is this the best list of really harmful crimes, given clear evidence on the nature and consequences of such crimes? Maybe not completely so, considering the well-documented counter-effective results of criminalising drugs. As already stated in the second part to this chapter, criminalising drugs also leads to financial and other facilitation of trafficking in human beings and sexual exploitation. Financial fraud is also driven by drug money, and so on. Thus, European and national crime catalogues ought to be reformed, if protection of freedom, security and justice by administration of criminal justice really comes first.

Such reform is of course to be directed against inflation of criminalisation of human conduct as well, as witnessed all over Europe. So why not go for an exclusively binding European catalogue of crime, limiting criminalisation of more or less undesirable conduct by national jurisdictions? Such far-reaching limitation of federal subsidiarity may not be politically feasible yet, although it might make good sense.

In fact, Europe is not really clear and consistent on these issues yet. Thus the 2011 Commission Communication suggests more criminal legislation, while the European Council and the European Parliament seem more reticent here.[7] It may therefore be time for more principled priorities here too, it seems.

Less criminal law may go together well with less administration of criminal justice, as in fact suggested by Articles 83 and 325(4) TFEU. So why is the European Public Prosecution Office to operate according to the 'principle of legality', prescribing prosecution of all crime falling under its competence and brought to its attention? This is at odds with proportionality and subsidiarity of and in the administration of criminal justice rightly endorsed in other European statements like the 2011 Commission Communication on criminal policy.[8]

If punishment as infliction of pain is really to be *ultimum remedium*, then there ought to be no prosecution by any European or national prosecution office of crime *qua* crime without investigation into other means to prevent and redress consequences of crime. This holds good not just for crimes under imperfect positive law senselessly criminalising ever more human conduct, but also for crime according to law suitably reformed.

So both catalogues of crime and catalogues of sanctions need to be reformed. Real and really wrongful harm only ought to be punished – that is, if no other ways of handling such harm are feasible – and punishment ought to be as reparative as possible, in the interest of crime victims, offenders and of all concerned.

And if there is still need for administration of criminal justice, it ought to be

7 See for example, the European Council Statement 15936/09, and the European Parliament's Report on an EU approach to criminal law (24 April 2012).

8 European Commission, 2011, note 2 above.

just, and not only in the sense of proportional, fair and efficient. Federal subsidiarity may therefore also be curbed by the need to protect European individuals and (other) bodies in national jurisdictions against human rights violations in the name of criminal justice. What may Europe do, both formally and informally, against police, public prosecution and criminal judicial laziness, incompetence, corruption, fraud and outright injustice?

Ought not this to lead to some or other limitation to federal subsidiarity? At least Article 82(1)(c) TFEU may be invoked here: 'measures are to be adopted to support the training of the judiciary and judicial staff.' Such training ought to include legal ethics of criminal investigation and criminal procedure as well. Also, informal pressure may be applied in order to 'force' more than a few European jurisdictions in directions of more justice and fairness in the administration of criminal justice.

The European Court of Human Rights is doing good work here too, but much more needs to be done to curb so much criminal injustice from the start. In terms of available European means in terms of proportionality and subsidiarity, federal and otherwise, these issues may be rather more pressing than other issues high on official European agendas.

European integration of crime prevention and public administration serving freedom, justice and security in general

Indeed freedom, security and justice and in fact protection of human life and rights in general are to be served by much more than just administration of criminal justice. If protection of such basic rights and fundamental values is to come first, then administration of any criminal justice, or of whatever justice, may not come first at all. Any sensible determination of proportionality and subsidiarity of the administration of criminal justice is to heed this, also against ever more punitive public opinion and politics.

Again, other public policies may be much cheaper and rather more effective against violations of human life and rights than so much administration of criminal justice. Preventing wrongful harm to human life and rights from the start should have top priority. Or, rather, any rational criminal administration should be integrated into rational public administration in general. Much more thought and action is needed in the redistribution of public means spent on administration of criminal justice as compared to protecting and furthering human life and rights by other often less costly and more effective means.

Europe needs more federal and liberal integration of the administration of criminal justice into rational public administration at large, subject to sensible standards of proportionality and subsidiarity. This implies more rational and constructive sanctioning, relegating punishment as infliction of pain to its rightful marginal role as *ultimum remedium* only. What counts is the promotion, by the best possible means, of freedom, security and justice for all Europeans (and for all citizens of the world, of course, which, alas, is another matter).

Beccaria's dream of the rational public administrator balancing all concerned interests and forces like a skilled architect balances all relevant factors in order to create buildings as stable as they are beautiful (like those of the Natolin Centre), may still be far away. But if freedom, security and justice really matter, like in fact the protection and furthering of all human life and rights, then it ought to be more than just a dream. And in any case, European or in fact any civilisation ought to be measured by the marginality of criminal justice.

Part of this can be practically simplified: do not start any criminal procedure whatsoever, from legislation up to and including individual prosecution and punishment, without clear consideration of all costs and benefits concerned. Therefore, criminalise truly *mala fide* wrongful harm only, mete out any punishment only if there are no other ways to handle such crime and, if need really arises, go for the cheapest and most constructive reparative punishments possible. And avoid punishment as infliction of pain as long as crime can be addressed any other way.

Keep in mind that any administration of criminal justice, or justice in general for that matter, is never an end in itself. Punitive populism and its oftentimes false resentments go against this grain. We should try to do something against this as well, at least by duly explaining that administration of criminal justice may not be the one and only way to forestall crime and other dangers.

Just as there ought to be more serious public debate on real priorities in Europe and elsewhere, freedom, security and justice, and the best ways to realise them, ought to come first. Even these supreme values are no ends in themselves, presuppositions as they are for human flourishing as the ultimate end of any public administration or in fact of life itself.

7 EU criminal law and *effet utile*: a critical examination of the Union's use of criminal law to achieve effective enforcement

Vanessa Franssen

Introduction

In recent years, the EU has increasingly obliged its Member States to provide for criminal sanctions in order to enhance the *effet utile* of EU law. The Treaty of Lisbon expanded the Union's competences in this respect, by introducing an explicit legal basis for EU 'functional criminalisation'[1] in Article 83(2) TFEU. The EU focus on effectiveness is far from new but raises some delicate questions in the context of criminal law.

As may be seen clearly from legislative and policy documents, the EU's preference for criminal sanctions is based on the assumption that criminal sanctions send out a powerful message of disapproval and therefore exert a stronger dissuasive or deterrent effect than administrative or civil sanctions or measures. In consequence, criminal enforcement is considered more effective than other, 'softer' types of enforcement. However, the underlying reason *why* criminal sanctions convey a powerful societal message remains implicit and is hardly the subject of debate at the EU level.[2] The EU legislator appears to take the expressive function of criminal sanctions for granted and essentially focuses on the instrumental function of criminal sanctions.

The Union's instrumental approach to criminal sanctions is not so surprising, considering the originally economic ambitions of the European integration process. However, this effectiveness-driven logic creates tensions with more traditional conceptions and fundamental principles of criminal law. While no one will deny that effectiveness is a relevant criterion for any type of enforcement, effectiveness is hardly a stand-alone justification for criminalisation.[3] In fact, effectiveness is rather the desired outcome and depends on a number of factors,

1 Mitsilegas, V. (2014), 'EU Criminal Law Competence after Lisbon: From Securitised to Functional Criminalisation', in: Acosta Arcarazo, D. and Murphy, C. C. (eds), *EU Security and Justice Law: After Lisbon and Stockholm*, London: Hart Publishing, 111 and 117–18.

2 Even in its crucial policy statement in its Communication of 2011, *Towards an EU Criminal Policy: Ensuring the effective implementation of EU policies through criminal law*, COM (2011) 573 final, 20 September 2011, the European Commission did not explain why (or under which conditions) criminal sanctions have a stronger dissuasive effect than other types of sanctions.

3 Cf. Herlin-Karnell, E. (2011), 'The Development of EU Precautionay Criminalisation', *EuCLR*

not just (and perhaps not even primarily) the law on the books. This raises the question whether EU criminalisation (i.e. criminalisation imposed upon Member States by the EU) should not receive a stronger justification than merely ensuring the *effet utile* of EU law.

This chapter will argue that criminal law should not be used for mere regulatory purposes,[4] as a seemingly 'easy solution' whenever the existing enforcement tools – for whatever reasons – fail. Instead, it should ideally[5] only be used when strictly necessary, as a last resort. Deciding whether criminal sanctions are really necessary requires more than a mere effectiveness assessment, even in the field of economic and financial crime and even with respect to legal persons; this 'need' should be evaluated in light of the protected legal interests and values. Criminal law is, or should be, essentially an expression of society's core values and norms, also at the EU level. Therefore, as the EU pursues its ambition of further integration (despite the difficult political climate), time has come to reflect upon European-wide norms and values which truly merit criminal law protection. In other words, EU criminalisation requires a careful balancing exercise between effectiveness on the one hand and the *criminal law* principles of proportionality and subsidiarity on the other.

The discussion will be structured as follows. It will first sketch the explicit and potentially implicit powers of the EU with regard to substantive criminal law. Next, it will illustrate the growing reliance of the EU legislator on criminal sanctions by means of the new legal framework for market abuse. Then, it will analyse the risks and pitfalls of the current EU approach, from a theoretical and practical perspective. Based on this analysis, the following section will make suggestions for a more solid justification for future EU criminal law instruments, taking into account the fundamental principles of criminal law and the core functions of criminal law.

1, 149, 162 (arguing that 'the very notion of effectiveness as a template for criminalisation is generally considered to be a difficult parameter when justifying legislation').

4 For an analysis of the EU's regulatory powers and how criminal law is used as a 'policy tool' for financial regulation, see Herlin-Karnell, E. (2015), 'Constructing Europe's Area of Freedom, Security, and Justice through the Framework of "Regulation": A Cascade of Market-Based Challenges in the EU's Fight against Financial Crime", *German Law Journal*, 16, 49.

5 Of course, in reality national legislators too do not always observe this principle. See e.g. Ouwerkerk, J. W. (2012), 'Criminalisation as a Last Resort: A National Principle under the Pressure of Europeanisation', *NJECL*, 3, 228, at 229–32, with reference to the last resort principle in Dutch criminal law. It also appears that the focus on the principle of *ultima ratio* has been less strong in common law jurisdictions: Harding, C. (2015), 'The Interplay of Criminal and Administrative Law in the Context of Market Regulation: The Case of Serious Competition Infringements', Chapter 9 in: Mitsilegas, V. *et al.* (eds), *Globalisation, Criminal Law and Criminal Justice*, Oxford: Hart Publishing. However, this chapter will take a principled approach to analyse and evaluate the criminalisation efforts of the EU.

The powers of the EU with regard to criminal law

Criminalisation powers based on Article 83 TFEU

The powers of the EU to approximate national (substantive) criminal law used to be limited to certain types of serious crime with a cross-border dimension.[6] In 2009, the Treaty of Lisbon significantly increased those powers in two respects. On the one hand, the Treaty of Lisbon extended the list of so-called 'Euro crimes'[7] in Article 83(1) TFEU. On the other hand, and more importantly for the purpose of this chapter, the Treaty incorporated in Article 83(2) TFEU the case law of the EU Court of Justice (hereinafter: CJEU), thereby providing for a legal basis for 'functional criminalisation'[8] or the creation of 'EU *effet utile* crimes'. Without exaggerating, one may say that Article 83(2) TFEU dramatically expands the scope of EU criminal law. Both 'spheres' of EU criminal law should be clearly distinguished from one another.

Approximation of national criminal law on the basis of Article 83(1) TFEU deals with offence definitions and sanctions regarding kinds of behaviour which, due to their particular serious nature, are usually already defined as criminal offences in most Member States.

The Union's powers under this provision are based on a *numerus clausus* system, which means that only offences belonging to one of the ten pre-defined offence categories can be subject to EU approximation measures.[9] The aim is to align the definition of (existing) criminal offences and to ensure that national criminal sanctions are of a similar type and level. The underlying criterion for such approximation is the *'particularly serious'* nature of the offences listed in Article 83(1), para. 2 TFEU, in combination with their 'cross-border dimension resulting from the nature or impact of such offences or from a special need to combat them on a common basis'. In other words, Euro crimes are based on a consensus about the seriousness and wrongfulness of the behaviour and the need to take joint action at EU level in order to combat crime that often (though not necessarily in every individual case)[10] has a transboundary nature or impact.

Despite the impression the use of an exhaustive list might create, the Union's

6 Former Article 29 EU Treaty (version of the Amsterdam Treaty).

7 The term which is used, for instance, by the European Commission in its 2011 Communication, note 2 above, at 5. For a discussion of the genesis and gradual acceptance of this term as part of a broader European penology, see e.g. Daems, T. (2013), 'Punishment and the Question of Europe', in Daems, T. *et al.* (eds), *European Penology?*, Oxford/Portland: Hart Publishing, 27, at 37.

8 Mitsilegas (2014), note 1 above, at 111.

9 The Council may add other types of serious cross-border crime to this list, based on a unanimous decision and the consent of the European Parliament (Art. 83(1), para. 3, TFEU).

10 It has been argued indeed that the scope of the EU's powers under Article 83(1) TFEU is 'not limited to transnational criminality' and includes 'areas of crime which have a cross-border dimension but which do not involve cross-border or transnational criminality as such.' The approximation of criminal definitions and sanctions on the basis of Article 83(1) TFEU may thus also concern 'criminality conducted purely at national level.' See Mitsilegas (2014), note 1 above, at 116.

power to approximate national criminal law on the basis of Article 83(1) TFEU is quite broad. For one, the provision includes fairly open categories of crime, which may encompass a variety of different offences.[11] For another, it appears the scope of application of this provision is not limited to offence-specific legal instruments,[12] but extends to more general, cross-sectorial instruments. An example thereof is the Directive on the freezing and confiscation of instrumentalities and proceeds of crime[13] on the basis of Articles 83(1) and 82(2) TFEU, which applies to a whole range of serious criminal offences that have been subject to EU approximation.[14] Moreover, it may be expected that the implementation of this cross-sectorial Directive in national criminal law will have some spill-over effects on other 'purely national' criminal offences.

Whereas Article 83(1) already provides for a quite broad legal basis for EU criminal law, Article 83(2) TFEU enables the EU even more to set out its own criminal law policy:[15] it allows the EU to oblige the Member States to criminalise certain types of behaviour that are not yet covered by national criminal law.

As indicated above, Article 83(2) TFEU codifies the case law of the CJEU. In the so-called Environmental Crime Case[16] and the subsequent Ship-Source Pollution Case,[17] the Court endorsed the European Commission's view that the EU (then EC) legislator was allowed to require the Member States to adopt effective, proportionate and dissuasive *criminal* sanctions with regard to former First Pillar policy areas. Article 83(2) TFEU now explicitly states that the EU legislator may establish minimum rules for the definition of criminal offences and sanctions in any area of Union policy 'which has been subject to harmonisation measures', provided that such approximation of national criminal law 'proves essential to ensure the effective implementation' of that policy.

In principle, the approximation of national criminal law based on Article 83(2) TFEU concerns *any* policy area for which the EU shares competence with its Member States[18] and may adopt harmonising measures. Actual or full harmonisation is required by Article 83(2) TFEU.[19] While some have stressed that this criterion 'may serve to limit the scope of EU's competence on Article 83(2)

11 *Ibid.*, at 116–17.

12 See for instance: Directive 2011/36/EU of the European Parliament and of the Council on preventing and combating trafficking in human beings and protecting its victims, and replacing Council Framework Decision 2002/629/JHA, OJ, L 101, 15 April 2011, 1; Directive 2011/92/EU of the European Parliament and of the Council on combating the sexual abuse and sexual exploitation of children and child pornography, and replacing Council Framework Decision 2004/68/JHA, OJ, L 335, 17 December 2011, 1.

13 Directive 2014/42/EU of the European Parliament and of the Council on the freezing and confiscation of instrumentalities and proceeds of crime in the European Union, 3 April 2014, OJ, L 127, 29 April 2014, 39.

14 Article 3, Directive 2014/42/EU, note 13 above.

15 To this end, the European Commission issued its Communication of 2011, note 2 above.

16 Case C-176/03, *Commission v. Council*, 13 September 2005.

17 Case C-440/05, *Commission v. Council*, 23 October 2007.

18 Art. 4 TFEU.

19 Mitsilegas (2014) note 1 above, at 118, and the references mentioned there.

TFEU',[20] it nevertheless seems that 'EU *effet utile* crimes' may concern a great variety of policy areas and specific behaviours.

With respect to all those policies, approximation of national criminal laws is possible whenever this 'proves to be essential' for the 'effective enforcement' of EU law. Whenever the EU legislator thus deems minimum rules for criminal offences and sanctions are 'essential' to ensure such effective enforcement, Member States may be compelled to criminalise certain behaviour and to adopt specific criminal sanctions. The criterion of 'effective enforcement' thus drives EU criminal law based on this legal basis. This raises the question as to what extent other factors, such as the seriousness of the infringement (including its abstract and concrete harmfulness and the degree of culpability) and the societal value of the protected legal interests[21] can and should be taken into account before having recourse to EU criminalisation. In other words, the question arises whether the *effet utile* of EU law can, and should, be the main criterion for criminalisation instigated by the EU, or whether it should be balanced against other principles of EU (criminal) law. These questions will be addressed in more depth in the discussion later on in this chapter.

Other criminalisation powers?

In addition to the explicit two-fold legal basis for EU criminalisation in Article 83 TFEU, one may wonder whether the EU could still adopt criminal law instruments *outside* the scope of the foregoing provision, in particular to ensure the *effective* enforcement of Union law. Based on a systematic interpretation[22] of the Treaty, one could argue that the powers of the EU with regard to criminal law are now clearly defined in Chapter 4 of Title V of the TFEU and that other potentially confusing references to criminal law elsewhere in the Treaty have been eliminated. Nevertheless, the division of powers with respect to substantive criminal law is less clear-cut than a systematic interpretation would suggest and still very much contested.[23]

First of all, would it be possible for the EU legislator to create criminal offences for the purpose of effectiveness in other policy areas that are strongly 'Union centred'?[24] For instance, could the EU legislator use Article 325 TFEU as a legal

20 Mitsilegas, V. (2014), 'From Overcriminalisation to Decriminalisation. The Many Faces of Effectiveness in European Criminal Law', *New Journal of European Criminal Law*, 416, 421.

21 Cf. Grandi, C. (2011), 'The "Qualities" of Criminal Law – Connected to National and European Law-making Procedure', *European Criminal Law Review*, 1, 285, at 303.

22 Cf. Seibert, T. (2008), 'The European Fight against Fraud – The Community's Competence to Enact Criminal Laws and Its Power to Approximate National Criminal Law by Directives', *European Journal of Crime, Criminal Law and Criminal Justice*, 16, 89, at 101.

23 See e.g. Mitsilegas (2014), note 1 above, 118–21; Klip, A. (2011), 'Towards a General Part of Criminal Law for the European Union', in Klip, A. (ed.), *Substantive Criminal Law of the European Union*, Antwerp/Apeldoorn/Portland: Maklu, 26.

24 European Commission, Proposal for a Directive on the fight against fraud to the Union's financial interests by means of criminal law (hereinafter: 'Proposal for the Financial Interests Directive'), COM(2012) 363 final, 11 July 2012, 7.

basis to oblige Member States to criminalise fraud against the Union's financial interests? In its initial proposal for a Directive that is meant to replace the 1995 'PIF' Convention, the European Commission took the view that Article 325 TFEU 'includes the power to enact criminal law provisions',[25] even though Article 325 TFEU does not explicitly mention criminal sanctions. Of course, neither does this provision explicitly exclude 'the application of national criminal law', contrary to the wording of former Article 280(4) TEC.[26] What is more, the Commission held that the requirement of '[d]eterrent, effective and equivalent protection comprises by nature, and historically (see PIF Convention of 1995), a criminal law dimension.'[27]

Clearly, the Council did not share this viewpoint, as it quite quickly changed the legal basis for the proposed directive on the Union's financial interests into Article 83(2) TFEU.[28] This modification of the legal basis confirms the potentially very broad scope of application of Article 83(2) TFEU. Whereas the Commission interpreted Article 325 TFEU in the light of the *effet utile* principle, assuming that the Union has all powers that are needed to ensure the effectiveness of EU law, the Council unambiguously gives preference to the principle of conferral of powers: any powers that have not been explicitly delegated to the Union remain with the Member States.[29] The choice between Article 325 and Article 83(2) affects the extent of the Union's criminalisation powers: while both provisions allow the EU to harmonise national criminal law to protect the Union's financial interests, the former legal basis imposes less restrictions and a stronger obligation

25 European Commision, Proposal for the Financial Interests Directive, COM(2012) 363 final, 11 July 2012, 7.

26 In the past, the meaning of the so-called 'non-affection clause' of Article 280(4) TEC, precluding the (then) EC legislator from adopting *'necessary measures . . . affording effective and equivalent protection in the Member States'* which concern *'the application of national criminal law'*, provoked a lot of discussion; see e.g. Fromm, I. E. (2008), 'Ius Puniendi: The Right of the Institutions of the EC to Protect the Financial Interests of the EC from Fraud (Art. 280 paragraph 4 EC Treaty', *European Journal of Crime, Criminal Law and Criminal Justice*, 16, 125, at 135–8; Siebert, T. (2008), 'The European Fight against Fraud – The Community's Competence to Enact Criminal Laws and Its Power to Approximate National Criminal Law by Directives', *European Journal of Crime, Criminal Law and Criminal Justice*, 16, 89, at 98–102. However, even if the EC legislator did not have the power to oblige Member States to use criminal law, the Member States themselves already agreed to use criminal sanctions for the protection of the financial interests of the EC in the so-called PIF Convention. The crucial difference is, of course, that the PIF Convention is an international agreement to which the Member States subscribed voluntarily, whereas the Commission's current proposal for a directive would impose a top-down obligation to create criminal offences, which could be enforced before the CJEU.

27 Proposal for the Financial Interests Directive, COM(2012) 363 final, 11 July 2012, 6–7. Interestingly, a similar position was adopted by Advocate General Kokott in her opinion in Case C-489/10, *Łukasz Marcin Bonda*, 15 December 2011, para. 18.

28 Council, Amended Proposal for a Directive of the European Parliament and the Council on the fight against fraud to the Union's financial interests by means of criminal law, 2012/0193 (COD), 10 June 2013, 2–3.

29 Article 4(1) TEU.

to legislate.[30] Hence, the importance of the discussion is far from being merely theoretical.[31]

While the proposal for the future 'PIF' Directive is still under discussion, it is noteworthy that the CJEU recently joined the legislative debate, albeit it of course in an indirect way.[32] In *Taricco*,[33] a case concerning Italian VAT fraud legislation, the Court recalled that:

> Article 325 TFEU obliges the Member States to counter illegal activities affecting the financial interests of the European Union through effective deterrent measures[34]

and that:

> [a]lthough the Member States have freedom to choose the applicable penalties – which may take the form of administrative penalties, criminal penalties or a combination of the two . . . criminal penalties may nevertheless be essential to combat certain serious cases of VAT evasion in an effective and dissuasive manner.[35]

Moreover, under the currently applicable 'PIF' Convention, the Member States are already obliged:

> to take the necessary measures to ensure that conduct constituting fraud affecting the European Union's financial interests is punishable by effective, proportionate and dissuasive criminal penalties, including, at least in cases of serious fraud, penalties involving deprivation of liberty.[36]

For sure, this judgment does not resolve the legislative discussion between the Commission and the Council as far as the legal basis of the new Directive is

30 Mitsilegas (2014), note 1 above, 119.

31 Furthermore, under Article 325 TFEU, the UK, Ireland and Denmark could not benefit from the opt-outs they negotiated with respect to Title V of the TFEU, including Article 83(2) TFEU. See Protocols No. 21 and 22 to the Lisbon Treaty. See also Herlin-Karnell, E. (2015), note 4 above, 55.

32 The CJEU 'intervention' did not escape the attention of the Luxembourg Presidency of the Council: see, Council, 'Proposal for a Directive on the fight against fraud to the Union's financial interests by means of criminal law (PIF Directive) – Judgment in case C-105/14 (Taricco)', Interinstitutional file 2012/0193 (COD) of the Presidency to CATS, Brussels, 17 December 2015, 12088/15.

33 Case C-105/14, *Taricco*, 8 September 2015. For a first analysis of the judgment, see Lasalle, M. (2015), 'Taricco Kills Two Birds with One Stone for the Sake of the PIF', *European Law Blog*, 27 October 2015, consultable at: http://europeanlawblog.eu/?p=2954.

34 Case C-105/14, *Taricco*, 8 September 2015, para. 37.

35 *Ibid.*, para. 39.

36 *Ibid.*, para. 40.

concerned.[37] But it does mark, once again, the (perceived) importance of criminal sanctions for the effective protection of the Union's interests, in particular its financial interests.

In sum, for the time being, the issue whether Article 325 TFEU contains an implicit legal basis for EU criminalisation remains unsettled. In the future, once the new 'PIF' Directive has been adopted, the CJEU may be called upon to clarify the matter.

A second, even more delicate question is whether the EU would have the power to adopt criminal measures in areas belonging to the Union's exclusive competence. Sporadically, this possibility has been suggested by some scholars.[38] Moreover, in its 2011 EU criminal law policy Communication, the European Commission announced that it would further explore 'the potential role of criminal law as a necessary tool to ensure effective enforcement' in 'other harmonised policy areas', adding as 'indicative examples' 'customs rules concerning the approximation of customs offences and penalties' and 'fishery policy, where the EU has adopted a "zero tolerance" campaign against illegal, unreported and unregulated fishing'.[39] The Commission thereby seems to suggest that certain aspects of policy areas belonging to the exclusive competence of the EU could be covered by Article 83(2) TFEU.

Nevertheless, it seems quite unlikely that this legal basis could be stretched as to include exclusive competences of the EU. One may invoke several arguments against such an extensive interpretation of Article 83(2) TFEU. First of all, from an historical and teleological perspective, Article 83(2) TFEU is based on case law which dealt with shared competences (in particular transport and environmental

37 The judgment may have important repercussions on the scope *ratione materiae* of the future Directive though, because the CJEU quite heavily insisted on the fact that VAT fraud should be considered fraud against the Union's financial interests; see Case C-105/14, *Taricco*, 8 September 2015, paras 38 and 41.

38 See e.g. Wils, W. P. J. (2007), 'Is Criminalization of EU Competition Law the Answer?', in: Ehlermann, C.-D. and Atanasiu, I. (eds), *European Competition Law Annual 2006: Enforcement of Prohibition of Cartels*, Oxford/Portland: Hart Publishing, 315 (arguing that Art. III-271 (2) of the (rejected) Constitutional Treaty, which was very similar to Art. 83(2) TFEU, 'could undoubtedly be used to criminalize the enforcement of EU antitrust law in all the Member States'). See also Corthaut, T. (2012), *EU Ordre Public*, Alphen aan den Rijn: Kluwer Law International, 160 (contending that 'the fact that certain areas have become the exclusive competence of the Union make it virtually inevitable that EU law also determines certain crimes' and thereby referring to the example of counterfeiting euro bills, because it relates to the Union's exclusive competence for the 'monetary policy for the Member States whose currency is the euro' (Art. 3(1), (c) TFEU). Since the Lisbon Treaty, counterfeiting of (any) means of payment has, however, become one of the Euro crimes listed in Article 83(1), para. 2 TFEU (contrary to former Art. 29 TEU), thereby explicitly giving the EU the power to approximate national criminal law on this subject. See in this respect the Directive of 15 May 2014 on the protection of euro and other currencies against counterfeiting by criminal law, and replacing Council Framework Decision 2000/383/JHA, OJ L 151, 21 May 2014, 1. Whether the general argument made by Corthaut still stands for other areas of policy which are not explicitly included in Art. 83 TFEU, is probably doubtful. That being said, as illustrated above, the scope of Article 83(1) is definitely interpreted broadly by the EU legislator.

39 European Commission, Communication, note 2 above, 10–11.

policy). Second, the wording of Article 83(2) TFEU refers to policy areas that have been subject to 'harmonisation measures', a term that is used with regard to areas of shared competence (see e.g. Art. 114 TFEU). Third, Article 83(3), para. 2 TFEU includes the possibility of enhanced co-operation in case Member States cannot reach an agreement, and enhanced co-operation is explicitly excluded for fields of exclusive competence (Art. 329(1) TFEU and Art. 20(1) TEU).

That being said, even with respect to areas in which the EU has exclusive competence, the enforcement of Union rules often relies to a large extent on the action of the Member States. In light of the principle of sincere co-operation,[40] laid down in Article 4(3) TEU, the Member States have to help the Union 'in carrying out tasks which flow from the Treaties'. Moreover, in accordance with settled case law of the CJEU, Member States are compelled to use criminal sanctions when enforcing certain aspects belonging to the Union's competence if similar infringements of (purely) national law are also punished with criminal sanctions (principle of assimilation or equivalence).

Provisional conclusion

At the end of this section, one may conclude that the EU has quite broad powers to legislate in the area of substantive criminal law. In addition to the legal basis for the so-called Euro crimes (Art. 83(1) TFEU), the Treaty provides the EU legislature with an explicit legal basis for functional criminalisation (Art. 83(2) TFEU), whose precise scope is however still to be clarified. In addition, there are some doubts as to whether this legal basis might be supplemented by Article 325 TFEU to ensure the effective protection of the Union's financial interests.

The next question to address is how the Union legislature has been using its powers for functional criminalisation so far, in particular its powers based on Article 83(2) TFEU, and to explore which criteria have been used to justify the resort to criminal law.

The Union's appetite for criminal law: a new legal framework for market abuse

Since the entry into force of the Treaty of Lisbon,[41] the EU legislature (in fact, primarily the European Commission) has taken a couple of important legislative

40 Case 68/88, *Commission v. Hellenic Republic* (so-called *Greek Maize* case), 21 September 1989, paras 23–4.

41 Notorious pre-Lisbon examples of the EU legislation designed to enhance the effectiveness of EU law by means of criminal law are the Environmental Crime Directive and the Ship-Source Pollution Directive: Directive 2008/99/EC on the protection of the environment through criminal law, 19 November 2008, OJ, L 328, 6 December 2008, 28; Directive 2005/35/EC on ship-source pollution and on the introduction of penalties, including criminal penalties, for pollution offences of 7 September 2005, as amended by Directive 2009/123/EC of 21 October 2009, OJ L 255, 30 September 2005, 11. Other examples are the Directive on sanctions and measures against employers of illegal immigrants and the (not-adopted) proposal for a Directive on criminal sanc-

initiatives which aim at introducing minimum rules for definitions of criminal offences as well as criminal sanctions in order to tackle the ineffective enforcement of certain areas of EU law. The most notable example is the Commission's proposal to introduce criminal sanctions against insider dealing and market manipulation when committed intentionally,[42] which led to the adoption of a new Market Abuse Directive[43] (hereinafter: 2014 MAD) and a Market Abuse Regulation[44] (hereinafter: MAR), replacing the 2003 Market Abuse Directive[45] (hereinafter: 2003 MAD). Our objective is *not* to analyse the substance of the new legal framework, as this is the subject of another chapter in this volume,[46] but to study the dual-track approach adopted by the EU legislature and the underlying justification for EU criminalisation.

A dual-track approach for market abuse

The dual-track (or two-pronged) approach of the EU legislature for the new market abuse legal framework consists in combining an administrative track (where national and supranational authorities co-operate with one another to enforce EU law) with a criminal track (where national authorities are in charge). Of course, the enforcement of EU law by a combination of administrative and criminal law is as such not new; it suffices to refer to the field of competition law, where the European Commission exercises administrative investigative and sanctioning powers at the supranational level and where national authorities have similar powers of an administrative and/or criminal nature.[47] However, it is the

tions for the enforcement of intellectual property rights: Directive 2009/52/EC of the European Parliament and of the Council providing minimum standards on sanctions and measures against employers of illegally staying third-country nationals, 18 June 2009, OJ L 168, 30 June 2009, p. 24; European Commission, Proposal for a Directive of the European Parliament and of the Council on criminal measures aimed at ensuring the enforcement of intellectual property rights, COM(2005) 276 final, 12 July 2005; European Commission, Amended proposal for a Directive of the European Parliament and of the Council on criminal measures aimed at ensuring the enforcement of intellectual property rights, COM(2006) 168 final, 26 April 2006.

42 European Commission, Proposal for a Directive of the European Parliament and of the Council on criminal sanctions for insider dealing and market manipulation (hereinafter: Proposed MAD), COM(2011) 654 final, 20 October 2011, Art. 3–4; European Commission, Amended Proposal for a Directive of the European Parliament and of the Council on criminal sanctions for insider dealing and market manipulation, COM(2012) 420 final, 25 July 2012.

43 Directive 2014/57/EU of the European Parliament and the Council on criminal sanctions for market abuse, 16 April 2014, OJ L 173, 12 June 2014, 179.

44 Regulation (EU) 596/2014 of the European Parliament and the Council on market abuse and repealing Directive 2003/6/EC of the European Parliament and the Council and Commission Directives 2003/124/EC, 2003/125/EC and 2004/72/EC, OJ L 173, 12 June 2014, 1.

45 Directive 2003/6/EC of the European Parliament and the Council on insider dealing and market manipulation (market abuse), 28 January 2003, OJ L 96, 12 April 2003, 16.

46 See the discussion by Blachnio-Parzych, Chapter 15. See also Luchtman, M. J. J. P.and Vervaele, J. A. E. (2014), 'Enforcing the Market Abuse Regime: Towards an Integrated Model of Criminal and Administrative Law Enforcement in the European Union?', *New Journal of European Criminal Law*, 5, 202–20.

47 For a more extensive analysis, see the discussion by Günsberg, Chapter 14.

first time that the EU legislature adopts two closely interconnected legal instruments to ensure national enforcement of EU law by means of administrative tools on the one hand and by criminal sanctions on the other. It is interesting to analyse the differences between the administrative and the criminal track, as it may tell us something about the functions and objectives of EU criminal law.[48]

The MAR contains a highly elaborated regime of administrative enforcement, which is directly applicable at the national level. It contains far-reaching supervisory and investigative powers for (national) competent authorities,[49] and reinforces the co-operation between those authorities and ESMA, i.e. the European Securities and Markets Authorities.[50] Some of these powers are almost comparable to the investigative powers judicial authorities have (e.g. they may require existing recordings of telephone conversations, electronic communications or traffic data held by investment firms, credit institutions or financial institutions),[51] or may potentially require the intervention of judicial authorities (e.g. the search of premises and seizure of documents).[52]

Furthermore, the Regulation requires that Member States give their national competent authorities the power to impose a wide variety of specific administrative sanctions and measures,[53] including quasi-criminal sanctions such as the disgorgement of the profits,[54] a temporary ban of a person discharging managerial responsibilities or responsible for the infringement from exercising managerial responsibilities in investment firms,[55] and fines up to 5,000,000 euro for natural persons[56] and up to 15,000,000 euro or 15% of the total annual turnover for legal persons.[57] Although the MAR imposes such administrative sanctions, it does not entirely annihilate the choice between administrative and criminal sanctions which Member States used to have under the 2003 MAD.[58] The administrative sanctions laid down in the MAR are indeed only a minimum; Member States may decide to adopt criminal sanctions instead.[59] Therefore, one may conclude that the MAR as such does not impose limits on national criminal law.[60]

48 For a somewhat similar approach to EU competition law, see Harding, C. (2015), note 5 above.
49 Art. 23(2) MAR.
50 Art. 24-25 MAR.
51 Art. 23(2), para.1, (g) MAR.
52 Art. 23(2), para. 1, (e) and para. 2 MAR.
53 Art. 30(2) MAR.
54 Art. 30(2), (b) MAR.
55 Art. 30(2), (f) MAR.
56 Art. 30(2), (i) MAR.
57 Art. 30(2), (j) MAR.
58 The 2003 MAD merely required 'effective, proportionate and dissuasive' measures, 'without prejudice to the right of the Member States to impose criminal sanctions' (Art. 14(1)). For an application of this requirement, see e.g. Case C-45/08, *Spector v. CBFA*, 23 December 2009.
59 Art. 30(1), para. 2 MAR.
60 Before the adoption of the MAR, some scholars argued that the dual-track approach of the EU legislator with respect to market abuse may place limits on national criminal law to ensure the effectiveness of EU law. The preference of the EU legislator for administrative sanctions to address certain harmful market practices would limit Member States' possibilities to criminalise such behaviour, as a harsher criminal law approach would undermine the effectiveness of EU

In some cases, Member States are, however, obliged to use criminal law to enforce the EU market abuse rule. The 2014 MAD creates the obligation for Member States to criminalise insider dealing, unlawful disclosure of inside information and market manipulation *'at least in serious cases and when committed unintentionally'*[61] and defines those criminal offences.[62] In addition, the 2014 MAD imposes upon the Member States minimum rules for the maximum term of imprisonment for natural persons,[63] though not in case of aiding and abetting.[64] By contrast, as far as legal persons are concerned, the 2014 MAD does not require criminal sanctions.[65] The Directive only provides for minimum rules; 'Member States are free to adopt or maintain more stringent criminal law rules for market abuse.'[66] For instance, Member States may criminalise 'market manipulation committed recklessly or by serious negligence.'[67]

What justification for criminalising market abuse?

After this short overview of both legal instruments, one may wonder what the main distinguishing criteria between the administrative and the criminal track are, especially taking into account that some of the investigative powers under the MAR are in fact quite intrusive or coercive and that, similarly, some

law (Mitsilegas, V. (2014), 'From Overcriminalisation to Decriminalisation. The Many Faces of Effectiveness in European Criminal Law', *New Journal of European Criminal Law*, 416, 422–3). Eventually, the EU legislator did not make such a far-reaching decision. The MAR imposes administrative sanctions '[w]ithout prejudice to any criminal sanctions' (Art. 30(1)) and explicitly states that Member States 'may provide for higher levels of sanctions than those established' by the MAR (Art. 30(3)). Rather than imposing administrative enforcement for certain market abuse infringements, the EU only sets minimum definitions and sanctions. Member States may thus impose higher or more severe sanctions, even of a criminal nature, unless of course those sanctions would result in a disproportionate limitation of the freedom of movement or other fundamental rights. See e.g. Case C-387/93, *Domingo Banchero*, 14 December 1995, para. 58; Case C-348/96, *Calfa*, 19 January 1999, para. 28. More recently, the CJEU also evaluated the (dis)proportionality of national criminal law in the field of migration law, with respect to the implementation of the Returns Directive. See e.g. Case C-61/11 PPU, *El Dridi*, 28 April 2011, paras. 54–62. For an extensive analysis of this case and subsequent case law in the same field see: Mitsilegas, V. (2015), *The Criminalisation of Migration in Europe. Challenges for Human Rights and the Rule of Law*, London: Springer, 60–75.

61 Art. 3(1), 4(1) and 5(1) 2014 MAD.

62 A careful reading of the definitions in the 2014 MAD reveals some small differences with the definitions laid down in the MAR, which raises the question as to how these definitions will interact in the future.

63 Art. 7(2) and (3) 2014 MAD.

64 Art. 7(1) 2014 MAD.

65 In fact, the 2014 MAD contains the same standard clause for liability of legal persons (Art. 8) as several other post-Lisbon criminal law directives adopted on the basis of Article 83(1) TFEU and grants Member States the choice between criminal and non-criminal sanctions, provided that they are 'effective, proportionate and dissuasive' (Art. 9).

66 Recital (20) Preamble to the 2014 MAD.

67 Recital (21) Preamble to the 2014 MAD.

administrative sanctions are clearly punitive.[68] In other words, why did the EU legislature consider that certain forms of market abuse are worthy of criminalisation? At the end of the day, the most distinctive features of the criminal track appear to be the requirement of intent for criminal liability (although Member States may apply a lower threshold for criminal liability) and the possibility to impose a prison sentence.

An analysis of the initial proposal for the new MAD reveals a number of interesting elements in this respect. By introducing criminal sanctions, the Commission hoped to remedy the ineffectiveness of the pre-existing legal framework on market abuse, which was demonstrated in a report by the High-Level Group on Financial Supervision.[69] National definitions of market abuse offences differed greatly, which, due to the cross-border dimension of many of these offences, 'undermines the internal market'.[70] What is more, existing sanctions were 'lacking impact' and considered 'insufficiently dissuasive'.[71]

To justify criminalisation, the Commission argued that:

> criminal sanctions, in particular imprisonment, are generally considered to send a *strong message of disapproval* that could increase the *dissuasiveness* of sanctions.[72]

In particular:

> [m]inimum rules on criminal offences and on criminal sanctions for market abuse . . . can contribute to ensuring the *effectiveness of this Union policy* by demonstrating *social disapproval of a qualitative different nature* compared to administrative sanctions or compensation mechanisms under civil law.[73]

Furthermore:

> [c]riminal convictions for market abuse offences, which often result in *widespread media coverage*, help to improve *deterrence* [as] they demonstrate to potential offenders that the authorities take serious enforcement action which can result in imprisonment or other criminal sanctions and a criminal record.[74]

68 The EU legislator was clearly aware of the punitive nature of some administrative sanctions, as Recital 23 of the 2014 MAD warns Member States that the imposition of criminal sanctions and administrative sanctions should not lead to a breach of the principle of *ne bis in idem*.

69 Recitals (3) and (8) Proposed MAD; Explanatory Memorandum to the Proposed MAD, 2.

70 Explanatory Memorandum to the Proposed MAD, 3.

71 Explanatory Memorandum to the Proposed MAD, 3.

72 Explanatory Memorandum to the Proposed MAD, 2, emphasis added. See also: European Commission, Communication on reinforcing sanctioning regimes in the financial sector, COM(2010) 716, 8 December 2010, 9.

73 Explanatory Memorandum to the Proposed MAD, 3, emphasis added.

74 Explanatory Memorandum to the Proposed MAD, 3, emphasis added.

Finally, based on the impact assessment, the Commission concluded that:

> requiring Member States to introduce criminal sanctions for the most serious market abuse offences [is] *essential to ensure the effective implementation of the Union policy on market abused*.[75]

Briefly summarised, criminal sanctions are thus needed because they express stronger social disapproval and because they are more deterrent than other sanctions, thereby ensuring the effective enforcement of the EU rules on market abuse.

Whilst advocating the need to adopt criminal sanctions, the Commission also wanted Member States to apply more severe administrative sanctions to market abuse, including (non-intentional) insider dealing and market manipulation.[76] As a fact, a previous evaluation of national laws revealed that not all Member States provided for pecuniary administrative sanctions, and amongst those that did, the level of those sanctions varied hugely.[77] As indicated above, the adopted MAR includes an impressive list of administrative sanctions, some of which are definitely punitive and can be easily qualified as criminal sanctions under Articles 6 and 7 ECHR. One may therefore wonder why the EU legislature did not first introduce those more stringent administrative sanctions and await the outcome of those changes before upgrading to criminal sanctions. Would it not have made more sense to first introduce minimum rules for the types and levels of administrative sanctions to tackle national divergences? Put differently, was the approximation of national criminal law really *'essential'* to ensure a more effective enforcement of EU rules, as Article 83(2) TFEU requires? Still, the European Commission claimed that the adoption of administrative sanctions had 'proven insufficient to ensure compliance with the rules on preventing and fighting market abuse'.[78]

While the effectiveness justification of the Commission is clearly reflected in the preamble to the 2014 MAD,[79] it should nevertheless be pointed out that, interestingly, some further reasons for criminalisation were added. In particular, the 2014 MAD also highlights the serious impact (even attempted) insider dealing, unlawful disclosure of inside information and market manipulation may have on 'the integrity of the market'[80] and 'investor confidence in [financial]

75 Explanatory Memorandum to the Proposed MAD, p. 4, emphasis added.

76 European Commission, Proposal for a Regulation of the European Parliament and of the Council on insider dealing and market manipulation (market abuse) (hereinafter: Proposed MAR), COM(2011) 651 final, 20 October 2011. The European Parliament further enhanced the already severe administrative sanctions proposed by the Commission (Art. 26) and refined the criteria for determining the type and level of those sanctions (Art. 27). See European Parliament, Legislative resolution on the proposal for a regulation of the European Parliament and the Council on insider dealing and market manipulation (market abuse), 2011/0295 (COD), 10 September 2013.

77 Recital (4) Proposed MAD, 8.

78 Recital (5) Proposed MAD, 8.

79 See in particular recitals (3) and (5)–(8) Preamble to the 2014 MAD.

80 Recitals (11)-(12) Preamble to the 2014 MAD.

markets'[81], the 'actual or potential profit'[82] which may be obtained from such behaviour, and the 'potential for widespread damage on the lives of millions of peoples',[83] as illustrated by the financial crisis and in particular the Libor scandal.

Furthermore, criminal sanctions imposed for such offences should take into account 'the concrete circumstances in each individual case' and 'should be proportionate, taking into account the profits made or losses avoided by the person held liable as well as the damage resulting from the offence to other persons and, where applicable, to the functioning of the market or the wider economy'.[84] In other words, criminal sanctions must be individualised and proportionate to the objective seriousness or harmfulness of the offence. Thereby, the Directive seems to go a small step further than Article 49(3) Charter of EU Fundamental Rights,[85] which states that criminal sanctions 'must not be ***disproportionate*** to the criminal offence'.[86]

In short, one may say the Commission's initial focus on the effectiveness of EU law is somewhat counterbalanced against other criminal law concerns, namely the seriousness of the behaviour, based upon the underlying protected values (market integrity, investor confidence) and the need for proportionate sanctions.

Criminal sanctions for market abuse, but not for cartel offences?

On a final note, the EU legislator's step towards criminal sanctions in the field of market abuse is nevertheless somewhat remarkable when compared to the (punitive) administrative approach in EU competition law.[87] One may indeed question whether insider dealing and market manipulation are really so much more serious and harmful than cartels to justify the introduction of criminal sanctions. In fact, at first sight, these infringements appear to be fairly comparable: the underlying legal interest is the protection of investors/consumers and the integrity of the market,[88] the required *mens rea* is intent, and the harm is usually widespread, affecting both individual victims and the market system as a whole.

81 Recitals (13) Preamble to the 2014 MAD.
82 Recitals (11)–(12) Preamble to the 2014 MAD.
83 Recitals (7) Preamble to the 2014 MAD.
84 Recital (24) Preamble to the 2014 MAD.
85 Recital (27) Preamble to the 2014 MAD explicitly refers to this principle.
86 Emphasis added.
87 With respect to the 'criminal' nature of EU fines imposed for cartels in light of the Article 6-7 ECHR, see Franssen, V. (2013), *European Sentencing Principles for Corporations*, doctoral dissertation, Leuven, KU Leuven, 307–14.
88 See e.g. European Commission, Communication on reinforcing sanctioning regimes in the financial sector, COM(2010) 716, 8 December 2010, 10. Admittedly, there is some ambivalence about the objectives of EU competition law and the main legal interests it protects. But consumer protection has been put high on the political agenda by former EU Competition Commissioners Monti and Kroes; see Parret, L. (2010), 'Shouldn't We Know What We Are Protecting? Yes We Should! A Plea for a Solid and Comprehensive Debate about the Objectives of EU Competition Law and Policy', *ECJ*, 6, 339, at 339–40 and 355–8; Franssen (2013), note 87 above, at 326.

Hence, would it not seem logical to send a similar message of strong social disapproval with respect to cartel offences? Would a similar enforcement approach in both fields not strengthen the internal coherence of EU (criminal) law, which the European Commission acknowledged to be an important objective of future EU criminal law policy?[89] Internal coherence is considered 'a necessary condition if criminal law is to be able to reflect the values held to be important by society collectively and by individuals and their understanding of justice' and 'necessary in order to ensure acceptance of criminal law.'[90] Besides, to impose minimum rules for the definition of criminal offences and the applicable criminal sanctions in case of market abuse but not for cartel offences, might upset the existing 'ordinal proportionality'[91] of national offences.

The adoption of different enforcement strategies with respect to (serious) market abuse and cartel offences therefore seems a missed chance. It seems that the enforcement strategies pursued by the respective Directorates-General of the European Commission are less the result of a well-considered coherent and consistent policy choice, based on a common understanding of the need to protect the underlying legal interests and values by means of criminal law, but rather the outcome of institutional dynamics and effectiveness concerns. The administrative enforcement of EU competition rules seems to function quite effectively, hence there is no need for criminal sanctions (assuming that the EU would have the power to oblige Member States to introduce criminal sanctions, which (as discussed above) is far from certain).

It remains to be seen whether this distinction is sustainable in the long run, and whether the desired deterrent effect and strong social disapproval with respect to market abuse will actually result from the simple adoption of criminal offences. The latter aspect will be further discussed in the following section.

How problematic is the current approach to EU criminalisation based on effectiveness concerns?

As said before, the main aim of EU legislation approximating national criminal laws on the basis of Article 83(2) TFEU is to ensure a more effective implementation of EU policies. Particularly, EU criminal law will kick in when 'the enforcement choices in the Member States do not yield the desired result and levels of enforcement remain uneven'.[92] EU criminal law is therefore not primarily

89 European Commission, Communication of 2011, note 7 above, at 3–4 and 12.

90 European Criminal Policy Initiative, 2014, 'The Manifesto on European Criminal Policy in 2011', *European Criminal Law Review*, 4, 86, at 91.

91 Proportionality can be subdivided in ordinal and cardinal proportionality: the former 'refers to the relative seriousness of the different types of offences, and involves comparative assessments of gravity' while the latter 'refers to the relationship between the seriousness of the offence and the severity of the penalty.' Van Zyl Smit, D. and Ashworth, A. (2004), 'Disproportionate Sentences as Human Rights Violations', *Modern Law Review*, 67, 54, at 559.

92 European Commission, Communication of 2011, note 7 above, at 3.

founded on the need to protect core moral or social values, but on an instrumental need to strengthen the *effet utile* of EU law.

Nevertheless, at the same time, the above example of market abuse shows that the EU legislator invokes the strong dissuasive and even deterrent effect of criminal sanctions as a reason why sanctions of a criminal nature are needed to ensure more effectiveness. Compared to administrative and civil sanctions, criminal sanctions are deemed to send out a more powerful message of disapproval, particularly in case of imprisonment.

Let us now analyse more closely the different justifications for EU criminalisation, taking into account the EU constitutional legal framework and some of the core functions and principles of criminal law. To what extent is EU 'functional criminalisation' problematic?

The constitutional background of EU effectiveness

From a historical and institutional perspective, the EU's predominant focus on effectiveness is, of course, not at all surprising. The Union's entire functioning is aimed at achieving its objectives, which calls for the effective implementation of its actions. Hence, the institutional framework of the Union is designed to 'ensure the consistency, effectiveness and continuity of its policies and actions'.[93] The Commission, when launching new legislative proposals, should be interpreted against this constitutional background.

Furthermore, based on the principle of sincere (or loyal) co-operation,[94] Member States are required, both by the Treaties and by the case law of the CJEU, to 'take all measures necessary to guarantee the application and effectiveness of Community law'.[95] Article 4(3), para. 2 TEU now states that the 'Member States shall take any appropriate measure, general or particular, to ensure fulfilment of the obligations arising out of the Treaties or resulting from the acts of the institutions of the Union.'

To this end, ever since the *Greek Maize* case, Member States must ensure equivalent protection of EU law, meaning that 'infringements of Community law are penalised under conditions, both procedural and substantive, which are analogous to those applicable to infringements of national law of a similar nature and importance and which, in any event, make the penalty effective, proportionate and dissuasive.'[96] The need for effective and dissuasive sanctions is thus deeply rooted in EU constitutional law.

Consistent with the overall Union logic of effectiveness, legal instruments based on Article 83(2) TFEU can go a step further and oblige Member States to adopt effective, proportionate and dissuasive *criminal* sanctions, or even impose more specific requirements for criminal sanctions.

93 Art. 13(1), para. 1 TEU.

94 Art. 4, para. 3 TEU (previously Art. 10 EC).

95 Case 68/88, *Commission v. Hellenic Republic*, 21 September 1989, para. 23.

96 Case 68/88, *Commission v. Hellenic Republic*, 21 September 1989, para. 24.

Dissuasive or deterrent sanctions to ensure effectiveness

In justifying *criminal* sanctions, the European Commission has pointed to the need 'to send a *strong message of disapproval* that could increase the *dissuasiveness* of sanctions'[97] and argued that '[m]inimum rules on criminal offences and on criminal sanctions . . . can contribute to ensuring the *effectiveness of [a] Union policy by demonstrating social disapproval of a qualitative different nature* compared to administrative sanctions or compensation mechanisms under civil law.'[98] The Commission thus relies on the deterrent and expressive (or symbolic) functions of criminal law, which are indeed both key objectives of criminal sanctions.

Yet, whether criminal sanctions are actually *more effective* than other sanctions, is far from obvious.[99] While the EU legislature apparently has a great deal of faith in the effectiveness of criminal law enforcement, this optimism is probably not shared by many criminal lawyers and criminologists.[100] As a fact, civil or administrative enforcement may very well be (much) more effective than criminal enforcement. Effective enforcement depends on a wide range of factors, not just on the label or nature of the sanction.

For instance, administrative and civil sanctions might be more effective as they may be better adjusted to the socially undesirable behaviour than the typical ('iconic') criminal sanction of imprisonment (for natural persons) or fines (for legal persons). For instance, an investment firm might be more deterred by the risk of losing its license or authorisation than by a high fine, as the impact of the former sanction is most likely more far reaching. Nevertheless, the withdrawal of a license is an administrative sanction for market abuse imposed by the MAR,[101] whereas (criminal or non-criminal) fines are the only compulsory sanctions for legal persons committing the (serious and intentional) market abuse criminal offences under the 2014 MAD.[102]

Besides, under administrative or civil law, authorities may be able to react more swiftly as the burden of proof is less high and procedural safeguards for 'suspects' are less strong, thereby making the investigative and sanctioning process less burdensome and less costly.

97 Explanatory Memorandum to the Proposed MAD, at 2, emphasis added. See also European Commission, Communication on reinforcing sanctioning regimes in the financial sector, COM(2010) 716, 8 December 2010, 9.

98 Explanatory Memorandum to Proposed MAD, p. 3, emphasis added.

99 See e.g. also Oberg, J. (2014), 'Do We Really Need Criminal Sanctions for the Enforcement of EU Law?', *New Journal of European Criminal Law*, 5, 370, at 378.

100 See e.g. Van Swaaningen, R. (2013), 'Reversing the Punitive Turn: The Case of the Netherlands', in Daems, T. *et al.* (eds), *European Penology?*, Oxford/Portland: Hart Publishing, 354–5, with reference to Loader (2010) ('We expect too much of punishment, and insufficiently acknowledge the negative side-effects, whether in prison or in society') and 356 ('It is also worthwhile to simply point at negative effects of punitiveness, such as the overburdened criminal justice system, the high costs of a largely ineffective penal system').

101 Art. 30(2), (d) MAR.

102 Art. 9 2014 MAD.

Very often administrative authorities or agencies are also more specialised in a certain matter than judicial authorities and they may have more opportunities to build up case experience, which is crucial with respect to complex crimes in the field of economic and financial law. For instance, criminal convictions for insider trading are notoriously hard to get because the investigations require specialised knowledge and sufficient experience. Moreover, intent is so hard to prove in these cases that many investigations lead to a dead end or, in a less worse scenario, to an out-of-court settlement between the authorities and the suspect.[103] As indicated above, the Commission invoked the 'extensive media coverage' of market abuse offences as a factor which will help 'to deter potential offenders'.[104] Yet, will this also be the case when the media report – once again – on failed investigations or trials?[105]

Furthermore, whether sanctions are effective tools to ensure enforcement of EU law, and thus ultimately to ensure law-abiding behaviour, also depends on the probability of being caught. The higher the chance of detection, prosecution *and* punishment, the higher the deterrent effect of certain prohibitive rules is. Hence, a (very) severe sanction which is hardly applied will have a lesser deterrent effect than a less severe sanction which is applied with a high degree of certainty. Moreover, deterrence-based punishment can only function properly if potential offenders are *aware* of the threat of punishment *before* engaging in criminal activities[106] and *act* on this threat.

Finally, whether a sanction is 'deterrent' also depends to some extent on the personality of the individual perpetrator: for instance, his or her attitude towards

103 For instance, in Belgium a notorious criminal case of insider trading (in the context of the takeover of Fortis Bank by the Belgian State in 2008) ended in a settlement with the public prosecutor. This way, the investment company *Bois Sauvage* and some of its executives were able to avoid a criminal conviction and a criminal record. The settlement received a lot of negative attention in the media and was considered a bargain for the company and its executives. However, according to the Minister of Justice and the Secretary of State in charge of the fight against fraud, the upside of the story was that the Belgian Treasury received about 9 million euro. See BELGA/AVE, 'Minnelijke schikking Bois Sauvage was beste slechte oplossing', *Knack Online*, 28 November 2013.

104 Recital (11) Proposed MAD, 8. See also Explanatory Memorandum to Proposed MAD, p. 3.

105 For similar reasons, the European Economic and Social Committee warned the European Commission that a better detection of market abuse would not necessarily result in more effective enforcement, as the main problem under the 2003 MAD regime seemed to be that 'an overwhelming majority of cases are either not prosecuted or are dropped in exchange for payment of a fine. It is possible that public prosecutors' offices in Member States lack specialist departments in this area.' (At para. 4.10: Opinion of the European Economic and Social Committee on the Proposal for a Regulation of the European Parliament and the Council on insider dealing and market manipulation and on the Proposal for a Directive of the European Parliament and the Council on criminal sanctions for insider dealing and market manipulation, O.J., C181, 21 June 2012, 64.)

106 Von Hirsch, A., Bottoms, A. E., Burney, E. and Wikstrom, P.-O. (2009), 'Deterrent Sentencing as a Crime Prevention Strategy', in: Von Hirsch, A. *et al.* (eds), *Principled Sentencing. Readings on Theory and Policy*, Oxford/Portland: Hart Publishing, 3rd ed., 57, 58–9.

risk and towards unlawful behaviour. As a result, one and the same sanction may give different incentives to different perpetrators.

In sum, as criminologists and criminal lawyers know well, the effectiveness of criminal law and criminal sanctions may vary widely. For sanctions to be *deterrent*, punishment must be certain, severe and swift, *and perceived* as such by potential perpetrators.[107]. This definitely holds true for natural persons, but also for legal persons. The EU obligation to create criminal provisions and minimum sanctions will not resolve practical enforcement issues, such as the difficulty to prove market abuse, the lack of expertise with the public prosecutor's office, or the simple fact that market abuse cases are not a prosecutorial priority.[108] The EU legislator seems quite well aware of this,[109] but nevertheless asserted that criminal sanctions are essential to ensure the effective implementation of EU market abuse rules.

Sanctions sending out strong disapproval to ensure effectiveness

Furthermore, the choice for EU criminalisation is also based on the symbolic or expressive function of criminal law and criminal sanctions. The expressive function of criminal punishment is probably the main distinguishing feature compared to administrative and civil sanctions,[110] and is often closely connected to morality. As a renowned American scholar once aptly wrote:

> the factor that most distinguishes the criminal law is its operation as a *system of moral education and socialization*. The criminal law is obeyed not simply because there is a legal threat underlying it, but because the *public perceives*

107 For a much more extensive analysis see Franssen (2013), note 87 above, 40–5, and the references there.

108 For instance, in Belgium no less than 97 per cent of the investigations into market abuse and other securities offences result in a dismissal of charges. The principal reasons are the lack of interest in these offences on the part of the police and the public prosecutor's office, the existence of a two-tier administrative and criminal law enforcement system in accordance with the EU approach (!) and the absence of clear agreements between the Financial Services Regulatory Authority ('FSMA') and the public prosecutor's office which deals with such cases. See Bové, L., 'Gerecht negeert beurscriminelen', *De Tijd Online*, 24 July 2012.

109 For instance, recital (19) Preamble to the 2014 MAD emphasises that '*Member States should ensure that law enforcement, judicial authorities and other competent authorities responsible for investigating or prosecuting*' market abuse offences have '*effective investigative tools*', and the European Commission stressed that the effectiveness of criminal sanctions depends on whether '*they are appropriately applied by the criminal justice system*' (Explanatory Memorandum to Proposed MAD, 2), (emphasis added).

110 See e.g. Buruma, Y. (2004), 'Grenzen aan de strafrechtelijke aansprakelijkheid', in: Groenhuijsen, M. S. and Simmelink, J. B. H. M. (eds), *Glijdende schalen. Liber amicorum J. de Hullu*, Nijmegen: Wolf Legal Publishers, 71, 90; Gutwirth, S. and De Hert, P. (2011), 'Punir ou Réparer? Une fausse alternative, in: Tulkens, F *et al* (eds), *La peine dans tous ses états. Hommage à Michel van de Kerchove*, Brussels: Larcier, 93, 95–6, emphasis added ('Nous sommes convaincus que *la peine doit d'abord être symbolique et surtout marquer le rejet de l'acte (non de l'auteur)* ainsi que le rétablissement de l'ordre bafoué.').

> *its norms to be legitimate and deserving of compliance*. Far more than tort law, the criminal law is a system for *public communication of values*.[111]

Another scholar added: '[p]unishment is not just a way to make offenders suffer; it is a special social convention that signifies moral condemnation.'[112]

Advocate General Jacobs described the distinguishing feature of criminal sanctions as follows:

> Criminal penalties, also, seek to dissuade; but it does not follow that every dissuasive sanctions is penal. Typically, *the purpose of a criminal sanction exceeds that of simple deterrence*, and will normally involve such matters as the *stigma of social disapproval or the attribution of moral blame*. Thus, the amount of the penalty, in a criminal case, will often reflect the extent of society's disapproval of the conduct in question, *rather than any more pragmatic consideration*.[113]

Nowadays, criminal punishment is clearly no longer confined to *moral* issues: it has evolved into a strong enforcement mechanism of social norms that are *essential* to the functioning of any system based on the rule of law.[114] Whereas moral norms are based on a fundamental conception of goodness and wrongfulness, social norms are the result of social convention.

Ideally, criminal enforcement is limited to the essential rules of a society, i.e. rules which by the majority of a given society are deemed so important that their violation deserves a strong social message of disapproval. The less frequently criminal law is used, the stronger the message of disapproval will naturally be. By contrast, if criminal law is instrumentalised for less important rules, resulting in an inflation of criminal offences, this threatens to undermine the expressive function of criminal law and punishment as a whole.

Due to its expressive or symbolic function, criminal punishment is also said to have a stigmatising and reputational effect.[115] Stigma[116] is the expression of

111 Coffee, J. C. (Jnr) (1991), 'Does "Unlawful" Mean "Criminal"?: Reflections on the Disappearing Tort/Crime Distinction in American Law', *B.U. L. Rev.*, 71, 193, at 193–4, internal references omitted and emphasis added. The quote continues as follows: 'As a result, the criminal law often and necessarily displays a deliberate disdain for the utility of the criminalized conduct to the defendant. Thus, while tort law seeks to balance private benefits and public costs, *criminal law does not* (or does so only by way of special affirmative defenses), *possibly because balancing would undercut the moral rhetoric of the criminal law*' (emphasis added).

112 Kahan, D. M. (1996), 'What Do Alternative Sanctions Mean?', *University of Chicago Law Review*, 63, 591, at 593.

113 Opinion of Advocate General Jacobs, Case C-240/90, *Germany v. Commission*, 3 June 1992, para. 11, emphasis added.

114 See also Harding, C. (2015), note 5 above.

115 See e.g. Uhlmann, D. M. (2009), 'After the Spill Is Gone: The Gulf of Mexico, Environmental Crime, and the Criminal Law', *Michigan Law Review*, 109, 1413, at 1452–3 ('But whether [the expressive function of punishment is] viewed as a standalone theory or as a corollary to deterrence or retributive theory, there is no question that criminal prosecution has a stigmatizing effect that civil enforcement does not.').

116 Etymologically, stigma means 'to mark with a brand' (OED).

internalised norms and is associated with moral or social disapproval.[117] It affects the offender's social identity in a negative way.[118] Stigma is, however, not apportioned by a court: rather it is a social, informal effect of criminal punishment and the formal criminal process more in general.[119] Not all offences may trigger the same stigmatising effect, as they are not perceived equally socially undesirable or harmful.[120] Moreover, it appears some criminal sanctions have a stronger expressive or stigmatising effect than others.[121] Typically imprisonment sends a much stronger message than a fine,[122] even if both are imposed by a criminal court.[123]

It is notoriously difficult to grasp this expressive or symbolic mechanism of criminal punishment in all its complexities as it is based on a subtle interaction between moral and social norms, conventional perceptions and the law.[124] Yet, one thing is sure: it is not enough to attach a criminal label to a certain behaviour to trigger strong social disapproval, whatever (national or EU) legislators may hope for, and notwithstanding the fact that the law can have a norm-shaping effect in the long run.[125] Unlike legal rules, moral values and core social norms are internalised ('inculcated') norms which develop slowly, are usually not very detailed and cannot be changed overnight.[126]

The expressive function of criminal law is thus strongly connected to the importance of the underlying social values that require protection and with the (perceived) harmfulness or undesirability of conduct infringing upon those values in a given society. In this respect, the problem with respect to EU effectiveness-driven criminalisation seems to be three-fold.

117 For a more extensive discussion of stigma see e.g. Ball, W. D., 'Civil, Criminal, or Mary Jane: Stigma, Legislative Labels, and the Civil Case at the Heart of Criminal Procedure', draft available at http://ssrn.com/abstract=1628950, 32–38. See also Goffman, E. (1963), *Stigma. Notes on the Management of Spoiled Identity*, Harmondsworth: Penguin, 11–31.

118 *Ibid.*

119 Bentham regarded the stigma of conviction 'as the "moral or popular" sanction [which] operates . . . through the adverse reactions to the conviction of persons in the community'. See Kadish, S. H. (1963), 'Some Observations on the Use of Criminal Sanctions in Enforcing Economic Regulations', *University of Chicago Law Review*, 30, 423, at 434, with reference to Bentham.

120 See e.g. Dan-Cohen, M. (2010), 'Sanctioning Corporations', *Journal of Law and Policy*, 19, 15.

121 According to some, stigma is not so much linked to a certain form punishment, but to the criminal conviction as such *and* its severity in general. See Posner, R. A. (2003), *Economic Analysis of Law*, New York: Aspen, 223.

122 Some say that a conviction resulting in a fine has a very limited stigmatising effect, even in the case of a criminal fine. See Posner (2003), note 121 above, at 222 and 224. Cf. Posner, R. A. (1998), 'Social Norms, Social Meaning, and Economic Analysis of Law: A Comment', *Journal of Legal Studies*, 27, 558.

123 Kahan (1996), note 112 above, at 593 ('Not all modes of imposing suffering express condemnation or express it in the same way. The message of condemnation is very clear when society deprives an offender of his liberty. But when it merely fines him for the same act, the message is likely to be different.').

124 Cf. e.g. Tonry, M. H. (2006), 'Purposes and Functions of Sentencing', *Crime & Justice*, 34, 12 ('communication, is the most complex and multifaceted [purpose]').

125 See e.g. Shavell, S. (2002), 'Law versus Morality as Regulators of Conduct', *American Law and Economics Review*, 4, 227, at 254–5.

126 *Ibid.*, 234–6.

First, when the EU legislator adopts rules imposing criminalisation and/or minimum rules for criminal sanctions, there is strikingly limited reflection – or at least no open debate – about what exactly determines the strong message of disapproval sent out by criminal sanctions. The EU legislator seems to take the expressive function of criminal sanctions for granted, as if the criminal label would suffice to trigger such strong disapproval. Put differently, while the EU legislator invokes the strong social disapproval that criminal sanctions carry as a justification for EU criminal law, he does not fundamentally question, from a criminal law perspective, the importance of the underlying norms or values.[127] As discussed above, the distinction between Euro crimes and EU *effet utile* crimes is precisely that there is a EU-wide consensus about the seriousness and harmfulness of the crimes listed in Article 83(1) TFEU, whereas this is not the case for functional criminalisation on the basis of Article 83(2) TFEU. The mere fact that criminal sanctions are used to ensure the effective implementation of EU policies does not imply that the underlying legal interests are really essential enough to justify the use of criminal law.

The second problem is closely related to this first one. Criminal law is traditionally perceived as being typical of a particular society, because every society has its own norms and values as well as customs, even if some norms and values are widely shared. The EU is however not a homogeneous society, but a pluralist political entity with a common cultural heritage. This also explains why EU action in the field of criminal law has always been quite delicate. Member States do not like to give up their sovereign power to decide which misconduct is a violation of society's fundamental norms and values. What is fundamental in one society may be less important in another one.[128]

Nevertheless, Article 83(2) TFEU clearly enables the EU to set its own criminal policy agenda. In principle, the Union legislator can decide to criminalise any behaviour which is subject to EU harmonising measures, even if at the national level similar types of behaviour are (usually) not governed by criminal law. By doing so, the EU also excludes the possibility for Member States to decriminalise such behaviour at a later point in time,[129] even if this would be desirable in the light of the internal coherence of the national system (e.g. to safeguard the ordinal proportionality of national sanctions).[130] Consequently, the EU's actions based

127 Cf. Grandi, C. (2011), note 21 above, at 302–3 (pointing out that criminalisation at the EU level is not based on the 'protection of a "bene giuridico" but [on] the effectiveness of an EU policy').

128 See e.g. Asp, P. (2011), 'The importance of the Principles of Subsidiarity and Coherence in the Development of EU Criminal Law', *EuCLR*, 1, 50 ('[C]riminal law is a legal area which is closely connected to national culture and national values and to national understandings of complex ethical questions . . . [T]here are important differences between the Member States on such ethical questions . . . [S]uch differences are not only technical in character, but . . . they reflect deeply rooted understandings of different problems and the way they should be solved. Since criminal law forms part of a system of values built on fundamental understandings of this kind it should be considered as part of the national identities of the Member States, which, according to article 4(2) of the Treaty on European Union, should be respected.').

129 See also Grandi (2011), note 21 above, 303.

130 Some scholars however point out that 'overcriminalisation is not a one-way-street' and that 'the application of the principle of effectiveness in European criminal law may lead us to a totally

on Article 83(2) TFEU could potentially upset national conceptions of criminal law and disturb the internal coherence of national criminal justice systems, which are expressions of national identities.

The European Commission expressly acknowledged this in its 2011 EU criminal law policy Communication:

> While EU criminal law measures can play an important role as a complement to the national criminal law systems, it is *clear that criminal law reflects the basic values, customs and choices of any given society*. The Lisbon Treaty accepts this diversity. For this reason, it is particularly important to ensure that EU legislation on criminal law, in order to have a real added value, is *consistent and coherent*.[131]

The key question is, however, how the EU legislator can reconcile the essence of criminal law as an expression of 'basic values, customs and choices of any given society' with the need for EU effectiveness? In any event, a debate and reflexion about the EU-wide societal importance of the underlying values seems crucial. The EU should only use criminal law for effectiveness purposes when the underlying values are considered essential enough to use the strongly expressive and powerful tool of criminal enforcement. For sure, Article 83(2) TFEU already contains an essentiality test,[132] but this test concerns the effectiveness of EU, not the essential character of the underlying value or legal interest. Otherwise EU criminal law based on *effet utile* concerns may result in an undesirable increase of criminal offences, which will be detrimental to the expressive function of criminal law. This constitutes the third (potential) problem of EU functional criminalisation.

In sum, the effectiveness-based approach to EU criminalisation creates three concerns: the expressive function of criminal sanctions is assumed without really questioning the importance of the underlying social values; the EU legislator should make more efforts to identify common core values which truly merit criminal law protection; and functional criminalisation might lead to an increase of criminal provisions.

Some key elements for future EU criminal law

In order to address the above concerns adequately, the Union's criminalising efforts need to be conditioned by other qualitative criteria and principles, in addition to the effectiveness criterion.

different direction, that of decriminalization': Mitsilegas, V. (2013), note 60 above, 418. This idea is based on the reasoning that national criminal legislation may not disproportionately limit the rights of free movement, a reasoning which the CJEU has followed on a number of occasions. Member states should refrain from using criminal law in such a way that it limits the effective enjoyment of the free movement rights.

131 European Commission, Communication of 2011, note 7 above, at 3, emphasis added.

132 See also Oberg (2014), note 99 above, 370.

In a first step, it seems highly desirable for the EU legislator to engage more explicitly in a debate about pan-European core values. This will help the EU legislator identify which values truly merit a criminal law approach.

To identify such pan-European core values, it may help to define a European identity with respect to criminal law and punishment. Some have observed in this respect that 'our ideas on punishment are imbedded in our commitment to social welfare, democracy and human rights.'[133] While this is undeniably true, this approach will probably only provide a minimum common denominator for criminalisation, not a more comprehensive set of qualitative criteria. Indeed, although all EU Member States subscribe to the Charter of Fundamental Rights of the EU and the European Convention on Human Rights, these instruments only provide for general minimum standards, which need to be supplemented with more detailed regulations, for instance to ensure adequate protection of procedural safeguards in criminal proceedings throughout the EU.[134] The same argument can be made with regard to substantive criminal law.

Others have argued in favour of an EU public order which accommodates both EU-wide values and national sensitivities: '[T]here is *no such thing as EU culture*, which could inspire the EU *ordre public*, *though there is undoubtedly a European cultural heritage* which the post-Lisbon EU Treaty explicitly recognizes.'[135] Although the concept of EU public order is by no means limited to the sphere of criminal law, it could offer an interesting approach to single out a common normative basis for the creation of criminal offences ensuring the implementation of EU law.

Of course, it is less obvious for the EU to call upon a common societal disapproval towards certain behaviour, due to its highly pluralist citizenship. The EU is *not* a State, or a homogeneous society. Nevertheless, one could successfully argue that the EU has many federal,[136] and increasingly also '"state"-like features, such as sanctioning powers'.[137] As the norms and values of the EU Member States gradually converge, there may also be a growing consensus about basic EU-wide norms and values. Consequently, it should not be that difficult any more to elaborate EU criminal legislation which is consistent with the Member States' core norms and values. This is also what the European Commission explicitly strives to be: consistent with the Member States criminal law systems, as well as internally and externally coherent.[138] However, putting this into practice appears to be a challenge.

133 Van Swaaningen (2013), note 100 above, at 357, with reference to Snacken and Dumortier (2011).

134 Spronken, T. (2011), 'EU Policy to Guarantee Procedural Rights in Criminal Proceedings: An Analysis of the First Steps and a Plea for a Holistic Approach', *EuCLR* 1, 213, at 217.

135 Corthaut, T. (2012), note 38 above, 443.

136 See e.g. Claes, M. and De Visser, M. (2012), 'The Court of Justice as a Federal Constitutional Court', in: Cloots, E. *et al,* (eds), *Federalism in the European Union*, Oxford/Portland: Hart Publishing, 84–5.

137 Herlin-Karnell, E. (2015), note 4 above, 72.

138 European Commission, Communication of 2011, note 7, at 3.

But the EU legislator should nevertheless try to identify such common essential norms. To impose criminalisation without a fair basis of common societal disapproval is not a good idea. Without public support and sufficient awareness at the national level, it is highly unlikely that law enforcement authorities will be willing to enforce criminal law provisions imposed by the EU level. When criminal rules remain black letter rules, they are also ineffective. Criminalisation of a certain conduct can of course have a norm-shaping effect, but this takes time, a lot of time.[139] Whether this long-term norm-shaping effect can justify the need for EU criminalisation is anything but obvious.

Second, the EU legislator should balance (legitimate) effectiveness concerns more carefully against the criminal law principles of proportionality and subsidiarity. These principles should be distinguished from the proportionality and subsidiarity as general principles of EU law, which apply to the exercise of powers by the EU in relation to its Member States.[140] As criminal law principles, proportionality and subsidiarity put limits on the interference of the (national and supranational) authorities with the fundamental rights of suspects. Proportionality requires that the use of criminal law and the severity of criminal sanctions is proportionate to the objective and subjective seriousness of the conduct. The subsidiarity principle implies that criminal law is chosen as a last resort, when absolutely necessary, i.e. when other enforcement tools prove to be insufficient.[141]

For sure, the European Commission already identified both principles as guiding principles in its 2011 EU criminal law policy Communication.[142] However, when analysing the EU legislator's practice, it seems further improvements are to be made to make sure that future legislative instruments live up to those guiding principles. For instance, as already mentioned, the Preamble to the 2014 MAD highlights the seriousness of the criminalised conduct, based upon the underlying protected values, as well as the need for proportionate sanctions. Yet while the integrity of the market and investors' protection are key values which the EU legislator wants to protect by imposing minimum rules for criminal offences and sanctions for some forms of market abuse, those same values are apparently less important when it comes to cartels, despite the similarities between both forms of 'economic criminality' (see above). Therefore, the EU legislator should make further efforts to evaluate the seriousness of the conduct in light of the importance of the underlying values and to do so in a coherent and consistent way across all EU policies.

139 See e.g. Shavell, S. (2001), note 125 above, 254–5.

140 See also Franssen, V. (2013), note 87 above, at 197–8. Cf. Herlin-Karnell, E. (2014), note 4 above, at 45–51, and in particular at 50, where the author explicitly raises the question of whether subsidiarity is different in the Area of Freedom, Security and Justice as compared to EU law in general.

141 For a nuanced view on the restrictive potential of the principle of *ultima ratio*, see Böse, M. (2011), 'The Principle of Proportionality and the Protection of Legal Interests', *EuCLR* 35, 1, 3942. See also Ouwerkerk, J. W. (2012), 'Criminalisation as a Last Resort: A National Principle under the Pressure of Europeanisation', *New Journal of European Criminal Law*, 3, 228, pointing out that national legislators too do not always observe the principle of *ultima ratio* and expressing the hope that EU law might rein in the national legislator.

142 European Commission, Communication of 2011, note 7 above, 6–8.

The European Commission also emphasised that 'criminal law must always remain a measure of a last resort.'[143] However, to make this policy claim come true, future legislative proposals would require more solid empirical evidence that non-criminal enforcement tools are really not sufficient.[144] In case of market abuse, the choice for criminal sanctions was made on the basis of a rather thin subsidiarity assessment. As mentioned above, the Commission's legislative initiatives with respect to market abuse were launched after an assessment of the existing enforcement problems in the Member States. That assessment showed, for instance, that national competent authorities did not have effective supervisory and sanctioning powers and that national administrative sanctions varied greatly.[145] Rather than jumping right away to criminal sanctions, it would have made more sense, in light of the subsidiarity principle, but also for the purpose of effectiveness (as discussed above), to first strengthen and approximate the administrative enforcement tools. Criminal sanctions could still be introduced in a later stage, had the MAR not resulted in the desired effects.

Conclusion

Despite its broad powers under Article 83(2) TFEU, the EU should strive to establish a supranational consensus with regard to the moral wrongfulness or strong social undesirability of a certain behaviour *before* obliging Member States to adopt criminal sanctions. The mere situation that the enforcement mechanisms in a policy area that has been subject to EU harmonisation measures appear to be ineffective should *not* be a sufficient reason for EU criminalisation. In addition to the need for effective enforcement of Union law, the EU legislator should assess more carefully the need for criminal sanctions in light of the criminal law principles of proportionality and subsidiarity (including the *ultima ratio* principle). Such assessment requires an in-depth and evidence-based analysis of the reasons why existing enforcement tools are not effective. It is illusory to think that criminalisation will help solve a lack of resources or expertise, which are often root causes of ineffective enforcement.

Moreover, the EU legislator should realise that an instrumental use of criminal law entails a number of risks. For one, it may lead to inflation in the use of criminal law, thereby undermining the very expressive and strongly deterrent function of criminal law. For another, the mere use of a criminal label does not necessarily trigger a strong social disapproval, even if it may sometimes have a norm-shaping effect in the long run. Without social disapproval and public support for criminal law enforcement, law enforcement authorities may also have less incentive to actually enforce criminal provisions. In sum, a merely instrumental use of criminal law may be counterproductive.

143 *Ibid.*, 7.
144 See also Oberg, J. (2014), note 99 above, 379–80.
145 Proposed MAR, 12–13, and 21.

8 Tasks for criminology in the field of EU criminal law and crime policy

Christopher Harding

Epistemic communities

While it is now possible to describe EU criminal law as a burgeoning field of activity, in terms of policy, legal development, commentary and legal scholarship, there is as yet little criminological voice in this domain of action. Leaving aside the question of role and identity – whether such activity is a matter of new criminal law in its own right or a significant co-ordination and direction of national criminal law and criminal justice – there is no doubt regarding the practical and theoretical significance of what is happening at the European and more specifically EU level in this respect. But, as is now well noted, this is an area of policy and legal development with complex and diverse origins and has developed in an incremental, almost stealthy and arguably haphazard fashion, and for that reason continues to take many by surprise.[1] Indeed, it has taken some time for many experts in criminal law and criminal procedure, often very much rooted in a national perspective of their subject, to come to terms with and take seriously this European dimension (and after all, crime policy and criminal law was in EU terms the reserved area of national sovereignty *par excellence*). In that perspective, then, what appears as a lack of engagement with or by criminologists should seem less surprising. For practising and academic lawyers and legal officials, there was at least the established fact and model of the EU legal order to act as an entry point and ladder within the field, and there may be a readier empathy with the vocabulary of approximation, mutual recognition and minimum rules. But for criminologists, the field of European integration may have seemed a strange and foreign land, and continues as such, while those involved in the business of integration will have related more quickly to expertise in the areas of governance, law and political science rather than those of sociology and criminology.

Therefore, what may be reported at this stage is a growing and increasingly rapid engagement on the part of legal practitioners, officials in the area of criminal

1 See: Baker, E. and Harding, C. (2009), 'From Past Imperfect to Future Perfect: A Longitudinal Study of the Third Pillar', *European Law Review*, 34, 25; Harding, C. (2015), 'EU Criminal Law under the Area of Freedom, Security and Justice', Chapter 32 in: Arnull, A. and Chalmers, D. (eds), *The Oxford Handbook of EU Law*, Oxford: Oxford University Press.

justice and criminal law enforcement, and legal scholarship with the policy and practice of the EU dimension of criminal law. A quick and rather cursory testing of this observation may be supplied by a brief analysis of the membership of two 'expert groups' dealing with EU criminal law and crime policy. The first is the European Commission's Expert Group on EU Criminal Policy, established in 2012.[2] The role of this group, as outlined in Article 2 of the Commission's decision setting up the group, is to advise on legal questions but also on the gathering of factual evidence for the assessment of the necessity of EU criminal law measures. The group comprises twenty members and its initial (and current) membership may be categorised as ten academics, three lawyers and seven criminal justice officials (mainly judges or prosecutors). The ten academics are as a matter of formal description professors of criminal law or criminal justice and based in law faculties.[3] The second group is an international (or more exactly, European) research collective known as the 'European Criminal Policy Initiative' (hereafter ECPI), self-constituted, and comprising fourteen university professors working in the field of criminal law. The ECPI published a *Manifesto on European Criminal Policy* in 2009, updated in 2011, containing principles and guidelines 'for a reasonable criminal policy' at the European level'.[4] Strikingly, five members of the ECPI are also members of the Commission's expert group. Thus, two significant expert bodies in this context have what may be described as a clear 'law school' provenance, and a degree of overlap which suggests the emergence of some degree of academic hegemony in this particular field. Despite the mission statement for its expert group in Article 2 of the Commission's decision, including what might be considered a typical task for criminologists, the motor of informed and critical work within both groups would seem to be legal rather social scientific scholarship. This is important not just regarding the content and direction of such expert and critical work, but also as a comment on the emergence and character of epistemic and expert communities.

On the other side of the disciplinary divide, another snapshot of the extent of interest and awareness may be gained from a glance at the programme of the annual conference in 2015 of a leading European academic organisation in the field of criminology, the European Society of Criminology (ESC).[5] The theme of the 2015 conference was: 'Criminology as Unitas Multiplex: Theoretical, Epistemological and Methodological Developments', responding, in the view of the conference organisers, to 'clear signs of increasing crosstalk between elements

2 Commission decision of 21 February 2012 on setting up an expert group on EU criminal policy, OJ 2012, C53/9. See also the Commission's Register of Expert Groups and Other Similar Entities, http://ec.europa.eu.

3 Admittedly some of these will have some familiarity with the method and practice of criminology, and the latter may be a subject within some of those faculties, but the bulk of the work of these academic members is doctrinal legal scholarship.

4 See: 'The Manifesto on European Criminal Policy in 2011' (2011), *European Criminal Law Review*, 86.

5 Held in Porto in September 2015. European Society of Criminology (ESC). See: at www.esc.eurocrim.org.

which had remained separated for a long time'. But a view of the programme plenary sessions does not suggest that such crosstalk relates to what is happening in the context of the EU or the European integration project – what are listed as main topics for debate are the proliferation of theories, the links between biological and social sciences, chronic physical violence, the humanity of biosocial criminology, drug policies and security issues. All of these are undoubtedly important matters and it may well be that the discussion of the last two issues may relate to European strategies. But a specifically European dimension is not signalled in any way in the main programme, and in fact the word 'European' appears only in the title of the body organising the event. That is not to say that there is no awareness at all among European-based criminologists of a European dimension – there is a kind of festival fringe, in particular now a small number of research groups with an interest in crime and crime control in a specifically European context. A notable recent example is the network of criminologists whose discussion led to the publication of a collection of papers in 2013 under the title *European Penology?*[6] Some of the contributions to that collection contemplate a distinctively European aspect to crime policy and criminal law sanctions, and in some cases even a distinctive EU role and activity (for instance, Estella Baker on the emergence of the EU as a penal actor, Roland Miklau on approximation of sanctions within the EU and Dario Melossi on processes of criminalisation of migrants and the EU as a land of immigration).[7] As another example, one of the research groups under the aegis of the European Society of Criminology is the European Sourcebook Research Group, involved in the collection of criminal statistics and other data across Europe.[8] The European Sourcebook project[9] was initially promoted by the Council of Europe, and the role of the latter organisation in this field will be discussed further later on in this chapter. But much of the data collection and analytical research resulting from Council of Europe initiatives has naturally enough focussed on a comparison of national policy, law and practice and not a specifically EU dimension – comparative criminology rather than EU criminology.

Such contemporary empirical snapshots raise an interesting question. If there are indeed distinct epistemic communities, as represented by the 'expert groups' on EU criminal law on the one hand, and the European Society of Criminology and the researchers meeting at Onati on the other hand, to what extent are they aware of each other's role and existence, and to what extent do they feel that they need to or could learn from each other's expertise? Or, to put such a question in more specific terms: should the European Commission take on board contemporary discussion of the relation between biological and social scientific explanations of criminality, and should the criminologists talking to each other in Porto strive

6 Daems, T., van Zyl Smit, D. and Snacken, S. (eds) (2013), *European Penology?*, Oxford: Hart Publishing. The network organised a workshop in July 2010 at the Onati International Institute for the Sociology of Law and the publication emerged from that discussion.

7 *European Penology?*, note 6 above, Chapters 4, 5 and 6.

8 See: the further discussion later on in this chapter on the problem of gaining such statistical information.

9 See: further discussion later.

to understand more the institutional and legal framework emerging in Brussels and at the EU level?

The need for criminology

The argument being made here is that, certainly at its present stage of development, EU crime policy and criminal law is in need of both information and research conclusions of a criminological nature. Indeed, this may be said to have been the case for some time, even pre-dating the explicit emergence of crime policy and law on the EU agenda. As one example, the now well-established set of criteria embodied in the concept of effective, proportionate and dissuasive sanctions to be used in support of the implementation and realisation of EU policies may be cited as something calling out for evidence, much of which could be categorised as criminological. This legal mantra of implementation (a component of the broader underlying principle of Member State 'loyalty' or 'sincere co-operation')[10] was articulated in its classic form (the so-called 'trias') by the European Court of Justice in 1989 in the *Greek Maize* Case:

> Whilst the choice of penalties remains within [the Member State's] discretion, they must ensure in particular that infringements of Community law are penalized under conditions, both procedural and substantive, which are analogous to those applicable to infringements of national law of a similar nature and importance and which in any event, make the penalty effective, proportionate and dissuasive.[11]

It is clear enough in a very general sense what may be understood by such criteria – it is a matter of achieving a desired outcome by appropriate means. But a determination of what may be actually effective, proportionate or dissuasive in any given case or situation is another matter. Are these purely legal concepts and to what extent is the fulfilment of such criteria a matter of legal testing? Of the three elements, proportionality might appear to have the highest legal content, but in its application would still require a search for evidence of some kind, and assessment of such evidence, which would be an exercise of social scientific rather than a legal nature, regarding the sufficiency, circumstances and impact of the action being reviewed. At the very least, the application of such criteria raises questions concerning the relation between legal and social scientific evaluation and the issue of socio-legal impact. In an earlier discussion, Harding had referred to the idea of effective enforcement of legal norms as a chimera,[12] indicating the elusive character of both the substance of the concept and the evidence of

10 As embodied in Article 4(3) of the Treaty on European Union (TEU).

11 Case 68/88, *Commission v. Greece* (1989) ECR 2965, at 2985.

12 Harding, C. (1997), 'Member State Enforcement of European Community Measures: The Chimera of "effective" Enforcement', *Maastricht Journal of European and Comparative Law*, 4, 5.

achieving such aims. In the conclusion to that study of national enforcement of European norms, it was argued that:

> Member State divergences therefore *need to be assessed* and different ways of responding to *undesirable* outcomes of divergence considered rather than insisting on a widespread programme of harmonization and assimilation which may . . . for a number of reasons be incapable of realization in any event. Such a pragmatic strategy, based on a fuller knowledge and understanding of enforcement activity, may be the most sensible way forward for the purpose of achieving 'effective' enforcement of Community measures.[13]

That statement proposed an agenda for searching out information and developing an informed understanding of the process of legal enforcement. Naturally, enforcement is undertaken with the aim that it should be effective, but what counts or can be proved as effective depends upon a largely social scientific evaluation of how enforcement works in practice. That is even more the case regarding the search for a dissuasive outcome – what turns the subjects of enforcement towards desistance and compliance, and in particular what kind of sanction may have such an outcome, is a classic task for penology and criminology, often summed up as the business of measuring deterrent effect. In other words, any serious attempt to answer questions about the outcome of legal enforcement or implementation should engage the research efforts of sociologists, criminologists, political analysts and other relevant social scientists.

More recently, the European Commission itself appears to have admitted as much in general terms. In its 2011 Communication on EU criminal policy,[14] the Commission sounded a cautionary note regarding a resort to criminalisation in support of EU objectives.[15] To quote in full the relevant part of the Communication:

> Criminal investigations and sanctions may have a significant impact on citizens' rights and include a stigmatising effect. Therefore criminal law must always remain a measure of last resort. This is reflected in the general principle of proportionality (as embodied in [Article 5(4) of] the Treaty on European Union and, specifically for criminal penalties, in [Article 49(3) of] the EU Charter of Fundamental Rights). For criminal law measures

13 *Ibid.*, at 24.

14 European Commission: 'Towards an EU Criminal Policy: Ensuring the Effective Implementation of EU Policies through Criminal Law', COM(2011) 573 final. For some critical discussion of this document, see: Klip A. (2012), 'Editorial: European Criminal Policy', *European Journal of Crime, Criminal Law and Criminal Justice*, 20, 3; Harding, C. and Banach-Gutierrez, J. B. (2012), 'The Emergent EU Criminal Policy: Identifying the Species', *European Law Review*, 37, 758.

15 Actually, something of a switch from the emphasis on effective and dissuasive measures towards an application of *ultima ratio*, already strong in the longer-term European legal tradition (see: the contributions by Lahti, Chapter 5, and Kaptein, Chapter 6, in this volume).

> supporting the enforcement of EU policies [as laid down in Article 83(2) TFEU], the Treaty explicitly requires a test of whether criminal law measures are 'essential' to achieve the goal of an effective policy implementation.
>
> Therefore, the legislator needs to analyse whether measures other than criminal law measures, e.g. sanction regimes of administrative or civil nature, could not efficiently ensure the policy implementation and whether criminal law could address the problems more effectively. This will require a thorough analysis in the Impact Assessments preceding any legislative proposal, including for instance and depending on the specificities of the policy area concerned, an assessment of whether Member States' sanction regimes achieve the desired result and difficulties faced by national authorities implementing EU law on the ground.[16]

This constitutes, in the Commission's view, 'step one' of a criminalisation decision, stipulating in effect a criminologically informed impact assessment. There would appear to be important implications here for criminalisation (and decriminalisation) policy across the European spectrum. Strictly speaking, the statement applies to the use of criminal law within the area of the EU's own directive competence (i.e. based on Article 83 of the TFEU). But it is nonetheless sending a signal regarding approaches to criminalisation and in particular urging the use of impact assessment in deciding on the use of criminal law and sanctions, and at the very least may be seen as a soft law indication of good practice. And in this context, such impact assessments will inevitably have to draw upon criminological knowledge, expertise and research findings.

A case study of commissioned research: the implementation of EU requirements at national level

It should be recalled that one of the European Commission's important institutional roles is itself to guarantee and monitor the implementation and enforcement of EU policies and rules (under Article 17(1) of the Treaty on the European Union), again as part of the obligation of sincere co-operation, and to that end may need to engage in fact-finding and commission studies so as to ensure the 'application of the Treaties'. One example of this is provided by the study funded by the Commission into the implementation of a number of criminal law Framework Decisions, relating to a number of serious criminal activities having a transnational character: child pornography; drug trafficking; money laundering; fraud with no cash means of payment; support for irregular entry, transit and residence ('illegal entry').[17]

16 Communication, note 14 above, section 2.2.1

17 European Commission, *Study on Criminal Sanction Legislation and Practice in Representative Member States, Final Report*, 2014, Doi: 102838/20190. The co-ordinators of the study were Kai Ambos, Lorena Bachmaier Winter, Theodora Christou, Luis Francisco, Jorge de Mesas and Nicola Selvaggi. Aspects of this study are reported on in the contribution by Edwards to this volume, Chapter 16 (Jennifer Edwards was a national expert in the study, for the UK).

The brief for this study was to report back on action taken to implement the EU measures by formal legislative action and by practice, and consider whether the level of approximation was sufficient in relation to serious crimes with a cross-border dimension, and then the extent of any need for common definitions and sanctions.[18] The underlying objective of the investigation was stated in the report of the study in these terms:

> The EU wants to ensure that when adopting new legislation there is real added value and that it increases consistency and coherence.[19]

As carried out,[20] the investigation at the first, legislative level was mainly a matter of legal research and, as Edwards reports in relation to the UK (or England and Wales), proved to be a challenging enough research task in itself.[21] But it was correctly envisaged that any attempt to monitor and 'ensure application of the Treaties' should address questions of 'practice'; and in particular, it may be said, investigate ground-level enforcement, or seek to explain or understand any revealed deficiencies or inconsistencies in legislative implementation. Implementation at a legislative level is but one stage in a longer process and, although not without some problems (mainly of a political or constitutional nature), is on the whole easier to monitor and more certain of achievement. Ground-level application and enforcement is more difficult to penetrate and more prone to hazard – such as differential resources, diverse legal and enforcement cultures,[22] the commitment, expertise and energy of officials, and the strategies, delaying tactics and obstruction on the part of the targets of legal action. The discovery and proof of what happens at ground level in the context of crime policy and criminal law enforcement is likely to be a more daunting process but would qualify as a classic task in criminological research.

The reported experience of the researchers in this project is instructive, showing in particular how far such an enquiry into the practice of implementation could be taken within the time limit and resources of a single project and as an indication of some problems and obstacles in data collection. The report from the study also reveals some interesting assumptions and expectations regarding the matter of practical implementation.

For instance, in relation to evidence of sentencing as an indication of practice,

18 The formal basis for such investigation lay in the 'Stockholm Programme' established by the Council of the EU in December 2009 (OJ 2010, C115), and then in the words of the *Final Report*, the fact that the new legal framework under the Lisbon Treaty required a more in-depth and up-to-date analysis with a stronger focus on practical implementation (*Final Report*, note 17 above, at 6).

19 *Ibid.*, at 5.

20 Eleven 'representative' (in terms of major legal system and tradition) Member States were chosen for the study: Cyprus, France, Germany, Hungary, Italy, Latvia, Poland, Romania, Spain, Sweden and the UK – a first limitation in the research.

21 See: Chapter 16 of this volume.

22 See: the contribution by Harding and Banach-Gutierrez to this volume, Chapter 4.

a first approach was made to gain statistical data, and encountered great difficulty. In the words of the report:

> Most of the Member States studied do not keep complete statistical data on the criminal justice system in general let alone with regard to the sanctioning of each of the type of offences. The difference in the level of accuracy and detail between the eleven Member States is enormous and the different statistics refer to diverse time periods. Whilst Germany and the UK have a very developed statistical system, other countries only provide general numbers and regarding to general categories of offences . . . or do not provide separate information on non-custodial sanctions or suspended sentences. This significant inconsistency between Member States has imposed an additional difficulty in making an appropriate assessment of the real practice of sanctioning and prosecution of the offences studied and on the effective implementation of the European legal instruments.[23]

The researchers attempted further data collection by first of all reviewing judicial decisions (which proved useful only in the case of Spain and Italy, but not elsewhere, owing to the lack of official sources); and second by interviewing practitioners. The latter method, however, provided only 'an approximate snapshot' of practice, based only on what those interviewed had seen in their own courtroom or on their general impression. This led to the rueful conclusion that, in all those countries without the relevant statistics, 'no conclusive data can be obtained in the timeframe of the project'.[24]

Yet elsewhere the report does attempt some confident and firm conclusion. Thus it is stated:

> The data collected reveals a clear difference between the penalties foreseen in the laws and the actual penalties imposed by the courts. The actual penalties imposed in practice are usually at the lower end of those foreseen in the law and often not anywhere near the maximum penalties. The data collected in this study shows that the maximum penalties are rarely pronounced.[25]

Presumably this conclusion is based on data from that minority of States with the available data, probably four of the eleven, including the UK. But it is also based on some assumption regarding sentencing practice in relation to statutory maximum penalties. When the latter are set at a high level, as in the case of the UK, sentencers may well aim for a norm well below the maximum, so that a general expectation that sentences will usually be located close to the maxima may run counter to established national practice, even in the case of more serious offences. This suggests two gaps in the research finding: first, relating to the representative

23 *Final Report*, note 17 above, at 307.
24 *Ibid.*, at 303.
25 *Ibid.*, at 307.

nature of the data (in relation to all eleven States in the study, let alone all EU Member States); and second in relation to a consideration of national sentencing practice and culture in relation to the use of maximum penalties in legislation. But the research finding as stated above in the report leads to a recommendation there for minimum penalties to be laid down in EU directives for 'those relevant aggravating factors directly connected with the legitimate purpose of the Directive'.[26] This recommendation was quickly taken up by the Commission, on the ground that the investigation had shown that some Member States provide for very different sanctions for these serious crimes 'with the effect that some crimes are punished more leniently in some Member States than others'.[27] It may be questioned to what extent that conclusion is substantiated and whether this qualifies as decision-making based on carefully informed and tested criminological argument.

There are further examples in the report's findings of some slippage from hypothesis to conclusion, without very much substantiating data or evidence, while at the same time acknowledging the need for further research and data collection. Thus the report states, under the heading of 'settlement of minor cases', that:

> It is believed that harmonization at the level of sanctions and substantive law may be hindered by the different praxis in closing cases or discontinuing prosecutions. It is recommended that a common definition of a 'minor case' be established or alternatively that the threshold for applying diversionary measures allowing for the non-prosecution of a certain offence be set out. Consideration should be given to whether the subsidiarity principle would allow the establishment of EU guidelines on the grounds for exercising prosecutorial discretion with regard to the offences studied.[28]

It should be noted that these recommendations are not based on any further research evidence relating to the actual effect of any differences in prosecutorial praxis. But then the following paragraph in the report does appear to call for further research into some aspects of this question to consider how far differences in discontinuing prosecution and the procedural handling of cases may lead to spill-over effects, forum-shopping, inequality before the law and possible impunity of offenders. In turn, the Commission then drew from the report the existence of an incentive and possibility for offenders to engage in Member State forum-shopping in an active search for 'safe havens', as a justification for a legislative move towards minimum rules on offence definition and sanctions.[29]

Thus the report of this study, after all the effort of research, leads to an amalgam of hypothesising conclusion on the one hand, and on the other, a

26 *Ibid.*, at 306.
27 Commission, Press Release of 3 March 2014, EXME 14/03.06.
28 *Final Report*, note 17 above, at 308–9.
29 Press Release, note 27 above.

cautionary note regarding the need for more research. Regarding the latter, there is one especially telling paragraph which convinces and should command attention:

> If the Union deems it desirable to evaluate the impact of its legislation in practice, it is recommended that the EU requires the collection of precise and complete statistics on criminal offences. At the very least these should be in reference to the offences which have been regulated at EU level. It is acknowledged that this recommendation entails financial costs and training but it is considered essential for the effective assessment of EU criminal policy, its justification and its effectiveness, as well as for the advancement of a higher level of harmonization.[30]

In its tone, this is a forceful recommendation and accords with the Commission's own commitment to legislative impact statements, and adherence to the principles of proportionality and subsidiarity as stated in its Communication on Crime Policy in 2011. It will be interesting to see whether it bears fruit in the form of any proposed EU legislation, ahead of any legislation on minimum rules. Were it to do so, it would at the least improve the employment prospects for statisticians and criminological researchers.

Criminological research under the aegis of the Council of Europe

As part of this discussion it should be noted that for some considerable time now the Council of Europe (CE), as part of its mandate for dealing with social and legal problems, has promoted research and discussion of crime and criminal justice in a broadly European context and in that way supported and funded a large number of criminological projects. In 1958 the CE established the European Committee on Crime Problems (CDCP), whose role has included the elaboration of conventions, recommendations and reports and the organisation of criminological research conferences and other meetings.[31] In turn, in 1961 the CDCP established a Criminological Scientific Council (PC-CSC), a standing body of seven 'criminal science experts' to advise the CDCP in the preparation and implementation of the Council of Europe's programme in the field of crime problems. The Scientific Council sought close relations with the European Society of Criminology when that body was set up in 2001. However, due to budgetary limitations the Council has been inactive since 2005.[32] But overall during a period of fifty or more years, this Council of Europe activity has fostered academic and research links, meetings, reportage, research and critical analysis

30 *Final Report*, note 17 above, at 308.

31 See: the website of the CDCP: www.coe.int/CDCP.

32 For some overview discussion, see: Barberet, R. and Joutsen, M. (2010), 'Crime and Justice', Chapter 7, in: Immerthal, S. and Therborn, G. (eds), *Handbook of European Societies*, New York: Springer.

of crime problems, crime control and the operation of criminal justice and penal measures, within and between its Member States across Europe, and informed a large body of policy and legal development. But while this may be seen as an impressive intergovernmental outcome, it remains possible to speculate to what extent the emergent criminology has been European or a collection of national criminologies. As Barberet and Joutsen have commented, as a field of enquiry European criminology has a heterogeneous nature and is more like a sum of national criminologies.[33] Typically, many of the research reports in this area of activity are drafted by national rapporteurs, which then foster comparative analysis and findings, in some respects resonating with the intergovernmental nature of the CE as the sponsoring organisation. At the very least, however, there is now a large fund of 'comparative criminal justice' research and findings on a spectrum of issues and across most of the continent.

As remarked elsewhere, the European domain of crime control, criminal justice and penal systems is characterised by a wide diversity, which may be seen as a strength but also a challenge in a context of integrating governance. This is true of both legal and research culture, and so also in turn it is a feature of information relating to crime and crime control – the existence, location, retrieval and management of that information. As Harrendorf has observed: 'collecting comparable data on registered crime and on criminal justice across countries is a complex, almost impossible task.'[34] It has already been shown that a recent large-scale research project commissioned by the EU quickly encountered difficulty regarding the collection of essential data within a significant number of the Member States, and this was one of its major matters of report back to the EU Commission. But there has been naturally enough awareness of this issue for some time in the context of the Council of Europe. This problem lay behind the setting up of the European Sourcebook project, initially promoted by the CE in the mid-1990s. The Sourcebook (ESB)[35] is a reference tool, comprising statistics and other quantitative data, and then associated reports and analyses. This data collection initiative was established in 1993 under the umbrella of the CE and has since 1996 produced five editions of statistical data, although the work of its experts and national correspondents was later funded by a number of CE Member States and also the EU Commission. The ESB's website was hosted first by the Dutch Ministry of Justice and then by the University of Lausanne, and its

33 *Ibid.*, at 14.

34 Harrendorf, S. (2011), 'How to Measure Punitiveness in Global Perspective: What Can Be Learnt from International Survey Data?', in: Kury, H. and She, E. (eds), *Punitivity: International Developments, Vol 1: Punitiveness: A Global Phenomenon?*, Bochum: Universitätsverlag Brockmeyer, at 125.

35 *European Sourcebook of Crime and Criminal Justice Statistics*, website at: http://wp.unil.ch/europeansourcebook. See also 8 (2000) and 10 (2004) *European Journal on Criminal Policy and Research*, special issues on the results of sourcebook data. For a convenient account of the development and progress of this project, see the preface to the most recent, fifth, edition of data collection, as published by HEUNI (the European Institute for Crime Prevention and Control) in Helsinki, September 2014.

activity has been brought together as the European Sourcebook Research Group, and the last, as noted above, is linked to the European Society of Criminology. The whole project comprises therefore a network of individual and organisational activity.[36]

This brief overview of the CE criminal science aegis prompts two main observations. First, its focus has largely been the traditional and longstanding questions of criminology, as perceived in a national perspective, and then any broader research agenda has been predominantly comparative in nature. Second, comparative research has naturally enough identified and started to address the problem of comparability of national data. But since the CE is an organisation of co-operation rather than integration, it has not steered research activity towards the needs of ever more integrating policy and governance, that is, of the EU. But there is an important heritage and body of criminological research within the aegis of the CE that the EU, in its development of crime policy and criminal law, could and should draw upon and link with. Especially as the EU Commission and other bodies become more concerned with the problem of data deficit and comparability, the experience and work done already under the umbrella of the CE is very pertinent.

Working out an EU research agenda

A strategy of impact assessment in the development of crime policy and criminal law, whether at the national or European level, presupposes the availability and usability of information regarding crime and criminal law enforcement. Taking the example of a few key questions of the present moment – the need for common minimum sanctions in relation to certain categories of offending, the need to criminalise a business activity such as cartel collusion, the imposition of criminal responsibility on corporate persons, or the use of criminal sanctions in relation to different aspects of person trafficking – all of these matters should be taken forward in the form of new policy or rules, not only with an appreciation of their cross-European dimension, but also as a fully informed exercise. Understanding the European dimension and being fully informed both require full and rigorous interdisciplinary research, in particular on the justification for the use of criminal sanctions in normative and social scientific terms.

The EU institutions appear to have a strong awareness of this argument. On the one hand, there are the calls for impact assessment or evidence-based policy as put forward for instance in the Commission's Communication on Criminal Policy in 2011 (above). On the other hand, the data deficit and problems of comparability have led to calls for a criminological 'esperanto', or conceptual and

36 For an account of the ESB's methodology, see: the General Introduction to the Fifth Edition Report (HEUNI), note 35 above, and also the discussion by Harrendorf, S. (2012), 'Offence Definitions in the European Sourcebook on Crime and Criminal Justice Statistics and Their Influence on Data Quality and Comparability', *European Journal of Criminal Policy Research*, 18, 83.

terminological harmonisation, which might enable a meaningful and informed comparison and analysis of national data and sources. Thus, in the 'Millenium Strategy' in 2000 the Member States called for the elaboration of criminal statistics and for the Commission to launch studies in this area,[37] then in the Hague Programme of 2005 the European Council welcomed the Commission's initiative to establish instruments on the collection and analysis of crime data,[38] in 2006 the Commission's Action Plan on Crime Statistics emphasised the importance of establishing an EU-level offence classification system,[39] and at the same time the Commission established an Expert Group on the Policy Needs for Data on Crime and Criminal Justice.[40] The major policy and research hurdles at the EU level are summarised by the Commission in the following terms:

> Statistics on crime and criminal justice are indispensable tools for developing evidence-based policy at EU level. Impact assessments, evaluations of the implementation of EU legislation from the Member States and assessment of the effectiveness of new laws are only some examples of the use of statistical information. While the need for factual statistics has long been recognised by the Member States and the European Commission, there is still a lack of reliable and comparable statistical information.[41]

But it is not just a matter of quantitative data and establishing an esperanto for its effective use. There is also a need to appreciate and understand cultural differences and preferences in relation to criminality, criminal justice and criminal law enforcement – regarding, for instance, the response of offenders to the application of sanctions, judicial preferences in sentencing policy, or official and professional choices in relation to the practice of prosecution.[42] Such qualitative issues also raise challenges for researchers, especially at a supranational level.

This reflection suggests that there is a long distance to travel in future research in this area, but important reasons to follow that route. And in doing so there are likely to be significant challenges. First, there are methodological and conceptual issues to confront – for instance, working out a satisfactory European

37 OJ 2000, C 124/1.
38 OJ 2005, C 53/11.
39 Communication from the Commission to the Parliament and Council, *Measuring Crime in the EU: Statistics Action Plan 2011–14*, 18 January 2012, COM(2011) 713 final. See: de Bondt, W. and Vermeulen, G. (2009), 'Esperanto for EU Crime Statistics: Towards Common European Offence Definitions in the EU-Level Offence Classification System', at 87 in: Cools, M. *et al.* (eds), *Readings in Criminal Justice, Criminal Law and Policing*, Apeldoorn: Maklu and Governance of Security Research Group.
40 Commission decision 2006/581/EC.
41 Communication on Measuring Crime in the EU, note 39 above, at 2. See further: the enumeration of reasons for limited progress, *ibid.*, at 4–5.
42 See for instance: the recent study by Harding and Edwards, seeking an understanding of the impact of sanctions used to deal with illegal business cartels, by reference to such 'cultural' factors: Harding, C. and Edwards, J. (2016), *Cartel Criminality: The Mythology and Pathology of Business Collusion*, Aldershot: Ashgate.

level offence classification system or research and policy Esperanto.[43] Second, there is the need to situate policy within the European normative framework of subsidiarity, proportionality and legitimacy. Third, there is the mundane question of time and resources – much of this kind of research is long term and will need funding from somewhere.[44] And finally, there is a need, at the supranational level, for organisational grip and efficiency, or to put the matter more bluntly, to ensure that all such activity is coherent and joined in a meaningful way. This last point is a call not just for sensible cohabitation as between the CE and the EU, but also for mutual awareness and information as between the emergent experts – for instance as between the EU Expert Groups on EU Criminal Policy (EO2760), on the Policy Needs for Crime Data (EO2837), and on Trafficking in Human Beings (EO2722), and the project on criminal sanction legislation and practice (above).[45] In conclusion, there is no shortage of tasks for criminology in this context, but also considerable scope for discussion still as to how those tasks may best be carried out.

43 See: Harrendorf, note 36 above; and de Bondt and Vermeulen, note 39 above.

44 Consider, for example, the successive sponsoring and funding arrangements for the European Sourcebook project and its publications, referred to above.

45 On the face of it, there is no obvious mutual cross-referencing or collaboration between these groups, but arguably they ought to be informed by each other's work. It is interesting to speculate on the expectations of the Commission in this regard.

Part II

Stocktaking progress, achievements and prospects

9 Reflections on the prospects for regional criminal courts: Europe and Africa compared

Harmen van der Wilt

National criminal law enforcement and international criminal justice increasingly face competition of an intermediate institutional device: regional criminal courts. While the establishment of a European Criminal Court currently has no priority, Article 86 of the Treaty on the Functioning of European Union (TFEU) explicitly mentions a European Prosecutor, who would have the competence to investigate, prosecute and charge criminal offences involving the infringement of the financial interests of the European Union. On 12 March 2014, the European Parliament approved the proposal to organise such a European Public Prosecutor's Office. Section 4 of Article 86 envisages the extension of the mandate of the EPPO with serious crimes, having cross-border dimensions. The proposals still provide for decentralised law enforcement before national courts, but the establishment of a European Prosecutor can be a stepping stone for the birth of a European Criminal Court.

Meanwhile, the African Union has shown more boldness in proposing to equip the African Court of Justice and Human Rights with a Criminal Chamber wielding jurisdiction over individuals responsible for international crimes. This suggestion has obviously emerged from growing resentment of the International Criminal Court's (ICC) focus on African suspects and situations and the indictment of African leaders. The plans are generally considered as a trick to outwit the ICC.[1] But whatever the motives for this initiative may be, they deserve serious discussion.

In this reflective discussion, we can consider the justification for such instances of regional criminal justice. Do we need it? Is it useful? How can it be sustained, both legally and politically? As frame of reference, this chapter will borrow from Anthony Duff's recent digressions on criminal law and community.[2] According to Duff, an important purpose of criminal law is to create an institutional framework

1 Compare du Plessis, M. (2012), 'Implications of the AU Decision to Give the African Court Jurisdiction over International Crimes', Institute for Security Studies, Paper 235, June 2012 and Bhoke Murungu, C. (2011), 'Towards a Criminal Chamber in the African Court of Justice and Human Rights', *Journal of International Criminal Justice*, 9, 1067–88.

2 Compare Duff, R. A. (2011), 'Responsibility, Citizenship and Criminal Law', in: Duff, R. A. and Green, S., *Philosophical Foundations of Criminal Law*, Oxford: Oxford University Press; and Duff, R. A. (2010), 'Authority and Responsibility in International Criminal Law', in: Besson, S.

'through which perpetrators of public wrongs can be called to account for those wrongs'.[3] Responsibility is a key concept in this process and Duff employs the idea in a double – reciprocal – sense: the social environment – community – responds to the public wrong by urging the perpetrator to 'answer for his crime', by holding him to account for his actions. But that obviously begs the question of who has the authority to hold someone to account. Criminal law, so Duff argues, presupposes a normative, political community to which both caller and called belong. It requires a shared language and normativity, because only in that case can the offender understand the charge. The main point that Duff intends to make is that the concept of political community serves to demarcate the spatial realms of states against undue mutual influence and in this respect dovetails with the paradigm of a society of sovereign states. We do not interfere with a murder committed by a foreigner abroad, not because we do not find the act morally and legally objectionable or repulsive, but because it is none of our business. We have no authority over it and this provides one basic rationale for the territoriality principle.[4] It also explains that domestic criminal law of nation states is still the salient paradigm of criminal law.

If the international community, by proxy of the ICC or other international criminal tribunals, intervenes, it obviously overrules the state's prerogatives. By what right, by what authority does it require the perpetrator to 'answer for his crimes'? Is the international community a political community in a similar sense as that described above? Duff denies that it is, because the global community lacks close (cultural) ties or deep structures of richly shared interests. The ICC is a default option that only intervenes if the state forfeits its prime obligation to render life and security to its citizens, either by oppressing them or by neglecting them (the 'failed state' scenario). This is neatly expressed in the complementarity principle that allows the ICC to interfere only if a state has proved to be 'unwilling or unable' to genuinely pursue criminal investigations and prosecutions. The international community can therefore be best portrayed as a moral community that comes to the rescue of trampled and humiliated persons, by virtue of a shared humanity.[5]

Duff has been criticised for presenting a too facile and schematic picture of normative communities.[6] Certainly his theory would benefit from more sophisticated refinements, but it has the charm of simplicity and can be considered as a workable hypothesis for the purposes of this discussion. The issue here is whether regional criminal courts and solutions operate at the service of a political

and Tasioulas, J. (eds), *The Philosophy of International Law*, Oxford: Oxford University Press, 589–604.

3 Duff (2011), 'Responsibility, Citizenship and Criminal Law', note 2 above, 126.

4 Duff (2011), note 2 above, 134.

5 Duff (2010), 'Authority and Responsibility', note 2 above, 600.

6 Chetman, A. (2010), 'Citizenship v Territoriality: Explaining the Scope of Criminal Law', *New Criminal Law Review*, 13(2), 427–48; Long, R. (2014), 'Responsibility, Authority and the Community of Moral Agents in Domestic and International Criminal Law', *International Criminal Law Review*, 14, 836–54.

community, or rather as an extension of a moral community. We can shed some light on this question, so it can be argued, by exploring the institutional structures in which these courts are expected to develop, by examining the comments of stakeholders/protagonists of such regional courts and – most importantly – by investigating the nature of the crimes that qualify for being processed by those courts. This discussion will integrate these aspects, putting emphasis on the last issue.

As is well known – and has been briefly observed before – the European Union does not put its cards on increased centralisation – let alone the establishment of a European Court – in the realm of criminal law. It has rather opted for the principle of mutual recognition of judicial decisions, adopted during the Summit in 1999 in Tampere, that presupposes (a certain degree of) normative and legal pluralism. Member States are expected to co-operate magnanimously, *n'en déplaise* their different values and opinions of what constitutes a criminal offence. That obviously does not create a climate for centralised regional law enforcement. However, many scholars have observed that mutual recognition requires some minimum harmonisation, as too divergent criminal laws would make states reluctant to render mutual assistance, blindly accepting each other's idiosyncrasies. Article 82 of the Treaty on the European Union acknowledges this relationship by stipulating that judicial co-operation is predicated on the principle of mutual recognition of judicial decisions, which encompasses the approximation of the legal and administrative provisions of the Member States. More in particular, Article 83 identifies a number of specific categories of very serious crime with a cross-border dimension that would be amenable to harmonisation in respect of constituent elements and sanctions, by means of directives:

- Terrorism
- Trafficking in human beings and sexual exploitation of women and children
- Unlawful drug trafficking
- Illicit trafficking in arms, ammunition and explosives
- Illegal money-laundering activities
- Corruption
- Forgery of money and means of payment
- Computer crime
- Organised crime.

It is interesting to note that nearly all these crimes feature on the list of crimes that define the competence of both Europol and Eurojust.[7] It is a policy of 'small steps'. First, we abolish the requirement of double criminality for extradition/surrender and other forms of international co-operation in criminal matters. That comports with the spirit of the principle of mutual recognition. Next,

7 A notable exception is terrorism, but that special category is the subject matter of a special Council Decision 2005/671/JHA on the exchange of information and co-operation concerning terrorist offences, Brussels 20 September 2005, OJ 2005, L 253/22.

we create institutions – Europol and Eurojust – that are expected to assist and streamline multinational criminal law enforcement, in respect of those crimes for which double criminality has been abolished. Third, we decide to harmonise a number of very serious crimes, obviating the need for abolition of double criminality. Fourth, we consider the establishment of a European Prosecutor's Office. And finally, we ponder – in our wildest dreams – on creating a European Criminal Court. At each step the number of crimes dwindles, epitomising the mental obstacles and resistance against further unification and centralization of European criminal law: the European Prosecutor's Office has only competence over one crime (fraud against the financial interests of the European Union) and the European Criminal Court is still a phantom.

What do we make of the crime categories that should be subject to harmonization and would qualify for being brought under the jurisdiction of a European Criminal Court in formation? Some of them really strike at the communal interests of the European Union – fraud against EU financial interests, counterfeiting of the euro, arguably corruption, in view of the increasing practice of European tendering. Recalling Duff's ideas on political community and criminal law, it makes sense that perpetrators should answer for their crimes before a forum that represents the European Union as such. Other crime categories – trafficking in human beings, drugs, arms, money laundering, computer crime – are often, if not by definition, transnational crimes. These are volatile, elusive offences which are notoriously difficult to repress, in view of the scattered evidence, perpetrators, victims and witnesses over several jurisdictions. States have a *shared,* rather than a *common*, interest to join hands and reinforce co-operation. If that can be accomplished by smoothing requirements for mutual assistance, they will probably not be prepared to walk the more laborious way of engaging in common institutions risking a further erosion of their sovereignty. In respect of these crimes, the European Union probably does not represent a political community.[8] Terrorism arguably constitutes a status apart, as it most closely resembles the 'core crimes' under the jurisdiction of the International Criminal Court. Whether the European Union might be considered as a regional moral community that would justify the creation of a European Court which would call the perpetrators of terrorist offences to account in the name of the European citizens is still a matter for further discussion.

Compared to Europe, the African Union has acted in a straightforward manner, skipping all the intermediate steps in the protracted development towards a

8 Duff's account of the State as a political community that is predicated on collective interest again serves as an insightful analogy: 'However, if we are to understand the criminal law not simply as a set of prohibitions, but as a practice through which wrongdoers are called to public account, we must be able to ground it in some kind of community – a "we" who call them to account. This "we" requires not merely an aggregate of individual interests in such matters as security, but a collective interest that is "our" interest. A collective interest, however, requires more than a collection of people who happen to find themselves in the same geographical territory; it requires people who can see themselves as being engaged in a common enterprise of living not just alongside each other, but together.' Duff (2011), note 2 above, 137.

regional criminal court. Obviously, the African Union lacks the sophisticated institutional framework of the European Union that grounded the intensified co-operation in criminal matters. The starting point of the African Union is radically different. Rather than the possible culmination in a line of frustrated attempts to improve criminal law enforcement, based on inter-state co-operation, it has been presented as a device to eclipse the International Criminal Court. This difference in background shows up in the subject matter jurisdiction. The International Criminal Law Section of the African court shall have the power to try persons for the following crimes:

- Genocide
- Crimes against humanity
- War crimes
- The crime of unconstitutional change of government
- Piracy
- Terrorism
- Mercenarism
- Corruption
- Money laundering
- Trafficking in persons
- Trafficking in drugs
- Trafficking in hazardous wastes
- Illicit exploitation of natural resources
- The crime of aggression
- Inchoate crimes.[9]

While Article 83 of the EU Treaty and Article 28 of the AfCHPR Protocol have a number of crimes in common – terrorism, corruption, money laundering, trafficking in persons and trafficking in drugs – the differences are more conspicuous. For one thing it is remarkable – but not surprising – that the African Union has incorporated the core crimes (including aggression). After all, this move demonstrates the clear intention to challenge the ICC.[10] Most of the other categories are exemplary of the manmade disasters that have vexed Africa for ages: piracy, mercenarism, trafficking in hazardous wastes, illicit exploitation of natural resources. By far the strangest customer is the crime of unconstitutional change of government, not only because it surely will give rise to and will aggravate political tensions, but also because it has not and nowhere been recognised as an international crime. The inclusion of this crime has prompted the African Union to postpone the enactment of the Protocol.

9 Amended Protocol on the Statute of the African Court of Justice and Human Rights, Article 28B-N (International Jurisdiction of the Court).

10 Murungu (2011), note 1 above, 1079, explicitly acknowledges that dissatisfaction with the ICC has triggered the decision to create the ICL Section: 'it is the AU decision not to cooperate with the ICC that has led to the call for establishment of a Criminal Chamber within the African Court to prosecute African individuals who commit international crimes in Africa.'

The duplication of the jurisdiction in respect of 'core crimes' is problematic, because it raises questions as to the proper division of labour between the ICL section of the African Court and the ICC. Any priority of the regional court cannot, under the current Rome Statute, be defended on the basis of the complementarity principle, as Article 17 only refers to 'states' and not to other courts.[11] The African Union has so far chosen to ignore the issue, by simply omitting any reference to the ICC.[12]

Some final reflections

Where do we currently stand with regional criminal courts? It is difficult to consider regional criminal courts as the representatives of – in Duffian language – either a political or a moral community. The very fact that, for the time being, the EU Member States are only prepared to outsource the prosecution of fraud against the EU financial interests to the EPPO demonstrates their limited perception of collective interests of a political community that deserve centralised protection. A sudden disaster, like the terrorist attack of 9/11, may set the issue afloat, but meanwhile the Member States give preference to intensified inter-state co-operation.[13]

At first blush, the prospects for an African criminal court as representative of a moral or political community are even bleaker. An institution cannot simply 'out of the blue' declare itself the spokesman of an entire continent. The Rome Statute is a consensual instrument that has been ratified by many African states. Those states should first abjure their former commitments or at least indicate how they envisage the ICC and the African Criminal Court to be inter-related. As demonstrated above, none has occurred. Some scholars attribute the real added value of the African Court in its dealing with precisely those crimes that the ICC does not cover.[14] That may be true, but it requires a common understanding that these crimes affect the collective interests of the African people and that, in turn, requires a minimum agreement on the content of those crimes. Max du Plessis has quite rightly observed that 'The predicate for according an international

11 Compare Du Plessis (2012), note 1 above, 11 and Murungu (2011), note 1 above, 1075. Murungu is slightly more optimistic in the assessment of solutions to this problem, where he opines that 'Nevertheless, a progressive interpretation of positive complementarity might, for the purpose of closing impunity gaps, infer that even regional criminal courts could have jurisdiction over international crimes within the ICC jurisdiction' (1081).

12 Du Plessis (2012), note 1 above, rightly uses strong language by contending that 'it is unfathomable that the draft protocol nowhere mentions the ICC, let alone attempts to set a path for African states that must navigate the relationship between these two institutions' (at 10).

13 On the triggering capacity of calamities, see: Klip, A. (2010), *European Criminal Law: An Integrative Approach*, Intersentia: Cambridge-Antwerp-Portland, 481(e).

14 Compare Abass, A. (2013), 'The Proposed International Criminal Jurisdiction for the African Court: Some Problematical Aspects', *Netherlands International.Law Review*, 60, 49: 'The fact that the Rome Statute does not cover such crimes as corruption, unconstitutional changes of governments, mercenarism and so on, which affect the majority of African states, is perhaps the strongest case in favour of the prosecution of international crimes by the African Court.'

court criminal jurisdiction in respect of crimes is that the substantive elements of the crimes are generally agreed upon – at the very least, that there is consensus amongst African states regarding these crimes and their elements.'[15] The harmonisation of criminal law, including international crimes, in Africa is far less advanced compared to Europe.

These sobering remarks do not disqualify regional criminal justice. In principle, regional criminal courts are commendable. Their physical and psychological proximity, their potential to generate expertise and their reputation for unbiased and impartial adjudication all contribute to their legitimacy.[16] It is interesting to see that African proponents of the Court invoke these qualities, when they stress the necessity of ownership and participation. African problems should be left to Africans to deal with, which implies that African criminals are to be judged by their fellow Africans in Africa.[17] It would be unfair to jettison such statements as merely cheap rhetoric. They remind us of Duff's contentions that perpetrators are to answer for their crimes to a forum that has the authority to call them to account and may be evidence of an incipient political community. To be sure, the advocates of a regional African Court use the arguments of political and cultural unity to sustain their claim that regional courts are morally justified to prosecute the most serious international crimes. In that sense, we may witness a blending of a moral and political community.

Of course, it remains to be seen whether a regional criminal court will live up to the expectations. Perhaps a modest approach would be preferable, in favour of small steps rather than the creation of a fully fledged (permanent) court that would devour huge resources and might be difficult to get rid of, when once established. The Extraordinary African Chambers in the Senegalese Courts that have recently been launched in order to try former Chad dictator Hissin Habré, after protracted quarrels between Senegal and Belgium, provides an example in kind.[18] Its performance and its reception by the African population may be an adequate indicator of the viability of an African criminal court.

15 Du Plessis (2012), note 1 above, 7.

16 For a positive assessment of the potentials of regional criminal justice, see: Burke-White, W. W. (2003), 'Regionalization of International Criminal Law Enforcement: A Preliminary Exploration', *Texas International Law Journal*, 38, 729–61.

17 Compare in particular Murungu (2011), note 1 above, 1079.

18 On the background and establishment of these Chambers, see Williams, S. (2013), 'The Extraordinary African Chambers in the Senegalese Courts: An African Solution to an African Problem?', *Journal of International Criminal Justice*, 11, 1139–60.

10 The practice of plea bargaining in the Nordic context

Patrick S. Günsberg[1]

Reservations about plea bargaining

The discussion here addresses the issue of plea bargaining in the Nordic context. Special regard will be paid to the system of plea bargaining that was recently adopted in Finland.[2] By way of introduction it may be noted that 'plea bargaining' as used here refers to the compromise reached between the prosecutor and the defendant, who admits guilt in order to gain a reduction in sentence (simple plea bargaining).[3]

Harding noted regarding plea bargaining that 'the compromise of retributive values has resulted in a greater European wariness of such an approach, based on concerns about coercion of vulnerable defendants, the compromise of defence rights and the presumption of innocence, and historical association with the use of torture.'[4] In the US, harsh penalties and the unpredictability of jury trials tend to incentivise guilty pleas. What is more, by providing evidence against those on the upper rungs, a white-collar defendant might get a greatly reduced sentence – this practice has been referred to as the crown witness system and has been sharply rejected in Finland.[5] A Finnish Government Bill dating to the early 2000s

1 This paper draws on the author's doctoral dissertation entitled 'Criminalizing Business Cartels in Europe – A Comparative Perspective', which he defended on 4 May, 2015 at the University of Helsinki.

2 A consultation exercise by the Finnish Ministry of Justice regarding the introduction of plea bargaining in Finland revealed that roughly one fifth of the respondents were in favour of some form of limited plea bargaining, another fifth of the respondents were neither in favour nor against, and the rest of the respondents rejected the idea. The number of responses amounted to twenty-nine. See: Oikeusministeriö, Arviomuistio syytteestä sopimisesta (plea bargain). Lausuntotiivistelmä, 2010, 11. See the Finnish Government Bill 58/2013, 'Hallituksen esitys eduskunnalle syyteneuvottelua koskevaksi lainsäädännöksi ja syyttämättä jättämistä koskevien säännösten uudistamiseksi', 4.

3 Other forms of plea bargaining include charge bargaining where for instance as a trade-off one charge (of many) is discarded where the defendant enters a guilty plea. Fact bargaining refers on the other hand to the discriminatory introduction of facts in exchange for admitting guilt; see Lawrence, J. *et al.* (2008), 'Hardcore Bargains: What Could Plea Bargaining Offer in UK Criminal Cartel Cases?',*Competition Law Journal*, 19–20.

4 Harding, C. (forthcoming 2016), 'The Role of Whistleblowing and Leniency in Detecting and Preventing Economic and Financial Crime: A Game of Give and Take?' at 8.

5 Koponen, P. (2012), 'Talousrikokset ja syytteestä sopiminen', in: Hyttinen *et al.* (eds), *Rikoksesta*

argued in a rather spirited fashion that the reliability of information obtained as a result of reduced sentences is questionable. It was argued that this conundrum would not be as obvious if the defendant produced evidence as to his own behaviour. A reduced sentence following the defendant's confession concerning his own offences may indicate that feelings of guilt warrant forgiveness. A crown witness system on the other hand would reinforce an environment that encourages whistle-blowing, thus implying the idea that if one can inform on other people's even worse offences, one is pardoned. The Government Bill put forward that only compelling circumstances would warrant such a moral compromise and that the ethics that criminal law reflects were at stake.[6] Such an unyielding position may not be entirely justified, however.[7]

More recently a Finnish working group had in a quite unprecedented move proposed adopting a system of plea bargaining.[8] Subsequently a Finnish Government Bill suggested the introduction of rules concerning plea bargaining.[9] The previous debate concerning plea bargaining had laid much weight on the legal principles in a way that perhaps was not helpful for a discussion regarding criminal policy.[10] The negative attitudes concerning plea bargaining in Finland according to Oikarainen were prompted especially by the principles of mandatory prosecution and *ex proprio motu*, the latter meaning that the court should on its own initiative protect the rights of the parties, a duty which is independent of the preferences of the persons involved.[11]

The prosecutor could in an effort to secure a suspended prison sentence overlook the more blameworthy qualities of a given conduct that would call for an unsuspended prison sentence.[12] One can also imagine that the defence side

rangaistukseen, juhlajulkaisu Pekka Viljanen 1952 – 26/8 – 2012, University of Turku, Faculty of Law, 67.

6 See the Finnish Government Bill 44/2002m at182; some commentators refer to a 'dog-eat-dog' environment, for instance, Baker, D. I. (2001), 'The Use of Criminal Law Remedies to Deter and Punish Cartels and Bid-Rigging', *George Washington Law Review*, 69, 708.

7 Koponen (2012), note 5 above, at 68.

8 Oikarainen 'Syyteneuvottelu ja tunnustamisoikeudenkäynti oikeuspoliittisena kysymyksenä – uhka vai mahdollisuus?' *Lakimies* 5/2012, 742; Finnish Ministry of Justice, 'Syyteneuvottelu ja syyttämättä jättäminen', 26/2012.

9 It may be noted that there is no accurate Finnish expression for the concept of plea bargaining; see the Government Bill 58/2013, note 2 above, 4. An amendment to the Criminal Investigations Act would, in Chapter 3, section 10a, provide *inter alia* that the prosecutor could decide upon the recommendation of the leading investigating police officer that the preliminary investigation would not concern all the offences committed when it is suspected that the perpetrator has committed several offences, if the perpetrator has entered a guilty plea and thus contributed to the investigation and no public or private interest requires that the preliminary investigation should be conducted. The prosecutor could subsequently demand a sanction according to a more lenient penalty scale. Importantly the foregoing would only apply to offences that carry a maximum custodial sentence of six years, except for offences that target life and health, children or sexual offences: Government Bill 58/2013, note 2 above, 1. See also Oikarainen, 2012, note 8 above, 748.

10 Oikarainen (2012), note 8 above, 746.

11 *Ibid.*, 744.

12 See Koponen (2012), note 5 above, 63.

would seek to exploit the system by strategically choosing the most convenient moment to enter a plea bargaining agreement. Yet it would seem that one should recognise that strategic planning on both sides infiltrates the whole judicial system even in the absence of plea bargaining.[13]

Plea bargaining could be characterised as a legal transplant that has been adopted in various forms around the world. Finland is one of the more recent countries to join the movement. In Linna's view, the shape that plea bargaining has taken in Finland is reasonably well adjusted to the Finnish system of criminal procedure. The successful implementation of plea bargaining would depend on the balance that is struck between the defendant's legal protection on the one hand, and the effectiveness of the proceedings on the other.[14]

Forms of plea bargaining have been introduced *inter alia* in Norway, Denmark and Germany, while Sweden and Iceland have rejected it. In Europe, it seems that due to the financial crisis, effectiveness, as an objective, is important in the context of court proceedings. These considerations are reflected in the Finnish legislator's rhetoric too. On a critical note, Ervo argued that 'the novelty has not been put into philosophical context or into the systemic context of criminal proceedings.' However, this shift in policy would seem to be evidence of 'more coherent trends' as well.[15]

One could argue that while the State pursues efficiencies, as a by-product the procedure might become 'privatised'.[16] Far-reaching procedural changes have taken place since the 1990s particularly when it comes to civil matters. Yet criminal proceedings have not entirely escaped such tendencies. Nowadays the judge's role seems to have evolved towards one of an assistant to the parties, the judge himself taking a backseat with respect to the exercise of judicial powers. According to Ervo, there has been 'a big change from the adjudication, ideals of material law and a substantively correct judgment towards the ideal of negotiated law and pragmatically acceptable compromise.'[17] The long-established objective was to establish the material truth, yet the outcome of a given case is the product of procedural truth that specifically is derived from the evidence available at

13 Lawrence *et al.* (2008), note 3 above, 27.

14 Tuula, L. (2015), 'Syytteen muuttaminen ja tarkistaminen, syyteneuvottelu ja oikeusvoima', *Defensor Legis No 3/2015,* 435; see also the discussion in Máximo, L. (2004), 'From Legal Transplants to Legal Translations: The Globalization of Plea Bargaining and the Americanization Thesis in Criminal Procedure', *Harvard International Law Journal*, 45, 1–64.

15 Ervo, L. (2014), 'Plea Bargaining as an Example of the Recent Changes in the Finnish Criminal Procedural Paradigm', *Baltic Journal of Law & Politics*, 7, 97–8, 104, 105; for a Swedish committee deliberation, see 'Ett effektivare brottmålsförfarande – några ytterligare åtgärder', SOU 2005:117, 61; for another Swedish contemplation, see 'Brottmålsprocessen', SOU 2013:17, 241–2.

16 Ervo (2014), note 15 above, 99.

17 Moreover, in contrast to what used to be the case, now rather than chasing merely 'normative procedural justice', it seems that all the stakeholders should perceive the proceedings to be just. This change would reflect a change in how the parties are viewed – they now have a more important part to play as 'clients': Ervo, 2014, note 15 above, 100–1.

trial.[18] Thus there has been a shift that lays more emphasis on procedural truth rather than on the material kind.[19]

Due process concerns

Plea bargaining as a concept has been subject to criticism, since it could undermine the defendant's legal protection.[20] Linna and Oikarainen have argued that the one crucial question is whether the defendant can give up his right to a fair trial and under what conditions.[21] It could severely hurt the legitimacy of the criminal justice system if an innocent person enters a guilty plea.[22]

Linna, who has viewed plea bargaining as almost inherently problematic from a due process perspective, has underlined that importantly the defendant should enter plea bargaining negotiations with full knowledge and willingness. In her view, the plea bargaining agreement itself should have its basis in factual evidence that the prosecutor has.[23]

As Oikarainen pointed out, the Finnish Working Group proposal on plea bargaining (and along the same lines the Government Bill that followed it) sought to alleviate the due process concerns associated with plea bargaining by ensuring that the prosecutor does not merely rely on the guilty plea of the defendant, but has evidence beyond that as well. Oikarainen argued that if the prosecutor does not have sufficient evidence to prosecute the case, the defendant should not be induced to enter a guilty plea.[24]

18 Ervo (2014), note 15 above, 102.

19 *Ibid.*, 104.

20 Oikarainen (2012), note 8 above, 754.

21 Linna, T. (2010), 'Puntarissa plea bargaining – vastassa oikeusturva ja itsekriminointisuoja', *Oikeustiede – Jurisprudentia* XLIII, 260; Oikarainen, 2012, note 8 above, 755.

22 Koponen (2012), note 5 above, 62.

23 Linna (2010), note 21 above, 227; Oikarainen (2012), note 8 above, 754. It may be feared that procedural safeguards of the defendants suffer as a result of the plea bargaining agreement, as it might require that the defendant agrees to refrain from claiming his rights. In order to alleviate such worries, the court could have a look at the plea bargaining agreement and at least ascertain that the defendant with full knowledge agreed to the terms of the agreement; see Lawrence *et al.* (2008), note 3 above, 26.

24 Oikarainen (2012), note 8 above, 755–6; Government Bill 58/2013, note 2 above, 45. The Working Group had also proposed that as a starting point the defendant should always have legal assistance available. Furthermore, the prosecutor would have to observe evidence that is favourable to the defendant: Finnish Ministry of Justice, 'Syyteneuvottelu ja syyttämättä jättäminen', 26/2012, 52. The prosecutor must explain the contents of the sentence proposal and other related matters, as per Chapter 5b, section 3. As per section 4, the court would have to observe the tenets of the proposal regarding the sentence if it agrees with the sentence proposal, provided that the defendant has entered the guilty plea and there is no reasonable doubt left regarding the accuracy of the guilty plea and that the defendant voluntarily entered it: Oikarainen (2012), note 8 above, 757. Linna noted that the proposal by the Working Group did not suggest that the agreement between the prosecutor and the defendant would accurately prescribe the sentence that the court will impose – thus while the court would have to adopt a more lenient scale of penalties with a view to its sentence consideration (the imposed sentence may not exceed three quarters of the ordinary sentence), it would not be bound by the plea bargain agreement. The Government Bill indicated

If the defendant enters a guilty plea at an early stage of the investigations, the gains are the greatest in terms of resource savings. The delayed proceedings are to a notable extent caused by interruptions at the stage of preliminary investigations.[25] Yet it is also then that the defendant tends to be poorly informed, and making a decision with full appreciation of the situation is difficult. Similarly, the prosecutor might not be sufficiently knowledgeable to make a considered decision in the early phases of the investigation.[26] One could argue that the more quickly the defendant is to enter a guilty plea, the greater his reward should be – for instance in Norway the most substantial reward is offered when the defendant produces evidence that was not available to the police. While it matters what the defendant would assume that the police could prove, it is irrelevant how things stand in reality in this respect.[27] This situation could then induce the defendant to enter a guilty plea. The foregoing is in contrast to the position that would not have the defendant decide whether to enter a guilty plea before the prosecutor can actually prove that the defendant committed the offence. Further on this view the defendant should be able to assess the evidence that the prosecutor has obtained. Such standards may appear to be beyond reach, as Koponen points out.[28]

Making the sentence discount depend on the extent that the guilty plea facilitates the inquiry into the matter may derive justification from the idea the defendant displays remorse. As opposed to that, a situation where the prosecutor has already obtained convincing evidence would make the defendant in a way compelled to accept the facts – in that case the guilty plea would not appear to reflect genuine regret in a similar fashion.[29]

The court needs to indicate the sentence that would have been handed down in the absence of a guilty plea. In Linna's view, this prevents the possibility that the sentence imposed would not differ from the sentence that would be given in the absence of a plea bargaining agreement.[30] Importantly the Government Bill sets out that if plea bargaining fails or if the court would not decide the case in accordance with the sentence proposal, the statements made in the course of the proceedings by the defendant may not be employed as evidence.[31] In spite of the foregoing, the fact that the defendant had entered

that the defendant must be informed that the court is not bound by the sentence proposal made by the prosecutor. Yet the sentence proposal should indicate the kind of sentence that the prosecutor proposes and the severity of the sentence, something that may be indicative of future practice, as Linna argued. The court is, however, bound by the type of offence prescribed in the plea bargaining agreement: Linna (2012), note 24 above, 129; see also the Government Bill 58/2013, note 2 above, 25, 32.

25 Koponen, note 5 above, 64.

26 *Ibid.*, 64–5.

27 *Ibid.*, 65.

28 *Ibid.*, 65, 71; Linna (2010), note 21 above, 254.

29 Koponen (2012), note 5 above, 65.

30 Linna (2012), note 24 above, 129.

31 Government Bill 58/2013 vp, note 2 above, 15.

plea bargaining negotiations, which were never concluded, could be perceived to reflect culpability.[32]

At the end of the day, despite efforts to observe the right against self-incrimination, one may always ask whether the offer by the prosecutor is such that it leaves little choice but to enter a guilty plea. There could be the risk that an innocent person would have to choose between a guilty plea and a fully fledged trial and would be persuaded to enter a guilty plea. This could be avoided by determining the culpability of the defendant in advance in a similar fashion as is done at trial. In Linna's view, the infringement of Article 6 of the European Convention on Human Rights (hereinafter ECHR) (the right to a fair trial) in terms of inappropriate pressure may be escaped only if prior to the conclusion of the plea bargain negotiations, the prosecutor was already in the possession of evidence sufficient for a conviction.[33] The gap between the outcomes of a trial and a guilty plea should not be of such magnitude that in reality one could not speak of a voluntary decision.[34] It may be noted that the amendment (as per the Government Bill) to the Finnish Criminal Code in Chapter 6, section 8a provides that the court must announce what the sentence would have been in the absence of a guilty plea.[35]

The European Court of Human Rights (hereinafter ECtHR) has also addressed the due process questions in relation to plea bargaining: the ECtHR has taken the stance that plea bargaining agreements are not in violation of the ECHR and indisputably benefit the defendant, the injured party and the 'administration of justice'.[36] In one ruling, the ECtHR noted that while plea bargaining is more frequently used in the US, European legal systems provide for reductions in sentences in exchange for a 'guilty plea', which may necessitate the existence of an understanding between the defendant and the prosecutor as to the content of the guilty plea. The Court said that it may not be viewed as 'oppressive conduct' and thus in violation of Article 6 ECHR that the judge or the prosecutor lets the defendant know beforehand what the sentence would be if the defendant entered a guilty plea or alternatively if the defendant did not enter one. Article 6 ECHR could be violated, in the Court's view, if the sentence following the guilty plea deviated so much from the sentence that would follow if the defendant did not enter one that it could be regarded as exerting inappropriate pressure on the defendant – thus inducing him to enter a guilty plea, while the defendant is innocent. In such circumstances the right against self-incrimination could be impaired or Article 3 ECHR could be violated (the ban on torture and inhuman

32 Linna (2012), note 24 above, 130; see also Lawrence *et al.* (2008), note 3 above, 25. See also Stephan, A. (2008), 'The UK Cartel Offence: Lame Duck or Black Mamba?', University of East Anglia Centre for Competition Policy Working Paper, 8–19, 23ff.

33 Linna (2010), 253–4; Linna questions whether any resources would be saved after all as a result of introducing a system of plea bargaining. See also Linna (2010), note 21 above, 253–4.

34 Linna (2010), note 21 above, 253–4, 260, 261.

35 See Oikarainen (2012), note 8 above, 757.

36 Government Bill 58/2013, note 2 above, 10; see ECtHR, decision as to the admissibility of Application No. 39672/03, *Nikolay Milanov Nikolov v. Bulgaria*, 28 September 2010, at para 11.

or degrading treatment or punishment) if the defendant perceived the guilty plea as the only way to avoid the penalty.[37] The ECtHR noted that it is up to the defendants to enter plea bargaining agreements and judges in the US to seek to ensure that defendants enter such agreements voluntarily.[38]

White-collar crime and plea bargaining

The European Court of Human Rights has on several occasions found Finland guilty of delayed proceedings – especially when it comes to the time-consuming proceedings related to white-collar offences.[39] Indeed the desired resource savings have induced rapid changes in terms of shaping policies.[40] With regard to equal treatment it is regrettable if delayed proceedings have the effect that by chance some defendants escape an unsuspended prison sentence.[41] It stems from the idea of equality that white-collar criminals also should be subject to criminal sanctions, not only the perpetrators who commit traditional criminal offences.[42] In order to cope with challenging criminal law proceedings, introducing plea bargaining could be considered.[43] It may be mentioned that the time-consuming proceedings prompted the Council of Europe to suggest already in 1987 that its Member States should widen the scope of prosecutorial discretion whenever possible. It referred to the requirements of Article 6 ECHR. The Council of Europe specifically underlined that countries with a tradition of mandatory prosecutions should take note of the recommendation.[44] A trend that highlights fair trial values seems to have brought about an emphasis on procedural truth in criminal trials.[45]

Plea bargaining seems to have its primary catalyst in ever more complex and time-consuming criminal proceedings. Furthermore, the more complex and costly the criminal proceedings are in a given country, the more commonly, it appears, plea bargaining is being employed.[46] Prior to the twentieth century the great majority of the criminal cases within common law jurisdictions faced jury trials instead of guilty pleas. Before the mid-nineteenth century plea bargains

37 Government Bill 58/2013, note 2 above, 10; ECtHR, partial decision as to the admissibility of application Nos 24027/07, 11949/08 and 36742/08, *Babar Ahmad and others v. UK*, 6 July 2010, at para 168.

38 The Court found in this particular case that it was not inappropriate for the prosecutors to discuss in advance the potential sentences with the defendant; see ECHR, *Babar Ahmad*, note 37 above, at para 169.

39 Government Bill 58/2013, note 2 above, 9; see also Constitutional Law Committee Report 7/2014 (prompted by the Government Bill 58/2013), 2.

40 See Koponen (2012), note 5 above, 60.

41 *Ibid.*, 63–4.

42 *Ibid.*, 62.

43 *Ibid.*, 62.

44 Council of Europe, 1987, Recommendation No R (87) 18, of the Committee of Ministers, concerning the simplification of criminal justice, at 3.

45 Koponen (2012), note 5 above, 63.

46 Combs, N.A. (2002), 'Copping a Plea to Genocide: The Plea Bargaining of International Crimes', *University of Pennsylvania Law Review*, 151, 8.

were infrequent. Guilty pleas were regarded as insufficient. It was only the first decades of the twentieth century that saw the wider adoption of plea bargaining agreements in the US. A drastic increase in their employment had taken place during the decades following the American Civil War.[47] In 1908 roughly 50 per cent of the cases were disposed of through plea bargain agreements, and already by 1925 90 per cent, a figure that has remained static to this day.[48]

The Finnish Government Bill recognised the US origins of plea bargaining, and that typically a court ultimately reviews the plea bargaining agreements and hands out the sentences. Also, other common law countries, and notably more recently several civil law countries such as France, Germany and Estonia, have adopted systems of plea bargaining. Plea bargaining practices in Denmark and Norway have their own peculiarities.[49] Previously a guilty plea by the perpetrator had not provided much grounds for sentence reduction in Finland.[50] Hammond has pointed out, referring to the US context, that despite plea bargaining being occasionally portrayed in a less flattering light, in terms of cartel cases it is rarely criticised. Plea bargaining benefits the government, the parties to the case, the judiciary, the injured parties and the public at large, as the defendants co-operate promptly.[51]

Rautio, an official at the Finnish Ministry of Justice, has listed some advantages of plea bargaining in a memorandum, noting *inter alia* that such practice makes obtaining evidence easier.[52] Lawrence *et al.* argued that allowing bargaining in criminal cartel cases is useful in light of the limited resources available. [53] Similarly the Finnish Government Bill pointed out that resources would be saved in terms of the preliminary investigation, the workload of the prosecutor and court proceedings.[54] Especially, the investigation of serious white-collar offences is resource intensive.[55] It was argued that due to the complexity of the white-collar offences, adopting a system of plea bargaining would be advantageous.[56]

Consequently, arguably more resources would be left to detect offences that otherwise could go unnoticed, which in turn would profit deterrence, presumably even more so than the severity of the sanctions.[57] A reduction in sentence

47 Combs (2002), note 46 above, 12.

48 *Ibid.*, 13, footnote 32.

49 Government Bill 58/2013, note 2 above, 4.

50 *Ibid.*, at 5.

51 Hammond, S. D. (2006), 'The U.S. Model of Negotiated Plea Agreements: A Good Deal With Benefits For All', OECD Competition Committee Working Party No. 3, October 17, 2006, 2; see also Furse, M. (2012), *The Criminal Law of Competition in the UK and in the US*, Cheltenham: Edward Elgar, 152.

52 Rautio, J. (2010), 'Resursseja säästävä menettely, jossa rikoksen varhainen tunnustaminen voisi läpinäkyvässä menettelyssä johtaa rikoksesta muutoin seuraavaa rangaistusta lievempään rangaistukseen', OM 20/41/2009, 15 January 2010, 13–14.

53 Lawrence *et al.* (2008), note 3 above, 18.

54 Government Bill 58/2013, note 2 above, 11.

55 *Ibid.*, 12.

56 *Ibid.*, 14.

57 While the proposal would reflect the concepts of sentence bargaining and count bargaining, it does not cover charge bargaining or fact bargaining; see Government Bill 58/2013, note 2 above, 13.

and expedited proceedings would incentivise defendants to enter a guilty plea. Also the improved predictability would benefit defendants, the Government Bill envisaged.[58]

Oikarainen has noted that it may be doubtful whether white-collars offenders are sufficiently motivated to enter guilty pleas in Finland. For instance, in terms of tax fraud offences, mostly suspended prison sentences have been handed down. Arguably, then, the appeal of entering plea bargaining negotiations for white-collar offenders lies essentially in the less-time consuming proceedings. It is possible, as Oikarainen says, that only the availability and enforcement of harsher penalties, especially unsuspended custodial sanctions, could make plea bargaining more attractive for white-collar offenders.[59] It may be noted, however, that rather than the duration of the prison sentence, it appears that it is the actual imposition of one that counts to many.[60]

Furthermore, one can argue that sentence discounts for guilty pleas might undermine the deterrent effect. Conversely, an increase in the amount of prosecutions could offset such a problem. It is not obvious, however, that deterrence is generally weakened. As Lawrence *et al.* note, the European Commission Decision in relation to the *Gas Insulated Switchgear* cartel recognised that 'Japanese and European providers of GIS coordinated the allocation of GIS projects worldwide, with the exception of notably the USA and Canada', and the US is notoriously the land where plea bargaining is entrenched.[61]

Vuorenpää has pointed out that the general preventive effect draws on the certainty that sanctions will be imposed and the legitimacy of the criminal justice system.[62] Oikarainen argued that while plea bargaining may reinforce the former, the legitimacy of the system could suffer if in the public's view white-collar offenders receive special treatment.[63] Yet as Lawrence *et al.* point out, while concerns may be expressed that perpetrators do not get their 'just deserts', it is also true that the condemned conduct may not have even been uncovered in the absence of plea bargaining.[64]

58 Government Bill 58/2013, note 2 above, 11.

59 Oikarainen (2012), note 8 above, 761.

60 Lawrence *et al.* (2008), note 3 above, 26.

61 See Summary of Commission Decision, 24 January 2007, Case COMP/38.899, *Gas Insulated Switchgear*, OJ, 2007, C 5/7. For more anecdotal evidence, made known by a Department of Justice official, that seems to indicate that cartels have specifically avoided operations in the US, see: Hammond, S. (2004), 'Cornerstones of an Effective Leniency Program', *ICN Workshop on Leniency Programs*, Sydney Australia, 8; Lawrence *et al.* (2008), note 3 above, 25–6; see also Baker (2001), note 6 above, 709.

62 See Mikko, V. (2007), *Syyttäjän tehtävät, erityisesti silmällä pitäen rikoslain yleisestävää vaikutusta*, Vammala, 26; Oikarainen (2012), note 8 above, 761–2, footnote 54.

63 Oikarainen further notes that for certain offences such as the drink-driving offences, the creation of the deterrent effect is not categorically dependent on the kind of penalty that is available – imposing a driving ban may be much more effective than a fine or even a suspended prison sentence: see Oikarainen (2012), note 8 above, 762.

64 Lawrence *et al.* (2008), note 3 above, 26.

Anti-cartel enforcement

The battle against hard-core cartels, a form of unlawful white-collar activity, may benefit both from a crown witness system and from plea bargaining. It seems then that it could be helpful to consider the discussion concerning negotiated justice with respect to cartel behavior, as it may provide a good case in point.

A former official at the Swedish competition authority, Norgren, recognised the value of 'a crown witness system whereby the suspected company representative may get amnesty if sufficient information and co-operation is provided, not only about own involvement in the alleged cartel but also about the other cartel members'. According to him, such an arrangement in Sweden would be unacceptable 'on legal and moral grounds'.[65] Amnesty and leniency mean that immunity against criminal prosecution is granted to the first cartel member that reports the cartel.[66] While conceptually detached, both a crown witness system and plea bargaining may be discussed in the same context, as both are targets of similar criticism. Such practices contradict for instance the principle of mandatory prosecution, as they would provide for immunity against prosecution or a sentence reduction.[67] As per the Nordic tradition, with regard to penal sanctions, expressing disapproval has been more important than a confession by the perpetrator.[68]

The Swedish Government explicitly refused to consider the introduction of a crown witness system in the context of a proposed criminalisation of cartel conduct.[69] Andersson and Legnerfält have pointed out, however, that while a prison sentence is a more serious sanction than a director disqualification order, it may be questioned from a principled point of view why immunity is available against director disqualification orders in Sweden, but could not be introduced in terms of prison sentences.[70] In contrast, in Denmark the revised leniency rules

65 Norgren Claes, Director General, Swedish Competition Authority, 'Criminal Enforcement of Antitrust Laws', Fordham Law Seminar, New York, 14 September 2006.

66 'Amnesty' refers to the Leniency Program Operated by the Department of Justice, and the terms 'amnesty' and 'leniency' will be used interchangeably hereinafter; see Lawrence *et al.* (2008), note 3 above, 17, footnote 2.

67 See Swedish report 'En ny konkurrenslag', SOU 2006: 99, 530–3; Petri, K. (2012), *Uusi Kilpailuoikeus*, SanomaPro, 73–4; Oikarainen (2012), note 8 above, 744. Incidentally, according to Wagner-Von Papp, the German arguments against granting immunity are '(1) that they infringe the rule of law, because they prevent imposing the sanction that justice requires; (2) that they infringe the principle of equality; (3) that they infringe the principle of mandatory prosecution; (4) that they destabilize the public trust in a just legal order; (5) that deals with criminals are immoral; and (6) that such provisions foster unreliable evidence.' See: Wagner-Von Papp, F. (2011), 'What If All Bid Riggers Went to Prison and Nobody Noticed? Criminal Antitrust Law Enforcement in Germany', in: Beaton Wells, C. and Ezrachi, A. (eds), *Criminalising Cartels*, Oxford: Hart Publishing, 176.

68 See Petri, K. (2006), *Uusi kilpailuoikeus*, Helsinki: WSOYpro, 66; *Regeringens proposition* 2007/08:135, 151. See also Government Bill 58/2013, note 2 above, 4.

69 The idea of criminalising cartels in Sweden was not followed through; see *Regeringens proposition* 2007/08:135, 151.

70 Andersson, H. and Legnerfält, E. (2008), 'Effektivare kartellbekämpning genom ny konkurrenslag?', *Europarättslig Tidskift*, 3, 617.

grant immunity against criminal prosecution to the first leniency applicant.[71] In Denmark, most members of a task force took the position that immunity against custodial sanctions should be automatically granted to the whistle-blower.[72] Norway favoured a model that would make the criminal prosecution of an individual dependent on the Competition Authority's request or alternatively would be prompted by a strong public interest.[73]

While the primary aim of leniency programs appears to be the detection of cartels and the production of evidence, the chief purpose of plea bargaining would seem to be the facilitation of prosecution.[74] Cartels are intrinsically unstable, and plea bargaining could offer a way to further upset the stability of cartels. Plea bargaining increases the chances that a penalty will be imposed – even if full immunity cannot be obtained and the cartel has been detected, potentially a fellow cartel member could co-operate with the authorities.[75]

Arguments have been put forward in the UK context to this effect. Plea bargain agreements could be offered to cartel members who do not qualify for full immunity.[76] Currently such a system is absent in England and Wales.[77] The now-defunct Office of Fair Trading was the first prosecutorial body in the UK to have the competence to grant immunity against criminal prosecution to the whistle-blower. It seems that it was acknowledged that this measure was needed in the fight against cartels.[78] Following that line of thought, it might be argued that plea bargaining would also have its merits, especially from a deterrence perspective.[79]

71 The runners-up would be subject to the rules of the Penal Code regarding settlements; see Forslag til Lov om ændring af konkurrenceloven og straffeloven, 26 October 2012, 11. The immunity against criminal prosecution takes the following form in the Danish Competition Act, section 23 a. – (1): 'Anyone who acts in breach of Section 6 of this Act or Article 101(1) TFEU by entering into a cartel agreement shall upon application be granted withdrawal of the charge that would otherwise have led to a fine or imprisonment being imposed for participating in the cartel, in case the applicant, as the first one, approaches the authorities about the cartel, submitting information that was not in the possession of the authorities at the time of the application.' Further, subparagraph 11 of the same provision spells out that: '[a]n application from an undertaking or an association shall automatically cover current and former board members, senior managers and other employees provided that each person satisfies the requirements . . .' See Danish Competition Act, Consolidation Act No. 23 of 17 January 2013.

72 'Rapport fra udvalget om Konkurrencelovgivningen', March 2012, available at: www.evm.dk/~/media/oem/pdf/2012/pressemeddelelser-2012/10-04-12-konkurrencelovsudvalget/rapport-fra-konkurrencelovsudvalget-marts-2012.ashx.

73 Prop. 75 L (2012-2013), Proposisjon til Stortinget (forslag til lovvedtak) Endringer i konkurranseloven, at para 4.4.

74 Lawrence *et al.* (2008), note 3 above, 22.

75 Lawrence *et al.* (2008), note 3 above, 23–4. See also Furse, M. (2012), *The Criminal Law of Competition in the UK and in the US*, Cheltenham: Edward Elgar, 151–2.

76 Furse (2012), note 75 above, 151; Wardhaugh, B. (2012), 'The Cartel Offence Within a "World Class" Competition Regime: An Assessment of the BIS Consultation Exercise and Its Results', *European Competition Journal*, 588.

77 Lawrence J. *et al.* (2008), 'Hardcore Bargains: What Could Plea Bargaining Offer in UK Criminal Cartel Cases?' *Competition Law Journal*, 17.

78 Lawrence *et al.* (2008), note 3 above, 18.

79 Lawrence *et al.* (2008), note 3 above, 23–4; Furse, 2012, note 75 above, 151–2.

Furse pointed out that US-style plea bargaining is not available in Ireland either and quoted a report which said that while the defendant may enter 'charge bargaining', it 'will not result in certainty about a particular sentence, except insofar as the charges pleaded to define the outer limits of range of sentence that may be imposed'.[80] While in Ireland the courts have it in their discretion to take note of the co-operation provided by runners-up in the leniency race, the extent of sentence discount is not predictable.[81]

In the US most defendants who do not qualify for amnesty enter plea bargaining agreements.[82] Stephan argued that the US enforcement is greatly facilitated by the plea bargaining agreements. While informal settlements are available in the UK, they cannot be compared with direct settlements in the US[83] – subsequently every case in the UK will be disposed of by means of a trial.[84] A British report had noted too that the US enforcement record was indebted to the system of plea bargaining that the UK lacked.[85] The practice of plea bargaining and sentencing guidelines in the US give a good idea to defendants and prosecutors alike how things will turn out if a guilty plea was entered. Indeed where the Department of Justice (hereinafter DOJ) has been forced to proceed to a trial, it has been successful in less than half of the cases. The dependence on the evidence provided by the whistle-blower, whose testimony may not be perceived to be the most reliable, may plague the trial cases.[86] Proving a case 'beyond reasonable doubt' is challenging, and the risk of failure is remarkable if the case progresses to trial.[87]

The defendants in the US are normally offered either of two types of plea bargain agreement. In the one case, the agreement may be altered by the court, while the defendant cannot pull out from the agreement irrespective of the changes made by the court. In the other, the agreement is binding on the court.[88] Hammond has noted that 90 per cent of the defendants accused of

80 Galbreath, C. (2010), 'Criminal Enforcement of Competition Laws in Ireland, A Look At Enforcement To Date', 2010, available at: www.tca.ie/images/uploaded/documents/2010-01%20Criminal%20Enforcement%20of%20Competition%20Laws%20in%20Ireland.PDF, at 8; Furse (2012), note 75 above, 172.

81 Furse (2012), note 75 above, 175; Galbreath (2010), note 80 above, 7.

82 Lawrence *et al.* (2008), note 3 above, 17.

83 Stephan takes the position, however, that a sustained success for the UK criminal cartel regime may at the end of the day depend on the competition authority's impact on the general public's awareness regarding the harmful nature of cartels, as such awareness would induce compliance and corroborate prosecutorial efforts; see Stephan, A. (2008), 'The UK Cartel Offence: Lame Duck or Black Mamba?', University of East Anglia Centre for Competition Policy Working Paper 8–19, 33.

84 Stephan (2008), note 83 above, 4.

85 Office of Fair Trading (OFT), *Proposed Criminalization of Cartels in the UK*, report prepared for the Office of Fair Trading by Sir Anthony Hammond KCB QC and Roy Penrose OBE QPM, OFT 365, November 2001, 30.

86 Beaton-Wells, C. (2011), 'Cartel Criminalisation and the Australian Competition and Consumer Commission: Opportunities and Challenges', in: Beaton Wells and Ezrachi (eds), note 67 above, 183.

87 Lawrence *et al.* (2008), note 3 above, 24.

88 *Ibid.*, 28.

antitrust violations during the past two decades have agreed to plea bargaining arrangements.[89]

Stephan suggested that the appeal of plea bargaining agreements is reflected in the foreigners who have on their own accord returned to the US only to be imprisoned in accordance with a plea bargain agreement.[90] Reindl has pointed out that the grand jury investigation benefits the prosecution and makes it 'relatively easy to obtain indictments against a defendant'. This in turn induces defendants to embrace plea bargaining. As a result the prosecution rarely has to meet the 'beyond reasonable doubt' threshold.[91]

According to Stephan, as a further incentive for the defendants the amount of information that is subject to publicity may be limited in plea agreements. This may be useful in view of potential private actions. Plea bargaining arrangements allow also the concurrent settlements of 'corporate and individual liabilities'. Having entered a plea bargaining agreement, the defendant gives up the right to contest the case. The plea bargain agreements may entail specifics that relate to the location of the prison and even amenities.[92] Defendants may also appreciate that the case could be speedily resolved. Certain defendants could regard the aforementioned gains as equally important as the duration of the sentence.[93]

As a result, the DOJ is able to ensure the regular enforcement of the offence – the laborious trials and appeals are avoided, which leaves vacant resources for further use. Stephan has pointed out, however, that while the plea bargaining agreements secure a certain level of enforcement in the US, the system has been accused of being unfair, and is the product of a lengthy evolution. Thus it is filled with features that originated in the US legal culture.[94]

On a more general note, Reindl argued that the US system could not easily be transplanted to Europe. Subsequently the expected benefits of a criminal anti-cartel regime might not materialise.[95] Stephan noted that since the apparent US success in pursuing cartels may be attributed to the system of plea bargaining, it is possible that the UK, lacking such a system, will not be able to bring many criminal cartel cases.[96] Lawrence *et al.* argued that while US-specific plea

89 Hammond, S. D. (2006), 'The U.S. Model of Negotiated Plea Agreements: A Good Deal With Benefits For All', OECD Competition Committee, Working Party No. 3, 17 October 2006, at para 1.

90 Stephan (2008), note 83 above, 24.

91 In addition, Reindl notes the uniquely strong investigatory powers in the US, namely, grand jury subpoenas, grand jury investigations and indictments, and a competition authority that prosecutes and does not have to depend upon public prosecutors: Reindl, A. P. (2006), 'How Strong Is the Case for Criminal Sanctions in Cartels Cases?' in: Cseres, K. J., Schinkel, M. P and Vogelaar. F. O. W (eds), *Criminalization of Competition Law Enforcement, Economic and Legal Implications for the EU Member States*, Cheltenham: Edward Elgar, 118.

92 Stephan (2008), note 83 above, 23–4.

93 Lawrence *et al.* (2008), note 3 above, 25; see also Stephan (2008), note 83 above, 23.

94 Stephan (2008), note 83 above, 25.

95 Reindl (2006), note 91 above, 119.

96 Stephan (2008), note 83 above, 25–6.

bargaining has its own characteristics that do not apply to the UK, a system of plea bargaining could offer notable advantages.[97]

While the courts do not embrace plea bargaining in the UK, the overall approach would appear to be nowadays more accommodating. In *R. v. Goodyear*[98] the judge pointed out that the judge himself should not participate in plea bargaining.[99] The UK Government, however, rejected plea bargaining in the context of anti-cartel enforcement, arguing that implications for the criminal justice system should be cautiously examined.[100]

By way of conclusion, it seems that there are some good reasons to introduce a system of plea bargaining, especially when it comes to the demanding criminal proceedings that concern, for instance, hard-core cartel conduct. Despite its demerits, it is increasingly accepted that plea bargaining could be a useful tool in the fight against white-collar crime.

Conclusion

The Finnish choice to adopt a system of plea bargaining represented something of a sea-change in policy. The European Court of Human Rights has found Finland guilty of delayed proceedings on several occasions, especially when it comes to white-collar crimes. To an extent it would seem that the resource-intensive nature of criminal cases prompted the introduction of plea bargaining.

Detractors could argue that such practices come into direct conflict with the principle of mandatory prosecution. Denmark and Norway have had more relaxed attitudes toward plea bargaining and a crown witness system, or at a least something that approaches one when compared to Finland and Sweden. A crown witness system in particular has brought about associations with moral compromise. However, introducing plea bargaining in Finland may indicate that the official stance is evolving on the issue.

The bigger picture tells us that the objective of material truth in court proceedings has been given a less important role while more pragmatic considerations pave the way for negotiated justice. Ultimately a given court ruling is based on facts available in one specific instance, and the outcome of the case is rather the product of procedural truth.

One of the concerns related to plea bargaining has to do with the defendant's legal protection. The legitimacy of a criminal justice system could be gravely undermined if innocent individuals were persuaded to enter guilty pleas. Interestingly the ECtHR has said that plea bargaining agreements do not violate the ECHR and may benefit the defendant. The Council of Europe had already in

97 Lawrence *et al.* (2008), note 3 above, 38.
98 2005 EWCA Crim 888, at para 67.
99 See Furse (2012), note 75 above, 152.
100 Department of Business, Innovation and Science, *Growth, Competition and The Competition Regime, Government Response to Consultation*, March 2012, at para 7.40.

1987 suggested that its Member States should widen the scope of prosecutorial discretion where possible.

In the anti-cartel context it could be desirable to provide cartel members who do not benefit from immunity the opportunity to enter plea bargain agreements. For instance, in the US, defendants frequently enter plea bargains – when the DOJ has been compelled to take a case to trial, it has succeeded in less than half of the cases. Indeed it is the challenging nature of criminal prosecutions in relation to white-collar conduct that highlights the advantages that plea bargaining carries. It appears that this perception is now gaining ground in the Nordic context as well.

11 The EU Criminal Intelligence Model: problems and issues

Artur Gruszczak

EU criminal law and crime policy in the past decade have evolved towards a co-operation regime facilitating cross-border proceedings and increasing effectiveness of criminal justice. As part of judicial co-operation in criminal matters, EU Member States have developed various collaborative projects aiming to strengthen and widen the scope of cross-border prevention and fight against transnational crime. With the Treaty of Lisbon, the field of judicial co-operation in criminal matters and law enforcement has acquired enhanced capabilities to make the Union more effective in tackling the problem of cross-border criminal activities. The shift from *locus regit actum* principle to *forum regit actum* principle, epitomised in EU legal instruments relevant to judicial co-operation in criminal matters, made Member States aware of utility of intergovernmental settings for their legal and normative regulations and encouraged EU institutions, particularly the Commission, for launching proposals which pretended to enlarge the scope of EU judicial co-operation.

Today's facets of criminality in the EU and outside its borders are highly disquieting, or even in their most radical expressions just alarming. Transnational global 'crime corporations' built around powerful criminal groups from as distant countries as Nigeria, Russia, Japan, Colombia, the United States, India or South Africa have penetrated economic, financial and social systems of EU Member States with increasing assertiveness and intensity. They became involved in both traditional forms of organised criminality, such as drug trafficking, corruption, extortion, fraud, gambling, racketeering, trafficking in human beings, trade in engendered species, pornography, theft and robbery, and novel forms exploiting modern tools and 'dual-use' communication technologies which exploded at the time of the computer revolution in the 1980s and the subsequent network revolution and globalisation. Financial networks, the Internet, cellular telephony and global communication made criminal organisations even more sophisticated and dynamic than ever before. Hence, new serious and challenging forms of transnational crime emerged, including money laundering through electronic transactions, cybercrime, intellectual property theft and counterfeiting.[1] The

1 Abraham, I. and van Schendel, A. (2005), 'Introduction: The Making of Illicitness', in: van Schendel, A. and Abraham, I. (eds), *Illicit Flows and Criminal Things. States, Borders, and the*

pervasiveness of criminal organisations made Western societies feel trapped due to the fact that the expansion of illegal activities met with the increasingly decisive response of governments that did not hesitate to introduce harsh control and surveillance measures affecting whole societies.

One of the new elements in the developments of EU crime policy since the beginning of the twenty-first century has been the focus on enforcement and obligations of Member States in this respect.[2] Legal instruments in criminal law adopted by EU institutions not only must be implemented in the national criminal justice systems, but also duly and effectively enforced by competent national authorities supported – which is characteristic for the EU – by supranational institutions and agencies.[3] The specific institutional and normative framework for EU co-operation in criminal matters is reflected both in substantial and procedural criminal law of the Member States. The exchange of information with respect not only to regulations, normative measures and legal instruments, but also to ongoing criminal proceedings, investigation and prosecution, has been considered as a value added to national efforts by EU agencies and bodies.

Nowadays the essential part of criminal procedure and crime policy is the investigation of crime and criminals by using the intelligence and relevant information collected by competent agencies and services. A European criminal policy has to put a proper emphasis on this fact and stimulate proposals and solutions which could effectively meet requirements and needs of Member States, yet at the same time strengthen the role of EU institutions, agencies and regulations. The European Criminal Intelligence Model (ECIM) is an example of the search for possible synergies between EU criminal law and crime policy and national criminal justice systems. The scope of synergy-building is fairly modest and confined to organisational and technical matters. However, the ECIM has underpinned numerous initiatives and projects launched recently with a view to curbing most dangerous forms of transnational and organised crime through the wide-range involvement of EU institutions and agencies in close co-operation with EU Member States.

This chapter will focus on the European Criminal Intelligence Model as a methodological framework for criminal intelligence and information exchange on EU level. It proceeds as follows. In the first section, the notion of criminal intelligence is elaborated, with special attention devoted to the meaning of this term in EU legal texts. In the following section, the European Criminal Intelligence Model is presented as a project adopted by the Council of the EU with the aim of enhancing effectiveness of terrorist and criminal prevention. The

Other Side of Globalization. Bloomington-Indianapolis: Indiana University Press, 3–6. Winter, H. (2008), *The Economics of Crime. An Introduction to Rational Crime Analysis*. London and New York: Routledge. Yar, M. (2006), *Cybercrime and Society*. London-Thousand Oaks-New Delhi: SAGE Publications.

2 Klip, A. (2012), Editorial: 'European Criminal Policy.' *European Journal of Crime, Criminal Law and Criminal Justice*, 20, 8–9.

3 Cools, M. *et al.* (2010), *EU and International Crime Control. Topical Issues*. Antwerp-Apeldoorn-Portland: Maklu.

next section analyses the process of integrating the ECIM with the policy cycle for organised and serious international crime. The last section offers an analytical look at methodology employed for the purposes of criminal intelligence at EU level. It describes in detail the methods, techniques and tools used in the policy cycle, Europol's OCTA/SOCTA threat assessments, and COSPOL/EMPACT as platforms for coordinating and implementing joint actions of Member States and EU agencies involved in the prevention and fight against serious and organised crime. In conclusion, the EU criminal intelligence model is assessed as a working formula useful for developing and implementing strategic blueprints to tackle current problems of internal security and prepare for future anticipated threats and hazards.

What is criminal intelligence?

For centuries, the collection and storage of information about crime and criminals have been a core part of criminal justice development. Criminal police and magistrates stockpiled variegated information as a source of important knowledge about the phenomenon of crime as well as about individuals and groups with illegal records. However, its practical use was largely reduced due to the lack of effective tools of information management and processing and, in many cases, low quality of the acquired data. Moreover, national interests of sovereign nation states were in many cases contrary to the principle of information sharing and intelligence exchange.

In the 1960s the US authorities realised that national security should not be solely identified with defence against Soviet spy networks active worldwide or Communist agents in Western democracies. It should equally take into account the problem of crime and delinquency, having indigenous root causes yet proliferating beyond national territories and state borders.[4]

Already in the mid-1970s, the US National Advisory Committee on Criminal Justice Standards and Goals proposed a definition of criminal intelligence. It was formulated as 'the product of systematic gathering, evaluation, and synthesis of raw data on individuals or activities suspected of being, or known to be, criminal in nature'.[5]

Policy recommendations, in-depth reports and well-intentioned advices notwithstanding, the practice of law enforcement showed numerous limitations to the application of intelligence analysis. Data collection was more oriented towards evidence gathering than information acquiring, processing and collation.

4 DeLuca, J. (1991), 'Intelligence Analysis: Planning and Executing Complex Criminal Investigations', in: Fijnaut, C. J. C. F. and Jacobs, J. B. (eds), *Organized Crime and Its Containment: A Transatlantic Initiative*, Deventer: Kluwer Law & Taxation, 142.

5 National Advisory Committee on Criminal Justice Standards and Goals (1976), *Organized Crime: Report of the Task Force on Organized Crime*, Washington, DC: National Advisory Committee on Criminal Justice Standards and Goals, 122.

Today's criminal intelligence encompasses techniques and solutions that enhance investigators' natural deductive abilities and cognitive processes, described often as the 'natural intuition', or 'hunch', which quite subconsciously is in use all the time. According to a definition contained in the National Criminal Intelligence Sharing Plan, a document issued in October 2003 in the framework of the Global Justice Information Sharing Initiative, sponsored by the Office of Justice Programs of US Department of Justice, criminal intelligence is identified as 'Information compiled, analyzed, and/or disseminated in an effort to anticipate, prevent, or monitor criminal activity'.[6]

The real and decisive value of the criminal intelligence is measured by the scope and depth of information analysis and the quality of the final 'product' as a tool having a direct application to the investigation.

The authors of a manual of criminal intelligence prepared for the UN Office on Drugs and Crime share the following opinion:

> The basic problem for intelligence analysts is putting intelligence and information together in an organized way so that the difficult task of extracting meaning from the assembled information is made easier. Only when the proper explanation of what the original information means has been derived can this intelligence be put to practical use. The techniques and systems embodied in this manual are practical tools, which can be of value in any investigation.[7]

Criminal intelligence engages in the fight against serious and organised crime. It is linked to criminal investigations, which aim at producing evidence that can result in conviction in a court of law. It is not, however, the one and only objective. Criminal intelligence enables law enforcement services to adopt a proactive stance with regard to threats and perils brought about by various forms of criminality, organised or not. Identifying elements of crime environment and understanding *modi operandi* of criminal groups is a strong prerequisite for threat assessment and crime forecasts allowing for anticipation and prevention of possible future criminal activities. 'Intelligence provides the knowledge on which to base decisions and select appropriate targets for investigation. While the use of criminal intelligence analysis is appropriate to support investigations, surveillance operations and the prosecution of cases, it also provides law enforcement agencies with the ability to effectively manage resources, budget, and meet their responsibility for crime prevention.'[8]

The acquisition of information in the pre-trial investigation phase is one of the most salient procedural elements.[9] Given sensitivity of the issue of ownership of

6 US Department of Justice, (2003), *National Criminal Intelligence Sharing Plan*. Washington, DC: US Department of Justice, Office of Justice Programs, available at: www.cops.usdoj.gov/files/ric/CDROMs/LEIntelGuide/pubs/National_Criminal_Intelligence_Sharing_Plan.pdf.

7 UNODC, (2011), *Criminal Intelligence. Manual for Analysts*. New York: United Nations, 7.

8 *Ibid*.

9 Kaiafa-Gbandi, M. (2010), 'Harmonisation of Criminal Procedure on the Basis of Common

the information and criminal data, it is hardly possible to collect and process them without a clear consent from the country of their origins.

The above-mentioned disclaimer was particularly valid with reference to European *acquis* related to criminal intelligence in the area of judicial co-operation in criminal matters. For decades, it was fairly modest due to certain political prerequisites and substantial impediments imposed by Member States. As a result, what is intelligence was by no means an obvious question for EU officials and representatives of Member States. The plenty of conceptualisations, definitions and formulations circulating in the scholarly world or applied by national intelligence services of Member States precluded putting forward a single definition of intelligence. EU institutions became engaged in this undertaking only in the mid-2000s when the Commission adopted an official interpretation of what is information and what is intelligence. In a 2004 communication on enhancing access to information by law enforcement agencies, there is a curious remark (added, by the way, in a footnote): 'For the purpose of this Communication the expression "data" or "information" means "data, information and intelligence" unless otherwise indicated; the term "intelligence" refers to "criminal intelligence".'[10] Such imprecise depiction of intelligence did not facilitate efforts to work out a comprehensive approach to the co-operation of EU Member States and institutions in exchanging information and data relevant for cross-border activities of law enforcement agencies. Incentives to specify the meaning of intelligence in EU policy were included in the European Council multi-annual programme of strengthening the area of freedom, security and justice, adopted in November 2004. An intelligence-led approach to EU law enforcement co-operation in the prevention and combating of threats to internal security and public order demanded a clear concept of intelligence. The Council pointed out that exchange of information and intelligence on crime and criminal activities is the basis for law enforcement co-operation in the European Union.[11] In 2006, the Council, acting on the initiative of Sweden, adopted Framework Decision 2006/960/JHA on simplifying the exchange of information and intelligence between law enforcement authorities of Member States. One can find such a peculiar provision in Article 2(d)(i) of this Framework Decision:

> information and/or intelligence:
>
> - any type of information or data which is held by law enforcement authorities; and

Principles. The EU's Challenge for Rule-of-Law Transnational Crime Control', in: Fijnaut, C. and Ouwerkerk, J. (eds), *The Future of Police and Judicial Cooperation in the European Union*. Leiden-London: Martinus Nijhoff Publishers, 366–7.

10 European Commission (2004), *Communication from the Commission to the Council and the European Parliament. Towards Enhancing Access to Information by Law Enforcement Agencies*, COM(2004) 429 final (16 June), 5.

11 Mitsilegas, V. (2009), *EU Criminal Law*. Oxford: Hart Publishing, 252.

- any type of information or data which is held by public authorities or by private entities and which is available to law enforcement authorities without the taking of coercive measures.[12]

A question remained whether this wording provided a precise and operational definition of intelligence. As many experts underline, information is not synonymous with intelligence. Information and data are raw materials while intelligence is a processed information and data and cross-checked against other available sources of information and knowledge. From a functional standpoint, criminal intelligence executed at national level used to be identified with supporting evidence-led inquiry: gathering information for the police investigation, structuring the evidence for courts or revealing the nature of crime phenomena. International collaboration in criminal justice involves strategic intelligence: evaluation of threats, assessment of criminality's impact, anticipation of future threats and risks. EU experience has proved viability of the strategic dimensions of criminal intelligence given the limitations in operational activities and barriers maintained by respective national authorities with regard to data sharing and information exchange. This is why the idea of an EU criminal intelligence model emerged in specific circumstances of elevated threat to national security of Member States following terrorist activities in the EU.

The European Criminal Intelligence Model – origins, principles and evolution

The events of 9/11 highlighted the critical importance of intelligence for effective prevention and combating of terrorism and transnational crime. However, it did not have any special impact on the capabilities of EU legal and institutional arrangements to establish a genuine criminal intelligence model. Attempts at intensifying and enlarging the scope of judicial co-operation in criminal matters at EU level resulted in the adoption of several legal instruments and the pressure on the Member States to implement the existing EU legal measures in this field. Efforts aimed to encourage a more intense and effective exchange of criminal information, and intelligence did not yield the expected results, mostly due to the lack of unanimity and the deficit of trust among the Member States.[13]

In the immediate aftermath of the 11 March 2004 terrorist attack in Madrid, EU institutions placed particular emphasis on the exchange of information and intelligence between law enforcement authorities of Member States and called for

12 Council of the EU (2006a), Council Framework Decision 2006/960/JHA of 18 December 2006 on simplifying the exchange of information and intelligence between law enforcement authorities of the Member States of the European Union, *Official Journal of the European Union*, L 386 (29 December).

13 Bures, O. (2006), 'EU Counterterrorism Policy: A Paper Tiger?' *Terrorism and Political Violence*, 18, 62–3. Müller-Wille, B. (2006). 'Intelligence and Democratic Accountability: A Blessing, not a Curse.' *European Security*, 15, 491–506; Duke, S. (2006), 'Intelligence, Security and Information Flows in CFSP.' *Intelligence and National Security*, 21, 619–20.

the improvement of mechanisms for co-operation and the promotion of effective systematic collaboration between police, security and intelligence services. The European Commission in its Communication in June 2004 listed the main shortcomings of hitherto co-operation in the field of information and intelligence exchange among the Member States and with EU bodies. The Commission enumerated the following negative features:

- Variety of stakeholders
- Compartmentalisation of information
- Lack of a clear policy on information channels
- Legal, technical and practical problems hindering exchange between Member States.[14]

Having reviewed thoroughly the obstacles to an effective exchange of information between law enforcement authorities in Member States, the Commission concluded that they can only be effectively addressed on the basis of a firm commitment of Member States to set up a European Criminal Intelligence Model.[15] This model would comprise a common methodology of a reliable threat assessment. It would eventually render intelligence-led law enforcement effective and allow for enhanced co-operation in the field of criminal justice. EU criminal intelligence would assist the competent national authorities in the performance of their strategic or operational tasks in order to prevent and combat terrorism and other forms of organised crime.

The European Council in the Hague Programme of November 2004 established the goal of 'setting up and implementing a methodology for intelligence-led law enforcement at EU level'.[16] Member States also agreed to develop a criminal intelligence model which should become a core concept of intelligence-led policing and provide methodology to tackle organised crime. They started from the assumption that the national law enforcement agencies within the European Union, as well as those already established at the European level, had an incomplete and rather poor awareness of serious and organised crime. The direct consequence of the lack of information or its incompleteness was the incapacity of law enforcement to evaluate and predict risks and, subsequently, create response strategies as well as work out tailor-made tactical and operational blueprints.

Terrorist attacks in London in July 2005 stimulated Member States to take up the issue of generating criminal intelligence capabilities at EU level. A British proposal submitted to Interior Ministers from EU Member States gathered at an informal meeting in September 2005 contained what may have been considered

14 European Commission (2004), *Communication from the Commission to the Council and the European Parliament. Towards Enhancing Access to Information by Law Enforcement Agencies*, doc. COM (2004) 429 final (16 June), 3–4.

15 *Ibid.*, 8.

16 European Council (2004), 'The Hague Programme: Strengthening Freedom, Security and Justice in the European Union', *Official Journal of the European Union*, C 53 (3 March), 9.

the 'missing link' in the creation of a potential EU intelligence tradecraft. A consultation paper delivered by the UK Home Office introduced the idea of a European Criminal Intelligence Model (ECIM) based on the principles of intelligence-led policing and evidently inspired by the UK's National Intelligence Model.[17] According to the UK Presidency, an ECIM should benefit EU Member States by:

- Improving knowledge of serious and organised crime through more effective collection, exchange, and analysis of information
- Increasing the effectiveness of Europol and other relevant EU bodies
- Achieving better operational results
- Allowing all Member States as well as EU institutions to observe a common methodology for tackling serious and organised crime in the EU.[18]

The ECIM was marked by a 'shift from reactive policing to a problem-solving approach, based on analysis, by developing action plans (focused on crime prevention as well as on repressive action) and involving multiple actors (both private and public partners)'.[19] According to Brady, 'the ECIM sets out how the EU can achieve this by ensuring national police forces, Europol's criminal intelligence analysts and the police chiefs' operations work together against the same criminal threats.'[20] Intelligence-led policing principles, which were the critical underpinning for the ECIM, were based on the assumption that EU agencies and institutions in strict co-operation with Member States must first improve its knowledge of various aspects of cross-border and international criminality, while also developing an intelligence cycle leading to strengthened and accurate operational capabilities.[21]

The original concept of the European Criminal Intelligence Model indeed took the shape of an intelligence cycle which relied on inputs from Europol and Member States contributing either directly or through appropriate institutional or working schemes as provided in EU law. The elements of that cycle were the following:

- Setting strategic priorities on the basis of threat assessments delivered by appropriate EU bodies, mainly Europol
- Identifying knowledge gaps

17 UK Presidency (2005), *A European Criminal Intelligence Model.* Paper issued by the 2005 UK Presidency of the EU.

18 *Ibid.*, 1.

19 Council of the EU (2010a), *Result of the 'Harmony' project – 'A Generic European Crime Intelligence Model' – Bringing Together the Existing Instruments and Strengthening Europol's Central Role*, doc. 14851/10 (25 October), p. 8.

20 Brady, H. (2008), 'Europol and the European Criminal Intelligence Model: A Non-state Response to Organized Crime', *Policing*, 2,106.

21 Nunzi, A. (2007), 'Exchange of Information and Intelligence Among Law Enforcement Authorities: A European Union Perspective' *Revue internationale de droit pénal*, 78, 148.

- Producing intelligence requirements facilitated by Europol
- Launching a proactive collection programme in Member States
- Storing and analysing intelligence in Europol
- Producing specialist threat assessments to improve knowledge in priority areas
- Identifying top criminals and networks
- Targeting top criminals and networks by Member States
- Recycling through Europol intelligence generated by investigations underway.[22]

This cycle required operational excellence and demanded from national stakeholders (law enforcement agencies from Member States) full commitment to the principles of EU criminal intelligence co-operation and a strong capacity to deliver requested information and data. This was a highly demanding task and not every Member State was ready, capable and willing to meet these requirements and expectations. As a result, the European Criminal Intelligence Model did not achieve a full work capacity, and neither was it grounded on a comprehensive approach to intelligence tradecraft. One of the reasons behind the difficulties and delays in implementing the full criminal intelligence cycle was the lack of a single clear definition of intelligence. This shortcoming was evidenced in the European Union counter-terrorism strategy, adopted in December 2005. It contained numerous elements of criminal intelligence alluding to the ECIM model but its final version departed from earlier commitment to intelligence as a pivotal element of disrupting terrorist activities. It suggested putting into practice the principle of availability with regard to criminal information and law enforcement data.[23]

While in December 2006 the Council finally adopted, on the initiative of Sweden, the Framework Decision on simplifying the exchange of information and intelligence between law enforcement authorities of EU Member States, it neither significantly improved the efficiency of any information exchange system in the EU, nor contributed to the feasibility of the ECIM. A prospective solution to the challenge of granting mutual access to criminal records stored in the individual databases of the Member States, based on the principle of availability, formulated in the Hague Programme and contained in the Swedish initiative, collapsed in the face of the inherent bureaucratic inflexibility within the decision-making process at the EU level.

The 2009 Stockholm Programme sought to adopt a comprehensive approach to security, justice and mobility in the EU. It put emphasis on chances and opportunities as well as threats and systemic risks embedded in the complex structure of the EU as an international actor and as an area of freedom, prosperity

22 Council of the EU (2006b) *Comprehensive Operational Strategic Planning for the Police (COSPOL)*, doc. 5859/4/06 REV 4 LIMITE (10 October), p. 3.

23 Council of the EU (2005), *The European Union Counter-Terrorism Strategy*, doc. 14469/4/05 REV 4 (30 November).

and economic development. Avoiding a direct reference to the ECIM, it highlighted the necessity to establish a methodology based on common parameters in order to be able to analyse the threats at European level.[24]

The Stockholm Programme heralded a new strategic approach to internal security in the European Union. It was embodied in the EU Internal Security Strategy (EU ISS) adopted in early 2010 to further improve security in the EU, protect safety of citizens of the Union and tackle organised crime, terrorism and other threats. Building on some original premises of the ECIM, the new strategy focused on an intelligence-led, proactive approach to the challenge of terrorism, organised crime and both natural and manmade disasters. It highlighted prevention and anticipation as mechanisms aimed to detect future threats and prevent their happening. It called Member States to foster information exchange on a basis of mutual trust and share intelligence in time in compliance with the principle of information availability.[25] The authors of a study on the EU ISS submitted to the LIBE committee of the European Parliament, summing up the meaning of the strategy, stressed that 'The central articulation of the guidelines is between the emphasis on a proactive, intelligence-led approach, and the development of a comprehensive model for information exchange and operational co-operation.'[26]

The Internal Security Strategy thus offered a strategic framework and broad guidelines for a comprehensive approach to effective intelligence-led policing and enhanced criminal intelligence co-operation among EU Member States with a direct and active involvement of competent EU agencies and bodies.[27] It laid solid grounds for criminal intelligence conceived as a critical element of evidence-based co-operation in the area of criminal justice in the EU, supported by the best available assessments and risk analyses, and overwhelmingly accepted as a viable political option.

The ECIM and the policy cycle

The Treaty of Lisbon and the Stockholm Programme, enacted at the end of 2009, sought to give a strong impetus to EU co-operation in the fields of internal security and criminal justice. With the entry into force of the Treaty of Lisbon, the pillar structure was formally abolished, yet the area of internal security, namely police co-operation and judicial co-operation in criminal matters, retained its specific character, allowing Member States to keep a wide array of

24 European Council (2010), 'The Stockholm Programme – An Open and Secure Europe Serving and Protecting the Citizens.' *Official Journal of the European Union*, C 115 (4 May).

25 Council of the EU (2010b), *Internal Security Strategy for the European Union. Towards a European Security Model*. Brussels: General Secretariat of the Council.

26 Sherrer, A., Jeandesboz, J. and Guittet, P.-E. (2011), *Developing an EU Internal Security Strategy, Fighting Terrorism and Organised Crime*. Brussels: European Parliament, 32.

27 Bossong, R. and Rhinard, M. (2013), 'The EU Internal Security Strategy. Towards a More Coherent Approach to EU Security?' *Studia Diplomatica*, LXVI, 51–2. Horgby, A. and Rhinard, M. (2013). *The EU's Internal Security Strategy: Living in the Shadow of Its Past*, Occasional Paper no. 24. Stockholm: The Swedish Institute of International Affairs.

national competences in that area. As a result, collaborative schemes and working arrangements originating in national practices and depending on intergovernmental collaboration still required a strategic framework and flexible organisational setting on EU level, yet they could be also developed in an independent way, relying mostly on bilateral or multilateral agreements and pre-established co-operation patterns and practices.

In October 2009, Belgium launched an idea to link the various national strategies of the Member States with political decisions at EU level to create an effective way of carrying out operational activities between EU agencies and national law enforcement services. It crafted the *Harmony Project* in close co-operation with Europol, as well as the UK and the Netherlands, because of their experience in intelligence-led policing, so as to develop an integrated EU approach to crime prevention and combating terrorism through a comprehensive threat assessment and on this basis as an intelligence-led co-operation in action.[28]

The project envisioned linking all the requisite organisations within a horizontal approach, which would result in a better alignment between the activities of the EU agencies and be combined with a vertical approach, meaning that Member States could avail themselves of the opportunity to integrate EU tools and measures into their national strategies and policies. As a result, a genuine European policy cycle could be established on the grounds of the already existing EU instruments, policies and actions.

In October 2010, the Standing Committee on operational co-operation on internal security (COSI) agreed on the establishment of a EU policy cycle for organised and serious international crime on the basis of an intelligence-led policing approach. JHA Council adopted in November 2010 conclusions on the creation and implementation of an EU-wide policy cycle for organised and serious international crime. It was implemented in two stages: initial two-year policy cycle 2011–13 and fully fledged four-year policy cycle 2013–17.[29]

It is worth underlining that the policy cycle was considered to be the new embodiment of the European Criminal Intelligence Model, the next phase in its evolution since the mid-2000s. The Belgian Presidency asserted in July 2010 that its proposal was nothing but 'a generic European Criminal Intelligence Model that describes a multi-annual policy cycle and defines the roles, processes and products needed for the implementation thereof'.[30] The policy cycle sought to fill the gaps in the hitherto implementation of the ECIM and aimed to translate current strategies and political priorities into operational plans and appropriate activities. Although cyclical in its name, it was rather conceived as a temporally determined sequence of strategic assessments, political decisions and operational

28 Belgian Federal Police (2010), *Harmony Project*, Brussels: Belgian Federal Police.

29 Council of the EU (2010c), *Council Conclusions on the Creation and Implementation of a EU Policy Cycle for Organised and Serious International Crime*, 3043rd Justice and Home Affairs Council meeting, Brussels, 8 and 9 November 2010, available at: www.consilium.europa.eu/uedocs/cms_data/docs/pressdata/en/jha/117583.pdf.

30 Council of the EU (2010d), *Expert Group – EU Policy Cycle*, doc. 11814/10 Limite (5 July), 1.

plans intended to bring about a better systemic response to the current and emerging threats.[31]

The policy cycle thus could be perceived as a linear development of proactive, problem-oriented comprehensive approach to organised and serious international crime tackled at EU level with the active involvement of competent EU institutions and agencies. The ECIM, considered to be a traditional approach to intelligence-led law enforcement in the field of EU internal security, was envisioned as a vertically oriented methodological toolset shifting accordingly on the temporal axis of the policy cycle development to the pre-established elements of strategies, action plans and operational tasks. It is worth underlining that Europol's organised crime threat assessment was the point of departure both for the initial cycle as well as the subsequent fully fledged cycle. This meant that ECIM's intelligence-led orientation and threat assessment methodology was underpinning and permeating the logics of EU policy cycle for organised and serious international crime.

The policy cycle reorganised the institutional framework for EU criminal intelligence, referring directly to post-Lisbon EU architecture in the area of freedom, security and justice and taking advantage of new opportunities and chances. First of all, the responsibility for organisation and effective implementation of the policy cycle laid with COSI, whereas Europol's role was limited to producing threat assessments and giving inputs for the policy-making process specified by the policy cycle. This was contrary to the original concept of EU criminal intelligence model and needs further elaboration.

The ECIM took from its British pattern a centralised architecture with a central unit as the functional prerequisite for an efficient criminal data management. Therefore, Europol was pointed to as the 'central EU capability to receive, store and analyse this collected information'[32] and to support operational activities of the Member States based on Europol's earlier strategic assessments. The application of the ECIM was predetermined by Europol's capabilities, which had been reduced by legal provisions and organisational schemes, as well as Member States' inability to exercise a joint will or exhibit an openness for advanced co-operation in the exchange of information and intelligence in the area of transnational criminal justice. Europol, on the basis of the new Decision adopted in April 2009, was equipped with enhanced capabilities in the area of information management, intelligence production and sharing, as well as operational support for Member States. Europol's strategy for the period 2010–14 assigned this entity the role of EU criminal information hub and the centre for law enforcement expertise.[33]

31 Council of the EU (2010e), *EU Policy Cycle*, doc. 12657/1/10 REV 1 (3 September).

32 Council of the EU (2010c), *Council Conclusions on the Creation and Implementation of a EU Policy Cycle for Organised and Serious International Crime*, 3043rd Justice and Home Affairs Council meeting, Brussels, 8 and 9 November 2010, available at: www.consilium.europa.eu/uedocs/cms_data/docs/pressdata/en/jha/117583.pdf.

33 Busuioc, M., Curtin, D. and Groenleer, M. (2011), 'Agency Growth between Autonomy and Accountability: The European Police Office as a "Living Institution"', *Journal of European Public Policy*, 18, 848–67; Carrapiço, H. and Trauner, F. (2013), 'Europol and its Influence on

Most importantly, Europol was tasked to lead the further development of the ECIM. In this regard, it should develop a common EU approach for targeted collection and sharing of key criminal information, integrated analysis of financial intelligence linked to all crime phenomena and identification of top criminal targets. It should also improve and strengthen the OCTA methodology and promote ECIM principles among national authorities in the Member States as well as EU institutions and agencies.[34] Europol was also presumed in the EU Internal Security Strategy to bear responsibility for analysing future situations and scenarios and for preparing regular threat assessments.

The policy cycle sought to depart from a loose, often dispersed and fragmented architecture of EU multi-level co-operation in the face of criminal threats towards a centralised COSI-led institutional process engaging EU institutions and agencies in the prevention and fight against serious and organised crime.

In accordance with the policy cycle, COSI's competences include:

- Acting as a platform for a thorough discussion about the SOCTA methodology
- Submitting draft conclusions to the Council setting new priorities for the fight against organised and serious international crime
- Discussing and adopting strategic plans
- Monitoring the progress and validating operational action plans.

COSI's central role in the development, monitoring and reporting of the policy cycle stems from the political prevalence of traditional intergovernmental mode of governance in the field of EU internal security. While Europol as the 'EU criminal intelligence hub' has been tasked with information management and data analysis, COSI as the Council's body in charge of operational co-operation on internal security has a strong influence on the unfolding steering processes within the policy cycle and is entitled to a considerable part of the decision-making process in the course of coordinating the implementation of the fully fledged policy cycle.

The policy cycle reinvigorated the fading ECIM thanks to a flexible formula of EU internal security management and the reduction of the scope of criminal intelligence to serious and international organised crime. It also allowed for diversified methodological solutions more suitable to the complex nature of present dangers and the requirement of a proactive stance with respect to risks and threats to EU internal security.

EU Policy-making on Organized Crime: Analyzing Governance Dynamics and Opportunities', *Perspectives on European Politics and Society*, 14, 366–8.

34 Europol (2009), *Europol Strategy 2010–2014*, Europol Management Board, doc. 1424-73r1 (2 November).

ECIM methodology

The ECIM may be perceived as a framework for intelligence-led strategic, operational, organisational and institutional plans and activities aiming to tackle effectively most serious threats to internal security of the European Union.[35] As a methodological concept, it was formulated in general terms, as a common denominator for further actions, to get support from Member States and avoid prolonged discussion on detailed mechanisms and processes. As a result, the ECIM was proclaimed as a new common concept and methodology to tackle organised crime, although its application through the government management cycles (policy development, policy setting, implementation and monitoring, evaluation) simply required much more elaborated, detailed and goal-oriented directives. Evident shortcomings of the original EU criminal intelligence model were partially made up through the integration of the existing methodological solutions and the formulation of new proposals which reduced deficits embedded in the ECIM. They are briefly described in the following subsections.

The policy cycle methodology

The original policy cycle for serious international and organised crime established by the Council in 2010 consisted of four stages. For the purposes of criminal intelligence, the policy cycle included:

- A complete and thorough picture of criminal threats reflected in Europol's serious and organised crime threat assessment (SOCTA)
- Prioritisation of identified threats and adoption for each of the priorities of a Multi-Annual Strategic Plan (MASP) in order to work out a comprehensive response to the addressed threats involving preventive as well repressive measures
- Implementation of annual Operational Action Plans (OAP) built upon the COSPOL framework as the multilateral co-operation platform to address the prioritised threats
- A thorough evaluation of outputs and outcomes of the cycle contributing to the formulation of intelligence requirements for the next policy cycle.

The Council decided that the initial 'warming-up' two-year cycle should focus on crime priority areas commissioned by COSI, be based on the old-school Europol methodology employed in the OCTA assessments and organised within the reviewed COSPOL framework concentrated on single law enforcement issues instead of an integrated approach. The next, fully fledged, four-year cycle should start with a new SOCTA assessment produced by Europol of the basis of a

35 Gruszczak, A. (2013), 'EU Intelligence-led Policing: The Case of Counter-terrorism Cooperation', in: O'Neill, M., Swinton, K. and Winter, A. (eds), *New Challenges for the EU Internal Security Strategy*. Newcastle upon Tyne: Cambridge Scholars Publishing, 21–4.

new methodology. It will be developed in conformity with the presumptions of integrated and integral approach, engaging various categories of stakeholders: EU institutions (Council, Commission), EU agencies and bodies (Europol, Frontex, IntCen) and Member States (relevant national criminal intelligence or law enforcement services). It will support Member States in implementing national intelligence models through delivering training packages and streamlining specialised courses offered by the European Police College (CEPOL). It will put greater emphasis on the reporting and independent evaluation mechanisms.

The policy cycle, concentrating on serious international and organised crime, seeks to effectively implement the ECIM in its most practical meaning and thereby gain leverage in the overall EU strategy in the area of freedom, security and justice. However, it has to incorporate, in order to be productive and efficient, dispersed pieces of the methodological process accelerated by post-Lisbon developments in the field of EU internal security.

OCTA/SOCTA

The starting point of the initial and the next fully fledged EU policy cycle is a threat assessment in which Europol delivers analytical findings underpinning priorities, goals and action plans translated into EU policy on serious and organised crime. The necessity to have on EU level a reliable, aggregated, comprehensive evaluation of current trends in organised crime impacting the Union was strengthened after the 2004 terrorist attack in Madrid.

Following the European Council's conclusion in 2004 to set up and implement a methodology for intelligence-led law enforcement at EU level, a new role in this respect was assigned to Europol in the area of threat assessment and risk analysis. In 2006, the first Organised Crime Threat Assessment (OCTA) was published, replacing thereby the Organised Crime Report prepared annually since 1993. The then Director of Europol, Max-Peter Ratzel, described the OCTA as 'a core product of the intelligence-led policing concept'.[36] Through Europol, the EU sought to earn its own capacities to work out and deliver to EU and national stakeholders independent evaluations of threats from terrorism and organised criminality.[37]

However, the methodology of the OCTA and the quality of 'intelligence products' delivered by Europol raised certain reservations. Experts pointed out the lack of coherence and specification of the analytical language, the use of concepts without further explanation or example, questionable reliability and validity of the operational definitions.[38]

It was then clear, with a view to launching the policy cycle and improving

36 Europol (2006), *EU Organised Crime Threat Assessment 2006*. The Hague: Europol, 3.

37 Argomaniz, J. (2009), 'Post-9/11 Institutionalisation of European Union Counter-terrorism: Emergence, Acceleration and Inertia', *European Security*, 18, 160.

38 Van Duyne, P. C. (2007), 'OCTA 2006: The Unfulfilled Promise', *Trends in Organised Crime*, 10, 120–8. Zoutendijk, A. J. (2010). 'Organised Crime Threat Assessments: A Critical Review', *Crime, Law and Social Change*, 54, 63–86.

criminal intelligence capabilities developed in the EU, that the OCTA had to be reconceptualised. A European Union Serious and Organised Crime Threat Assessment (EU SOCTA) was envisaged as a precondition to the first stage of fully fledged policy cycle. It was expected that a new SOCTA should provide for a comprehensive and in-depth panorama of criminal threats and perils affecting security of the EU.

In June 2012 COSI approved the methodology used to produce SOCTA for the purposes of the policy cycle 2013–17. The SOCTA was defined as a present- and future-oriented threat assessment based on the analysis of the threatening features and aspects of serious and organised crime groups, areas of their activity and regional dimensions of those activities. It was relying on information and data provided by national law enforcement agencies as a response to intelligence requirements (questionnaires), delivered by third countries or organisations and extracted from open sources. The analysis starts from three focus points: organised crime groups, crime areas and the environment. These three aspects are intertwined with tailored indicators, which are used to assign their respective level of threat. In addition to these indicators, crime-relevant factors are also analysed with the use of horizon scanning as a method for identifying crime-prone social factors and future crime threats. The scaled indicators and crime-relevant factors underpin the next stage of the SOCTA methodology, which is data evaluation, assessment and analysis focused on present and future threats. The final result is an analytical ('intelligence') product comprising a list of recommended priorities supporting decision-making and the preparation of multi-annual strategic plans on organised crime groups and serious crime areas, in a later phase of the policy cycle.[39]

Europol's SOCTA plays an important and specific role at the stage of EU criminal intelligence co-operation. It is the leading tailor-made EU-legitimated intelligence product underpinning the policy cycle in a specific intelligence-led way, supporting political decision-making and ensuring that the most relevant threats in the EU are duly and effectively addressed.

COSPOL

COSPOL (Comprehensive, Operational, Strategic Planning for the Police) was adopted by the European Police Chiefs Task Force (EPCTF) in 2004, following the terrorist attack in Madrid, as a multilateral law enforcement instrument intended to achieve tangible operational results in the field of combating and dismantling criminal and terrorist organisations. It was originally conceived as a twin project to the ECIM, seeking to enhance and make better use of the potential of available actors and instruments for European operational police co-operation. COSPOL, responding to priorities and strategies in the fight against organised crime and terrorism as set by the Council of the EU and the European Council

39 Council of the EU (2012a), *Serious and Organised Crime Threat Assessment (SOCTA) – Methodology*, doc. 12159/12 (4 July).

in the period 2004–5, was subject to Europol's analytical and organisational support as well as concrete law enforcement measures agreed by the Member States via the so-called driver, i.e. a person nominated by the leading Member State to manage the given COSPOL project, especially regarding the operational coordination such as information and intelligence flow.[40]

The pivotal role in the successful implementation of COSPOL was performed by a person seconded by the leading Member State, the so-called driver, assisted by co-drivers, be it another Member State (or States) or an EU agency. The driver was responsible for drafting and producing in co-operation with the other Member States involved in a given COSPOL project (so-called forerunner countries) and Europol an action plan setting out aims and assigned tasks. Member States were expected to deliver required information and intelligence following a request through COSPOL in a timely and accurate fashion.

In the advent of legal and strategic transformation of the EU area of freedom, security and justice, COSPOL was relaunched on a new process-based foundation. The revised format for the COSPOL entailed:

- An integral and integrated approach to the criminal phenomena, based on prevention, proactive stance, preparation, repression, and partnership among various stakeholders of EU internal security
- Launch of new investigations and support to the ongoing investigations
- Facilitation of the cross-border investigation co-operation
- Enhancement of intelligence flow
- Prevention of serious and organised criminal and terrorist activities.[41]

The Council's decision to create the policy cycle had a direct impact on COSPOL. The ongoing COSPOL projects were incorporated into the policy cycle framework with a view to further improve it as the platform for multilateral co-operation to implement the multiannual strategic plans. However, despite the fact that COSI agreed on new terms of reference of the COSPOL framework, the Polish Presidency in the Council put forward a proposal for a new platform to effectively address in a multidisciplinary integrated way the prioritised threats through Multi-Annual Strategic Plans and annual Operational Action Plans. The new platform, so-called EMPACT, was approved by COSI in 2012 replacing thereby COSPOL at the stage of strategic and operational planning of the policy cycle.[42]

40 Council of the EU (2006b), *Comprehensive Operational Strategic Planning for the Police (COSPOL)*, doc. 5859/4/06 REV 4 LIMITE (10 October).

41 Council of the EU (2009), *COSPOL Projects*, doc. 13610/1/09 REV 1 (5 November), p. 6.

42 Council of the EU (2011), *Amending the COSPOL Framework into [EMPACT]*, doc. 15386/1/11 REV 1 (3 November).

EMPACT

EMPACT (European Multidisciplinary Platform Against Criminal Threats) started in 2012 as part of the intelligence-led approach to tackling organised crime, identifying priorities and setting out Operational Action Plans (OAPs) to combat the prioritised threats to internal security of the European Union.

EMPACT is the platform to coordinate and implement all joint actions of Member States and EU agencies resulting from a given pre-set goal reflected in a respective OAP and corresponding with general priorities for the fight against serious and organised crime set by the Council.

EMPACT is built on the organisational and procedural model inherited from COSPOL. It is based on project groups, led by the driver, supported by a unit established at Europol and a project support manager being a designated Europol official. COSI is responsible for evaluating the implementation of EMPACT, including the participation of Member States and other actors. National EMPACT coordinators bear responsibility for the implementation of EMPACT in a respective country.[43]

In 2013, eight EMPACT projects were launched following Council conclusions on setting priorities for the fight against serious and organised crime, adopted in June 2013.[44] These projects referred both to regional dimensions of international organised crime (the capacity and role of organised crime groups in West Africa and the Western Balkans), as well as certain areas of criminality identified as most salient issues in the context of action plans to combat selected forms of criminality (illegal immigration, trafficking in human beings, cybercrime) and organised groups engaged criminal activities (itinerant organised crime groups).

EMPACT, still in its initial development, should be seen for now as a relevant organisational element of the overall internal management of EU policy cycle. Its task is to translate political priorities into action plans and connect EU agencies with respective national authorities of Member States. Given the close working relationship with Europol, EMPACT projects would probably be more focused on concrete criminal problems and should organise data processing and analysis along the identified threats and established priorities, taking advantage of available intelligence capabilities on EU level.

Conclusions

The emergence and development of criminal intelligence had its roots in the very phenomenon of organised crime reflecting a dynamic process of transition from individual locally based criminality to transnational organised serious crime

43 Council of the EU (2012b), *EMPACT Terms of Reference*, doc. 14518/12 (3 October).

44 Council of the EU (2013), *Council Conclusions on Setting the EU's Priorities for the Fight against Serious and Organised Crime between 2014 and 2017*, Justice and Home Affairs Council meeting, Luxembourg, 6 and 7 June 2013, available at: www.consilium.europa.eu/uedocs/cms_data/docs/pressdata/en/jha/137401.pdf.

with powerful resources and a global reach. The European Union's institutions and Member States' relevant authorities reached in the mid-2000s a critical level of common awareness and mutual understanding with respect to the gravity of dangers posed by terrorist networks and transnational organised criminal groups. Strong political impulse sent by the European Council in the aftermath of the terrorist act in Madrid in 2004, enhanced in the Hague Programme, was orchestrated with the growing activeness and organisational stabilisation of EU agencies in the field of security and justice: Europol and Eurojust. UK initiative to 'Europeanise' its national intelligence model hit the needs of the new proactive intelligence-focused EU internal security policy.

EU institutions competent in the field of criminal justice and home affairs took over responsibility for adopting legal instruments and measures with regard to criminal intelligence. As mentioned above, the Council decided to put forward ECIM and to integrate this project with the policy cycle for organised and serious crime with the aim to improve efficiency of proactive strategy of tackling the problem of organised criminality through a comprehensive threat assessment and translation of identified goals into operational activities.

The European Criminal Intelligence Model is based on the assumption that the tasking and coordination processes at EU level should be fully dependent on the key intelligence products conceived as the 'deliverables' by which intelligence-led law enforcement can be implemented. All intelligence work should be supported by the knowledge products and system products as elements that provide quality assurance to the ECIM. In this regard, the functioning of EU-wide co-operation and liaison arrangements, centralised in Europol, is meant to provide support for analysis of organised crime.

The effective use of intelligence remains the domain of national law enforcement services and their ability to prevent and combat criminal groups. However, efficiency of criminal proceedings should take into account not only the operational aspects of law enforcement in a given Member State, but also some organisational prerequisites emerging at supranational level and embedded in general strategies and operational plans adopted in a consensual way. The EU Criminal Intelligence Model can be helpful in developing and implementing strategic blueprints to tackle current problems of internal security and prepare for future anticipated threats and hazards. It also offers respective national authorities the practical knowledge required for effective management of available resources. It can be developed in four dimensions: technological harmonisation, legal approximation, cultural exchange and organisational centralisation of information exchange. These aspects are envisaged in the policy cycle, which should be seen as a working formula that enables a more effective, better organised and well-established framework of criminal intelligence in the EU.

12 Victims as individuals with rights in the European Union: their protection and their legal standing[1]

Begoña Vidal Fernández

Introduction

'Let us not forget that any of us may be the victim of a crime.' This affirmation, found in a study on the rights and needs of victims,[2] is sufficiently vigorous, as a presentation to this work, to open our eyes abruptly. In fact, the European Commission estimates that some 75 million people are crime victims each year, and every year thousands of people perish in the one million traffic accidents or so that take place in the European Union.[3]

Given that what has been said is unquestionable, no less so is the fact that we all have an interest in knowing our rights and in knowing what we can and what we should do if we were ever to find ourselves in a similar situation. These rights are established in national laws.[4] However, in a shared common territory, which is the European Union, where not only freedom of circulation and of establishment are guaranteed, but also non-discrimination on the basis of nationality,

1 The author is a member of both of the research project funded by the *Ministerio de Economía y Competitividad del Gobierno de España*: Ref. DER2012-35862, 'Aproximación legislativa versus reconocimiento mutuo en el desarrollo del espacio judicial europeo: una perspectiva multidisciplinar' (M. Jimeno Bulnes, Dir.), and 'El Estatuto de la víctima. Propuestas para la incorporación de la normative de la Unión Europea', Ref. DER 2012-31549 (M. Hoyos Sancho, Dir). The author likewise wishes to express her thanks to Antony Ross Price for the English translation of this article.

2 Gordillo Santana, L. F., 'Derechos y necesidades de las víctimas', published on the web page of the *Oficina de Atención a las víctimas del Gobierno de La Rioja* (www.larioja.org/npRioja/default/defaultpage.jsp?idtab=821408, last accessed 30.11.2015).

3 Data obtained from the *Communication from the Commission to the European Parliament, The Council, The Economic and Social Committee and the Committee of the Regions*, 'Strengthening victims' rights in the EU', COM(2011) 274 final, 18.5.2011.

4 In Spain, these laws are quite complete, but they are dispersed not only in different legal bodies, but also come under the responsibility of different ministries. Thus, the protection of victims of terrorism and of violent crimes and against sexual freedom are matters for the Ministry of the Interior regulated by Law 29/2011 the assistance and protection of victims of terrorism [Ley 29/2011 la asistencia y protección a las víctimas de terrorismo], and by Law 35/1995, help and assistance to victims of violent crimes and against sexual freedom [Ley 35/1995, las ayudas y asistencia a las víctimas de delitos violentos y contra la libertad sexual]. The victims of gender violence come under the attention of the Ministry of Justice and benefit from the full protection of Law 1/2004 on integral protection measures against gender violence [Ley 1/2004 de protección integral contra la violencia contra la mujer]. In contrast, attention to victims of road traffic accidents comes under the General Directorate of Traffic.

and where, precisely for that reason, the risk of 'becoming' a victim is so great, whether in the country of residency or outside it, the existence of some standards of common protection, equal for all European citizens, is essential, alongside some mechanisms that reach beyond national territories.

The above shows that it is as much a national as a cross-border problem, requiring the actions of the European Union.[5]

Certainly, the needs of the victims of cross-border crime differ from those of the victims of crimes with no ramifications beyond the scope of national territory. But everybody shares the same basic necessities: respectful treatment of their person and dignity, the right to receive support, protection of their physical integrity and of their property, and access to justice, to seek the reparation and the compensation that they deserve.[6]

Evolution of the appearance of victims in the European panorama and their consideration

It may be asked why the victims have had enough of being the forgotten ones in the system, given that *ius puniendi* (the monopoly of the State to impose criminal law) was construed as compensation to the victim, in opposition to retribution and its excesses, which make the reconstruction of social peace impossible. The Democratic Rule of Law, the present dominance of the 'Rule of Law' is a consequence of the social pact in which citizens have freely decided to place *ius puniendi* in the hands of the State, the coercive power on those citizens who attack the peaceful conviviality of society. On the basis of that transference, we have passed on the responsibility of the citizen-victim to the State as opposed to the citizen-offender, who assumes the role of doing justice in the name of society, which is how the victim has slipped into a background role.[7] This step backwards for the victim has not only meant little or no consideration of the needs of the victim, but also the duty that is imposed upon the victim by the judicial criminal system, as a witness of a criminal offence.

Up until not so very recently, the victim of a crime or a serious infraction was found in the lamentable situation of having had to suffer the circumstances of the crime and of having to comply with the obligation of attending the proceedings as a witness, under the threat of being convicted for failing to co-operate with the justice system. Moreover, the victim was obliged to tell the truth under threat of a conviction for giving false testimony. In the meantime, the perpetrator of those misfortunes not only had the protection of certain fundamental laws, the violation of which would nullify the proceedings, and which also left the offender free from any obligation to co-operate with the justice system. The legal order

5 *Communication from the Commission to the European Parliament, The Council, The Economic and Social Committee and the Committee of the Regions*, 'Strengthening victims' rights in the EU' COM(2011) 274 final, 18.5.2011.

6 IP/11/585, Commission Press Release, 18.5.2011.

7 Gordillo Santana, note 2 above.

even allowed the offender to give false testimony without committing an offence. A situation that meant, in Spain, the suspension of a quarter of all trials due to the absence of the witness for the prosecution, the victim.[8] Serrano Masip warned that a statute for the victim would have to be prepared, in which the duties of the victim towards the Justice Administration would be joined to the status of the offended party, differentiating in this way the duties of any citizen to collaborate with the justice system.[9]

Over recent years, attempts have been made to renew the role of the victim in the criminal system, as a person with rights, as is the accused.[10] As Tardón made clear, it is not a question of contrasting their rights with those of criminals, nor of returning to a private conceptualisation of criminal law, but of finding harmony in criminal justice, a balance between the protection of the interests of society in general, the rights of the accused and the reparation of material and moral harm inflicted on the victim.[11]

Each victim is a unique person and should be treated as such.[12] In this area, the Commission has been working to present communications and proposals to make the needs of victims an essential part of the justice systems, together with the detention and punishment of offenders.[13]

The consideration of victims as individuals with rights in the European Union appears in the 1999 Council of Tampere, which establishes European policy on matters concerning the protection of victims of crime:

- Define the legal standing of the victim
- Guarantee an effective remedy for the harm that has been caused
- Create and develop social assistance systems that cover the most basic needs of victims.

8 Magro Servet, V. (2012), 'Preceptividad de la práctica de la prueba preconstituida con víctimas en el proceso penal', *La Ley Penal*, 92, April. The author clarifies that the non-appearance of victims in court is caused by the fear of declaring before the accused, as they do not wish to repeat what they have already previously said twice, to the police and before the examining magistrate.

9 Serrano Masip, M. (2013), 'La victima de violencia de género ante el deber de denunciar y declarar en el proceso penal', *Revista General del Derecho Procesal*, 29, 16.

10 On the interruption of the conception of restorative justice and the situation of Spanish criminal justice, see my (2008) work in: 'El estatuto de la víctima en el proceso penal en la Unión Europea/ The standing of the victim in criminal proceedings throughout the European Union', *El proceso penal en la Unión Europea. Garantías esenciales/Criminal Proceedings in the European Union. Essential Safeguards*, M. de Hoyos Sancho, M. (ed.) (bilingual edition), Valladolid: Lex Nova, 207–29.

11 Tardón Olmos, M. (2008), 'El Estatuto jurídico de la víctima', *Cuadernos de pensamiento político,* FAES, July–September.

12 Reding, V. (2011), 'Le droit des victimes', *Revue du Droit de l'Union Européenne*, 2, 173.

13 *Communication from the Commission to the European Parliament, The Council, The Economic and Social Committee and the Committee of the Regions*, 'Strengthening victims' rights in the EU', COM(2011) 274 final, 18.5.2011.

Lines of action and policy guidelines for the European Union were fixed in the Stockholm Programme[14] between the years 2010 and 2014 with the aim of achieving 'an open and secure Europe serving and protecting citizens'. The political priority of the Council over the coming years is 'to focus on the interests and needs of citizens'. Within this broad framework, it undertook to promote the rights of citizens in a Europe based on fundamental rights, 'living together in an area that respects diversity and protects the most vulnerable', among whom are found the victims of crimes.[15] So, the Council urged the Commission and the Member States to:

- Examine how to improve legislation and practical support measures for the protection of victims and to improve the implementation of existing instruments
- Offer better support to victims in other ways, possibly through existing European networks that provide practical help and put forward proposals to that end
- Examine the opportunity of making one comprehensive legal instrument on the protection of victims, by joining together Council Directive 2004/80/EC of 29 April 2004 relating to compensation to crime victims and Council Framework Decision 2001/220/JHA of 15 March 2001 on the standing of victims in criminal proceeding.[16]

For its application, the Commission presented the Communication 'Delivering an area of freedom, security and justice for Europe's citizens Action Plan Implementing the Stockholm Programme',[17] defining the policies and objectives noted by the Council in measures to be carried out within a set timetable. Consequent to its own plan of action, the following year, the Commission presented its Communication on 'Strengthening Victim's rights in the EU'[18], which proposes measures to adopt, in order to satisfy the needs of victims: a directive establishing minimum levels of rights, support and protection to victims, a regulation on the application of the principle of mutual recognition to protection measures in civil matters, and a review of the directive on compensation for victims of crimes in cross-border situations.

14 DO C 115, 4.5.2010.

15 Different classes of victim are listed under point 2.3.4. of the *Stockholm Programme* (DO C115, of 4.5.2010): 'Those who are most vulnerable or who find themselves in particularly exposed situations, such as persons subjected to repeated violence in close relationships, victims of gender based violence, or persons who fall victim to other types of crimes in a Member State of which they are not nationals or residents, are in need of special support and legal protection. Victims of terrorism also need special attention, support and social recognition.'

16 *Stockholm Programme*, point 2.3.4. cit.

17 COM(2010) 171 final, 20.4.2010.

18 COM (2011) 274 final, 18.5.2011.

The proposals of the Commission were accepted by the Council in its Resolution of 10.6.2011.[19]

The system for the protection of actual or potential victims' crime in the legislation of the European Union

We may all be victims, and it can happen to us in our State or residence or in the territory of another Member State. Regardless of whether a cross-border situation arises, all the citizens of the Union have the right to benefit from certain common standards for protection, minimum common regulations on protection and support. These common standards are established in Directive 2012/29/EU,[20] which contains an authentic common European status of victims' rights and protection of all types of crime, in criminal proceedings and on the fringes of all criminal proceedings. Other directives co-exist alongside it, which have specific objectives for protection (trafficking of human beings, victims of sexual abuse, child sexual exploitation, child pornography).[21]

The increasing exercise of the right to free circulation and residence has increased the number of people who have become victims involved in criminal proceedings in a Member State that is not their habitual residence,[22] who also have a right to satisfactory protection, and to payment of compensation. The Council of Europe adopted Directive 2004/80/EC, of 29 April 2004, on compensation to crime victims, which included victims of crimes in cross-border situations.[23]

Among the needs of victims, the need for protection stands out, above all when it is a question of especially vulnerable victims. The special vulnerability may be due to their individual characteristics (minor age, disability, fear, anxiety or personal, economic or social situation), or the type of crime (terrorism, organised crime, gender violence). The free circulation of these citizens aggravates their situation as victims, as added to the losses and general consequences of any victim are those that arise when the victims find themselves outside the area

19 *Roadmap for Strengthening the Rights and Protection of Victims, in Particular in Criminal Proceedings*, OJ C187, 28.6.2011.

20 *Directive Establishing Minimum Standards on the Rights, Support and Protection of Victims of Crime, and Replacing Council Framework Decision 2001/220/JHA*. OJ L315, 14.11.2012.

21 *Directive 2011/36/EU of the European Parliament and of the Council, of 5.4.2911, on Preventing and Combating Trafficking in Human Beings and Protecting its Victims, and Replacing Council Framework Decision 2002/629/JHA. Directive of the European Parliament and of the Council of 13 December 2011 on Combating Sexual Abuse and Sexual Exploitation of Children, and Child Pornography, Replacing the Council Framework Decision 2004/68/JHA*. On both instruments, see Hoyos Sancho, M. (2012), 'La armonización del Estatuto de las víctimas en la Unión Europea', *Garantías Constitucionales y Derecho penal europeo*, Madrid: Marcial Pons Publisher, 409–23.

22 Whereas clause (2) of the *Resolution of the Council, of 10.6.2011, on a Roadmap for Strengthening the Rights and Protection of Victims, in Particular in Criminal Proceedings*, OJ C187, 28.6.2011.

23 Salinero Alonso, C. (2005) undertook a complete study of this directive in 'La indemnización de víctimas de delitos. Comentario a la Directiva 2004/80/CE del Consejo, de 29 de abril de 2004, sobre indemnización a las víctimas de los delitos', *in iustel.com, RGDE*, 7, May.

of protection. The legitimate exercise of the right to circulate and to establish oneself freely throughout the territory of the European Union has increased the number of people who, having suffered victimisation in one State and having obtained the opportune protection, wish or have to move to another Member State with the ongoing need for their protection. This has highlighted the necessity for the protection given to a victim in one Member State to 'travel' with the victim, in any movements throughout the common European area.

New community reforms take account of the different nature of national regulatory norms on the protection of crime victims. It is articulated in some Member States through criminal procedures, in others through different types of (civil[24] or administrative[25]) regulations. Therefore, the instrument for issuing such an order is regulated at a community level in two ways: for States in which those measures are criminal law matters, Directive 2011/99, on the European Protection Order;[26] and, in those Member States in which that protection is granted through administrative or civil decisions, Regulation 606/2013 envisages mutual recognition of those decisions,[27] except for those adopted in matters concerning parental care (custody or visits) and subjects like the dissolution of matrimonial ties, to which regulation 2201/2003 applies.[28]

At present, therefore, there are numerous European and national normative instruments, which regulate the right and protection of the different kinds of victim in the European Union. There are, however, few basic norms: Directive 2012/29/EU, Directive 2011/99/EU, (EU) Regulation 606/2013 and Directive 2004/80/EC. These four legal measures guarantee, at a community

24 Austria, Germany, Sweden, Luxembourg and Finland.

25 Holland and Denmark.

26 *Directive 2011/99/EU of the European Parliament and of the Council* of 13.12.2011. Published in OJ L338, 21.12.2011.

27 *Regulation EU 606/2013 of the European Parliament and of the Council, of 12.6.2013, on Mutual Recognition of Protection Measures in Civil Matters.* OJ L181/4, 29.6.2013. At first the Commission proposed the application of the regulations on competence, recognition and execution in civil and mercantile matters (Regulation 44/2001, referred to as Brussels I) and in relation to marriage and parental responsibility (Regulation 2201/2003, referred to as Brussels II bis), for the recognition of 'civil protection orders'. However, the Brussels I Regulation recognises the authority of government employees who will never have the authority to issue certain measures on victim protection and, in turn, the Brussels II Regulation bis precisely excludes those measures insofar as they are ancillary to decisions on separation or the dissolution of matrimonial ties. Faced with the need to reform them to include these measures, the Commission finally opted for a new Regulation on the so-called cross-border recognition and enforcement of 'civil protection orders' (see Peyró Llopis, A. (2013) 'La protección de las víctimas en la Unión Europea: la orden europea de protección', *Revista de Derecho Europeo (REDE)*, 46, esp. 21–3).

28 *Council Regulation, of 20.11.2003, Concerning Jurisdiction and the Recognition and Enforcement of Judgments in Matrimonial Matters and the Matters of Parental Responsibility (Brussels Regulation II bis).* For a detailed picture of this instrument see amongst others Arangüena Fanego, C., Hoyos Sancho, M. and Vidal Fernández, B. (2011) in *European Civil Procedure*, London: Thomson Reuters – Aranzadi Publisher, 185ff. See, likewise Vidal Fernández, B., 'The child as an especially vulnerable victim in cases of transfrontier parental abduction: procedural community instruments', in *Guarantees and Rights of the Specially Vulnerable Victim in the Legal Framework of the European Union*, Valencia: Tirant lo Blanch, 2013.

level, the rights of victims, their rights in criminal proceedings, the extension of the personal protection of victims beyond the frontiers of one Member State and the right to compensation, also in cross-border situations.[29]

Community norms that seek to readjust the position of victims and to facilitate instruments for their recognition and for the exercise of their rights, which has been briefly described, paints a complex panorama. It is worth asking why a single regulatory instrument was not introduced on the legal standing of the victim in the European Union, which would cover all victims, their rights and duties in all proceedings and their protection through the most appropriate measures, whether of a criminal, civil, administrative or social nature.

Peyró Llopis[30] suggested that this panorama is the visible result of the institutional battle waged between the Council and the Commission, modified by the Treaty of Lisbon, in defence of the right to table legislation. Following the entry into force of the TFEU, the Commission saw its powers to propose regulation on mutual co-operation enlarged, at the same time as the Council saw its own reduced to the possibility of formulating proposals for directives and only if it had the support of a quarter of its Member States (today seven Member States).[31]

The European (criminal) protection order (EPO)

The European protection order is based on the fact that one person facing a threat of such dimensions that make it necessary to adopt a protection measure in the context of criminal proceedings, and wherever that threatening situation persists when that person decides to move to another Member State.[32]

Directive 2011/99/EU authorises States to issue those orders that can be enforced in any State of the EU[33] (the executing State), which will have to take the most acceptable measures (on the person causing the damage or the danger) in accordance with their legal orders (whether criminal or administrative), in order to pursue the protection of the person in question (obligation not to access

29 Except for victims of traffic accidents that occur in a Member State other than their State of residence, in which the protection is not satisfactory. They face an added problem, which is the different periods in the Member States within which compensation has to be claimed, in general too short for them to make use of this right. The importance of the problem has led the Commission to contract studies on national practice in the compensation of road traffic accidents, with the presentation of options to improve the position of cross-border victims (see the Report by ALBERT, presented on 30.11.3008, *Compensation of Victims of Cross-Border Road Traffic Accidents in the EU: Comparison of National Practices, Analysis of Problems and Evaluation of Cross-Border Victims*).

30 'La protección de las víctimas en la Unión Europea: la orden europea de protección', *op. cit.* 16 and 28. The author clearly expresses the reasons for the debate surrounding the proposal for a Directive on the European Protection Order, and the importance of its legal basis in Art. 82 of the TFEU.

31 Art. 73 TFEU.

32 Hoyos Sancho points to this as the real reason of this order (Hoyos Sancho, M., (2015) 'El reconocimiento mutuo de las medidas de protección penal y civil de las víctimas en la Unión Europea: la Directiva 2011/99, el Reglamento 606/2013, y su respectiva incorporación a los ordenamientos español y alemán', *Revista Aranzadi de Derecho y Proceso Penal*, 38, April–June).

33 Except Denmark and Ireland, which are not participants.

certain places or zones in which they live or not to visit the protected person, injunction or restrictions on any form of contact – telephone, email – with the protected person, injunction or restrictions on approaching the protected person beyond a certain distance, among other possible measures). And in case of incompliance by the person causing danger, the State of execution has the authority to impose penalties, whether criminal or otherwise.

The objective of the EPO (European Protection Order) is to improve the protection granted to victims of crimes who change residence between Member States of the European Union,[34] although the European supervision order as Arangüena Fanego[35] has observed, also serves this purpose.

Recognition and execution of 'civil' protection orders

Regulation (EU) 606/2013 on mutual recognition of protection measures in civil matters also offers protection to victims who move their residence to another Member State (except Denmark). The reason for this instrument is explained in the document that accompanies the proposal from the Commission: 'During the negotiations, it appeared that the mechanisms used in this instrument, based on Article 82 TFUE dealing with mutual recognition in criminal matters, is not compatible with the ambitious standard of mutual recognition already reached for civil matters, covered by Article 81 TFUE'.[36]

In matters of mutual co-operation in civil matters, the mutual recognition of legal and extrajudicial decisions has advanced by the lowering of restrictions placed upon them, until they are substituted by a standardised certificate that contains all the necessary information for the recognition of the accompanying decision and, if applicable, its execution. Having confirmed the efficacy of the mechanism included in the Brussels II bis Regulation,[37] the regulation on the recognition of civil protection orders establishes an automatic mechanism for

34 On the origin of this instrument see Hoyos Sancho, M. (2011), 'La orden europea de protección: estudio de la iniciativa con vistas a la adopción de la Directiva del Parlamento Europeo y del Consejo sobre la orden europea de protección', *Cooperación judicial civil y penal en el nuevo escenario de Lisboa*, Granada: Comares, 251–68. The author analyses the first proposal that did not go ahead, and highlights the points that made its modification necessary.

35 'La protección transnacional de la víctima por medio de la orden europea de vigilancia en el marco de las medidas cautelares no privativas de libertad aplicadas entre los Estados miembros de la Unión Europea', *Análisis de medidas para mejorar la protección policial y judicial de las víctimas de violencia de género*, nº 12 de la Colección contra la violencia de género. Documentos. Ministerio de Sanidad, política social e igualdad, Madrid, 79–92. And by the same author: (2013) 'Eficacia transnacional de medidas de vigilancia y de protección', in *Garantías y derechos de las víctimas especialmente vulnerables en el marco jurídico de la Unión Europea* (Hoyos Sancho, M. (dir.)), Valencia: Tirant lo Blanch, 327–52. And also Arangüena Fanego, C. (2013), 'Nuevos pasos para la tutela de la víctima en la Unión Europea: la orden europea de protección', *Derecho procesal en el espacio judicial europeo (Liber Amicorum Faustino Gutierrez-Alviz Conradi)*, Barcelona: Atelier, 43–66.

36 COM/2011/0276 final.

37 *Regulation (EC) 2201/2003, Jurisdiction, Recognition and Enforcement of Judgments in Matrimonial Matters and Matters of Parental Responsibility.*

these decisions when accompanied by the relevant forms, even though the measures that they contain are not contemplated in the law of the executing State. So that this may be possible, total trust has to exist between the national authorities, assisted by the standardised form, which may only be issued by an impartial judge out of respect for the fundamental rights and the defence rights of the person causing the danger.

The co-existence of civil and/or criminal cross-border protection measures leads to incoherent situations in real life, as the fact of requiring for recognition of an order set in other Member States what it is not required for domestic orders.[38]

Spain has implemented both the Directive 2011/99 (EPO) and the Regulation (EU) 606/2013, with the Law 23/2014, of 20 November 2014, of mutual recognition of criminal decisions in the European Union. Relating the Principle of Primacy of European Law, Hoyos Sancho (2015) considers that as far as this issue is not harmonised yet, national authorities charged of recognition of EPOs or 'civil protection orders' from other Member States have more freedom when recognising or not these orders and for adjusting them to their own legal system.[39]

The Directive on compensation to crime victims[40]

Among the needs of the victims identified by the Commission (in its Communication 'Strengthening Crime Victims' Rights in the European Union') is the payment of compensation and reparation.

Reparation leads to the contemplation of the possibility of offering restorative justice to victims. Mediation is of special relevance among the various reparative instruments. The Directive establishing minimum standards on the rights, support and protection of victims of crime includes their right to restorative justice.

Compensation, in contrast, refers to the payment of economic compensation, at first, by the offender, to the victims of crimes and accidents, which in some cases substitutes another type of compensation.

The legal orders of all Member States recognise the right of the victim to compensation, as does the Directive on minimum standards (2012/29).[41] The problem usually arises when the perpetrator of the offence is insolvent or can not be identified or convicted, and this is aggravated in cross-border cases, as it adds to the difficulties over claiming the compensation. So that this right of the victim is not overlooked, the Council approved the Directive on Compensation

38 The co-existence of civil and/or criminal cross-border protection measures can lead to inconsistency in relation to the recognition of such orders in different Members States. See: Hoyos Sancho (2015), note 32 above.

39 Hoyos Sancho (2015), note 32 above.

40 *Directive 2004/80/EC, of 29.4.2004, on Compensation to Crime Victims.*

41 Art. 16: '1. Member States shall ensure that, in the course of criminal proceedings, victims are entitled to obtain a decision on compensation by the offender, within a reasonable time, except where national law provides for such a decision to be made in other legal proceedings. 2. Member States shall promote measures to encourage offenders to provide adequate compensation to victims.'

to crime victims, in 2004,[42] which is applicable to all Member States, including Denmark.[43] On the basis of that regulation, it is possible to request compensation from authorities in the State where the victim resides, and the State in which the crime was committed has the obligation to pay it. In 2009, the Commission prepared the follow-up report on the application of the Directive,[44] in which there are two opposing ideas: the authorities that are expected to intervene hold a reasonably positive opinion on the functioning of the compensation regime that has been introduced, while those requesting compensation (the victims) consider the planned process lengthy and complicated. With this information, the Commission has proposed a review of the Directive that will make the compensation system more accessible. It will provide more information to citizens on its existence and on the procedures, ensuring compliance with language requirements, and greater clarity and transparency in the key elements of the compensation systems: the offences to be included in each national system and which injuries are covered.

The legal standing of victims of crime in the European Union

Directive 2012/29 of 25 October establishing minimum standards on the rights, support and protection of victims of crime, and replacing Council Framework Decision 2001/220/JHA

Directive 2012/29 substitutes the 2001 Framework Decision on the standing of victims in criminal proceedings, which although limited to criminal proceedings, signalled a great step forward; however, it did not reach the desired objective of harmonisation.[45]

Given that it substitutes the Framework Decision, no more than a reference is needed to the studies and works published in this area to see aspects of the

42 See the exhaustive study by García Rodríguez, M. J. (2005), 'Marco jurídico y nuevos instrumentos para un sistema europeo de indemnización a las víctimas de delitos', *Boletín de Información del Ministerio de Justicia*, 1980–81, Madrid, 7–32.

43 As it is not an instrument of mutual co-operation, it is outside the scope of the opt-out clause which applies to Denmark, since the signing of the Treaty of Maastricht in 1992. The Directive was adopted on the legal basis of the former Article 308 TEC (now Article 235 TFEU), which makes the Union responsible for reaching one of the objectives fixed in the treaties (in this case, of removing the obstacles to the free circulation of people and services throughout the Member States).

44 *Report from the Commission to the Council, the European Parliament and the European Economic and Social Committee on the Application of Council Directive 2004/80/EC Relating to Compensation to Crime Victims*, of 20.4.2009 (COM (2009) 170 final).

45 The *Report from the Commission Pursuant to Article 18 of the Council Framework Decision of 15 March 2001 on the Standing of Victims in Criminal Proceedings (2001/220/JHA) of 20.4.2009* (COM(2009) 166 final) highlighted the weakest point in the regulation: its origin under the Third Pillar, as a Framework Decision, which allowed many of the provisions to be applied through non-binding regulations, which in reality prevented any review of whether they were applied in practice.

new regulation that coincide with its earlier version.[46] But the Directive widens its field of application, both in extension as well as in intensity: it incorporates new rights and obligations, and reinforces those contemplated in the Framework Decision.[47]

By extension, it is a regulation directed at all victims, both those directly offended as well as those harmed by the crime. Thus, Article 2, when defining the 'victim', speaks about the person affected by the crime in the first paragraph, and those harmed by the crime in the second paragraph.[48] This conceptual breadth will necessarily be restricted to the determination of rights and procedural possibilities, which correspond to the different subjects affected by the illegal activity.[49] It also responds to all the victims, regardless of the type of crime[50] and to

46 See Vidal Fernández (2008), note 10 above, 307–31, in which the author undertakes a detailed study of the Framework Decision, on its interpretation by the European Court of Justice to its precepts, as well as a critical evaluation. See also the relevant bibliographic references.

47 These are new rights recognised for the victim's families, the right to access services of all types, to the return of property seized during criminal investigations, to an individual assessment of the degree of their vulnerability, to challenge a decision not to provide an interpreter or translator. With regard to the procedural rights, the right to file the complaint with the authorities of their state of residence, to obtain a copy of the complaint and statements made to the police, to give testimony immediately after an offence and with guarantees to respect their privacy, and to request a review of a decision not to continue with the proceedings.
Rights already recognised in the Framework Decision are reinforced, such as the right to information, the right to translation and interpreting, the right to criminal mediation (that is understood in a wider sense in the Directive as a right to any other measure of restorative justice), the obligation to give appropriate training to professionals and public employees who have frequent contact with crime victims.

48 Article 2 of Directive 2012/29 defines the 'victim' as: 'i) a natural person who has suffered harm, including physical, mental or emotional harm or economic loss which was directly caused by a criminal offence, and ii) family members of a person whose death was directly caused by a criminal offence and who have suffered harm as a result of that person's death.'

49 As will be seen further on, some of the rights that are recognised cannot apply to people who are merely affected by the crime: the right to services of restorative justice.
Galaín Palermo highlights the transcendence of the difference between a broad concept and strict concept of the victim on this point, where he covers the topic of victim reparation from a criminal perspective, as a third punitive line: 'A broad concept of the victim should be accepted, for the purposes of *ex delicto* civil liability, including everything seen to have been directly or indirectly affected by the harm that the crime caused, of course, as the offended party in the crime. The concept of the victim has to be restricted, for the purposes of criminal reparation that might arise from consensus and might constitute a functional equivalent to the sentence. The victim that can participate in a restorative justice agreement that leads to a resolution of the criminal legal conflict (legal concord) and that, in addition, could arrive at a resolution of the social conflict (social peace), can only be the person offended by the crime, who directly suffered the criminal behaviour or who is the legal owner of the legal goods that were damaged or endangered. . . . For the purposes of reparation as an equivalent function of the punishment that allows the legal conflict to be resolved and the social conflict, the person offended by the crime, who directly suffered the criminal behaviour or who is the legal owner of the legal goods that were damaged or endangered.' Galaín Palermo, P. (2010). *La reparación del daño a la víctima del delito*, Valencia: Tirant Publisher Monografías 684, 126 and 144.

50 Hoyos Sancho, M. (2012), 'La armonización del Estatuto de las víctimas en la Unión Europea', in *Garantías Constitucionales y Derecho penal europeo*, Madrid: Marcial Pons Publisher, 409–23,

the circumstances or the place where it was committed (as it establishes minimum common standards for all Member States, except Denmark).[51]

It is also broader with regard to the strength of the rights and the protection that are afforded to the victims. There is a change of view in the denomination of the victims: references are no longer to 'especially vulnerable victims', but to victims 'in need of special protection'. All victims have an important need for protection, each person who feels especially vulnerable after having lived the experience, but certainly not all of them need protection of the same intensity, whether because of the particular characteristics of the person (children, disabled people), type of crime[52] or the circumstances surrounding that person. That is because one person involved in a particular crime might not need special protection, but might in other circumstances (for example, an offence involving injury changes if caused by someone with a special personal relationship to the victim or another type of dependency). In consequence, before qualifying a victim as 'especially vulnerable', it is necessary to examine each personality and each situation in an individual way.[53] And the victims who are, after this individual assessment, considered to be in a situation of special vulnerability 'to secondary and repeat victimisation, to intimidation and to retaliation'[54] are also the subject of special protection measures.[55]

This special protection has important consequences in relation to criminal proceedings,[56] particularly the time, the number of repetitions and the form in which testimony is given by victims.[57] They have the possibility of making a

which contains the Directives approved in relation to specific crimes and completes a detailed study of Directive 2011/36/EU on preventing and combating trafficking in human beings and protecting its victims, as well as Directive 2011/92/EU E on combating child pornography and the sexual abuse and sexual exploitation of children, both from the point of view of the victims.

51 See whereas clauses 70 (United Kingdom and Ireland taking part), and 71 (Denmark opted out).

52 Terrorism, organised crime, human trafficking, gender-based violence, violence in a close relationship, sexual violence, exploitation or hate crime (Article 22.3 *in fine* of the Directive).

53 This change of focus and the introduction of this individual assessment was proposed by the European Economic and Social Committee (EESC) in its Opinion on the Communication from the Commission 'Strengthening victims' rights in the EU', (2012/C43/09), of 7.12.2011, published in OJ C43/2012. '1.8. The EESC accepts that certain victims are particularly vulnerable requiring specific treatment, but believes that rather than identifying certain "vulnerable victims", and thus potentially creating a hierarchy of victims, the Commission should propose that all victims of crime should have access to special measures by means of an individual assessment . . . to determine their vulnerability in relation to their personal characteristics, the nature of the crime, and relationship with the suspect.'

54 Article 22.1 *in fine* of the Directive.

55 Contained in chapter 4 of the Directive, Articles 18 to 24.

56 See, on this: Hoyos Sancho, M. (2013), 'El tratamiento procesal de las víctimas especialmente vulnerables en los últimos instrumentos normativos aprobados en la Unión Europea/The procedural treatment of especially vulnerable victims in current and recently proposed normative instruments in the European Union', in *Garantías y derechos de las víctimas especialmente vulnerables en el marco jurídico de la Unión Europea/Guarantees and Rights of the Especially Vulnerable Victim in the Legal Framework of the European Union* (Hoyos Sancho, M. (dir.)), Valencia: Tirant lo Blanch, 47–70.

57 Article 23 of the Directive.

statement before the trial begins, which – if possible – will be with a professional with sufficient training to take their statement. It should always be the same person in relation to crimes of gender violence[58] and, in the context of personal relations,[59] of the same sex as the victim. The possibility is also established of testifying in another room or by videoconferencing or other communication technologies, and of doing so as many times as may be absolutely essential.[60] The possibility of recording their first statement is available for children (under eighteen years old),[61] which may be used as evidence in court without any need for it to be repeated orally.

Strengthening the role of restorative justices is one way of satisfying the needs of victims who do not find themselves at ease in criminal proceedings. This procedure is considered more effective than the traditional punishments, to comply with its function of balancing the trust of citizens in the justice system, because it achieves the satisfaction of the victim and, moreover, confronts offenders with their behaviour and then its consequences, obliging them to assume responsibility for their actions.

However, the following factors must be taken into account, to avoid new harm to the victims, before taking a case to criminal mediation: the nature and severity of the crime, the degree of harm inflected, the repeated violation of physical, sexual and psychological integrity of a victim, inequality between both parties, age, maturity and the intellectual capabilities of a victim.[62]

Having verified those points, and as a safeguard for victims, the Directive establishes a series of valid conditions for mediation purposes:[63]

58 For the purposes of the Directive, gender violence is understand as violence directed at a person because of their sex, gender identity or expression, or which affects people of a particular sex in a disproportionate way. It is understand as a form of discrimination and a violation of the fundamental freedoms of the victim. And it includes: violence in personal relations, sexual violence (rape, sexual assault and harassment), trafficking in human beings, slavery, forced marriages, female genital mutilation, and so-called 'honour crimes' (whereas clause 17 of the Directive).

59 Violence committed by a person who is or has been the spouse or sentimental partner of the victim, or another relative of the victim . . . that may be physical, sexual, psychological and economic (Whereas clause 18 of the Directive).

60 Article 23.2 of the Directive. In the Spanish system, the victim is obliged to give testimony on multiple occasions: first of all to the police (whether or not the victim wishes to do so), for statements made in front of identity parades, once again before the examining magistrate and yet again at the trial.

61 Article 24.1a of the Directive, which includes in this precept the jurisprudence of the European Court of Justice delivered in the Pupino judgment, case C-105/03, of 16.6.2005, in relation to statements made by children in criminal proceedings. See Vidal Fernández, B. (2008), note 10 above. In the Spanish system at present, case law has accepted the pre-trial testimony of children, but it is practically impossible for an examining magistrate to agree on pre-constituted evidence for an adult victim, however much the latter may contend that taking the witness stand in a trial will cause personal trauma (Magro Servet (2012), note 8 above).

62 Whereas clause 46 of the Directive.

63 Article 12 of the Directive.

- They should be in the interests of the victim
- The consent of the victim has to be freely given (and may be retracted at any moment, ending the mediation process) and informed (especially, of the consequences of the agreements and of other possible outcomes, such as non-compliance, and if the agreement that is reached may be taken into account in other criminal proceedings)
- The offender has to acknowledge the basic facts
- The conversations will be confidential.

Obscure and clear points of Directive 2012/29

In addition to the positive results in the preceding sections, the interest in shaping a really useful instrument for victims should be stressed. The first point, for whoever may be in that situation, is to know where to go to ask for help and information on what should be done. On this point, the Directive urges Member States to set up services in various bodies, following the principle of a 'single access point' or a 'one-stop office', which cover the different needs of the victims and avoid going around in circles from one administrative service to another.[64]

Another clear point is the insistence of satisfactory training for professionals who respond to the victims, from their initial contact with the authorities (police, administrative and judicial), and with lawyers, but also doctors and nurses, social workers, etc. The purpose is to improve their protocols for action to guarantee impartial, respectful and professional treatment of victims.[65] Here, it is worth stressing the content of the Opinion of the Committee of the Regions on the packet of measures proposed by the Commission,[66] bearing in mind that routine procedure when a person has fallen victim to a crime is for that person to go to the nearest law enforcement body (the municipal police or the civil guard in Spain) to 'report' what has taken place. This fact is highlighted in the Opinion of the Committee of the Regions, as well as the fact that it is usually the local administrations (municipal councils) that from the very beginning provide refuge for the victim. In consequence, it is proposed to give greater relevance to the training of law enforcement agents, social workers and other professionals who operate at a local level. These indications are accompanied by a need for financing to turn them into reality.

In third place, the treatment that is given to cross-border victims deserves mentioning – in other words, the treatment of those people who have found themselves in this situation when moving within the territory of another Member State. In the community regulation, this circumstance is considered to generate a need for special support,[67] and in consequence expressly refers to their

64 Whereas clause 33 of the Directive, *in fine*.

65 Article 25 of the Directive.

66 *Opinion of the Committee of the Regions*, 16.2.2012. OJ C113, of 18.4.2012 (2012/C 113/11).

67 Whereas clause 38 of the Directive: 'Persons who are particularly vulnerable or who find themselves in situations that expose them to a particularly high risk of harm, such as persons subjected to . . .

rights.[68] Factors are added to the needs of all victims of crime, which arise from their transnational nature, such as differences in the language, the distance from the state of residence, the judicial and administrative system. The possibility of their complaint being presented in the State of residence or of origin of the victim is therefore important, as well as the possibility of giving testimony in a videoconference.[69]

In relation to these cross-border situations, the Opinion of the Committee of the Regions put forward a proposal to establish an 'emergency telephone number for victims in the EU', which as well as providing assistance at the place of the crime, can serve as a means of contact for the authorities in this country, when the victims return to their state of residence.[70] The proposal is interesting, but the proliferation of common and specific emergency telephones might lead to an excess of information that will finally serve little purpose due to its extension.

Among the obscure points is the possible violation of the presumption of innocence of the accused. Particularly, the regulation on victims with special protection needs in the Directive includes exceptions to the procedural regulations relating to testimony by the prosecution, allowing it to be given without the need for a courtroom presence. Moreover, throughout the regulation, measures are foreseen in favour of those who identify themselves as victims, and investigations start at that point. However, as the European Criminal Bar Association has made clear, 'when a person reports being a victim to a crime, we are unaware as to whether that person has been the victim of a crime that constitutes the object of the proceedings, and whether the person has been the victim of a crime committed solely by the accused or by others'.[71] It should be acknowledged that the Directive appears to have taken into account the recommendations pointing in that direction, as the most delicate precepts started with the expression: *Without prejudice to the defence rights . . . .*

A very large and obscure point is the lack of common regulations in matters of compensation, in the case of cross-border accidents (rail, air and maritime, as well as road traffic accidents). In addition, it is necessary to speed up such painful procedures as the repatriation of the corpses of victims, which requires harmonisation

crime in a Member State of which they are not nationals or residents, should be provided with specialist support and legal protection.'

68 In Article 17 of the Directive.

69 Articles 17.2 and 17.1b of the Directive, respectively.

70 *Opinion of the Committee of the Regions on the Package of Measures on the Rights of Victims*, of 16.2.2012.

71 *Statement on the Draft Directive Establishing Minimum Standards on the Rights, Support and Protection of Victims of Crime* (October 2011). One of its principal conclusions stands out: 'For the draft Directive, this case law means that all rights granted to "victims" and "vulnerable victims" should not unfairly interfere with the right of the defendant to exercise his right to challenge and question these same "victims" and "vulnerable victims" as witnesses against him. In individual cases, the specific circumstances of that case can lead to a different outcome when deciding how such competing interests can be respected. The ECBA finds that the proposed wording of the Directive does not sufficiently reflect this need to consider these potentially conflicting rights on a case to case basis.'

of national legislation setting up common procedures and plans. An example based on a real case illustrates this gap.[72] Some years ago, a resident of a village of Valladolid travelled to Germany to inquire about the price of a second-hand Audi car. The person in question took out an 'in-transit insurance policy' with a large insurance company providing insurance cover in Spain and in Germany to cover the risks of driving the automobile (valid up until arrival in Spain). While on a German motorway, another car, travelling in the wrong direction down the same motorway lane, crashed headlong into the Audi, resulting in instant death. The deceased Spaniard in Germany left two children and a widow. Criminal proceedings were initiated in Germany, of which the widow was informed. Her family initiated, from Spain, the administrative proceedings for the repatriation of the corpse, as well as the claim for compensation to the insurance company. At that point, the difficulties began. The first serious difficulty was evidently the language, but having surmounted that, the lawyer from Valladolid was unable to establish the information on how to take legal action in Germany, on German criminal proceedings, on the rights of crime victims recognised in the German legal system, and on their standing in criminal proceedings: whether they have to appear as a party to the proceedings or whether the Public Prosecutor will act on their behalf. Neither was information available on the timeframes for taking legal action or acting, or whether they had to lodge claims for compensation in the same criminal proceedings or in a separate civil case. The only road left open was to search, through friends and relations, for a German lawyer to gain such information, after which, to their great surprise, they found a system of restorative justice for the victim that took account of totally different parameters than the Spanish system, and with binding timeframes for the right to claim that were also very different from those established in Spain.

The European judicial network on civil matters was not up and running at the time of the events. At present, all the data on the German system in these matters may be obtained through the information contained in that network, provided that they were aware of its existence, of course. But even relying on this tool, the problem remains of having to present writs and other documents to the German courts, as well as having to appear at hearings. In this situation, on the one hand there is a clear need to improve the training of European lawyers to confront cross-border cases in a satisfactory matter, and on the other hand, the need for communication between the lawyers of the Member States of the European Union. Today, it is practically impossible for a European lawyer not to have some case with a cross-border element. I therefore believe it would be appropriate for all the Bar Associations of the Member States to plan a kind of 'specialised duty office in cross-border cases in the European Union', with sufficient training in these legal norms. In addition, these 'specialised offices' could be connected between each other through contact points, forming an information network that would function in a similar way to those that exist for judges, prosecutors

72 Example already used in another earlier work on the rights of victims, which continues to be equally valid (see Vidal Fernández (2008), note 10 above).

and law enforcement agencies. A 'European network of lawyers' that would organise and facilitate access to all the information needed by lawyers to value, in an effective way, the rights of the victims on whose behalf they act.[73]

Transposition of the Directive into the Spanish legal order: comments on the Standing of Crime Victims legislation

The timetable for implementation extended up until 16 November 2015. The European Union regulation had the virtue of giving a definitive push to the trend of recovering victims' role in criminal proceedings, which was lost when the States assumed the monopoly of *ius puniendi* focused on crime and criminal pursuit, and took their right to a full judicial protection away from them.

At present, the comprehensive protection of crime victims is constructed in Spain by the Standing of Crime Victim Law 4/2015, in force since 28 October 2015. The rights included in this law are applied to all victims of crimes committed in Spain or indictable in Spain, regardless of their nationality or whether they are legal residents or not.[74] But it does not apply to third persons damaged as a consequence of crime.[75]

The legal order in Spain already complied with the majority of the obligations arising from the community directive, with even greater protection in certain aspects. The great inconvenience of the Spanish regulation was its scattered and fragmented references. The Standing of Crime Victim Law improves the former situation of victims by considering, among other issues, the situation of victims of crimes committed in other Member States of the EU.[76] It is also worth pointing out the legislator's special sensitivity when taking into account measures designed to repair the so-called 'political' damage, by binding public powers to improve campaigns to increase social awareness and sensitivity in favour of victims, as well

73 It is true that there is a network of criminal lawyers established for collaboration between five Member States (France, Italy, Hungary, Romania and Spain): PenalNet, with the initial aim of facilitating the application of the European Arrest Warrant. Through PenalNet, EU lawyers can establish channels of communication and exchange documents with their colleagues in a completely safe, effective and confidential way over the Internet. In addition, PenalNet offers encrypted multivideo conferencing to lawyers that will allow the organisation of virtual meetings between lawyers at different points in Europe, guaranteeing the security of their communications for the lawyer and confidentiality for their client. The network of safe communications, PenalNet, began a second phase of the project in 2011, called PenalNet Plus, in which a delegation of PenalNet representatives went on a tour around Belgium, Holland, Germany, the Czech Republic, Austria, Luxembourg, Greece, the United Kingdom and Poland to present the platform and the advantages of joining the first network of European criminal penalists and the benefits that it offers lawyers, and therefore citizens, in their daily work (see www.penalnet.eu).

74 Explanatory Preamble Law 4/2015.

75 Article 2 *in fine,* Law 4/2015. It is intended to exclude with this provision a victims' group considered in other legal systems: the so-called 'good samaritans' (people who help victims, or help the police to prevent a crime or to catch the criminal) and the 'passed-by' (people accidentally harmed by the crime). Vid. *Commission Green Paper on Compensation to Crime Victims* (COM(2001) 536 – C5-0016/2002 – 2002/2022(COS)).

76 Article 17. It is also considered international co-operation (Art. 33).

as imposing mass media to respect their dignity, privacy and all other victim's rights.[77] With the same aim, it is established that lawyers cannot provide their professional services to victims of major aircraft accidents or other great catastrophes until forty-five days have passed.[78]

The best way to improve the standing of crime victims requires that every person in touch with the victim (agent, social services, health services, criminal justice services, etc.) works in coordination with each other. Article 31 of the Law 4/2015 states the possibility for public authorities and Bars, Colleges and Chartered Institutes, to prepare action protocols to make more effective their protection and support.[79]

From a procedural point of view, this norm inserts the possibility for victims' associations and legal bodies with legal legitimacy in law to defend certain rights, to take legal action.[80] It is a particularity of our system and was introduced to 'save' the legal regulations on gender violence drawn up by the autonomous regions, insofar as it is a procedural matter and is therefore the exclusive competence of the State.

Article 25 of the Standing of Crime Victims (Law 4/2015) lists a wide range of protection measures to observe in relation to children and vulnerable victims when acting in criminal proceedings, during the judicial inquiry as well as during the trial, in order to prevent secondary victimisation (avoiding repeated appearances to make statements on the facts, taking statements by specialised agents, avoiding visual confrontation with the criminal, respecting privacy of victims, etc.).[81] The Spanish Law 4/2015 leaves the door open to the practice of preparing evidence in advance *('prueba preconstituida')* in relation to the testimony of children and especially vulnerable victims (Article 26: pre-trial statements can be recorded and used in the oral hearing as evidence), which had been firmly requested by judges, academics, etc.).[82]

The final issue of the new Spanish regulation that needs to be emphasised is that of the new faculties recognised towards crime victims in the enforcement of

77 Article 72 *Estatuto de la víctima del delito.*

78 Article 8 Ley 4/2015.

79 Spain has developed several action protocols regarding special victims (gender violence victims) with very good results, coordinating the police action with the judicial one, or with the Bar. See García Rodríguez, M. J. (2015), 'Buenas prácticas para la protección y asistencia a las víctimas en el sistema de justicia penal', Madrid, *Boletín del Ministerio de Justicia*, 2174.

80 The First Final Disposition *(Disposición Final Primera)*, that modifies the criminal procedural Spanish law, inserts a new Article 109 bis, of which number 3 states: 'The associations of victims of the specific punishable act that is the object of criminal proceedings and the legal persons that are legitimately recognised in law to defend the rights of their members or third parties may bring criminal causes and civil actions as independent parties to the prosecution and may bring civil actions as a civil party.'

81 See also Articles 19 to 22 Spanish Law 4/2015, which establish similar protection measures to all crime victims.

82 See Magro Servet, V. (2012), 'Preceptividad de la práctica de la prueba preconstituida con víctimas en el proceso penal', *La Ley Penal*, 92, April; Burgos Ladrón de Guevara, J. (2015), 'La tabla de garantías de la víctima en el proyecto de reforma del proceso penal español', *Diario La Ley*, 8518, 14 April.

sentence phase.[83] The Spanish Law 4/2015 increases the crime victim's participation in enforcement of sentences to an active prominence in two levels: ***direct*** (by allowing them to appealing some enforcement judgements) and ***indirect*** (allowing them to request particular judicial measures for criminals on probation to guarantee their security).[84]

The Charter of Fundamental Rights of the European Union establishes in its Article 47 (first paragraph): 'Everyone whose rights and freedoms guaranteed by the law of the Union are violated has the right to an effective remedy before a tribunal in compliance with the conditions laid down in this Article.' An effective remedy before a tribunal is a crime victim's right, as important as guarantees of a fair trial for criminals. The Directive 29/2012 has put this issue on the agenda of all legislators of the European Union. Justice is a right of every citizen. States have the obligation to make justice, not only by pursuing the guilty or responsible, but also by compensating victims for its mistake in not maintaining social peace and security. It is important to pay attention to this point, as it means that ruling on the standing of crime victims in criminal proceedings cannot be substituted by other means of dispute resolution, as restorative justice. This tool can sometimes be useful in satisfying crime victims, but national legal systems cannot avoid their obligation of doing justice, and so, of establishing the legal frame with which to do this in criminal proceedings.

Spain already had a good regulation in place for the crime victim's procedural rights, but this was scattered within multiple regulations. The Directive has driven the Spanish legislator to set definitively the Standing of Crime Victims Law, a rule with a very long way to go.

83 All in Article 13, Spanish Law 4/2015.

84 Nistal Burón, J. (2015), 'La participación de la víctima en la ejecución penal. Su posible incidencia en el objetivo resocializador del victimario', *Diario La Ley*, 8555, 5 June.

13 Exploring the impact of legal culture in shaping the role of the European Public Prosecutor: the prospects for penal moderation

Constantina Sampani

Introduction

The entry into force of the Treaty of Lisbon revived the debate concerning the establishment and action of the European Public Prosecutor's Office (EPPO) which was initially triggered by the *Corpus Iuris* proposals in the 1990s.[1] The political and legal hue of the issues arising from the concept of the 'supranational' mosaic of this proposed institution has generated criticism and resistance from the Member States.[2] A reflection on the historical evolution of the negotiations for the introduction and formation of the institution of the European Public Prosecutor leads to the observation of two conflicting trends: on the one hand the persistent recognition of the need for the establishment of this institution and on the other the reaction of the Member States to its 'supranational' trait. The reservations of the Member States to the emergence of such an institution is attributed to their concern for issues related to good governance and its potential influence on the priorities of the daily work of national practitioners at the national level, given that the European Public Prosecutor will have to operate in close co-operation with the national prosecutors.[3] In setting the profile and main rationale of this future institution, the European Public Prosecutor will be a body that will investigate and prosecute offences against the Union's financial interests.[4] Article 86 of the Treaty on the Functioning of the European

1 In the second half of the 1990s, the European Commission funded an academic study which proposed a so-called *Corpus Iuris* whose aim would be to fight fraud affecting the Community's financial interests. The *Corpus Iuris* was a mini criminal code that contained definitions of various criminal offences (e.g. fraud, money laundering, corruption) and provisions on criminal procedure, part of which was the controversial proposal for the establishment of the institution of the European Public Prosecutor's Office. See Mitsilegas V. (2009), *EU Criminal Law*, Oxford: Hart Publishing, 67.

2 See contents of the follow-up report on the Green Paper on the criminal law protection of the financial interests of the Community and the establishment of a European Prosecutor, COM(2003) 128 final, Brussels, 19 March 2003.

3 Ligeti, K. and Simonato, M. (2013), 'The European Public Prosecutor's Office: Towards a Truly European Prosecution Service?', *New Journal of European Criminal Law*, 4, at 8–9.

4 Proposal for a Directive of the European Parliament and of the Council on the fight against fraud

Union (TFEU)[5] provides that '[i]n order to combat crimes affecting the financial interests of the Union, the Council . . . may establish a European Public Prosecutor's Office from Eurojust'.[6] A primary impediment in establishing the proposed institutional model is that the extent of the offences against the financial interests of the EU is not supported by reliable statistics and, therefore, the need for the problem to be addressed is not justified. The counter-arguments, however, are that the EPPO would guard more effectively against offences with a growing cross-border dimension and the national practitioners will investigate and prosecute only the national part of the offence.[7]

It was to this effect that the European Commission, at the Nice Intergovernmental Conference, proposed a robust reaction to the phenomenon of transnational crime against the finances of the European Union by highlighting the fragmented picture of the European law enforcement mechanism and reaffirming the need for the establishment of the EPPO.[8] The concern for the protection of the financial interests of the European Commission has consolidated the request for a response that would transcend traditional judicial co-operation.[9] The lack of statistical data alone was not considered to negate the existence of a serious problem that demanded mutual legal assistance.[10]

Alongside these considerations, apprehension regarding the idea for the development of the institution of the EPPO – as direct criminal law enforcement at the level of the Union – should be considered within the wider, continuing and deepening development of the European Union's criminal justice agenda and the deployment of criminal law at European level. The recent development of EU criminal law forms the legislative environment within which the European Public Prosecutor will operate and as a current trend in Member States for pan-European coordination in creating a unified emergent policy and law within the EU system. In a Green Paper published in 2001, the European Commission[11] expressed its desire to harmonise the criminal laws of the Member States only

against the Union's financial interests by means of criminal law, COM(2012) 363 final, Brussels, 11 July 2012.

5 Article 86, Treaty on the Functioning of the Union (TFEU).

6 Eurojust is an agency of the EU, based in The Hague, dealing with judicial cooperation in criminal matters.

7 Ligeti and Simonato (2013), note 3 above, at 9.

8 Commission's opinion under Article 48 of the Union Treaty presented on the convening of the Conference of Representatives of the Governments of the Member States on the forthcoming revision of the Treaties, *Adapting the Institutions to Make a Success of Enlargement*, 26.1.2000, COM(2000) 34, point (5)(b). It was followed by the Additional Commission contribution to the Intergovernmental Conference in regards to constitutional reforms, *The Criminal Protection of the Community's Financial Interests: A European Prosecutor*, 29.9.2000, COM(2000) 608.

9 Kuhl, L. and Combeaud, S. (2002), *From the Corpus Juris to the European Public Prosecutor*, Presentation given in 2002 at the Centre for European Legal Studies, Faculty of Law, Cambridge, UK, available at: www.cels.law.cam.ac.uk/publications/occasional%20papers/Paper_7.pdf.

10 See contents of the preliminary report of the 'EuroNEEDs study', available at www.mpicc.de/shared/data/pdf/euroneeds_report_jan_2011.pdf.

11 See contents of the Green Paper on criminal law protection of the financial interests of the

to the extent necessary for the smooth operation of the EPPO, which was yet another confirmation of the mutually accepted need for the institution despite the resistance due to sovereignty arguments.

This discussion will consider the envisaged role of the European Public Prosecutor in the context of recent developments and trends in EU criminal law and whether its role can be extended to embrace the extra-judicial competence of restorative justice. An increasing number of jurisdictions within the EU, such as England and Wales, the Netherlands, Germany, Finland, France, Italy and Sweden, have incorporated out-of-court settlement procedures in their criminal procedural law. The aim of this tendency appears to be three-fold: a) to derive benefit from the pivotal role of the prosecution service in the administration of criminal justice system in order to reduce court caseload and improve cost-effectiveness in prosecutions; b) to 'socialise, humanise and rationalise the administration of criminal justice';[12] and c) to reflect the increasing political legitimacy that restorative justice has gained in various jurisdictions as a 'valuable alternative to tackle victim's rights even in the wake of horrendous crimes'[13] and respond efficiently to the individual offender's needs – all of these being considered measures that have an impact on the efficacy and perceived legitimacy of the criminal justice system. The emphasis on the need, challenges and profile of this emerging institution and the benefits and complexities of restorative justice mechanisms have been established through previous research. However, there is lacking a body of literature that poses questions as to whether, and how, to exploit the position of the European Public Prosecutor as a gatekeeper of the criminal justice system. This could include making an efficient use of restorative justice mechanisms and establishing a mutually shared legal culture of confidence in the European Public Prosecutor's role within the diverse legal cultures of the EU Member States. The purpose of this chapter is, therefore, to address and respond to this gap.

It would, consequently, be helpful to preface this account by posing the following four probing questions: a) What will be the profile of the European Public Prosecutor and what are the challenges it will face and the potential it will have when interacting with the European criminal justice system and national prosecutors, considering that it will be a key actor amid the diverse legal cultures (i.e. formal and informal law mechanisms) of the Member States? b) How will the status and role of the European Public Prosecutor sit in relation to varied attitudes towards crime and the diverse levels of punitiveness in the criminal justice systems of the Member States? c) How, after having examined these parameters in the position and environment of interaction of the European Public Prosecutor, can the restorative justice mechanism merge into the European Union picture?

Community and the establishment of a European Prosecutor, COM(2001) 715 final, Brussels, 11 December 2001.

12 Tak, P. J. P. (2008), 'Methods of Diversion Used by the Prosecution Services in the Netherlands and other Western European Countries', 135th International Senior Seminar Visiting Experts' Papers, Resources Material Series 74, January at 54–6.

13 Snacken, S. (2010), 'Resisting Punitiveness in Europe?', *Theoretical Criminology*, 14(3), 274.

d) What will be the nature of the European Public Prosecutor's involvement in this process?

This quest derives its significance from the recognition of the European Court of Justice, on the judicial level, and the ECHR on the legislative level, of the approach of a greater degree of decriminalisation and the resulting enhancement of restorative justice as an effective alternative. The role of the public prosecutor therefore attracts the spotlight, as from the criminological point of view it is part of a criminal justice system that is increasingly under pressure to respond to a high number of cases in which the prosecution service has the decisive role in the decriminalisation factor. From the organisational-sociological point of view, the investigation focuses on how the prosecution service can improve its efficiency when dealing with a large number of cases.[14]

Historical context: how the need for a European Public Prosecutor emerged

The European Commission had 'visualised' and supported the establishment of the EPPO through various channels for years. At the outset, therefore, some historical background may be useful in explaining the contradictory dynamics of this development.

A starting point was the study initiated and funded by the European Commission in the 1990s, as part of the fight against EU fraud. This initiative enjoyed the consistent support of the European Parliament and resulted in the *Corpus Iuris* proposals published in 1997.[15] The latter comprised a form of criminal code with a focus on the protection of EC financial interests, contained offence definitions and provided procedures for prosecution, trial and sanctions across the territory of the Member States as a single 'European Legal Area'. These ambitious ideas encountered strong resistance from certain Member States as a reflection of the anxiety emerging from the challenge to domestic criminal law sovereignty.[16] The Second Report on Reform of the Commission by the Committee of Wise Men[17] in 1999 repeated the need of the European Union for a body such as the EPPO, which would represent the interests of the general public. The competence of the European Public Prosecutor was envisaged as strictly oriented to the investigation and prosecution of crimes related to EU financial interests. The design of

14 Jehle, J. M., Wade, M. and Elsner, B. (2008), 'Prosecution and Diversion within Criminal Justice Systems in Europe. Aims and Design of a Comparative Study', *European Journal on Criminal Policy and Research*, 14, 93–9.

15 Zwiers, M. W. (2011), *The European Public Prosecutor's Office. Analysis of a Multilevel Criminal Justice System*, Cambridge-Antwerp-Portland: Intersentia, 2.

16 Harding, C. (2015), 'EU Criminal Law under the Area of Freedom, Security and Justice', in Arnull, A. and Chalmers, D. (eds), *The Oxford Handbook of European Union Law*, Oxford: Oxford University Press, 856–8.

17 On 17 July 2000 the European Council instituted a group of independent experts, the so-called Committee of Wise Men on the Regulation of European Securities Markets, with the aim to develop proposals for making the regulatory process for EU securities legislation more flexible, effective and transparent.

the EPPO was based on the idea of concentrating on its essential competence to present criminal cases relating to EU fraud, but with a simultaneous respect for the jurisdiction of national courts without implying any fundamental effects on national legal systems. The report also mentioned that it would be part of the responsibilities of the European Public Prosecutor to ensure the co-operation and coordination of national prosecution services and the prosecution before different national courts. The model was considered to be of a hybrid nature with a view to protecting national jurisdiction and keeping the Community structure to a bare minimum, but with the European Public Prosecutor being able to direct how prosecutions are to be 'selected, prioritised and conducted independently from instructions emanating from national services'.[18]

To advance the public debate on the issue of the European Public Prosecutor, the European Commission published a Green Paper on 11 December 2001 with the title 'Criminal law protection of the financial interests of the Community and the establishment of a European Prosecutor'.[19] A considerable onward movement of the Green Paper was that it widened the debate and raised questions for all interested parties (including practitioners, judges and prosecutors in Member States) on the need for a European Public Prosecutor, its institutional organisation and relationship with existing bodies, legal powers, harmonisation of substantive criminal law and rules of procedure.[20] In 2003, a follow-up report to the Green Paper was published in which several contributions were made by governmental and non-governmental actors. Member States' opinions on the need for a European Public Prosecutor were divided, with government bodies appearing more cautious about the European Public Prosecutor than other groups as, for instance, representatives from NGOs active in this field and organisations of defence lawyers.[21]

The legal basis, however, for the establishment of the European Public Prosecutor[22] was first set up when the representatives of the then twenty-five Member States of the European Union signed the Treaty establishing a Constitution for Europe (TCE).[23] The Constitution for Europe failed to complete the ratification procedure, due to its rejection by France and the Netherlands in 2005, but the Treaty of Lisbon[24] retained the legal basis for the establishment of the EPPO and the wider amendments to the field of European criminal law.[25]

18 Committee of Independent Experts, Second Report on Reform of the Commission, Volume II, 10 September 1999, 36–7, available at: www.europarl.europa.eu/experts/default_en.htm.

19 Green Paper, note 11 above.

20 *Eurojust News*, Issue 8, May 2013, 1–2, available at: www.eurojust.europa.eu/doclibrary/corporate/newsletter.

21 Kuhl and Combeaud (2002), note 9 above.

22 Article III-274 of the Constitution for Europe.

23 Treaty establishing a Constitution for Europe, OJ C 310, 16 December 2004.

24 The Treaty of Lisbon (or Lisbon Treaty) consolidates the two treaties that formed the constitutional basis of the European Union, the Maastricht Treaty and the Treaty establishing the European Community, which was renamed the Treaty on the Functioning of the European Union (TFEU).

25 For instance, the list of crimes provided has been extended in comparison to the previous regulation. According to Article 83(1) TFEU: 'These areas of crime are the following: terrorism, trafficking

After a period of uncertainty, the Treaty of Lisbon, i.e. the Treaty on European Union (TEU) and the Treaty on the Functioning of the Union (TFEU), entered into force on 1 December 2009.

In December 2009, the European Council also approved the Stockholm Programme for 2010–14, according to Article 68 TFEU, focusing on 'an open and secure Europe serving and protecting the citizens'. The Stockholm Programme acknowledged the need for a systematic reduction of the vulnerability of the financial system due to the availability of opportunities for organised crime as a consequence of the globalised economy. Reference to the EPPO is made under point 3.1.1. of the Stockholm Programme:

> In the field of judicial cooperation, the European Council emphasises the need for Member States and Eurojust to implement thoroughly Council Decision 2009/426/HA of the 16 December 2008 on the strengthening of Eurojust, which, together with the Lisbon Treaty, offers an opportunity for the further development of Eurojust in the coming years, including in relation to initiation of investigations and resolving conflicts of competence. On the basis of an assessment of the implementation of this instrument, new possibilities could be considered in accordance with the relevant provisions of the Treaty, including giving further powers to the Eurojust national members, reinforcement of the powers of the College of Eurojust or the setting-up of a European Public Prosecutor.

In April 2010, the European Commission proposed an Action Plan which implemented the Stockholm Programme and confirmed the intention to prepare for the establishment of the EPPO with the core responsibility to investigate, prosecute and bring to judgment offences against the EU's financial interests.

The European Commission then announced its parallel action in reforming the regulation for Eurojust and setting up the EPPO with new proposals made in 2013.[26]

The Commission's Communication on better protection of EU financial interests of 2013 acknowledged once again the urgent need to 'afford effective protection' to the rights of the individuals and companies affected by fraud, particularly in times of fiscal consolidation, where 'every euro counts'. This obligation of protection provided in the EU treaties and the case law of the European Court of Justice was reaffirmed in contrast to the remaining insufficient protection in Member States of fraud, corruption and other offences affecting the EU budget. The same Communication mentioned that research[27] and statistics[28] indicate that

in human beings and sexual exploitation of women and children, illicit drug trafficking, illicit arms trafficking, money laundering corruption, counterfeiting of means of payment, computer crime and organised crime.'

26 *Eurojust News*, note 20 above.

27 Euroneeds study. A preliminary report of this study is available on the website of the Max Planck Institute for Foreign and International Criminal Law (www.mpicc.de).

28 OLAF ten-year activity report.

criminal investigations into fraud are frequently obstructed by divergent legislation, uneven enforcement efforts, lack of sufficient national resources and the recurrent need to gather evidence outside the national territory of the Member States.[29] To this end the Proposal for a Council Regulation on the establishment of the European Public Prosecutor's Office sought to define the competences and procedures of the EPPO with the aim of correcting the deficiencies of the current enforcement regime and of creating consistency and coordination to these efforts. The general consensus of all debates is also reflected in the latest proposal confirming the need for an EPPO that holds a core cross-boundary role but is independent from the Member States and other European institutions, respects the boundaries of national jurisdictions and co-operates and coordinates with the national prosecution services.[30]

An overview of the developments towards the establishment of the European Public Prosecutor leads to two core observations: one is the manifested respect to the individuality and boundaries of national jurisdictions as a reassuring response to the sovereign resistance of the Member States, and second, the cautious attempt to form an institution for a coherent reaction to financial crime that will gain legitimacy through building up the mutual trust of national jurisdictions and to acquire a European identity. The dual nature of this agenda poses further significant but challenging questions: can this emerging institution encapsulate efficiently 'varying structures and convergent trends'[31] of the diversified European formal legal systems and informal legal cultures? Should consideration be dedicated to local debates and 'palace wars' that reveal persistent differences?[32] Which actors will translate national into transnational features and standards in shaping the EPPO and in what sense will the actors who are involved in the making of these common features and standards be representative of others in their legal cultures?[33] And even further, would there be normative and cultural cross-cultural issues and values amongst the Member States that would support the extension of competence of the European Public Prosecutor to consider alternatives to formal criminal procedure, such as administrative procedures and restorative justice?

The aim of posing these questions, with the view of bringing about common features and standards in the design of the EPPO, is to gain an in-depth

29 See Communication from the Commission to the European Parliament, the Council, the European Economic and Social Committee and the Committee of the Regions, *Better Protection of the Union's Financial Interests: Setting up the European Public Prosecutor's Office and Reforming Eurojust*, 17 July 2013, COM(2013) 532, 3.

30 See Proposal for a Council Regulation on the establishment of the European Public Prosecutor's Office, 17 July 2013, COM(2013) 534, 2.

31 Jehle, J.-M., Wade, M. and Elsner, B. (2000), 'Prosecution in Europe: Varying structures, convergent trends', *European Journal on Criminal Policy and Research*, 8, 27–42.

32 Dezalay Y. and Garth, B. G. (2002), *The Internationalization of Palace Wars. Lawyers, Economists, and the Contest to Transform Latin American States*, Chicago and London: University of Chicago Press, 7.

33 Merry, S. E. (2005), *Human Rights and Gender Violence. Translating International Law into Local Justice*, Chicago: Chicago University Press, 224–5.

understanding of whose standards are likely to be reflected in the profile of this institution and the potential effects of doing so on its legitimacy. And more specifically, the speculation of extending its traditional role to alternatives to formal criminal procedure is to be explored between and within different legal systems and cultures without falling into the trap of what can be 'learned' for immediate policy purposes from existing arrangements in certain jurisdictions.[34]

The profile of the European Public Prosecutor and its position in the broader context of the European law enforcement area

The recognition of the key role of the European Public Prosecutor as a public authority, who 'on behalf of society and in the public interest ensures the application of the law where the breach of the law carries a criminal sanction',[35] is directly reflected in the formal heading of Chapter 4 in the TFEU 'Judicial Cooperation in Criminal Matters' and the following Chapter 5 'Police Cooperation', which suggest an attempt for co-operation further than the creation of a conventional criminal code or catalogue of criminal offences.[36]

The emergence of EU criminal law has caused the surprise or even objection of many people on the basis that criminal law was outside the agreed competence of the Community[37] and should, therefore, remain exclusively a political and legal reserve of national sovereignty.[38] The Member States, however, have since the 1970s showed an increasing interest in co-operating in the field of criminal law in the context of the European Union, in addition to the traditional environment of the Council of Europe. At its dawn, the co-operation was based on specific initiatives (e.g. the 'Trevi Groups' established in 1975 by the European Council)[39] rather than elaborate programmes. The deepening of the economic integration of the Member States had a considerable influence on the rapid expansion of the co-operation in the field of criminal justice. The dynamic of a continuously intensifying co-operation in the area of criminal law commenced with the Schengen instruments of 1985 and 1990.[40] This was then continued with the 1992 Treaty

34 Nelken, D. (2013), 'Can Prosecutors Be Too Independent? An Italian Case Study', in Daens, T., Van Zyl Smit, D. and Snacken, S.(eds), *European Penology?*, Oxford and Portland, OR: Hart Publishing, 249.

35 See Recommendation Rec (2000) 19, *The Role of Public Prosecution in the Criminal Justice System*, adopted by the Committee of Ministers of the Council of Europe on 6 October 2000, 4.

36 Harding (2015), note 16 above, 848.

37 *Ibid.*, 838.

38 Turner, J. I. (2012), 'The Expressive Dimension of EU Criminal Law', *American Journal of Comparative Law*, 60, 555.

39 The Trevi groups were concerned with combating terrorism, police cooperation and exchange of information on police equipment, public order and football hooliganism, police training, forensic science and other scientific or technical matters and serious organised international crime. Bunyan, T., 'Trevi, Europol, and the European State' available at: www.statewatch.org/news/handbook-trevi.pdf.

40 The Schengen Treaties of 1985 and 1990 provided for the opening of borders to foreign police officers and information exchange.

of Maastricht,[41] the 1997 Treaty of Amsterdam[42] and the multi-annual European Council programmes (e.g. the Tampere and the Hague Programmes) and other developments for police and judicial co-operation in criminal matters.[43] All of these legislative and political measures prepared the ground for the provisions of the TFEU on the European Public Prosecutor's Office.[44]

In September 2011 the European Commission published a Communication that aimed to provide the framework for the further development of EU criminal policy in the dawn of the Lisbon Treaty.[45] This Communication is one in a series of documents and instruments published by European institutions, communications, resolutions, draft legislation and directives sketching a 'roadmap' towards an EU criminal law.

The deployment of criminal law at the European level attracts the attention of three major tensions: globalisation versus local diversity; security versus justice and rights protection; and criminalisation versus soft compliance.[46] In the Communication of 2011, the sensitivity of criminal law policy is recognised as a consequence of the substantial differences amongst the national systems regarding sanction types and levels and also in terms of the classification of certain conduct as an administrative or criminal offence. It is also acknowledged that the legal framework under the Lisbon Treaty provides fresh opportunities to develop EU criminal law legislation through mutual recognition and the harmonisation of national rules. But there is also the aim of maintaining the values of cultural and political diversity as an efficient response to the contemporary cross-border dimension of many crimes, and ensuring that criminals can neither escape through borders 'nor abuse the differences between national legal systems for criminal purposes'.[47] Another point of focus of the Communication is the balance between serving security interests and fulfilling the expectations for justice and rights protection, an objective that is intrinsic in the very terminology of 'freedom, security and justice'.[48]

An axiological tension within the Communication is manifested in relation to the enforcement culture; criminal investigations and sanctions are regarded as having a significant impact on citizens' rights and a stigmatising effect.[49] The 'strong' sanctions-based adversarial approach is therefore deemed to be a suitable

41 The 1992 Treaty of Maastricht introduced the 'Pillar' structure, which allowed for further criminal law cooperation through an intergovernmental format.

42 The 1997 Treaty of Amsterdam continued the development of the European criminal law cooperation with the introduction of the Area of Freedom, Security and Justice.

43 Zwiers, M. W. (2011), *The European Public Prosecutor's Office. Analysis of a Multilevel Criminal Justice System*, Cambridge-Antwerp-Portland, OR: Intersentia, 1–3.

44 Article 86 TFEU.

45 European Commission, 'Towards an EU Criminal Policy: Ensuring the effective implementation of EU policies through criminal law' COM(2011) 573 final.

46 Harding, C. and Banach-Gutierrez, J. B. (2012), 'The Emergent EU Criminal Policy: Identifying the Species', *European Law Review*, 37, 758–61.

47 European Commission (2011), note 45 above.

48 Harding and Banach-Gutierrez (2012), note 46 above, at 758–61.

49 European Commission (2011), note 45 above.

response to criminal conduct only when this is considered to be 'essential' to achieve an effective policy implementation and when no other civil or administrative sanctions can provide a sufficient response to it. The criminalisation and criminal procedure is assumed by the Commission to be a measure of last resort, an ***ultima ratio***, which will be criminologically informed by an impact assessment.[50] Alongside this approach the appropriate type of sanction is considered to be the one that reaches the global objective of being 'effective, proportionate and dissuasive' and hence depending on the seriousness and character of the breach of law, administrative sanctions may be more suitable, effective and speedy than criminal sanctions in achieving the desired enforcement level.

The Communication, however, prompts a further enquiry as to whether the picture of the European national legal systems' provisions on sanctions and penal policies are so uniquely individual that an attempt to grasp convergences and transform 'national into transnational' would be prohibited by fragmentation or whether there is a distinct 'European identity' in the overall approach, norms and values. Within the same context, the claims of the Communication pose the question as to whether the role of the public prosecutor has the same meaning and implications across the different legal systems and legal cultures of Member States and whether such a 'European' institution can reflect this diversity fairly and effectively. Finally, if one was to speculate that the 'institutional architecture'[51] of the European Public Prosecutor was to include a dimension in its competence to alternatives to formal criminal procedure, would this dimension deal efficiently with the complexities of punitive tendencies in different parts of Europe,[52] public attitudes to crime and the need to respond to fluctuations in 'wider social fears and insecurities'.[53] In other words, an investigation not only of the formal legal systems but also the underlying 'mentalities and sensibilities'[54] can provide insights and inform the construction of this emerging institution.

The EPPO and its interaction with the national prosecutors: challenges and potential

The EPPO will be expected to operate in close co-operation with the national prosecution services and its capacity to do so depends at least partially on the compatibility of this supranational institution with the national prosecution services.[55]

50 Harding and Banach-Gutierrez (2012), note 46 above, at 763–4. See also the discussion by Lahti in Chapter 5 of this volume.

51 The term 'institutional architecture' is used in Loader, I. and Sparks R. (2013), 'Knowledge Politics and Penal Politics in Europe', in Daems, T., van Zyl Smit, D. and Snacken, S. (eds), *European Penology?*, Oxford and Portland, OR: Hart Publishing, 55.

52 Daems *et al.* (2013), note 51 above, v–ix.

53 Nelken, D. (2011), 'Making Sense of Punitiveness: The 2008 Wiarda Inaugural Lecture', in Nelken, D. (ed.), *Comparative Criminal Justice and Globalisation*, Farnham: Ashgate, 12.

54 Loader and Sparks (2013), note 51 above, 54.

55 Zwiers, M. (2011), *The European Public Prosecutor's Office. Analysis of a Multilevel Criminal Justice System*, Cambridge-Antwerp-Portland, OR: Intersentia, 37.

This perspective becomes even more significant in the context of the European Public Prosecutor acting in a capacity as a guiding agency to alternatives to formal criminal procedure and especially restorative justice where the consensual element of the process prevails.

Prosecutors hold a key position in any country's criminal justice system. For a considerable number of jurisdictions, the prosecution decides on the crimes to be prosecuted, the person to be charged, what to charge, the stance it will take in seeking a conviction; and has a role in proposing the relevant sentence. While the police carry out arrests, it is the prosecutors who ultimately decide whether these arrests lead to charges. Judges preside over trials and sentence the convicted offenders, but the prosecution decides who to bring before the court.[56]

One of the challenges that the envisaged transnational feature of the European Public Prosecutor encompasses is that the context of the prosecutorial role differs substantially in every country. What the prosecutors do and the contents of their role in every criminal justice system relates to the national agenda and their respective professional background and culture. The expectations, therefore, in relation to their profile and role, differ according to the framework the criminal justice system they belong to has set for them. These fundamental differences can be generally categorised into the foundational characteristics of the continental European civil law (inquisitorial) and Anglo-Saxon common law (adversarial) systems, into systems characterised by the 'legality principle'[57] and the 'expediency principle' (or discretionary principle),[58] [59] and into criminal justice systems where political and public opinion influence on the prosecutorial role is or is not legitimate.

In civil law (inquisitorial) systems the prosecutor's authority extends to waiving the prosecution for reasons of public interest or settling criminal cases out of the court by means of 'transaction'[60] (The Netherlands) or 'conditional dismissals'

56 Tonry, M. (2012), 'Prosecutors and Politics in Comparative Perspective', in Tonry, M. (ed.), *Prosecutors and Politics. A Comparative Perspective*, Chicago, IL and London: University of Chicago Press, 41, 1.

57 'The primary premise of the legality principle is that prosecution must take place in all cases where sufficient evidence exists to prove guilt of a suspect, so long as no legal hindrances prohibit prosecution.' See Luna, E. and Wade, M. L. (2012), *The Prosecutor in Transnational Perspective*, Oxford: Oxford University Press, 146.

58 'The expediency principle . . . does not demand compulsory prosecution. Instead it allows the prosecution service discretion over the decision to prosecute, even when proof exists as to the crime and the identity of the offender and no legal hindrance bars proceeding with the matter.' See Luna and Wade (2012), note 57 above, 146.

59 A dichotomy was identified by the Council of Europe in its Recommendations of 2000 (See Council of Europe Recommendations, 'The Role of Public Prosecution in the Criminal Justice System', adopted by the Committee of Ministers of the Council of Europe on 6 October 2000, 2) across Europe between systems which are based on the 'legality principle' and those based on the 'expediency principle' prosecutions. See Zwiers (2011), note 55 above, 46.

60 Grounds to waive prosecution on the basis of public interest are, for instance, when the nature of the offence is such that would be disproportionate or ineffective to be prosecuted, or a disciplinary, administrative or civil measure would be a more effective response to the offence than a penal sanction. The 'transaction' is a form of diversion from further criminal prosecution and a public trial

(Germany), 'penal orders' (France, the Netherlands, Sweden), whereas in common law (adversarial) systems, the prosecutor is concerned with collecting evidence in order to establish whether the suspect is innocent or guilty, but sentencing is the responsibility of the judge.[61]

In most developed countries, prosecutors are career civil servants. For instance, in Sweden, Finland and Germany, legal and professional norms create the framework for prosecutors to have a reactive approach in the way they process cases. Prosecutors' decisions are based on whether they are satisfied that a crime has been committed; whether a particular individual has committed it; and whether there is sufficient admissible evidence to secure a conviction. In other countries, e.g. the Netherlands, the prosecutor has a wider scope of discretion as to what kinds of case and which individuals to prosecute.[62]

In certain Eastern and Central European countries, justice ministers may use the public prosecution service to achieve political aims. Western governments have severely criticised the practice of politically motivated prosecutions of former prime minister Yulia V. Tymoshenko in Ukraine[63] and Mikhail B. Khodorkovsky in Russia.[64] In states with long-established democratic regimes, political prosecutions are uncommon but not unheard of. In Western countries, decisions on prosecutions are expected to be made on the merits of each case independently from political considerations and preferences or emotions and the public opinion; the prosecutors are expected to be impartial, objective and protected from any political influence.

The diversified picture of the profile and role of the national prosecutors in the European scene, therefore, triggers an enquiry as to whether it is feasible to construct a model of a European Public Prosecutor that will meet the general acceptance of all Member States and, even more, whether such a model would attribute to the European Public Prosecutor the core role of determining whether cases should be referred to the court or employ alternatives to formal criminal procedure.

Despite the divergences in the role of national public prosecutors, however, in the past few decades national jurisdictions have conceded a gradual wane in the prescriptive power of mandatory prosecution under the principle of legality and a dramatic widening of the scope of the principle of expediency. For instance, although prosecutors in Germany are compelled to take action for every case before them, they are not bound to file public charges for all of them. The central limitation of resources has led to the development of a list of exceptions. Acting

by which the prosecutor offers the opportunity to the offender to settle a criminal case by paying voluntarily a sum of money to the Treasury or fulfil a financial condition(s) set out by the prosecution service. The transaction is excluded for crimes that carry a legislative prison sentence exceeding six years. See Tak, note 12 above, at 54–6.

61 Tonry (2012), note 56 above, at 7–9.

62 *Ibid.*, at 3.

63 Barry, E. (2011). 'Former Ukraine Premier is Jailed for 7 Years', *New York Times*, October.

64 Schwirtz, M. (2012), 'Russia Leader Orders Review of Oil Tycoon's Conviction', *New York Times*, 5 March.

under the principle of expediency, on the other hand, prosecutors are authorised to dismiss or defer criminal prosecution, depending on the specific circumstances, such as minor crimes with no significant public interest. A prosecutor may also consider it appropriate to impose a fine as a condition for not pursuing further prosecution.[65]

On the European level, although a Council of Europe Recommendation identified as early as 1987 the differentiating elements in the European criminal justice scene, the Committee of Ministers[66] aimed to address the issue of delays in the administration of criminal justice. This was attributed to the overcrowding of the courts due to the referral of an increasing number of criminal cases to them, including a substantial volume of crimes carrying minor penalties. The Committee of Ministers considered that the resulting delays had an impact on the reputation of the criminal law system and the 'proper administration of justice'.

The Committee of Ministers pursued the issue of lengthy delays in criminal proceedings by recommending that States should specifically focus their consideration and efforts on the more efficient use of resources and the clearer definition of criminal law policies. More specifically, the Committee of Ministers recommended that these issues could be remedied by introducing the principle of discretionary prosecution, using summary procedures, out-of-court settlements and simplified procedures for minor offences and simplifying ordinary judicial procedures. The Committee of Ministers primarily focused on the reduction of the burden on the system due to the high volume of minor crimes.[67] The proponents of the positivistic view of the law assert that whatever the discretionary power of the prosecutor, it will only be limited to low-level crimes and therefore the impact on the system's quest for truth will be insignificant. A glance at the volume of low-level crimes, however, contests such a view.[68]

The driving force in the increasingly changing trend towards alternatives to formal criminal justice, either on the European or national level, has been economics and the efficient distribution of resources. Criminal justice is costly and its expansion cannot continue indefinitely. 'Diversion' has been the watchword of the last few decades. The experience of formal criminal justice is that crime rates rise and that increasing resort to punitiveness rises geometrically with case load and costs. The escalation of overall costs reduces significantly the available resources of other services (e.g. social services, housing and schooling) and the community infrastructure that would have an impact on crime prevention and control. As for the offenders upon whom the criminal justice system has a direct impact, the court sentence frequently has very little influence in reinforcing the moral opprobrium as a major disincentive or crime preventative. In fact, the

65 Luna and Wade (2012), note 57 above, at 40–2.

66 The Committee of Ministers is the decision-making body of the Council of Europe. It is composed of foreign ministers of all forty-seven Member States. It has a dual function: it is a governmental body within which national approaches to European problems are discussed on an equal basis and a forum where collective responses to these challenges are attempted.

67 Zwiers (2011), note 48 above, at 44–6.

68 Luna and Wade (2012), note 57 above, at 40–2.

judicial avenue may be proved counter-productive as it conveys the message that the main reason for not committing crime is to avoid the unpleasant consequences of the system, rather than judge *a priori* the right or wrong of the action or consider the consequences for others.[69]

In light of this view of the Committee of Ministers and the changing landscape in individual European jurisdictions, the role of the public prosecutor could be viewed as a response to effectively reducing the large load of cases currently referred to the court. In parallel, the European Public Prosecutor can exploit the potential for the alternative to formal criminal procedure mechanisms as a means of minimising the danger in having procedures that are too fixed, incapable of evolving and irrelevant in responding to individual needs.

It is within the ambit of this recent approach that the introduction of the EPPO could be envisaged as a potentially powerful new actor on the European scene, not only in its traditional law enforcement role, but also as a gatekeeper in deciding whether to initiate or continue prosecutions before the courts, or extrapolate its competence in referring cases to alternatives to prosecution, as is already the practice in the criminal justice systems of certain Member States.

In considering the role of the European Public Prosecutor in this context, therefore, the aim is to establish whether, despite the distinctive differences, the prosecution services in different European countries can be categorised in groups with shared common characteristics. The figure of the European Public Prosecutor may then either reflect the amalgamation of these characteristics as perceived in different Member States and consistently with national systems, or emerge as a separate 'neutral' figure in the criminal justice system with the view of achieving wider acceptance and a more ready compliance among the Member States.

Using model countries

A comparison of criminal justice systems as a prelude to the harmonisation of institutional features for setting up a supranational institution such as the EPPO is required for gaining an in-depth understanding of criminal justice, not only as a formal legal system, but also as a social context within which law functions, and also of the perceptions, expectations and effects of law in society. A comparative approach serves the need of researchers and policy-makers to become aware of the challenges they may have to encounter if their conclusions are superficial or are value judgments based on prejudice as to which system is better, or the shortcomings of the other systems.[70]

69 Marshall, T. F. (1994), 'Grassroots Initiatives towards Restorative Justice: The New Paradigm?', in Duff, A., Marshall, S., Dobash, R. E. and Dobash, R. P. (eds.), *Penal Theory and Practice. Tradition and Innovation in Criminal Justice*, Manchester: Manchester University Press, 245–7.

70 Brants, C. (2011), 'Comparing Criminal Process as Part of Legal Culture', in Nelken, D. (ed.), *Comparative Criminal Justice and Globalisation*, Farnham and Burlington, VT: Ashgate, 50–3.

A comparison of criminal justice systems and the role of the national public prosecutor in different European jurisdictions based on reliable information stumbles over the obstacle of the lack of comparable statistical and legal information, as has been commented on in the chapter on public prosecution in the *European Sourcebook of Crime Justice Statistics.*[71] The enormous rise in the number of offences in Western, Central and Eastern European countries, coupled with the judicial (ECJ) and legislative (ECHR) trend to protect the recent shift of various jurisdictions not to extend criminalisation, however, makes it imperative to further explore the common threads in the prosecutorial role in various EU Member States, in an attempt to expand this recent tendency to alternatives to formal criminal procedure mechanisms.

The prosecution service is to be viewed as part of the criminal justice system – a system under the current pressure of a high volume of cases in which the prosecution level is increasingly expected to become the decisive decriminalisation stage. Integral to this is the exploration of how prosecution services can deal with a high volume of cases and proceedings, with the aim of reducing their workload and responding more effectively to individual needs.

In order to establish whether jurisdictions with common characteristics can form such groups, it is necessary not only to consider the prosecution service itself, but also to contemplate the criminal justice system as a complex whole, within which the competence and role of the prosecution service is to be evaluated. It is through this looking glass that one can observe the spectrum of the available decriminalisation and depenalisation options and the possibilities of discretionary decisions on case disposal at the level of police and prosecution services.[72]

The comparative study of different European jurisdictions strives to identify how substantial the divergences between common and civil law, Western and Eastern European criminal justice systems, are and whether there are any convergent trends that have the ultimate aim of developing an efficient and mutually accepted working mechanism in dealing with the increased number of criminal proceedings.

In order to give a representative picture of the prosecution services in Europe, one cannot ignore the historical or cultural marks on the various prosecution services, otherwise there are interpretation risks of being entrapped in oversimplified conclusions. For instance, Belgium and the Netherlands inherited their prosecution service from France, having been under its occupation. Spain, Italy and Greece changed their public prosecution services following their experience of dictatorial rule, whilst in Eastern European countries, mostly the role of public prosecution was formed after the demise of Communism.

71 Aebi, M., Aromaa, K., Aubusson de Carvalay, B., Barclay, G., Gruszcynska, B., Hofer, H. V., Hysi, V., Jehle, J.-M., Killias, M., Smit, P. and Tavares, C. (2006), *European Sourcebook of Crime Justice Statistics* (3rd ed.) The Hague: WODC. See also the discussion by Harding in Chapter 8 of this volume.

72 Jehle *et al.* (2008), note 31 above, 94.

Although the prosecution services of the EU Member States vary in their characteristics in a number of ways equal to the number of the Member States, certain models can be loosely distinguished. The criticism that may be anticipated in this attempt is that a further detailed analysis of the various levels of the systems may indicate more substantial differences amongst them than the one suggested by this classification. The context, however, of the introduction of the EPPO demands an overall approach to Member States' prosecution services with the aim of recognising the available general options without exhausting all efforts in pinpointing the details and also to combine constructive elements of various jurisdictions in the creation of the European Public Prosecutor.[73]

For the purpose, therefore, of exploring the generally available options without becoming mired in individual features, model systems can be identified. But the choice of these model jurisdictions does not imply that they are superior to other jurisdictions that may have a similar or different legal background.[74]

England and Wales can be exploited for an insight into a common law system that has introduced a separate prosecution service since the mid-1980s and which operates under a fairly rigorous requirement to bring a large number of cases before courts.[75] Within that system, the public prosecutor service does not lead the police, who have a broad discretion to deal with cases themselves, which results in a lower input to the prosecutorial level than in other jurisdictions.[76]

France provides a model for study of the oldest prosecution service in Europe and also an example for Romanic legal cultures, within which the prosecution service also includes a *juge d'instruction* (examining magistrate).[77] The countries which have adopted the French model function under relatively strict control of the minister of justice, who is responsible for giving general instructions to the service and positive and/or negative prosecution instructions in individual cases.[78]

Germany's traditional legal culture has been attached to the 'principle of legality' and mandatory prosecution. In past decades, however, an increasing number of exceptions have been allowed and the legislative ideal type is now, in reality, the exception.[79] The German model is similar to the French model. Both embody relatively stringent ministerial control, with the minister of justice usually possessing the competences to issue general and individual instructions.

73 Zwiers (2011), note 55 above, 48.
74 Fairchild, E. and Dammer, H. R. (2001), *Comparative Criminal Justice Systems*, Belmont, CA: Wadsworth Thomson Learning, 10.
75 Jehle *et al.* (2008), note 31 above, 98.
76 Zwiers (2011), note 55 above, 49.
77 Jehle *et al.* (2008), note 31 above, 98.
78 Zwiers (2011), note 55 above, 48.
79 Jehle *et al.* (2008), note 31 above, 98.

However, because these systems are based on the 'legality principle',[80] the minister's and the prosecutor's discretionary competences are restricted.[81]

The Eastern and Southern European model is a large one, as it includes a large group of countries, stretching from Portugal to Greece and north to Estonia. A historical characteristic that these jurisdictions share is that they have been subjected to previous dictatorial rule or Communist regimes, and therefore they were directly exposed to the experience of the abuses that an executive-controlled public prosecution service may generate. In an effort to eradicate the memory of this experience, these countries have separated the public prosecution service from ministerial control, or in certain jurisdictions, at most they allow general instructions by parliament or government minister. The Prosecutor General's position enjoys the same status and security of the judiciary. The Prosecutor General (the highest authority amongst the prosecutorial services), however, is appointed by the government or the parliament, for a fixed term. The prosecution service is rigidly hierarchical and operates primarily on the legality principle, although in a substantial volume of cases, a central policy covering discretionary elements in the application of law has been developed.[82]

The Netherlands provides a model of a smaller Western European country that is advanced in dealing with cases informally without a court hearing.[83] The prosecution service has final responsibility for investigations and also monitors the proper execution of court judgments. Public prosecutors are members of the judiciary.[84]

A discussion of key aspects of model criminal justice systems cannot claim to provide an informed account for the construction of a transnational institution unless considering two layers of value in every system of justice: the professed values and underlying values. The professed values are those that are officially announced through law as shared values of the participants in the system. For instance, equal justice for all citizens under the law is a professed value for most established systems of justice. A categorisation of justice systems according to the professed values, however, would be insufficient without a thorough consideration of the dynamics in a system that discloses the underlying values. Underlying values are those that, although are not openly announced, are nevertheless indicative of deep-seated patterns of behaviour and perceptions developed throughout a society's history, and govern actions within a given criminal justice system.

80 The concept of legality based on the core principle *nullum crimen nulla poena sine lege* (no crime or punishment can exist without an act of parliament) is to a large extent the outcome of the French Revolution and has been formulated as a particularly continental European concept. In Britain, the doctrine of 'legality' did not acquire the same specific connotation as in continental Europe; it rather merged into the broader notion of 'lawfulness' instead of the continental understanding. See Besselink, L., Pennings, F. and Prechal, S. (2011), 'Introduction: Legality in Multiple Legal Orders', in Prechal, S. (ed.), *The Eclipse of the Legality Principle in the European Union*, The Hague: Kluwer Law International BV, 5–6.

81 Zwiers (2011), note 55 above, 49.

82 *Ibid.*, 49.

83 Jehle *et al.* (2008), note 31 above, 98.

84 www.europol.europa.eu/content/memberpage/netherlands-789.

Efficiency, swift handling of cases, close adherence to rules or a contrasting flexibility may conflict with the value and diverse perceptions of what is equal justice under the law. Underlying values are harder to comprehend and distinguish than professed values and, on many occasions, have a greater impact on the perceived legitimacy of newly established processes and institutions.[85]

Considering legal culture: a step beyond structural comparison of legal systems

In comparing different legal systems, it is no longer enough to look narrowly at structural and rule-based interpretations. In the process of grouping legal systems into 'legal families'[86] and in the comparison of different legal systems, either with the purpose of law reform or unification of laws, the method should be to compare rules, but also to evaluate legal cultures.[87] The notion of legal culture has been a subject of debate between lawyers and sociologists. Friedman interpreted legal culture as:

> the ideas, values, attitudes and opinions people in some society hold, with regard to law and the legal system . . . Legal culture is the source of law – its norms create the legal norms; and it is what determines the impact of legal norms on society.[88]

Karl Klare provides a different approach to the definition of legal culture:

> By legal culture I mean professional sensibilities, habits of mind, and intellectual reflexes: What are the characteristic rhetorical strategies developed by participants in any given legal setting? What is their repertoire of recurring argumentative moves? What counts as a persuasive legal argument? What types of arguments, possibly valid in other contexts (e.g. in political philosophy), are deemed outside the professional discourse of lawyers? What enduring political and ethical commitments influence professional discourse? What are the understandings of and assumptions about politics, social life and justice? What 'inarticulate premises [are] culturally and historically ingrained . . . in the professional discourse and outlook'.[89]

A starting point when considering criminal justice systems and their various institutions, at least within democratic societies, is to avoid evaluating them as either better or worse than any other system. They are to be viewed as different, since they function within their own historical, political, social and legal context.

85 Fairchild and Dammer (2001), note 74 above, 11.

86 David, R. and Brierly, J. E. C. (1985), *Major Legal Systems in the World Today* (3rd ed.), London: Stevens, at 17–22.

87 Banakas, E. K. (1994), 'The Method of Comparative Law and the Question of Legal Culture Today', *Tilburg Foreign LR*, 119–24.

88 Friedman, L. M. (1994), 'Is there a Modern Legal Culture?', *Ratio Juris*,118.

89 Klare, K. (1998), 'Legal Culture and Transformative Constitutionalism', *SAJHR*, 167.

Criminal justice systems operate in a triangular dialectical relationship with the society they serve, the political circumstances that formulate their organisation and practice and the (criminal) law that defines its normative boundaries. Criminal justice systems differ, but the interrelationship of these components is what constitutes legal culture and this is what determines people's perception of what law and justice are.[90] Legal culture has a significant impact on people's expectations of criminal justice and its actors – how the procedures are organised and how their authority is manifested, how people judge whether an action or a decision is legitimate and effective; all grounds upon which people can decide whether in existing cases justice has been done. Awareness of, and sensitivity to, legal cultural issues is important if we envisage the legitimacy of an institution or criminal justice system, as these are dependent on social acceptance.[91] The term 'legal culture' is not to be considered as referring to 'insider culture' of those who study and practise the law or 'ideas, values, expectations and attitudes, beliefs towards law and legal institutions which some public or some part of the public holds'.[92] Such a definition enjoys the advantage of allowing the 'measurement' of legal culture by enquiring what beliefs, values, expectations a society holds, but it does not give an indication as to more specific questions and whether the answers would be interpreted in the same way in all cultural contexts. This approach also ignores the normative power of the dialectical relationship amongst the various components of legal culture: 'political, social and legal traditions, law and legal institutions, practice and the "structure of feeling"' which is the 'informal actual experience of legal culture – inside and outside of the legal community – and its relationship to deeply felt and ingrained attitudes about what law is and should be, and how it translates and should translate into institutions, institutional roles and the procedures and rules that govern them'.[93]

Therefore, when aiming to understand an area of a legal system or a legal institution, it would not suffice to seek optimal solutions in structure and rule in a sterile manner without considering the individual local legal cultures into which the new legal system/institution will be applied. The existing legal cultures within justice systems must inform such an undertaking. The distinct 'character' of a system is not actually to be found in formal legal rules but it is mostly to be sought in the day-to-day practice of the law.

The Anglo-Saxon systems are examples of the adversarial model, and the continental European systems of the inquisitorial model, but today almost no country has adopted a purely adversarial or purely inquisitorial system.[94] In the present

90 Cotterell, R. (1997), 'The Concept of Legal Culture', in Nelken, D. (ed.), *Comparing Legal Cultures*, Dartmouth: Aldershot, 13–32. Legal culture differs, of course, amongst individuals, local and social groups and jurisdictions, but such a discussion is outside the scope of this article.

91 Brants, C. (2011), note 70 above, 51–2.

92 Friedman, L. M. (1997), 'The Concept of Legal Culture: A Reply', in Nelken, D. (ed.), *Comparing Legal Cultures*, Dartmouth: Aldershot, 33–40.

93 Brants, C. (2011), note 70 above, 51–2.

94 The adversarial procedures have been criticised for not being sufficiently serious in the truth-finding process. In the view of Jackson, however, the adversarial and inquisitorial procedures

world of globalisation and ever-increasing interaction and consequent mutual influences, all legal systems are mixing in one way or another. Goldstein explains the matter in this way:

> These portraits of accusatorial and inquisitorial systems are, of course, idealised. European criminal procedures are no more purely inquisitorial than ours are purely accusatorial. Europeans too have accusatorial elements and mixed systems; they may tolerate more discretion than their literature concedes and may, in many instances, be moving towards greater role for counsel and more explicit protection for the accused. Nevertheless, these are central tendencies.' [95]

But even if one is to examine legal systems individually, one cannot ignore that they are the result of layered complexity. Legal systems have a dynamic nature; for instance, certain jurisdictions have 'borrowed' the legal system of one country and at the same time their historical experiences have influenced it and given it a distinct shape different to any other. Gambaro and Sacco, as quoted by Mattei, describe it thus:

> We should also consider an even larger difficulty that depends on the dynamic nature of legal systems; on the coexistence within them of different layers and sublayers; from that of different borrowings and receptions that divide the legal systems into different areas of law (e.g. public law based on the common law and private law based on the civil law as in many Latin American countries) and by different legal formants (e.g. case law and legal scholarship of a given system borrowing from sources of different legal systems such as in many modern European countries and such as in the United States during the age of legal formalism.[96]

People's willingness to comply with law and the attitudes towards the function of legal institutions seems to be more closely connected to their opinion about law, the role of the institutions and the values encapsulated in them. The core element therefore in encouraging acceptance and compliance is the shared founding values of the citizens and those who in a professional capacity practice law. The approach of using legal diversity constructively would consequently exclude the dynamic of 'lending' and 'borrowing' jurisdictions in their contribution to the creation of a common institution such as the European Public Prosecutor.

should not be compared but rather viewed in the context of two different systems with truth-certifying procedures in place, which developed through societal conceptions on how to settle disputes and enforce the law. See Van Der Walt, L. M. (1986), 'Comparative method: Comparing legal systems and/or legal cultures?', 52–3, available at www.academia.edu/933022/Comparative_method_comparing_legal_systems_or_legal_culture.

95 Goldstein, A. S. (1974), 'Reflections on Two Models: Inquisitorial Themes in American Procedure', *Stanford Law Review*, 1009.

96 Mattei, U. (1997), 'Three Patterns of Law', *American Journal of Comparative Law*, 14.

The new institution would stand a better chance of broader acceptance and fluidity in its operation with the national jurisdictions, especially in its potential role in the alternatives to formal criminal procedure, if it were to give sufficient insight into, and adopt elements of, diverse legal cultures – although there may be complexities in this endeavour to be resolved in an effective manner – so that European citizens can relate and refer to it.[97]

Framing the status and role of the European Public Prosecutor within an environment of diverse attitudes towards crime and levels of punitiveness

Drilling more deeply into the influence of culture and social structure in the formation of criminal and penal policies, the role of the European Public Prosecutor in restorative justice will now be explored with reference to the dynamic and complex European environment. The European Union comprises jurisdictions with different levels of punitiveness in their approach to criminal justice. They have different degrees of welfare expenditure, different elements of political economy, and they are constructed on different political structures that are pertinent to the existence or absence of populist punitiveness and any emphasis on human rights and dignity.

Recent criminological literature has extensively taken the approach that punitiveness in Europe has 'increased' or evolved in 'new' forms in the last twenty or thirty years.[98] 'Increased' punitiveness is said to be manifest through the decline of rehabilitative ideals, growing prison rates, harsher prison conditions, forms of punishment with a more expressive and emotional context with a greater emphasis on shaming and degradation, and a greater focus on victims' rather than offenders' rights.[99] Examples of 'new' forms of penal power are sex offender registration, mass incarceration and notification schemes.[100]

Contrary to the above, however, within the same period, the abolition of the death penalty has been proclaimed and observed in the whole of Europe, prison rates vary from increasing in certain European countries, to remaining fairly stable in others (Scandinavian countries, Germany), to decreasing in others (East European countries).[101] The case law of the European Court of Human Rights and the European Committee for the Prevention of Torture has reinforced prisoners' rights. Turning to victims, restorative justice – operating alongside or instead

97 Meintjes van Der Walt, L. (2006), 'Comparative Method: Comparing Legal Systems or Legal Cultures', *Speculum Juris*, 1, 51–64, available at www.academia.edu.

98 Snacken, S. (2010), note 13 above, 273.

99 Garland, D. (2001), *The Culture of Control: Crime and Social Order in Contemporary Society*, Oxford: Oxford University Press, 9 and 202–3.

100 Brown, M. (2005), 'Liberal Exclusions and the New Punitiveness', in Pratt, J. *et al.* (eds.), *The New Punitiveness: Trends, Theories, Perspectives*, Cullompton: Willan Publishing, 282–6.

101 The variation in prison rates over a period of time may be the result of changes in legislation, a political regime that supports a punitive climate, the economic conditions of a country and the general current culture towards crime.

of the judicial process – has gained political legitimacy in certain jurisdictions as a mechanism that respects their rights and satisfies their feeling that 'justice has been made'.[102] East European countries have now introduced non-custodial sanctions and measures; furthermore, offender rehabilitation programmes have been reintroduced based on the evidence produced by penal policies using the 'What Works' approach[103] in both West and East European countries.[104]

Reaching conclusions about the degree of 'punitiveness' in a given jurisdiction, however, involves both quantitative and qualitative aspects. Prison population rates per 100,000 inhabitants offers an indication of trends, but this information needs to be further refined by the consideration of 'attitudes towards punishment'. This should be interpreted (although not exclusively) through political debate, criminalisation in legislation, the decisions of practitioners involved in the criminal justice system (police, prosecutors, sentencers, release procedure personnel), 'popular' attitudes or public opinion towards punishment, and the attitudes of victims of crime towards revenge or forgiveness. Comparative studies of the penal systems of different countries, or the historical evolution within the same country, pinpoint that penal policies and approaches are not directly and solely related to crime rates. There is a constant and complex interaction between the decision-making of political and penal actors, and between the broader social and political changes that all West European societies experience in common and different developments in individual jurisdictions.[105]

Paradigms of diverse criminal and penal policies can be drawn between the Scandinavian countries, where prison rates are the lowest in Europe and welfare expenditures the highest, and the UK and East European countries, which have higher prison rates and lower welfare expenditure. The former appear to enjoy the highest levels of public trust and political legitimacy and lower levels of fear of crime, whereas the latter have lower levels of public trust and political legitimacy and higher levels of crime. High levels of public trust and legitimacy seem to be connected with welfare investment and social equality, rather than more punitive penal policies.[106]

Such an approach would also have to be considered in the light of political structures, as consensual democracies based on a more inclusive perspective are

102 Snacken, S. (2010), note 13 above, 273–4.

103 The author of this chapter borrows the term 'What Works' from the 'What Works Network' established by the UK Government (in 2013) with the aim of informing the decision-making of policy-makers, commissioners and practitioners by evidence-based information provided by independent specialist centres.

104 Canton, R. (2009), 'Taking Probation Abroad', *European Journal of Probation*, 1(1), 66–78.

105 Snacken, S., Beyens, K. and Tubex, H. (1995), 'Changing Prison Populations in Western Countries: Fate or Policy?', *European Journal of Crime, Criminal Law and Criminal Justice*, 1, 18–53.

106 Lappi-Seppala, T. (2007), 'Penal Policy in Scandinavia', in Tonry, M. (ed.), *Crime, Punishment and Politics in Comparative Perspective, Crime and Justice: A Review of Research*, Chicago, IL: Chicago University Press, 36, 217–96; and Lappi-Seppala, T. (2008), 'Trust, Welfare and Political Culture: Explaining Difference in National Penal Policies', in Tonry, M. (ed.), *Crime and Justice: A Review of Research*, Chicago, IL: Chicago University Press, 37, 313–87.

more welfare friendly and less prone to the populist attitude of the majoritarian democracies where increased levels of punitiveness attempt to provide an emotional response to the 'public'.[107] In the latter approach concepts such as 'penal populism' or 'populist punitiveness' refer to more punitive policies that are developed by politicians with the aim of satisfying public wishes and needs which are assumed to be punitive in character.[108]

Despite this diversity, however, the European Commission adopted in 2008 the 'Renewed Social Agenda' for the EU, in which welfare, solidarity, social cohesion and social inclusion have been described as distinct elements of the European identity.[109] In other words, the above values were recognised as providing a common thread linking the shared founding values of all European countries. The Commission undertook that:

> The fundamental social objectives of Europe have not changed: a strong commitment to harmonious, cohesive and inclusive societies respecting fundamental rights in healthy social market economies.

The Treaty of Lisbon of 13 December 2007 which entered into force in 2009 provides in Article 5a that:

> In defining and implementing policies and activities, the Union shall take into account requirements linked to the promotion of a high level of employment, the guarantee of adequate social protection, the fight against social exclusion, and a high level of education, training and protection of human health.

The consent of EU Member States to the above agenda and also the prerequisites, since the 1990s, of the abolition of the death penalty, ratification of the ECHR and the individual complaint procedure before the ECtHR, ratification of the European Convention for the Prevention of Torture and Inhuman and Degrading Treatment or Punishment (ECPT), before joining the Council of Europe (and eventually the European Union), demonstrates a convergent 'European identity' of social inclusion and a 'European community of sentiment'. The promotion of mediation as an approach to dispute resolution, coupled with the protection of the rights of victims, has now been taken up by the

107 Lappi-Seppala, T. (2010), 'Explaining National Differences in the Use of Imprisonment', in Snacken, S. and Dumortier, E. (eds), *Resisting Punitiveness in Europe?*, Cullompton: Willan Publishing; as in Snacken, S., 'Resisting Punitiveness in Europe?', *Theoretical Criminology*, 14(3), 277.

108 Bottoms A. (1995), 'The Philosophy and Politics of Punishment and Sentencing', in Clarkson C. and Morgan R. (eds), *The Politics of Sentencing Reform*, Oxford: Clarendon Press, at 17–49.

109 European Commission, 'Renewed Social Agenda: Opportunities, Access and Solidarity in 21st Century Europe', Communication from the Commission to the European Parliament, the Council, the European Economic and Social Committee and the Committee of the Regions, 2 July, COM(2008) 412 final.

EU and the Council of Europe as a strong indication of European endorsement of restorative justice practices.[110]

Conclusion

The institutional design of the European Public Prosecutor has been a subject of robust debate for several years. The EU Member States appear to be convinced of the need for its existence but are challenged by its supranational nature.

Considering the progress made so far towards the formation of the institution, coupled with increasing crime rates on the one hand and the growing tendency for decriminalisation on the other, an experimental discussion has been attempted for the extrapolation of the competence of the European Public Prosecutor to exercise its discretion in referring cases to alternatives to formal criminal procedure. The aim of this venture strives to respond to the need for penal moderation and more flexible and efficient responses to crime and individual offenders' needs. In attributing to the European Public Prosecutor such a role, however, one cannot adopt an oversimplified perspective. European States contain a wide range of divergent and subtle hues of social and political structure, historical experiences, legal culture and attitude in treating crime and offenders, but they also encompass shared fundamental values.

A difficulty involved in shaping the role of the European Public Prosecutor is the danger of being misled by an assumption that prosecuting authorities perform the same function in different jurisdictions because they bear the same name and the 'official' statement under which they operate gives a superficial indication that they are identical. The precise operation of the European Public Prosecutor can be envisaged constructively only when a researcher or a policy maker has an in-depth knowledge of the criminal justice systems within which the institution will operate and also the historical, political and cultural environments within which these systems and national institutions function. Language differences also impact on people's perceptions in the use of certain terms, and also the socio-political and cultural settings within which an institution operates produce very different outcomes. Considering these challenges, it is important to analyse an institution within a given jurisdiction at both the normative, formal level, and then also the substantive level at which the institution functions in practice.[111] An informed comparative approach would serve to 'emphasize the interdependence between law and other social phenomena'[112] and illustrate that the machinery of criminal justice and its institutions is an instrument of social control and is therefore influenced by, and influences, various aspects of social life.[113]

110 Snacken (2010), note 13 above, 285–6.

111 Cole, G. F., Frankowski, S. J. and Gertz, M. G. (1987), 'Comparative Criminal Justice: An Introduction', in Cole, G. F., Frankowski, S. J. and Gertz, M. G. (eds.), *Major Criminal Justice Systems. A Comparative Survey* (3rd ed.), Thousand Oaks, CA: Sage Publications, 16–17.

112 Kamba, W. J. (1974), 'Comparative Law: A Theoretical Framework', *International and Comparative Law Quarterly*, 23, 485.

113 Cole, Frankowski and Gertz (1987), note 111 above, 20.

Insights into legal cultural issues and subtleties will have a considerable impact on the construction of the European Public Prosecutor if we conceive this institution as one that will depend upon legal, political and social acceptance and which should generate legitimacy and its own expectations about what would be an acceptable role for it and how that may be achieved.[114]

A sensitive approach to this diversity and reinforcing the common threads of the European traditions will enable the European Public Prosecutor to respond constructively to crime by developing alternatives to formal criminal procedure mechanisms. This aim can be accomplished by building due process safeguards into procedures to monitor transparency, accountability and consistency in the operation and decisions of the EPPO and establishing fora where representatives of all Member States will exchange views and experiences on the operation of the EPPO and inform policy-makers who will actively engage with their reactions.

The idea of the EPPO is now a well-advanced concept and component of EU crime policy that has been given new impetus since the Treaty of Lisbon within the competence laid down in the TFEU, but is still a matter of ambivalent support on the part of many of the Member States. Enthusiasm for a more effective control of criminal activities affecting the financial interests of the EU remains tempered by a wariness regarding incursions into national prosecution policy and practice. Such an ambivalent attitude is to be expected in view of the existing diversity of prosecutorial tradition and practice across the Member States, and this complex jigsaw of legal culture needs to be considered carefully in the development of EU policy. At the same time, a number of competing trends jostle together in the evolution of this area of criminal policy – the efficient transnational management of certain types of crime, the deployment of limited resources, criminalisation and decriminalisation, and the promotion of alternatives to formal criminal procedure, such as administrative procedures and restorative justice. Therefore, the opportunity should be taken, in fashioning the role of the EPPO, to consider how and to what extent this emergent EU institution and process should accommodate what are now also being put forward as EU strategies of penal moderation and diversification in the methods of legal control of delinquent conduct.

114 Brants (2011), note 70 above, 52.

14 Exploring the case for criminalisation of business cartels in Europe

Patrick S. Günsberg[1]

Introduction

This chapter discusses a variety of arguments, which have been raised in the debate concerning EU anti-cartel enforcement and whether it would be desirable to introduce criminal penalties in this context. The discussion starts by asking whether cartels should be criminalised at the level of the EU institutions. Subsequently Article 83(2) of the Treaty on the Functioning of the European Union (TFEU), which is a possible legal basis for introducing harmonised EU-wide criminal law rules for hard-core cartels will be touched upon.[2] This elaboration then extends to some central criminal law principles, which have a bearing on a system of sanctions, the design of which should importantly be coherent. A particular justification for criminal sanctions, besides retribution, is their deterrent effect, especially in the context of anti-cartel enforcement, and a brief treatment of deterrence seems useful while contemplating what should be the EU's approach to hard-core cartels.[3] Finally, director disqualification orders (hereinafter DDOs) have been advanced as a viable alternative to criminal sanctions in the competition law enforcement arsenal and will be subject to scrutiny.

It may be helpful to mention that cartels could be first criminalised by individual Member States. This is something that Simonson has envisaged. In her view the problems concerning *inter alia* investigation and litigation favour a Member State-led cartel criminalisation project.[4] Further, Reindl has argued

1 This chapter draws on the author's doctoral dissertation entitled 'Criminalising Business Cartels in Europe – A Comparative Perspective', which he defended on 4 May 2015 at the University of Helsinki.

2 Those who have specifically discussed matters not far removed include, for instance, Harding, C. (2012), 'Hard Core Cartel Conduct as Crime: The Justification for Criminalization in the European Context', *New Journal of European Criminal Law*, 3, 138; Khan, A. (2012), 'Rethinking Sanctions for Breaching EU Competition Law: Is Director Disqualification the Answer?', *World Competition* 35; Öberg, J. (2011), 'Union Regulatory Criminal Law Competence after Lisbon Treaty', *European Journal of Crime, Criminal Law and Criminal Justice*, 19, 289.

3 Furse, M. (2012), *The Criminal Law of Competition in the UK and in the US*, Cheltenham: Edward Elgar, 29.

4 Simonsson, I. (2011), 'Criminalising Cartels in the EU: Is There a Case for Harmonisation?' in: Beaton Wells, C. and Ezrachi, A. (eds), *Criminalising Cartels*, Oxford: Hart Publishing, 216;

that a situation in which Member States criminalise cartels before the EU would be supported by the more thorough experience that the Member States have in prosecuting white-collars.[5] Indeed the former Commissioner for Competition, Almunia, has rejected the criminalisation of cartels at the EU level due to 'the current legislative framework (for instance, there are no EU criminal courts)'.[6] Furse has recently pointed out, however, that the UK's failure in its criminal prosecutions is likely to dissuade other Member States from taking the criminalisation path and that 'it is the very lack of harmonization and control at the EU centre that is responsible, significantly, for difficulties and limitations encountered in the operation of national criminal laws, at least in the UK, and Ireland.'[7]

EU criminal law and hard-core cartels

The European Community began as a peace project via economic integration. Through 'spillover', competences were extended to areas beyond the economic sphere, covering also criminal law.[8] Recently the Union's arguably broad formal competence[9] in the field of criminal law became evident with the introduction of Article 83(2) TFEU in particular. It provides that 'if the approximation of criminal laws and regulations of the Member States proves essential to ensure the effective implementation of a Union policy in an area which has been subject to harmonisation measures, directives may establish minimum rules with regard to the definition of criminal offences and sanctions.'

It has been argued that Article 83(2) TFEU is the very probable basis if an EU-wide harmonisation to criminalise cartels were to occur.[10] Indeed, Article 83(2) TFEU may be considered the chief legal basis for criminalisation under the Lisbon Treaty.[11] There are commentators who have, however, doubted whether

Reindl, A. P. (2006), 'How Strong is the Case for Criminal Sanctions in Cartels Cases?', in: Cseres, K. J, Schinkel, M. P. and Vogelaar, F. O. W. (eds), *Criminalization of Competition Law Enforcement, Economic and Legal Implications for the EU Member States*, Cheltenham: Edward Elgar, 127.

5 Reindl (2006), note 4 above, 126.

6 Rivas, J. (2011), 'Interview with Commissioner Almunia', *World Competition*, 34, 2.

7 Furse (2012), note 3 above. It should be noted that the final call will obviously be made by the Member States and the European Commission, if they should one day desire to proceed with the criminalisation of cartels at the level of the institutions and through harmonised rules at the Member State level; as Wils notes, the Treaty provisions may be amended to the liking of the Member States and the Commission: Wils, W. P. J. (2005), 'Is Criminalization of EU Competition Law the Answer?', *World Competition*, 28, 159.

8 Turner, J. (2012), 'The Expressive Dimension of EU Criminal Law', *American Journal of Comparative Law*, 60, 555.

9 Herlin-Karnell, E. (2012), 'EU Competence in Criminal Law after Lisbon', in: Biondi A., Eeckhout, P. and Ripley, S. (eds), *EU Law After Lisbon*, Oxford: Oxford University Press, 339.

10 See Furse (2012), note 3 above, 222. The Constitutional Treaty which was rejected included a wording very similar to Article 83(2) TFEU in Article III-271(2) and Wouter Wils argued that it 'could undoubtedly be used to criminalize the enforcement of EU antitrust law in all the EU Member States.' See Wils (2005), note 7 above, 159.

11 Öberg (2011), note 2 above, 315–16; harmonised penalties for competition law infringements could also possibly be adopted on the basis of Article 114 TFEU. Article 114 TFEU provides

a criminalisation of cartels would fulfil the criteria incorporated in Article 83(2) TFEU. Would the criminalisation prove to be 'essential' and is the criterion of a prior harmonisation fulfilled? [12] As Article 83(2) TFEU could be regarded as the chief legal basis for criminal measures, one may wonder whether such arguments are a pure 'lawyer's sophistry'.[13]

What seems to be problematic is that Article 83(2) TFEU appears to require that previous harmonisation should have occurred through legislative instruments. In case of competition law, the primary rules, Article 101 and 102 TFEU, are instead Treaty provisions. As noted by Dougan, this requirement may not have come about as a result of a deliberate planning by the Treaty drafters. Dougan argues that as Article 83(2) TFEU, due to its wording, does not seem to provide the possibility for introducing criminal penalties for competition infringements, it is possible that the derived powers acknowledged in the *Environmental Crime* case could be invoked.[14]

Khan has contended that while prior harmonisation in the field of competition law concerns the substantive rules, it does not concern the sanctions, and thus the Article 83(2) TFEU requirement of prior harmonisation would not be fulfilled.[15] Similarly, in Öberg's opinion it would be more rational to start by harmonising individual sanctions (as this is not done by Regulation 1/2003), and only after that introduce criminal penalties, if needed, in the field of competition law.[16]

that measures may be adopted 'for the approximation of the provisions laid down by law, regulation or administrative action in Member States which have as their object the establishment and functioning of the internal market.' See Frese, M. J. (2012), 'Sanctions in EU Competition Law: Principles and Practice' (dissertation, University of Amsterdam), at 113. Other possible legal bases could include Article 103 TFEU and Article 352 TFEU; see Khan (2012), note 2 above, 84–5. It may be mentioned that Article 83(1) TFEU reads as follows: 'The European Parliament and the Council may, by means of directives adopted in accordance with the ordinary legislative procedure, establish minimum rules concerning the definition of criminal offences and sanctions in the areas of particularly serious crime with a cross-border dimension resulting from the nature or impact of such offences or from a special need to combat them on a commmon basis. These areas of crime are the following: terrorism, trafficking in human beings and sexual exploitation of women and children, illicit drug trafficking, illicit arms trafficking, money laundering, corruption, counterfeiting of means of payment, computer crime and organised crime. On the basis of developments in crime, the Council may adopt a decision identifying other areas of crime that meet the criteria specified in this paragraph. It shall act unanimously after obtaining the consent of the European Parliament.'

12 See Khan (2012), note 2 above, 84; Öberg (2011), note 2 above, 313, 316.

13 Dougan, M. (2012), 'From the Velvet Glove to the Iron Fist: Criminal Sanctions for the Enforcement of Union Law, in: Cremona, M. (ed.), *Compliance and the Enforcement of EU Law*, Oxford: Oxford University Press, 109.

14 Case C-176/03, *Commission v. Council*, cited in Dougan (2012), note 13 above, 111.

15 Khan (2012), note 2 above, 84.

16 Öberg (2011), note 2 above, 315–16. It may be mentioned that Cseres said that '[t]he most important legal obligations that stemmed from Regulation 1/2003 for all the Member States were laid down in Article 3, namely the obligation for national competition authorities and national courts to apply Articles 101 and 102 as well as the convergence rule for Article 101, and in Article 35 in conjunction with Article 5, the obligation to empower national competition authorities'. Cseres, K. J. (2010), 'The Impact of Regulation 1/2003 in the New Member States', *Competition Law Review*, 6, 151.

Peers, however, observed that 'full harmonisation' in a particular area is not what is required.[17] Regarding the temporal criterion in Article 83(2) TFEU of a prior harmonisation, the English version of the Treaty seems to exclude the possibility of harmonising and criminalising at the same time, but according to Peers this interpretation should be doubted. As Peers points out, the 'effective implementation' of a Union policy could suffer if criminal law measures could be introduced only after harmonisation measures. Further, Peers notes that even if the temporal criterion of a prior harmonisation measure and subsequent criminalisation were strictly observed, no specific period of time between them has been prescribed. So practically it might be sufficient if the criminal measure was adopted instantly after the harmonisation measure.[18]

The arguments calling for further harmonisation in the area of competition law before the EU could invoke the criminal law powers enshrined in Article 83(2) would not appear persuasive. Nonetheless an eye should be kept on the broad EU criminal law powers – it would be desirable that the explicit basis for the EU to legislate criminal law in Article 83(2) TFEU would be respected in the context of any envisaged criminalisation of cartels.[19]

Herlin-Karnell characterises Article 83 TFEU as *lex specialis*, authorising the EU to legislate. She argues that Article 83(2) TFEU, if it is seen as a 'carte blanche', could be incompatible with the principle of using criminal law as the last-resort measure.[20] Herlin-Karnell points out that overcriminalisation goes against what is effective and calls for the observance of the principles of proportionality and subsidiarity in the field of criminal law.[21] Overcriminalisation risks undermining the normative influence of the law when the moral basis for criminalisation seems to be absent.[22] Thus concerns have been expressed about introducing criminal offences outside what has traditionally been perceived to be the core area of criminal law – more specifically it has been put forward that this worry may be especially relevant in terms of 'regulatory offences', such as

17 Peers, S. (2011), *EU Justice and Home Affairs Law*, Oxford: Oxford University Press, 775.

18 *Ibid.*, 776.

19 Öberg (2011), note 2 above, 316.

20 Herlin-Karnell, E. (2012), note 9 above, 339. Currently the Directive concerning market abuse is interesting in the sense that it offers a testing ground to show the boundaries of Article 83(2) TFEU. The market abuse Regulation No. 596/2014 and the Directive 2014/57EU regarding the criminalisation of market abuse went on to appear in the EU Official Journal – the regulation will enter into force in July 2016, whereas the Directive has a two-year implementation phase. To this effect see European Commission, *Daily News* of 12 June 2014; see also the Proposal for a Directive of the European Parliament and of the Council on criminal sanctions for insider dealing and market manipulation, Brussels, 20 October 2011, COM(2011) 654 final; Proposal for a Regulation of the European Parliament and of the Council on insider dealing and market manipulation (market abuse), Brussels, 20 October2011, COM(2011) 651 final; Herlin-Karnell, E. (2012), 'White-collar crime and European financial crises: getting tough on EU market abuse', *European Law Review*, 37, 485.

21 Herlin-Karnell (2012), note 9 above, 344–5.

22 Parker, C. (2011), 'Criminal Cartel Sanctions and Compliance: The Gap between Rhetoric and Reality', in: Beaton-Wells and Ezrachi (eds), note 4 above, 259. See also Harding (2012), note 2 above, 153.

antitrust violations.[23] Stucke has pointed out, however, that the overcriminalisation critique overlooks the educative role of criminal law – the society may come to condemn conduct that was once considered morally neutral, such as environmental offences.[24]

Besides material costs derived from criminal investigation, there is the risk that, a criminal prohibition notwithstanding, the cartel conduct would not appear to be affected or that criminal rules would not be applied. The outcome could be that the legitimacy of criminal sanctions suffers.[25] This possibility could be realised for instance if the prosecution is not continually funded and supported to a sufficient degree, subsequently resulting in the absence of prosecutions.[26]

What may be noted about criminal penalties is that arguably before the benefits of criminal cartel enforcement are likely to occur, the costs of such a system may take place.[27] The lack of criminal prosecutions in the UK may be understood to reflect this reality.[28] At an early stage of criminal enforcement there could be fewer convictions, which may raise questions as to the effective use of resources and therefore an advance awareness of this prospect would do good both among the public and policy-makers.[29] The US experience shows that the step-by-step development of criminal cartel enforcement by the Department of Justice (DoJ) began in the late 1950s and has been gradually improved with the help of the Congress. It was only after 1974 that a more severe treatment of the cartel infringements took place.[30] One may note that despite more than a century of the Sherman Act and the initial criminal prohibition of cartels, it was only during the past twenty years that the criminal enforcement has really been stepped up in the US, regularly sending executives to prison.[31]

The limits to EU criminal law competence

The debate whether Article 83(2) TFEU provides a legal basis to criminalise cartels is likely to continue. Besides that, it seems relevant for the present purposes to consider what are the limits on the EU's competence to legislate criminal law, whether explicit or non-explicit.

Criminal law may be seen to belong to the sovereign area of the Member

23 *Ibid.*, 144.

24 Stucke, M. E. (2006), 'Morality and Antitrust', *Columbia Business Law Review*, 2, 443, 537; see also Whelan, P. (2013), 'Cartel Criminalization and the Challenge of "Moral Wrongfulness"', *Oxford Journal of Legal Studies*, 33, 8.

25 Harding (2012), note 2 above, 142, 153.

26 *Ibid.*, 147.

27 Reindl (2006), note 4 above, 126.

28 Regarding the lack of criminal prosecutions in the UK, see Joshua, J. (2011), 'DOA: Can the UK Cartel Offence be Resuscitated?' in: Beaton Wells and Ezrachi (eds), note 4 above, 155.

29 Reindl (2006), note 4 above, 126.

30 Kovacic, W. E. (2011), 'Criminal Enforcement Norms: US Insights' in: Beaton Wells and Ezrachi (eds), note 4 above, 68.

31 Massey P. (2012), 'Criminalising Competition Law Offences, A Review of Irish Experience', *New Journal of European Criminal Law*, 3, 166.

States. The democratic deficit at the EU level arguably supports the idea that decision-making on criminal law should more appropriately take place at the national level to maintain legitimate criminal law.[32] Article 83(3) TFEU itself provides that if 'fundamental aspects' of a Member State's criminal justice system could be affected, the Member State may ask that the measure be suspended. This is the so-called 'emergency brake' in Article 83(3) TFEU, which may alleviate the Member State concerns about creeping EU criminal law powers.[33] Adopting criminal law measures against cartels under Article 83(2) TFEU therefore appears to be supported inter alia by the availability of the 'emergency brake' procedure, which may enhance the democratic legitimacy of the planned legislation.[34]

Article 83(2) TFEU requires that the proposed criminal measure is proven 'essential' for the effective implementation of a Union policy. Assessing whether this criterion is fulfilled does not come without difficulty.[35] The principle of *ultima ratio*, meaning that the criminal law should be used only as a last resort, is recognised by the Commission in the Communication 'Towards an EU Criminal Policy'.[36] Further, the Treaty on the European Union incorporates in Article 5(4) the principle of proportionality, which may also be of significance.[37] The EU Charter of Fundamental Rights calls for proportionality in the prescription of criminal penalties.[38]

In the context of the EU, where hard-core competition law infringements are already subject to administrative penalties, it may be useful to note regarding the principle of *ultima ratio* the following: if criminal penalties are introduced in an area where violations already attract administrative sanctions, it could be argued that the criminal penalties are adopted due to the experience that administrative penalties do not suffice. This way criminal law is not an alternative (which is the focus of the *ultima ratio* principle) but an additional measure.[39]

Interestingly, EU competition law could be regarded under the doctrine of the European Court of Human Rights (hereinafter ECtHR) as criminal law, (thus actually contradicting the statement in Regulation 1/2003, Article 23 that 'decisions taken pursuant to paragraph 1 and 2 shall not be of a criminal

32 Turner (2012), note 8 above, 4.

33 See Herlin-Karnell. E. (2010), 'What Principles Drive (or Should Drive) European Criminal Law?', *German Law Journal*, 11, 1117–18.

34 See Kaiafa-Gbandi, M. (2011), 'The Importance of Core Principles of Substantive Criminal Law for a European Criminal Policy Respecting Fundamental Rights and the Rule of Law', *European Criminal Law Review*, 1, 25.

35 Peers (2011), note 17 above, 775.

36 Communication from the Commission to the European Parliament, the Council, The European Economic and Social Committee and the Committee of the Regions, Towards an EU Criminal Policy: Ensuring the effective implementation of EU policies through criminal law, Brussels, 20 September 2011 COM(2011) 573 final, 7.

37 Article 5(4) TEU: 'the content and form of Union action shall not exceed what is necessary to achieve the objectives of the Treaties.'

38 See Article 49(3) of the Charter of Fundamental Rights.

39 Böse Martin, B. (2011), 'The Principle of Proportionality and the Protection of Legal Interests', *European Criminal Law Review*, 39.

nature')[40] and indeed the European Court of Justice (hereinafter ECJ) observes the principles set out by the ECtHR regarding criminal proceedings when dealing with competition law.[41] Melander has pointed out that the ECHR requirement set out in Article 6 may have a bearing on the principle of *ultima ratio*: 'the European procedural safeguards may still convert the solution adopted to be considered "criminal" – in the sense of the criminal charge mentioned in Article 6'[42] and Harding speaks of the 'tension between decriminalization values, as embodied in the *ultima ratio* principle, and due process values, as embodied in the primacy of Article 6 of the ECHR'.[43]

EU cartel sanctions and a 'consistent and coherent' EU criminal policy

The aforementioned Commission Communication underlines that as acknowledged by the Lisbon Treaty, diversity exists among the different societies that have their own 'basic values, customs and choices' that the criminal law reflects. Understandably this then means that EU criminal law needs to be consistent and coherent to render added value.[44] Such consistency was for example called for by criminal law professors from several Member States in 2009 in the 'Manifesto on the EU Criminal Policy of 2009'.[45] Such consistency requires due

40 See André Klip's book on European Criminal Law, where EU competition law is treated as criminal law: Klip, A. (2012), *European Criminal Law, an Integrative Approach*, Cambridge: Intersentia, 2. See also the judgment of the European Court of Human Rights, *A. Menarini Diagnostics S.R.L. v. Italy* (no. 43509/08), judgment of 27 September 2011.

41 Klip (2012), note 40 above, 3. Advocate General Sharpston has stated the following: 'I have little difficulty in concluding that the procedure whereby a fine is imposed for breach of the prohibition on price-fixing and market-sharing agreements in article 81(1) EC falls under the "criminal head" of Article 6 ECHR as progressively defined by the European Court of Human Rights. The prohibition and the possibility of imposing a fine are enshrined in primary and secondary legislation of general application; the offence involves engaging in conduct which is generally regarded as underhand, to the detriment of the public at large, a feature which it shares with criminal offences in general and which entails a clear stigma; a fine of up to 10% of annual turnover is undoubtedly severe, and may even put an undertaking out of business; and the intention is explicitly to punish and deter, with no element of compensation for damage' (see Case C-272/09, Opinion of Advocate General Sharpston of 10 February 2012, point 64, and Klip referring specifically to these points made by the Advocate General (see Klip (2012), note 40 above, 212).

42 Melander, S. (2013), 'Ultima Ratio in European Criminal Law', *Oñati Socio-Legal Series*, 3(1), 58.

43 Harding, C. (2015), 'The Interplay of Criminal and Administrative Law in the Context of Market Regulation: The Case of Serious Competition Infringements', in: Mitsilegas, V. *et al.* (eds), *Globalisation, Criminal Law and Criminal Justice*, Oxford: Hart Publishing, 218.

44 COM(2011) 573 final, note 36 above, 3; Herlin-Karnell, E. (2012), 'White-collar crime and European financial crises: getting tough on EU market abuse', *European Law Review*, 493; see also the discussion in Harding (2015), note 43 above. It may be noted that a Eurobarometer survey showed that the EU citizens were eager to see the EU put high priority on fighting crime, see COM(2011) 573 final, note 36, 2; Eurobarometer 75 (Spring 2011), available at http://ec.europa.eu/public_opinion/archives/eb/eb75/eb75_publ_en.pdf., 13.

45 See European Criminal Policy Initiative, 'A Manifesto on European Criminal Policy', *Zeitschrift für Internationale Strafrechtsdogmatic*, 12/2009 (and see also the discussion in Chapter 9).

respect of the principles of proportionality and the *ultima ratio*, which was also acknowledged by the aforementioned Commission's Communication.[46] The Commission states that there should exist a shared understanding of the guiding principles in the field of EU criminal law.[47]

In principle this cautious approach by the Commission is commendable, but, as pointed out by Herlin-Karnell, it might be undermined since 'consistent and coherent' criminal law could be understood to require increasingly more EU criminal law, which would conflict with the idea of giving space to the different values of the multiple societies within the EU. For instance the recent directive on market abuse does not convince everyone that this objective is being duly observed by the Commission.[48]

How should hard-core cartels be seen in this context, considering that they severely impede the functioning of the free market system and cause economic damage?[49] The legal interest that is being protected is the free market economy, which is arguably of the same calibre as several other legal interests that are protected by criminal law.[50]

In order to justify a criminal measure under the *ultima ratio* principle it is of foremost importance to demonstrate from a moral perspective the seriousness of the violation. In the most reprehensible cases only criminal law as the ultimate measure could provide sufficient condemnation, both from a normative and the actual damage perspective.[51]

Connor *et al.* point out that criminal sanctions for cartel conduct have a long history. In fact prohibitions of anticompetitive practices have been around since ancient times. They further argue that the historical origins of criminalising cartels indicate 'the universal moral reprobation of secret conspiracy, theft, deception, extortion and fraud'. Anticompetitive conduct has occasionally been punishable by death during times of great hardship such as famine – a trial was held in Athens in 326 BC regarding the imposition of capital punishment in relation to a cartel that raised grain prices.[52]

46 See the Manifesto under the heading '2. The ultima ratio principle', note 45 above; COM(2011) 573 final, note 36 above, 7.

47 COM(2011) 573 final, note 36 above, 12; Herlin-Karnell (2012), note 44 above, 493.

48 COM(2011) 654 final, note 20 above; Herlin-Karnell (2012), note 44 above, 493.

49 Harding notes that '[c]ertainly, there is now a well-established consensus that the economic impact of cartel activity is of such an injurious character to both markets and consumers as to justify strong legal control'; note 43 above, 222.

50 See Matikkala, J. (2009), 'Criminal Law and Competition Infringements', *Scandinavian Studies in Law*, 276.

51 Harding (2012), note 2 above, 142.

52 Connor, J. M., Foer, A. A. and Udwin, S. (2010), 'Criminalizing Cartels: An American Perspective', *New Journal of European Criminal Law*, 1, 205, 207, 217. Also Stucke has pointed out that attaining material gain unfairly at the expense of others has for a long time been censored: Stucke, M. E. (2006), 'Morality and Antitrust', *Columbia Business Law Review*, 498. It appears that already Aristotle acknowledged the detriments of excessive market power, by coining the term 'monopoly', and the late Roman Republic saw the *lex Julia de Annona*, a predecessor of modern competition laws, whereas the constitution of Zeno banned trade combinations in AD 483. For

Wardhaugh argued that cartels undermine in our society the institution that allows individuals to assure their own welfare and that the grounds for criminalising cartels could be derived therefrom.[53] Other commentators note *inter alia* that moral disapproval regarding cartels stems from the welfare losses that cartels bring about, the defiance of policy and collusion.[54] Harding points to the notion of crime that 'is about *conduct* as much as *harm*'. Considering this, it is interesting to note that the US approach is to target conspiracy and the attitudes of the cartelists rather than the economic effects of cartels and that in this sense the US model provides 'the convincing justification for using criminal law'.[55] Cartel behaviour may also be seen as delinquent, because the possibly significant economic power of a company is used to exercise private power over other private and public interests.[56] In an attempt to pin down the moral content of cartels and the legitimacy of subjecting cartel members to criminal penalties, one may also explore Green's noteworthy theory on white-collar crimes.[57]

Green has suggested that white-collar crimes in general could be examined from the perspective of everyday moral norms. Hard-core cartel conduct can be determined, for the purposes of his approach, to be virtually the same as a violation of the prevailing moral norms against cheating,[58] deceiving and stealing, which may be perceived to be a *mala in se* violation, something that would be perceived as wrong even in the absence of a statutory prohibition.[59] Beaton-Wells

further treatment of the truly ancient nature of cartel prohibitions, see (in Finnish) Kuoppamäki, P. (2012), *Uusi Kilpailuoikeus*, Helsinki: Sanoma, 20ff.

53 Wardhaugh, B. (2012), 'A Normative Approach to the Criminalisation of Cartel Activity', *Legal Studies*, 1. See also Matikkala, note 50 above, 276; Pöyhönen, J. (2003), *Uusi varallisuusoikeus*, 2nd ed., Helsinki: Talentum, 82–3; Harding, C. and Joshua, J. (2010), *Regulating Cartels in Europe*, Oxford: Oxford University Press, 274–5.

54 Harding (2012), note 2 above, 148–50; Wagner-Von Papp, F. (2011), 'What if all Bid Riggers Went to Prison and Nobody Noticed? Criminal Antitrust Law Enforcement in Germany', in: Beaton Wells, C. and Ezrachi, A. (eds), *Criminalising Cartels*, Oxford: Hart Publishing, 179; Connor *et al.* (2010), note 52 above, 210–11. See also: Whelan, P. (2007), 'A Principled Argument for Personal Criminal Sanctions as Punishment under EC Cartel Law', *The Competition Law Review*, 28.

55 Harding, C. (2006). 'Business Collusion as a Criminological Phenomenon: Exploring the Global Criminalisation of Business Cartels', *Critical Criminology*, 14, 200.

56 Harding and Joshua (2010), note 53 above, 275; Amato, G. (1997), *Antitrust and the Bounds of Power: The Dilemma of Liberal Democracy in the History of the Market*, Oxford: Hart Publishing, 3–4.

57 Green, S. (2006), *Lying, Cheating, and Stealin., A Moral Theory of White-Collar Crime*, New York: Oxford University Press.

58 Green defines cheating as follows: 'for us to say that X has cheated, X must (1) violate a fair and fairly enforced rule, (2) with the intent to obtain an advantage over a party with whom she is in a cooperative, rule-bound relationship.' The cheater manages to cheat and achieve an unfair advantage over others because the rule-abiding perceive themselves to be morally tied by the mandatory rule. See Green *supra* note 57, 57 and 60.

59 See Green (2006), note 57 above, 55–6 and 88ff. Deception could be deemed to be particularly conspicuous in bid-rigging cartels: the tenderers intend to convey the misleading message that the tenders were made independently, which is a false message. See Beaton-Wells, C. (2007), 'Capturing the Criminality of Hard Core Cartels: The Australian Proposal', *Melbourne University*

notes that under Green's approach, price-fixing may be perceived to be 'implicitly wrongful', therefore no further support for its wrongfulness would be needed.[60]

The concept of stealing, under Green's framework, seems to be applicable to the cartel overcharge that is extracted from the customers as a result of the cartel. It is clear that the cartel members intentionally sought to take the money away from the customers, who have the legitimate interest in the money.[61] Subsequently, one could argue that there is a certain appeal to the analogy between theft and cartel conduct. Harding has, however, pointed to the difference between theft and price-fixing, arguing that consumers do not feel the damage as directly as is the case with many other thefts.[62] Hence it seems that while the viability of say the concept of stealing for the context of cartel activity is not beyond criticism, it may have furthered the discussion and understanding regarding the inherent moral qualities of cartel conduct and might have made it that much more difficult to maintain a position that criminal law as a last-resort measure here is unwarranted.

The principle of coherence

As noted by a number of commentators and jurisdictions, the moral reprehensibility of cartels is arguably on a par with tax fraud, insider trading and intellectual property offences, which are mostly criminally prohibited in Western countries. Thus one may point to the principle that like cases should be treated alike and unlike cases differently.[63] Consequently, it may be asked whether it can be

Law Review, 31, 3; MacCulloch, A. (2012), 'The Cartel Offence: Defining an Appropriate "Moral Space"', *European Competition Journal*, 8, 73–93. Perhaps tellingly, bid-rigging is in Germany and Austria the only antitrust infringement to attract criminal penalties. See Dawes, A. and Lynskey, O. (2008), 'The Ever-longer Arm of EC Law: The Extension of Community Competence into the Field of Criminal Law', *Common Market Law Review*, 45, 153; Harding, C. (2010), 'A Pathology of Business Cartels: Original Sin or the Child of Regulation?', *New Journal of European Criminal Law*, 1, 48. See also the Irish case: *DPP v. Duffys and Anor* [2009] *IEHC* 208, where the judge considered cartels to be 'offensive and abhorrent, not simply because they are malum prohibitum, but also because they are malum in se', at para. 22. According to Stuart Green, viewing stealing merely as law-breaking would not sufficiently account for what is wrong about it. It would reduce it to the *malum prohibitum* category (Green, note 57 above, 89). See also the discussion in Connor *et al.* (2010), note 52 above, and Whelan (2013), note 24 above.

60 Beaton-Wells (2007), note 59 above, 698.

61 *Ibid.*, 700–1.

62 Harding (2010), note 59 above, 51–2.

63 Matikkala (2009), note 50 above, 278; see also Whelan (2007), note 54 above, 28. For a Swedish committee deliberation, see SOU 2006:99, 561. A Danish report weighed in on the issue as well, see 'Rapport fra udvalget om Konkurrencelovgivningen', March 2012, 39. For Norwegian thoughts, see Prop. 75 L (2012–2013), Proposisjon til Stortinget (forslag til lovvedtak) Endringer i konkurranseloven, Chapter 4, para. 4.1.2. Regarding the more recent Norwegian revision of competition laws, see the Amendment to the Competition Act that was adopted by the Norwegian Parliament on 28 May 2013. The Australian Cartel Project findings support this stance, indicating that those who thought that cartel conduct should attract criminal sanctions mostly saw the conduct in terms of similar seriousness to many other offences, including aforementioned types

objectively justified that individual cartelists go unpunished under the EU anti-cartel enforcement regime?[64]

The principle of coherence is important with respect to the emerging EU criminal law. While the principle of coherence does not get as explicit recognition in the Treaties as the principles of proportionality and subsidiarity do, for instance the Manifesto on European Criminal Policy referred to Article 11(3) TEU, which calls for coherent Union actions in the horizontal sense.[65] In this respect, it seems relevant that the EU Commission has made a proposal to introduce minimum criminal law rules concerning market abuses.[66] Duly observing coherence is important, as Asp points out: criminal law is not just a tool for attaining specified aims, but also a way of sending a moral message. When the latter function is undermined by a lack of coherence, then also the former ability of criminal law will suffer.[67] Certainly then the quest for a 'consistent and coherent' EU criminal policy should include an extensive overall evaluation of the control policy, where both the criminal penalties and administrative sanctions are compared.[68]

Moreover, as at the EU level the cartel control is administrative in name at least, and as the EU may take over serious cartel cases from national authorities, a question arises in cases where the national regime is based on criminal law: can it be considered to be 'a coherent and consistent criminal policy', as Harding asks, that an international cartel may be subject to corporate fines, whereas individuals at the local level may be jailed?[69]

An incoherent system of sanctions: Finland and Sweden – a case in point

In the Nordic context, several commentators have indicated that there seems to be an increasing need to develop a consistent approach as to the entire control policy, that would cover not only criminal penalties, but also administrative sanctions that are of a penal nature.[70]

The assumption in Finland seems to have been that administrative sanctions are more effective than criminal sanctions whose imposition may lag, and the higher standards of proof may even impede a conviction altogether. Thus a

of conduct. See Beaton-Wells, C. and Parker, C. (2012), 'Education Before Enforcement ?', *CPI Antitrust Chronicle*, October (1), 18.

64 See Matikkala (2009), note 50 above, 278; Whelan (2007), note 54 above, 28.

65 See European Criminal Policy Initiative, note 45 above, 709; Asp, P. (2013), *The Substantive Criminal Law Competence of the EU*, Jure Förlag Stockholm, 206–7.

66 COM(2011) 654 final, note 20 above.

67 Asp (2013), note 65 above, 207. See also on fair labelling, the discussion in Ashworth, A. (2009), *Principles of Criminal Law*, Oxford: Oxford University Press, 78.

68 See Lahti, R. (2011), 'Sanktionsavgifter eller straff', *Nordiska juristmötet: Stockholm, 39, 18–19 augusti*, 46.

69 Harding (2012), note 2 above, 146.

70 Lahti, R. (2012), 'Rikosoikeuden ultima ratio – periaatteesta ja hallintosanktioiden asemasta', in *Juhlajulkaisu Pekka Viljanen 1952 – 26/8 – 2012*, 9. See also the discussion by Warnling-Nerep, W. (2010), *Sanktionsavgifter – särskilt i näringslivet*, Norstedts Juridik, and Kiiski, K. (2011), *Hallinnollinen sanktiointi*, dissertation, University of Turku, 2011.

shift towards administrative sanctions could indicate that an increased control of a given conduct is pursued – this would owe to the perceived rigidness and ineffectiveness of the criminal regime.[71] The requirement of effective, proportionate and dissuasive sanctions in the implementation of EU law measures at the national level may have played a role here[72] – it seems that the legislator valued effectiveness, while it overlooked the requirement of proportionality.[73] This approach would seem to give rise to problems in relation to due process of law.[74] Sanctions should not be disguised as administrative ones, if in reality they are criminal, at least under the autonomous interpretation of the European Court of Human Rights.[75]

Partially the EU could be blamed for the confusion regarding the Finnish control policy – prior to the Lisbon Treaty the EU lacked general criminal law competence, which arguably brought about the expansion of the administrative law sanctions. Subsequently it can be argued that the system could have been more consistently developed if criminal law competences had been earlier available.[76]

The Swedish legal drafting on market abuse violations may by way of analogy provide a good starting point for rethinking the place of administrative sanctions in the fight against cartels and whether individual criminal liability should be available. It dismissed the idea of decriminalising insider trading and reasoned that the swifter nature of administrative sanctions would not give grounds to do so. Instead criminal law could shape the attitudes of society regarding the prohibited conduct.[77] As Harding points out, it is far from unheard of that public opinion is influenced by legal opinion and 'especially in relatively technical areas of conduct, and to this extent public opinion may need to be formed by expert opinion'.[78] All in all, it seems that the rationale behind an exclusively administrative enforcement scheme against hard-core cartels would contradict the objective of achieving a coherent system of sanctions. Specifically, one could argue that administrative sanctions against individuals should cover only minor offences, which would not include hard-core cartels.

Against this backdrop a more nuanced approach by the EU could be expected with regard to the dividing line between administrative and criminal sanctions,

71 Melander, S. (2008), *Kriminalisointiteoria: rangaistavaksi säätämisen oikeudelliset rajoitukset*, Helsinki: Suomalainen lakimiesyhdistys, 424.

72 Lahti (2012), note 70 above, 9–10. See also (in Swedish) Warnling-Nerep, W. (2011), 'Administrative sanktioner – sanktionsavgifter. Utövning av offentlig makt: fågel, fisk eller mittenmellan?', 119, available at https://helda.helsinki.fi/bitstream/handle/10138/29414/Administrativa_sanktioner_publication.pdf?sequence=1.

73 See Warnling-Nerep (2011), note 72 above, 119.

74 See Kiiski. K. (2011), *Rahamaksu rangaistuksena*, Edilex 2011/4, 1 March, 38–9.

75 See Herlin-Karnell, E. (2012), *The Constitutional Dimension of European Criminal Law*, Oxford: Hart Publishing, 58.

76 Matikkala (2009), note 50 above, 288.

77 Prop. 2004/05:142, 46-47; Warnling-Nerep (2010), note 70 above, 28–9.

78 Harding (2006), note 55 above, 200.

especially now that the Treaty of Lisbon has explicitly broadened the EU criminal law powers.[79]

Is individual accountability required in the area of competition law?

It has been suggested that cartel recidivism may be rampant in Europe. In a study of 389 recidivists over a period of twenty years, Connor identified a particularly high concentration of recidivists in Northern Europe and Japan.[80] This could mean that the current system of sanctions does not have the potential that is needed to prevent infringements. The European system of sanctions does not take into account the fact that individuals act in lieu of the company. This has prompted commentators to argue in favour of individual liability, which may include imprisonment, but also director disqualification orders and personal fines.[81]

The stigmatising effect of criminal law

Wils has pointed out in relation to the criminalisation of cartels, that criminal punishment is important with regard to the moral incentives that people get. Criminal punishment attaches a stigmatising label to the perpetrators and the message sent spreads across society, to the law-abiding citizens as well, subsequently promoting the sense of justice.[82] Corporate sanctions that currently are the mode of sanctions at the EU level fail to send as strong a message as individual criminal sanctions would. Further, punishing the company instead of the culpable executives undermines the signal regarding the seriousness of the violation.[83] As a result, a number of commentators acknowledge that criminal sanctions may deter, although measuring the deterrent effect is extremely difficult, thus making some commentators more sceptical than others.[84]

79 It appears that the lack of EU leadership may be problematic for the national anti-cartel regimes in other ways as well; see Furse (2012), note 3 above, 223.

80 Connor, J. M. (2010), 'Recidivism Revealed: Private International Cartels 1990–2009', *Competition Policy International*, 6, 101. Harding noted that '[t]here is now a body of evidence of cartel recidivism, the same actors continuing or repeating their cartel infringements, sometimes in the very same markets. More systematic surveys of legally established prohibited cartel activity are beginning to appear and serve to verify repeat offending on the part of some major players in certain markets, confirming a hitherto impressionistic reading of reported cases' (Harding, C. (2011), 'Cartel Deterrence: The Search for Evidence and Argument', *Antitrust Bulletin*, 56, 369).

81 See Öberg (2011), note 2 above, 308; Khan (2012), note 2 above, 78.

82 Wils, W. P. J. (2002), *The Optimal Enforcement of EC Antitrust Law: Essays in Law & Economics*, The Hague: Kluwer Law International, 216.

83 *Ibid.*, 217.

84 See Öberg (2011), note 2 above, 308; Parker (2011), note 22 above, 256; Wils (2005), note 7 above, 143; Frese. M. J. 2006, 'The Negative Interplay between National Custodial Sanctions and Leniency', in: Cseres, K. J. *et al.* (eds), *Criminalization of Competition Law Enforcement, Economic*

The debate on deterrence

Ginsburg and Wright have underlined that the managers and the shareholders may not abstain from price-fixing as it is profitable.[85] Fines alone as a sole form of sanction are problematic due to the infeasibility of levying optimal fines (insolvency cap).[86] Crucially, it is managers who initiate the collusion, and the members of the board or other superiors who fail to ensure the lawful operation of the firm. In Ginsburg and Wright's view, there should be a shift from corporate fines towards individual sanctions in order to increase deterrence in a cost-effective way.[87] Moreover, a possible deterrent effect gives incentives for the cartelists to become whistle-blowers, thus reinforcing the functioning of leniency programs.[88]

Consequently, the foregoing economic argument supports the supposed effectiveness of imprisoning individual cartel offenders,[89] and substantial corporate fines.[90] This line of argument may be traced to Becker's seminal paper in 1968 where he put forward the idea that it is better to rely on monetary sanctions than incarceration, as the former is less resource intensive.[91] Notably, Werden and Simon contested this view in the case of hard-core cartels, regarding prison sentence as the optimal sanction for price-fixers, *inter alia* referring to the aforementioned insolvency cap.[92] The optimal fine would be so high that companies or natural persons would not be able to pay it:[93] the likelihood of the cartelist getting caught is likely to be low[94] and the harm caused by the cartel considerable, which would make the optimal Beckerian fine beyond the ability of most defendants to pay it.[95]

A shadow of doubt has, however, been cast over the underpinnings of the above theory: behavioral economists have argued that the argument about optimal deterrence accompanied by the assumption of rational actors is limited in its ability to explain why people act a certain way.[96] As Stucke argues, 'it makes little

and Legal Implications for the EU Member States, Cheltenham: Edward Elgar, 208; Reindl (2006), note 4 above, 117; Whelan (2007), note 54 above, 33.

85 Ginsburg H. D. and Wright, J. D. (2010), 'Antitrust Sanctions', *Competition Policy International*, 6, 17.

86 Wils, W. P. J. (2008), *Efficiency and Justice in European Antitrust Enforcement*, Oxford: Hart Publishing, 56.

87 Ginsburg and Wright (2010), note 85 above, 17, at 22.

88 Harding (2011), note 80 above, 345.

89 Furse (2011), note 3 above, 41.

90 Harding (2011), note 80 above, 358–9.

91 Becker, G. S. (1968), 'Crime and Punishment: An Economic Approach', *Journal of Political Economy*, 76, 169–217.

92 Werden, G. J. and Simon, M. J. (1987), 'Why Price Fixers Should Go to Prison', *The Antitrust Bulletin*, winter, 917–37.

93 Furse (2011), note 3 above, 41.

94 The rate of detection has been estimated to be between 10 and 20%. See Bryant, P. G. and Eckhard, E. W. (1991), 'Price Fixing: The Probability of Getting Caught', *Review of Economics and Statistics*, 535.

95 Furse (2011), note 3 above, 41.

96 Harding (2011), note 80 above, 360; Öberg (2011), note 2 above, 306.

sense to assume that executives behave as rational profit maximisers who readily respond to incremental changes in criminal penalties.' Informal norms may have a strong impact on behaviour.[97] For instance, the concern that peers will disapprove may trump the inclination to fix prices – in the opposite case, the argument goes, where peers approve the unlawful behaviour, the deterrent effect of penalties may be undermined. Stucke acknowledges, however, the usefulness of the optimal deterrence theory in cases where individuals are not induced to refrain from unlawful conduct by informal norms.[98]

A further problem regarding the optimal deterrence theory is related to the difficulty of showing the full extent of cartel activity.[99] Although there exists no conclusive evidence as to the decrease of cartels, it is still not accurate to draw the conclusion that criminal sanctions would not reinforce compliance[100] or that the deterrent effect would definitely not be created.[101] The scholars who have questioned the reliability of the deterrence theory have still conceded that criminal sanctions may have an educative function by shaping the normative landscape thus contributing towards compliance. As Reindl puts it, 'sanctions can induce compliance with the law not only because of immediate deterrence-based value-maximizing considerations, but also indirectly by contributing to a subtle change in social norms.'[102]

There is anecdotal evidence from the United States indicating that sending people to prison attracts attention, which then arguably creates deterrence.[103] The OECD has cited in its report the US experience that individuals have offered to pay significant fines in order to escape prison sentences, but no one has ever preferred prison over fine.[104] Further, in the case of *United States v. McDonough* a defendant had committed suicide as he was convicted of price-fixing and sentenced to prison for a short period.[105]Arguably the deterrent effect of criminal penalties against white-collar offenders is unique, especially when compared to the narcotic addict. Bryan Allison, a convicted cartel offender, told while in shackles after the arrest, 'one of the other guys whispered to me, "This is so extreme."'[106] One can also imagine how the incarceration of Alfred Taubman, the chairman of Sotheby, as a result of price-fixing may have affected potential

97 Stucke, M. E. (2011). 'Am I a Price Fixer? A Behavioural Economics Analysis of Cartels', in: Beaton Wells, C. and Ezrachi, A. (eds), *Criminalising Cartels*, Oxford: Hart Publishing, 287–8.

98 See Stucke (2011), note 97 above, 287–8.

99 See Stucke, *ibid.*, 263, 287, 288; Harding (2011), note 80 above, 358–60.

100 Reindl (2006), note 4 above, 117.

101 Harding (2012), note 2 above, 152.

102 Reindl (2006), note 4 above, 117.

103 Baker, D. (2012), 'Deterring Cartels – The Criminalization Dimension', presentation at the Competition Law Enforcement Seminar in Dublin, 23 March 2012, 13.

104 The OECD Report, however, admits that systematic evidence as to the deterrent effect of criminal sanctions is absent: OECD, 2005, *Hard Core Cartels: Third Report on the Implementation of the 1998 Recommendation*, 27.

105 Werden and Simon (1987), note 92 above, 936.

106 Furse (2012), note 3 above, 44–5; O'Kane. M. (2011), 'Does Prison Work for Cartelists? The View from behind Bars, an Interview of Bryan Allison', *Antitrust Bulletin*, 56, 486.

price-fixers and what message they received.[107] That said, it may be concluded that the optimal deterrence model has been criticised and cannot be exclusively relied upon to support the criminalisation of cartels.

Possible alternative ways of measuring deterrence

One may seek to determine and measure deterrence of antitrust enforcement by identifying the number of potential offenders abstaining from cartel activities as a result of antitrust enforcement. The cartel abandonment rate may then be used to indicate the benefit that the enforcement activity brings – such a study was made by Deloitte for the UK's former Office of Fair Trading (OFT). Based on interviews with lawyers and companies, the company survey indicated that for every OFT decision, sixteen cartels were abandoned, and the survey of lawyers suggested that five cartels were abandoned every time the OFT reached a decision.[108] The OFT made also another study concerning the construction industry, which suggested that respondents could have been better informed of criminal sanctions and that improving the information on these sanctions would be beneficial in terms of deterrence.[109]

It could be taken to indicate deterrence that illegal activities are transferred to another country as a result of enforcement. Clarke and Evenett studied the US and EU enforcement of the Vitamins Cartels and indicated that 'the vitamins cartel raised prices more in nations without active cartel enforcement regimes.'[110] Anecdotal evidence corroborates such results, for instance that cartel meetings were held within jurisdictions regarded as 'safe'.[111]

Repeat offenders may offer another perspective on deterrence. Evidence of repeat offenders has been provided by Connor and Helmers, who found 174 cases of recidivism in a sample of cartels from 1990 to 2005. As already mentioned, perhaps tellingly, the worst recidivists came from the EU.[112]

All in all, measuring deterrence is difficult and it tends to be a crucial factor in anti-cartel enforcement. Thus further research on the deterrent impact is needed. Yet the available evidence seems to support the introduction of individual accountability into the EU anti-cartel enforcement regime.

107 Wils (2007), note 7 above, 143–4; Reindl (2006), note 4 above, 117.

108 For further treatment of cartel deterrence, see Harding (2011), note 80 above, 361; OFT, 2007, *The Deterrent Effect of Competition Enforcement by the OFT, A Report Prepared for the OFT by Deloitte* (OFT 962, November 2007).

109 Office of Fair Trading, 2010, *Evaluation of the Impact of the OFT's Investigation into Bid Rigging in the Construction Industry, A Report by Europe Economics*, June 2010, OFT 1240, 55; Harding (2011), note 80 above, 365.

110 Clarke, J. L. and Evenett, S. J. (2003), 'The Deterrent Effects of National Anticartel Laws: Evidence from the International Vitamins Cartel', *The Antitrust Bulletin*, 692.

111 Harding (2011), note 80 above, 367.

112 Connor, J. M. and Helmers, G. C. (2007), 'Statistics on Modern Private International Cartels, 1990–2005', AAI Working Paper, October, 23.

Director Disqualification Orders: a viable alternative to criminal penalties?

The OECD has recommended that its Member States should consider the option of introducing custodial sanctions for hard-core cartels, due to the insolvency cap with regard to optimal corporate fines and as anecdotal evidence speaks in favour of incarceration.[113] Yet the European Competition Commissioner has rejected the introduction of criminal penalties at the EU level.[114] In light of the foregoing and in an attempt to duly observe the *ultima ratio* principle, it could be asked whether there are any viable alternatives to the criminal penalties in order to bring about individual accountability into an antitrust regime that relies exclusively on corporate fines. Could the Director Disqualification Orders (DDOs) present a feasible alternative? It seems at least that this is what Sweden concluded when it introduced the DDOs, but no criminal liability.[115]

As DDOs represent a method of introducing individual accountability, they share some features with custodial sanctions and individual fines. DDOs introduce a certain period of time during which the offender may not be concerned in the management of a company. DDOs may not only be considered as an alternative to prison sentences, but the DDOs could also complement the prison sentences and fines in the array of sanctions available.[116] A DDO carries with it an opportunity cost as the offender will have to step down as a manager, which may affect the offender's salary and future ability to find employment. DDOs may also affect the reputation of the offender and could prevent recidivism.[117] Furthermore, Ginsburg and Wright suggest that DDOs may be useful against directors who, out of negligence, fail to implement compliance and are thus indirectly responsible for cartel activities.[118]

In Finland, however, the Committee that produced a memorandum prior to the adoption of the Competition Act did not propose the introduction of DDOs, due to the challenges involved in the surveillance and the identification of responsible individuals.[119] The problems of monitoring were noted by a Swedish committee as well.[120] The evidence from the UK is not encouraging: the

113 OECD (2003), *Hard Core Cartels, Recent Progress and Challenges Ahead*, 28; OECD (2005), *Hard Core Cartels: Third Report on the Implementation of the 1998 Recommendation*, 27, 39, 40; OECD (1998), *Council Recommendation Concerning Effective Action Against Hard Core Cartels.*

114 Rivas (2011), note 6 above, 2.

115 See (in Swedish) Regeringens proposition 2007/08:135, 156.

116 Ginsburg and Wright (2010), note 85 above, 19. Also Stephan argues in favour of a 'mixed' approach; see Stephan, A. (2011), 'Disqualification Orders for Directors Involved in Cartels', *Journal of European Competition Law & Practice*, 8.

117 Ginsburg and Wright (2010), note 85 above, 19; see also OECD (2011), *Roundtable on Promoting Compliance with Competition Law*, DAF/COMP (2011), 4, 17.

118 Ginsburg and Wright (2010), note 85 above, 19.

119 See Ministry of Employment and the Economy, *Kilpailulaki 2010* (Competitiveness 4/2009), 53.

120 SOU 2006:99, 574

imposition of a DDO under the Enterprise Act has yet to materialise. However, in the *Marine Hoses* case, DDOs were imposed under Company Directors Disqualification Act 1986.[121] As far as the author knows, no competition law DDOs have been imposed in Sweden. Actually it has been reported that it seems that the perpetrators may circumvent DDOs without much effort and that it appears compliance with the DDOs is not monitored to a sufficient degree.[122] If the Swedish solution to adopt DDOs seems unsatisfactory, the issue of criminalising cartels may well arise again in Sweden.[123]

In the UK context, Stephan has pointed to the difficulty of monitoring DDOs: a study regarding DDOs in cases of insolvency in 1997 indicated that DDOs did not present a significant obstacle for individuals seeking employment and that the perceived chance of getting caught running a firm once the DDOs had been imposed was not high. Stephan mentions also other studies, which indicate that the deterrent effect of DDOs is not great.[124]

Furthermore, in the EU context it is problematic that the EU law does not recognise DDOs, and in the absence of DDOs in the legislation of some Member States, the fact that a DDO is imposed in one Member State does not inevitably translate into a situation where the disqualified director could not assume a senior position in another Member State with no equivalent sanctions.[125]

The DDOs may disproportionately apply to small businesses, since it may be less plausible for a small company director to argue that he was not aware of the infringement.[126] The Swedish Government Bill predicted that DDOs may target disproportionately smaller firms, since in cartel conduct, the various individuals in the respective businesses may have comparatively speaking very different positions: for instance the individual engaged in cartel conduct from a smaller firm may be its owner or managing director, whereas a lower-ranking individual, who does not occupy any managerial positions, may be the human link between the bigger company and the cartel. The Government Bill suggested that while the blameworthiness of the individuals may be on an equal level, this runs the risk that only individuals employed by smaller companies would be subject to DDOs.[127]

It may be noted also that many of the problems associated with criminal sanctions may be present with regard to DDOs and personal fines, as individuals may have recourse to the full array of legal protections in a similar fashion as

121 Under this Act DDOs may be used in case of criminal offences; see Stephan (2011), note 116 above, 4.

122 Sveriges television, 'Brottslingarna kan enkelt kringgå näringsförbuden', 26 October 2011.

123 Bernitz, U. (2011), *Svensk och europeisk marknadsrätt I, Konkurrensrätten och marknadsekonomins rättsliga grundvalar*, Norstedts Juridik, 213.

124 Stephan (2011), note 116 above, 6.

125 OFT (2011), *The Impact of Competition Interventions on Compliance and Deterrence* (OFT 1391, December 2011), 36.

126 Stephan (2011), note 116 above, 5.

127 Prop. 2007/08:135, 158.

under a criminal regime.[128] The Swedish Government acknowledged that cases concerning corporate fines could become more cumbersome if the Competition Authority pursued a DDO due to reasons related to the collection of evidence: an individual who could be the possible target of a DDO could not be heard under similar conditions as previously.[129] The Swedish Government Bill noted that DDOs may be viewed as a criminal sanction under the European Convention of Human Rights.[130]

According to Wils, the stigmatic effect and moral message of DDOs could be stronger than that of fines. Wils considers DDOs to be a viable complement to imprisonment and 'a defensible second-best', but not a true alternative. In his view, imprisonment appears to carry a stronger deterrent effect. In the absence of other individual penalties, it is possible that for the offender the DDO may represent just a route to retirement: the company could still compensate for the loss of salary, etc.[131] Whelan noted that one disadvantage is that DDOs may target only directors, whereas individuals engaged in prohibited conduct, but who are not directors, escape DDOs – custodial sanctions do not suffer from a similar drawback.[132]

On a final note, a study commissioned in 2007 by the Office of Fair Trading showed that the surveyed companies regarded criminal penalties as the most important sanction, followed by DDOs, adverse publicity and fines.[133] This order of importance could indicate that companies view fines 'as a *cost* rather than as a penalty'.[134]

In conclusion, it seems that as a stand-alone sanction for individual offenders, the DDOs are not sufficient. However, using them as a complement to criminal penalties may be favoured.

128 See Furse (2012), note 3 above, 53–4.

129 Prop. 2007/08:135, 159.

130 What is more, Regulation 1/2003 sets out in Article 12 a restriction on the information exchange between Member State authorities when the evidence could be used in the pursuit of individual sanctions and therefore the Competition Authority must be careful not to use such information in a way that violates the rules of Regulation 1/2003, lest the future co-operation be undermined – see Prop. 2007/08:135, 168.

131 Wils (2008), note 86 above, 188; SOU 2006:99, 574.

132 Whelan took the position that DDOs should be used only to accompany criminal penalties; see Whelan, P. (2012), 'Strengthening Competition Law Enforcement in Ireland: The Competition (Amendment) Act 2012', *Journal of European Competition Law & Practice*, 6.

133 The study surveyed 202 UK companies; see OFT 962, note 108 above, 5 and 70–2. Another study commissioned by the OFT and undertaken by London Economics in 2011 attempted to assess the deterrent effect of competition intervention, thus sharing objectives with the earlier Deloitte 2007 survey. The businesses surveyed amounted to 809. The results were mostly in line with those of the Deloitte study. However, whereas the Deloitte study underlined the importance of individual sanctions, the newer findings suggested that reputational damage and fines are more important in the eyes of the businesses. See to this effect: OFT, *The Impact of Competition Interventions on Compliance and Deterrence* (OFT 1391 December 2011), 75.

134 Stephan (2011), note 116 above, 4.

A combination of measures as the ultimate solution?

Various commentators have postulated tentatively that a mixture of measures may be beneficial in achieving deterrence, instilling a culture that is attentive to antitrust rules.[135] The variety of sanctions, including criminal penalties, fines, private damage actions and disqualification orders, may possibly influence the management of a company to take the steps to change the corporate culture.[136]

As pointed out by Öberg, this is in keeping with the idea of the tit-for-tat strategy as advocated by Ian Ayres and John Braithwaite. Essentially it means that an array of punishments and persuasion is available.[137] Ayres and Braithwaite argue that as the toughness of the penalties increases, so does the level of compliance that the agency is able to achieve and that simultaneously the need to employ tough measures decreases: 'Regulatory agencies will be able to speak more softly when they are perceived as carrying big sticks.'[138] In their view, this approach embraces both the rational choice doctrine and sociological studies in combination, forming the basis of the tit-for-tat strategy.[139] Therefore at the EU level, according to this approach, penalties of varying severity should be available to the Commission, suggesting that individual penalties, besides the criminal ones, could include *inter alia* director disqualification orders and personal fines, but as complements, not as stand-alone sanctions.

Conclusion

While the EU exercises its criminal law competence, due respect should be given to the principle of *ultima ratio*, thus keeping in check the broad EU criminal law powers. A 'consistent and coherent' EU criminal policy, and a national one for that matter, should also aim to criminally prohibit violations of a similar penal value in order to support the credibility of the criminal justice system.

In the gravest cases, criminal law alone could communicate adequately the blameworthiness of a given conduct. Cartels impair one of the core pillars of our society, the market economy, on which individuals depend in an attempt to ensure their own welfare.

It seems that administrative sanctions could be properly adopted only against minor offences, whereas cartels as an egregious violation of competition law

135 Stucke (2011), note 97 above, 288; Harding favours director disqualification orders over prison sentences: Harding (2011), note 80 above, 375. See also Stephan (2011), note 116 above, 8; Wils (2005), note 7 above, 145, 147; Fingleton, J., Girard, M. and Williams, S. (2006), 'The Fight against Cartels: Is a "Mixed Approach" to Enforcement the Answer?', in: Hawk, B. E. (ed.), *International Antitrust Law & Policy*, New York: Fordham Competition Law Institute, 9ff.

136 See Harding (2011), note 80 above, 375.

137 Ayres, I. and Braithwaite, J. (1992), *Responsive Regulation, Transcending the Deregulation Debate*, New York: Oxford University Press, 5; Öberg has recently used the tit-for-tat argument in the context of antitrust violations; see Öberg (2011), note 2 above, 316.

138 Ayres and Braithwaite (1992), note 137 above, 6.

139 *Ibid.*, 19.

do not seem to fall within that category. One should not ignore the educative function of criminal law – public opinion could be shaped by experts' views in complex fields of law.

Arguably, cartel conduct warrants the ultimate condemnation provided only by criminal law. Other measures would not produce the stigmatising label on a par with criminal measures. Given that EU Member States have introduced criminal cartel offences, whereas similar rules are absent at the EU level, it may be noted that it would hardly make for a 'consistent and coherent' EU criminal policy if larger cross-border cartels did not prompt criminal liability whereas at the national level cartels were caught by criminal prohibition.

All things considered, there are several commentators who rightly acknowledge the value of a mixture of measures being available in the fight against cartels, including Director Disqualification Orders, fines and custodial sanctions.

15 The EU legislation on protection of financial markets against market manipulation and its implementation in Polish law

Anna Błachnio-Parzych

The genesis of the EU legislation on market manipulation

The accomplishment of the idea of integrity of financial markets in the EU requires an increase in investors' confidence. To establish a single market and to protect it in an effective way, a common legal and regulatory framework was needed. Because of wide differences between the EU countries regarding the functioning of the capital market, endeavours to approximate national regulations met with resistance.[1] The directives harmonising national legislation in the area of the capital market were adopted (for example the Capital Adequacy Directive,[2] the Public Offer Prospectus Directive,[3] the Insider Dealing Directive[4]), but the pace of market integration was slow. Therefore in 1999 the Financial Services Action Plan (FSAP) was announced. It pointed to the challenges created by the development of the modern market and the imperfections of the EU financial market legislation.[5] Many problems needed to be solved by uniform market conduct rules. It was also the time of big financial scandals (the cases of Enron and WorldCom) and the fight against market abuses needed the uniform rules. Therefore one of the FSAP aims was to adopt a directive that would define two most dangerous threats for capital market – insider trading and market manipulation.

At almost the same time, the EU Council set up the 'Committee of the Wise Men', which was to solve the problem of the slow pace of implementation of the EU financial markets legislation. The Committee formulated a four-level

1 Avgouleas, E. (2005), *The Mechanics and Regulation of Market Abuse*, Oxford: Oxford University Press, 244.

2 Council Directive 93/6/EEC of 15 March 1993 on the capital adequacy of investment firms and credit institutions, (1993) OJ L126/1.

3 Council Directive 89/298/EEC of 17 April 1989 coordinating the requirements for the drawing up, scrutiny and distribution of the prospectus to be published when transferable securities are offered to the public, (1989) OJ L124/8.

4 Council Directive 89/592/EEC of 13 November 1989 coordinating regulations on insider dealing, (1989) OJ L334/30.

5 Maloney, N. (2003), 'New Frontiers in EC Capital Markets Law: From Market Construction to Market Regulation', *Common Market Law Review*, 40, 811–13.

regulatory approach in the Final Report (the Lamfalussy Report).[6] The first-level directives should create only the core of implemented legislation, the general framework; the second level should concern implementing measures (more detailed technical provisions); the third, guidance of the operation of the directives in the EU countries; and the fourth, consistent application of the regulation in the EU countries. The last two levels have, in contrast to the first and the second, a practical character. While the first and the second levels create some theoretical frame and norms, the third and the fourth pursue the question of how to apply the norms.

The instrument that was aimed at strengthening credibility of the financial markets was the Directive 2003/6/EC of the European Parliament and of the Council of 28 January 2003 on insider dealing and market manipulation[7] (hereinafter referred to as the Market Abuse Directive or MAD I). It created a common frame to combat market abuse. The objective of the legislation was 'to ensure the integrity of Community financial markets and to enhance investor confidence in those markets. . . . A single Directive will ensure throughout the Community the same framework for allocation of responsibilities, enforcement and cooperation.'[8] The directive was the first level of regulation according to the Lamfalussy procedure.

In 2009 the High-Level Group on Financial Supervision in the EU concluded in its report that sanctioning regimes in Member States are heterogeneous. In consequence the protection against market abuses is weak. Therefore the EU Commission, after public consultation on the review of the Market Abuse Directive, prepared an assessment of contemporary regulations against market manipulation.[9] Gaps in the regulation of new markets, the regulator's lack of power to detect market abuses, and lack of clarity and legal certainty were pointed out as the main disadvantages. The idea was to enact not only a directive, but also a regulation which would have a direct application in domestic law. Currently therefore the EU legislation on market abuse consists of: Regulation (EU) 596/2014 of the European Parliament and of the Council of 16 April 2014 on market abuse (the Market Abuse Regulation,[10] hereinafter referred to as MAR), and the Directive 2014/57/EU of the European Parliament and of the Council of 16 April 2014 on criminal sanctions for market abuse (the Market Abuse Directive,[11] hereinafter referred to as MAD II). These two Acts create the system of protection against market abuse based on two pillars: administrative and criminal. An analysis of the differences in the description of behaviour treated

6 The Final Report of the Committee of Wise Men on the Regulation of European Securities Markets (Brussels, 15 February 2001).
7 (2003) OJ L 96/16.
8 Para. 12 of the MAD I Preamble
9 Commission Staff Working Paper Executive summary of the impact assessment, Brussels, 20 October 2011, http://ec.europa.eu/internal_market/securities/docs/abuse/SEC_2011_1218_en.pdf.
10 (2014) OJ L173.
11 (2014) OJ L173.

as manipulation and of the sanctions provided for in MAR and MAD II will help to understand the system.

The current and previous shape of anti-manipulation EU law

The definition of market manipulation

Before examining the way in which the EU legislator defined market manipulation, it is important to mention that market manipulation is sometimes called a 'virtual term of art',[12] because of the problems in describing the offence. They derive from the thin border between aggressive but legal behaviour of investors, and these kinds of behaviour that are called market manipulation. Sometimes the difference between them is based only on the intention of an investor. Therefore legislators aim for the most objective definition of market manipulation. The example of the endeavour is the definition enacted by the EU legislator.[13]

According to Article 12(1) MAR and Article 5(2) MAD II there are four main kinds of behaviour that should be treated as market manipulation: price manipulation, fictitious transactions, information-based manipulation and manipulation of the calculation of benchmarks. The same kinds of manipulation are provided for in Article 12(1) MAR. The previous Directive (MAD I) did not treat as manipulation the behaviour related to benchmarks. In fact it is formulated as a separate kind of manipulation, although the reason is not a specific mechanism, but its object. Therefore it will not be analysed here separately. Generally the difference between contemporary EU legislation and MAD I is that the former relates not only to financial instruments, but also commodity contracts, and MAR also to an auctioned product. The next important difference is that in MAR and in MAD II 'any other behaviour' has been added to 'entering into a transaction' and 'placing an order to trade in the description of price manipulation and fictitious transactions'. This means that not only behaviour that relates to the common activity of investors may be treated as manipulation, but also other kinds of behaviour, especially omissions – for example, refraining from placing an order. The definition of specific kinds of manipulation should begin with the provisions of MAR, because the regulation contains broader descriptions of the behaviour than MAD II. The MAR treats as manipulation not only behaviour that causes some effects, but also the risk and probability of some effect.

12 Avgouleas (2005), note 1 above, 104.

13 On the objective concept of the definition of market manipulation, see further: Błachnio-Parzych, A. (2014), 'The Concept of Defining and Combating Market Manipulation in Existing and Proposed EU Legislation', in: Brodowski, D., Espinoza de los Monteros de la Parra, M., Tiedemann, K. and Vogel, J. (eds), *Regulating Corporate Criminal Liability*, New York: Springer, 145–57.

Price manipulation

The first above-mentioned kind of manipulation is price manipulation. It is based on some specific orders or transactions. The essence is a 'direct assault on the integrity of a market's price formation (discovery) mechanism'.[14] According to the MAR, price manipulations are transactions, orders to trade, or any other acts which give, or are likely to give, false or misleading signals as to the supply of, demand for or price, or which secure, or are likely to secure, the price at an abnormal or artificial level (Article 12(1)(a) MAR). Such behaviour is not manipulation if the person who entered into the transactions or issued the orders to trade establishes that the reasons for so doing are legitimate and that these transactions or orders to trade conform to an accepted market practice. The 'accepted market practices' are established in accordance with Article 13 MAR. The provision stipulates criteria that shall be taken into consideration by the competent authority. The next important term for understanding the definition of the forbidden activity is the exemption on the basis of 'legitimate reasons', which was not defined by the EU legislator.

The EU legislation laid down in Article 12(2) MAR some examples of concrete behaviour that is encompassed by the general definition of the four kinds of market manipulation. According to the aforementioned provision, they constitute instances derived from the core definition given in Article 12(1)(a-d) MAR. One such is 'control over the market'. This kind of price manipulation is based not only one transaction. Usually it needs a number of activities, which often consist of transactions in the cash market and the futures market, refraining from activity in a certain situations. The investor also makes an effort to hide the fact that certain transactions are concluded by him or other parties are associated with him in a formal or an informal way.[15] It has to be underlined that control over the market is not only gaining a dominant position, but the specific use of this dominance.[16] The second example of price manipulation provided for in Article 12(2) MAR is the buying or selling of financial instruments at the opening or closing of the market, which is at least likely to have the effect of misleading investors acting on the basis of the prices displayed. This kind of manipulation constitutes an example of price manipulation. The character of the behaviour is connected with the period of closing the market, during which the close price is formed.

Other examples of price manipulation are misleading orders or transactions. The aim of the orders or transactions is to mislead other participants in the market. The success of the manipulation results from the irrational way of making decisions by investors, their fears, overconfidence and imitating others. According to the assumption known as *homo oeconomicus*, human beings act rationally, but

14 Avgouleas (2005), note 1 above, 131.

15 See further on control over the market: Błachnio-Parzych, A. (2011), *Kryminalizacja manipulacji instrumentami finansowymi*, Warsaw: Wolter Kluwer, 122–30.

16 See also: Friedman, R. D. (1990), 'Stalking the Squeeze: Understanding Commodities Market Manipulation', *Michigan Law Review*, 89, 34; McBride Johnson, P. (1981), 'Commodity Market Manipulation', *Washington and Lee Law Review*, 3, 730–1.

the research of Kahnemann and Tversky and the work of behavioural economists cast doubt on this assumption.[17] Investors are using simplified conclusions which constitute the base for decision-making. The difference between the misleading orders or transactions and the fictitious transactions lies in the fact that the perpetrator of this kind of manipulation is not acting with others who are buying or selling the same assets. Any possible co-operation with other perpetrators can be only on one side of the transaction – for example, the co-operation may rely only on applying orders to sell or only orders to buy.

According to Fischel and Ross this kind of manipulation is very rarely successful and the costs of establishing the responsibility for infringement of the prohibition are higher than the profits.[18] From the other side, it is extremely difficult to prove that the orders or transactions were made with the aim to mislead others.[19] Problems arise also in connection with the understanding of the term 'artificial price'. The kind of manipulation may be defined in different ways. The definition enacted by the EU legislator is an example of an objective approach, because the core of the definition is the term 'price at an abnormal or artificial level', in other words 'artificial price'.

The meaning of the term is not easy to define. It may seem that the artificial price is opposite to the natural price (natural change of the price), which responds to supply and demand.[20] However, every price which is presented in quotation is a consequence of supply and demand, because this relation is associated with the mechanism of quotation. From the perspective of the mechanism, the motivation which accompanies making the orders has no meaning.[21]

The attempts to define it in other ways are doomed to failure. When trying to describe it by referring to illegal practices,[22] it may be said that not all acts treated as manipulation constitute in themselves illegal practices. Other attempts to define the artificial price based on the concept of the lack of conformity with the price being the effect of other kinds of valuation than market valuation[23] are also doubtful. First, the difference may not be an effect of manipulation, but overreactions of market participants, their excessive optimism or pessimism. Second, the effects of the use of different kinds of valuation may differ. This raises the

17 Tversky, A. and Kahneman, D. (1974), 'Judgment under Uncertainty: Heuristics and Biases', *Science* (New Series), 185(4157), 1124–31; Cieślak, A. (2003), *Behawioralna ekonomia finansowa. Modyfikacja paradygmatów funkcjonujących w nowoczesnej teorii finansów*, Warsaw: Materialy I Studia, 51–7.

18 Fischel, D. R. and Ross, D. J. (1991), 'Should the Law Prohibit "Manipulation" in Financial Markets?', *Harvard Law Review*, 105, 503–53

19 *Ibid.*

20 Kuciński, R. (2000), *Przestępstwa giełdowe*, Warsaw: C. H. Beck, 122; Budzeń D. M. (1996), *Manipulacyjne kształtowanie cen papierów wartościowych*, *Glosa*, 9, 5.

21 More attempts to define the term 'artificial price' are presented in: Avgouleas (2005), note 1 above, 108–11, and Błachnio-Parzych (2014), note 13 above, 203–11.

22 Romanowski, M. (1999), *Prawo o publicznym obrocie papierami wartościowymi. Komentarz*, Warsaw: C. H. Beck, 873.

23 Easterbrook, F. H. (1986), 'Monopoly, Manipulation, and the Regulation of Futures Markets', *Journal of Business*, vol. 59(2), 118.

question of which kind of valuation should be treated as the one that is able to point the appropriate level of the price. The fact of the impact of a concrete transaction on the market price[24] also cannot be treated as a determinant for calling the price an artificial one. This kind of influence is inherently connected with the nature of the stock exchange, and without it the changes of market prices would not be possible.[25]

Therefore the term 'artificial price' cannot be defined in an objective way. The reasons behind distraction of market functions may be also be due to behaviour of market participants which comprise faulty decisions or decisions taken under the influence of excessive optimism or pessimism. The risk of fault is an element of market activity and it could be strange to punish people for their faulty investment decisions. However, manipulation is treated in another way because of the intent of the perpetrator. Therefore 'artificial price' should be treated as in fact a subjective element of the definition of market manipulation.

Fictitious transactions

The second kind of manipulation is fictitious transactions – the most known and the oldest kind of market manipulation[26] – defined as transactions, orders to trade, or any other activity or behaviour which affect or are likely to affect the price by the use of fictitious device or any other form of deception or contrivance (Article 12(1)(b) MAR). There is a difference between the way in which the EU legislator defined this kind of manipulation in MAR compared to MAD I. The previous Directive did not refer to the effect of the behaviour. Therefore it may be concluded that fictitious transactions were defined in MAR in a narrower way (Article 1(2)(b) MAD I). They may have an influence on other investors but their aim is to create or maintain the price on some specific level. It is possible because of the perpetrators' knowledge of the mechanism of completing transactions.

The perpetrators are sure that orders of selling or buying which do not differ in price and volume of the financial instruments, or differ to a little degree, will lead to a transaction. Two types of fictitious transaction are distinguished.[27] The first one is called 'wash sales'. The perpetrator of the manipulation enters both a buying and a selling order for the same financial instrument. The second type – 'matched orders' – consists of activities of two parties. The one enters an order to buy with the knowledge that the second will enter an identical or very similar selling order. It is important to remember that the effect of the fictitious transactions may be even short lived – sometimes that is enough for the manipulator to exploit it.

24 *Great Western Dustributors, Inc v. Brannan,* 201 F 2d 476 (7th Cir. 1953).

25 Siems, M. S. (2012), 'The EU Market Abuse Directive: A Case-Based Analysis', 27 September, available at: http://papers.ssrn.com/sol3/papers.cfm?abstract_id=1066603.

26 Avgouleas (2005), note 1 above, 130.

27 *Ibid.*, 129.

Information-based manipulation and manipulation of the calculation of benchmarks

The last kind of manipulation is information based, being connected not with orders or transactions, but with the dissemination of information, which gives, or is likely to give, false or misleading signals as to the supply, demand or price at an abnormal or artificial level, where the person who made the dissemination knew, or ought to have known, that the information was false or misleading (Aricle 12(1)(c) MAR). Similar to fictitious transactions, the definition of information-based manipulation in MAD I did not contain any condition concerning the effect of such dissemination of information.

Article 12(2)(d) MAR presents as an example of this kind of manipulation taking advantage of occasional or regular access to the traditional or electronic media by voicing an opinion. The condition for it to be treated as manipulation is having previously taken positions on that financial instrument and other stipulated objects, and profiting subsequently from the impact of the opinions voiced on them, without having simultaneously disclosed that conflict of interest to the public in a proper and effective way. In the example, the manipulator not only knows about the information, but he is an author of it. But if the conflict of interest is publicly and properly disclosed, responsibility is excluded.

The main difference between the way of defining manipulation in MAR and MAD II is that the latter requires the intent of the perpetrator. According to Article 5(1) MAD II, market manipulation shall constitute a criminal offence at least in serious cases and when committed intentionally. Moreover the EU legislator required criminalisation of only behaviour that leads to some effects. Meanwhile, MAR permits treating as manipulation behaviour that has probable effects.

Measures and sanctions

According to Article 14(1) MAD I Member States were obliged to ensure that the appropriate administrative measures or sanctions would be imposed against the persons responsible for market abuse. Deciding on the kind of the responsibility for infringement of prohibition of manipulation, the domestic legislator shall take into consideration whether the character and severity of the sanction is proportionate and may have effective and dissuasive character.[28] Although Article 14(1) MAD I provides that this was 'without prejudice to the right to impose criminal sanctions', the administrative measures and sanctions were of main significance.

The recent EU legislation aims at strengthening the response to market manipulation. The MAR provides for administrative measures against manipulation and insider trading. They have very diverse characters and the administrative pecuniary sanction is only one of them. Referring to the sanctions imposed on

28 See the discussion of these criteria in Harding, contribution to this volume, Chapter 8.

individuals (natural persons), it was laid down in Article 30(2) MAR that the following may be used: an order to cease the conduct and to desist from its repetition; the disgorgement of the profits gained or losses avoided due to the infringement insofar as they can be determined; a public warning; withdrawal or suspension of the authorisation of an investment firm. The maximum amount of administrative pecuniary sanctions is provided for in Article 30(2)(h) MAR as at least three times the amount of the profits gained or losses avoided because of the infringement. What is even more important, MAR stipulates also the concrete amount of maximum administrative pecuniary sanctions for the infringements described in the Regulation. In relation to market manipulation, it is at least 5 million euros or the corresponding value in the national currency.

MAD II requires the imposition of effective, proportionate and dissuasive criminal penalties for market manipulation at the national level. According to Article 7(2) MAD II, the maximum term of imprisonment has to be at least four years. In summary therefore, the EU legislator has provided for two parallel regimes of responsibility: administrative and criminal. It is worth mentioning that parallel regimes may be the source of the problem of overlapping. Depending on the assessment of the administrative responsibility as a 'criminal charge' according to the Article 6 of the European Convention on Human Rights, this situation may lead to an argument of infringement of the *ne bis in idem* principle.

Implementation of the EU legislation in the Polish legal order

Definition of market manipulation in Polish law

Member States were under an obligation to bring into force the laws, regulations and administrative provisions necessary to comply with MAD I not later than 12 October 2004. The Polish legislator enacted an amendment to the Act which regulated the Polish capital market (the Act of 21 August 1997 on public trading on securities)[29] on 12 March 2004.[30] The necessity for further changes was the reason to enact new regulations on the capital market. It was decided to divide the subject of the prior regulations into three Acts. The Act of 29 July 2005 on trading in financial instruments, called hereinafter TFI, included provisions against market manipulation.[31] Regarding MAD II, there have not yet been any further changes made in Polish law. The final deadline for transposition of the new Directive is 3 July 2016, but the current legal protection against market manipulation in Poland complies with the majority of obligations arising from this measure.[32]

It was further decided to dedicate one subchapter of the Act on trading in

29 Dz.U. No. 118, 754, with further amendments.

30 Act of 12 March 2004. on amendments of the Act on public trading in securities and other acts (Dz.U. No. 64, 594).

31 Dz.U. No. 183, 1538, with further amendments.

32 One of the amendments that will be necessary concerns the definition of manipulation behaviour related to the calculation of a benchmark.

financial instruments to the issue of market manipulation. According to Article 39(1) TFI, market manipulation is forbidden. The next paragraph explains the meaning of the term 'manipulation' in that Article 39(2), and points 1–4 contain equivalent content to Article 1(2) a–c MAD I. But that provision extends further to other kinds of behaviour, which is treated as manipulation. The reason why there are so many kinds of market manipulation is that separate points included provisions of MAD I which contain general definition of market manipulation, and also examples of them. These are the examples that were also stipulated in MAR for illustrating general definitions of market manipulation.

Assessing the Polish regulations simply in terms of implementation, it first should be noted that no provision of the previous Directive has been omitted. The implementation may be even described as a 'rewriting' of the Directive. This rewriting without consciousness of the meaning and the role of some concrete provisions of MAD I renders understanding of the regulation difficult. A presumption of legislative rationality during the process of interpretation of law requires some explanation of why provisions with general definitions are set down beside provisions as concrete examples of market manipulation. The legislation does not explain that the relation between Article 39(2) points 1–4 and others is like the relation between rules and examples. If the rewriting of Article 1(2) MAD I was accurate, that relation would be respected. The legislation should attach greater precision to the definition of market manipulation, since the more severe sanctions are consequences of infringements of the market manipulation prohibition. There are critical points regarding the earlier implementation of the Market Abuse Directive in Polish law.

Moreover, according to the definition of price manipulation stipulated in Article 1(2)(a) MAD I and in Article 12(1)(a) MAR, the behaviour does not constitute manipulation if the person who entered into the transactions or issued the orders to trade establishes that his reasons for doing so are legitimate and that these transactions or orders to trade conform to accepted market practices on the regulated market concerned. Laying down as separate kinds of manipulation practice that are examples within the EU rules, without adding the above-mentioned reservations, which exclude responsibility for manipulation, does not comply with the Directive. One of the examples of price manipulation mentioned earlier is the buying or selling of financial instruments at the close of the market with the effect of misleading investors acting on the basis of closing prices. This is regulated under Polish law as a separate kind of manipulation (Article 39(2), para. 7 TFI). As a result, the Polish regulation is more severe because of the lack of the possibility to exclude responsibility if the person had legitimate reasons and the behaviour conformed to accepted market practices.

One of the descriptions of manipulative behavior as formulated in the Polish law has an exceptional character: it does not derive from MAD I. According to Article 39(2), para. 5 TFI, manipulation is also the placing of orders or executing transactions while simultaneously misleading market participants, or using the fact that market participants are being misled, as regards the price of financial instruments. The condition of capital market liquidity is the existence of a different valuation of financial instruments. At the same time, one investor may suppose that the price of the concrete financial instrument will increase and another may suppose that it will decline. In fact, one of them is wrong and the other one is exploiting his fault, because he is sure that the other one is being misled. Investors do not have the right to mislead market participants, but they do not have an obligation to inform others that they are wrong. They also do not have to care about the source of their being misled, if it is not their behaviour. In fact the reason for this situation may be false valuation of the factors which determine the future change of the price. It is worth emphasising that the differences between investors' assessment of financial instruments are the engine of the market, the reason of exchange.

Sanctions

Polish law combined administrative and criminal responsibility for infringements of the market manipulation prohibition. This is not a similar solution to those that are in force in the United Kingdom, France or Germany. Models of describing manipulation differ in the regulations of these jurisdictions depending on the attribution of criminal or administrative responsibility. Therefore it may generally be said that these two regimes of responsibility overlap in relation to the same act. The difference between manipulation described as a crime or as an administrative offence is the element of intent on the part of the perpetrator, since this has to be proved in criminal proceedings. The model is similar to the one which can be derived from MAD II and MAR.

The solution in Poland is different. All kinds of manipulation stipulated in Article 39(2) TFI are divided into crimes and administrative offences. According to Article 183(1) TFI, criminal responsibility is a consequence of infringement of Article 39(2), paras 1–3, para. 4a and paras 5–7 TFI. But infringements of Article 39 (2), para. 4b and para. 8 TFI constitute an administrative offence (Article 172 (1) TFI).

Criminal sanctions which follow conviction for a crime of market manipulation are: a fine of up to 5,000,000 PLN or imprisonment between three months and five years or these two penalties combined (Article 183(1) TFI). According to Article 172(1) TFI, the Polish Financial Supervision Authority may impose a financial penalty of up to 200,000 PLN, or up to the amount of ten times the profits gained, or these two penalties together, on a perpetrator of the kinds of manipulation stipulated in the provision. The Polish legislator enacted an offence of conspiracy to commit a crime of manipulation as a separate crime (Article 183(2) TFI) and conspiracy to commit an administrative offence (Article 172(2) TFI). The only sanction is that the consequences of the responsibility for conspiracy to commit a crime of manipulation are lower. Sanctions for conspiracy to commit an administrative offence of manipulation are the same as sanctions for committing the criminal offence.

Comparing Article 183(1) TFI and Article 172(1) TFI, it has to be to concluded that the Polish legislator attached the greater importance to criminal responsibility and in consequence to criminal sanctions. The assessment of the sanctions against market manipulation leads to the conclusion that they are very punitive. Differently from Article 14(1) MAD and in the law of other EU states, the Polish approach has led to the use of criminal law as the main measure to combat market manipulation.

Conclusion

The changes made by the Polish legislation on market manipulation arising from the implementation of the EU law have some positive and negative features. Previously, market manipulation was defined as 'causing an artificial increase or fall in the price of securities'.[33] Such a description of a very complicated reality caused many problems for prosecutors, judges and for investors who wanted to know the legal limits of activity in capital market. The problem was the difficulty in interpreting the provisions concerning financial law and the need for some knowledge of the way capital market is functioning. There was little in the existing doctrine dedicated to the definition of manipulation according to that aforementioned provision.

Opposingly, the mistakes made during the implementation of MAD I should be pointed out. Some of these arise from imperfections in the EU legislation on market manipulation, for example the uncertainty regarding some terms ('legitimate reason', 'artificial price'). Moreover the Polish Financial Supervision Authority did not publish any kind of code of conduct, similar to the Code of Market Conduct published in United Kingdom, which would clarify the interpretation of any definition of market manipulation.

The EU legislator and, in consequence, the Polish legislator need to work out more effective solutions. The definition of price manipulation encompassed so many kinds of behaviour that it became difficult to apply. This does not serve the effectiveness of the regulation of market manipulation. The new proposals for the EU legislation against market manipulation will not change the situation. They have some positive aspects, as for example stronger protection of over-the-counter-market (OTC) and other new platforms of trading, and regulations concerning more effective investigations conducted by regulators, but the previous problems remain.

The Polish legislator has given more importance to criminal sanctions as measures to counteract market manipulation. Although this is not the best solution,[34] it is consistent with the direction chosen by the EU legislation in the new MAD II. According to the Preamble of the MAD II, the effectiveness of the sanctions

33 Article 177, Act of 21 August 1997 on public trading in securities (Dz.U. No. 118, 754).

34 See further on the choice of the legislator between administrative and criminal sanctions: Harding, C. (2015), 'The Interplay of Criminal and Administrative Law in the Context of Market Regulation: The Case of Serious Competition Infringements', in: Mitsilegas, V., Alldridge, P. and Cheliotis, C. (eds), *Globalisation, Criminal Law and Criminal Justice*, Oxford: Hart Publishing, Chapter 9. The author refers in the title to competition infringements, but his analysis has more general meaning and it is relevant also to market abuses.

is strictly connected with their severity.[35] However, the EU legislator seems not to notice that the issue of the effectiveness of law, especially criminal law, is much more complicated. Of significance is the clarity of the description of the forbidden behaviour. The lack of it causes problems with recognising the limits of permissible behaviour and with assessing if the crime has been committed. The severe sanctions linked with the prohibition of the behaviour, effectively rendering it an unprosecutable crime, will result in the criminal law as a symbolic measure. Taking into consideration that MAD II is one of the first Acts based on Article 83(2) of the Treaty on the Functioning of the European Union, this observation regarding the way in which the EU legislator perceives the criminal law is disquieting.

35 See point 6 of the Preamble to MAD II.

16 Transposing EU Framework Decisions into the United Kingdom's criminal law: the trials and tribulations of a researcher

Jennifer Edwards

Researching implementation and its context

What follows here is a researcher's reflexive report on working as a National Expert engaged in a European Commission-funded research project which set out to examine the implementation of EU criminal law, in the form of Framework Decisions, in Member State legal systems.[1] Such research serves the Commission's institutional role in monitoring the implementation and application of EU measures at the national level and ensuring the correct transposition of such instruments into national law. It was my role as a national rapporteur to examine five specific areas of UK criminal law – child pornography;[2] support of irregular entry transit and residence;[3] frauds with no cash means of payment;[4] drug trafficking;[5] and money laundering[6] – and to compose detailed reports for the Commission on whether, in those areas, the relevant Decisions had been properly implemented. Particular emphasis was put on the importance of discovering whether legislative changes had been made to accommodate them.

At first glance this seemed an easy task to accomplish. However, upon closer inspection I realised that there was a serious difficulty facing researchers who are tracking the way in which transpositions of this kind are effected in the United Kingdom. Simply put, finding a credible paper trail that allows one to follow a measure's journey from the Commission desk to the statute book is challenging, and it is the primary task of this discussion to explain this difficulty with reference to the findings of my research.

This, though, is not its only task.

1 European Commission, *Study on Criminal Sanction Legislation and Practice in Representative Member States, Final Report*, 2014, doi: 102838/20190. The co-ordinators of the study were Kai Ambos, Lorena Bachmaier Winter, Theodora Christou, Luis Francisco Jorge de Mesas and Nicola Selvaggi. See further discussion by Harding of this research and the report, in Chapter 8 of this volume.
2 Council Framework Decision 2004/68/JHA.
3 Council Framework Decision 2004/68/JHA.
4 Council Framework Decision 2001/413/JHA.
5 Council Framework Decision 2004/757/JHA.
6 Council Framework Decision 2001/500/JHA.

First, it has to be acknowledged that, at the time of writing, there has been and is within the United Kingdom a noted animus towards what the public at large perceive to be the pervasiveness of the European Union's presence – its scope and sphere of influence. The popular press in particular is scathing in its espousals. Below are a representative five:

'Ban shopping bags says EU'[7]
'Britain's Euro bill rockets by £2BN'[8]
'EU wants to merge UK with France'[9]
'75% say: Quit the EU now'[10]
'Get Britain out of Europe: We want our country back'[11]

This adverse feeling is not restricted to publications of a tabloid nature. Daniel Hannan, the MEP for south-east England, speaks in a similar vein, often from his seat in the European Parliament, and is on record as saying, while addressing the President of that body: 'See how the thicket of EU regulation grows. See how Brussels shoots its tendrils into every crevice, every nook of national life.'[12] He and others of his ilk (Nigel Farage and his UK Independence Party being perhaps the most well known) have long agitated for an 'In Out' referendum as a potential cure for this supposed intrusiveness; something that holds such sway with the general public that the Conservative Party, prior to its election in 2010 and re-election in 2015, included it as a central part of its political platform and scheduled the referendum for June 2016. As is often the case with such things, the earlier promise was reneged on, but that has done little to stymie the public's desire for the chance to make just that choice, or to quiet those like Mr Hannan who feel that the EU has no place dictating the content of national law – a feeling that is arguably even more potent given the 2015 election result[13] and the recent clashes regarding the economic impact[14] of illegal immigration that the crises at the Coquelles and Folkestone Eurotunnel sites have caused.[15]

7 Dana Glover, *Daily Express*, 20 May 2011, accessible at: www.express.co.uk/news/uk/247722/Ban-shopping-bags-says-EU.

8 Gabriel Milland, *Daily Express*, 24 August 2009, accessible at: www.express.co.uk/news/uk/122416/Britain-s-Euro-bill-rockets-by-2bn.

9 Macer Hall, *Daily Express*, 2 May 2011, accessible at: www.express.co.uk/news/uk/244206/EU-wants-to-merge-uk-with-france.

10 Alison Little, *Daily Express*, 22 October 2011, accessible at: www.express.co.uk/news/uk/278966/Three-quarters-of-Britons-say-quit-EU-now.

11 Accessible at: www.express.co.uk/web/europecrusade.

12 Daniel Hannan MEP, speaking at the European Parliament (accessible at: www.youtube.com/watch?v=HUfV3xALkow).

13 An interestingly large number of people cast their vote in favour of UKIP – the party which leans hardest towards leaving the European Union – a net gain of 9.5% over their 2010 total vote. www.bbc.co.uk/news/election/2015/results (accessed 26/07/2015).

14 www.telegraph.co.uk/news/uknews/immigration/11769718/Calais-crisis-live.html (accessed 26/07/2015).

15 See, for example, the following commentary: www.kentonline.co.uk/folkestone/news/police-on-standby-for-rival-41006/ (accessed 26/07/2015).

With this as the backdrop to my coming into the Commission's project, I could not but wonder on the potential for exploring this complex issue further. Thus, I posed myself the following question: does the EU's impact on UK law match the anti-EU rhetoric regarding intrusiveness and threats to national democracy?

I shall return to this question in due course. But first, before exploring the problem of the paper trail, there is another methodological point to make concerning jurisdictions.

The United Kingdom – three jurisdictions and the first hurdle

The UK is a deceptively complex subject for this kind of analysis. Not only is it a common law jurisdiction and therefore lacking any kind of codified, single source on the criminal law, it also subsumes three distinct internal jurisdictions – England and Wales, Scotland and Northern Ireland. Each of these has its own legal traditions, legislation, body of case law and structure, and as such, as I approached the Commission project, I felt I was faced with a challenge multiplied. As well as reviewing the jurisdiction that I am most familiar with – England and Wales – and seeking evidence there that the Decisions of the Commission had been properly transposed, I would have to repeat the process on much less familiar ground in the case of Scotland and Northern Ireland.

In this assumption, however, I was mistaken. I received a clarification early on in the project that made it clear that England and Wales was the only jurisdiction to be covered, and this, while being an honest relief to me in terms of the breadth of the research I would need to carry out, also raised questions about the more limited focus being laid down for the research. Although based on a pragmatic decision and consideration of time and resources, there may be points of comparative interest in relation to the three UK jurisdictions. The differences between them, particularly regarding Scotland – which, unlike England and Wales and Northern Ireland, is a distinctive hybrid of both civil and common law, and has its own substantive rules concerning civil law and criminal justice – are such that there is a real possibility that the process of implementing EU measures may be affected in noteworthy ways. Focusing on England and Wales misses this detail, and may present a skewed view of the way in which the UK has transposed the decisions under scrutiny.

That said, the decision on the 'sample' was final. The extent of the project was set, and will now be reflected in the present discussion.

Tracking transposition

The transposition of EU legislation into UK law is a lengthy process: fifteen steps, all told. They are summarised in the 2013 Transposition Guidance for Directives[16] as shown in Table 16.1.

16 H. M. Government (2013), *Transposition Guidance: How to Implement European Directives Effectively*, April.

Table 16.1 Transposition guidelines

Stage	*Function*
1. Pre-transposition	'Consider at the earliest possible stage how a proposal will be implemented. Consider resources and discuss the Directive with the negotiating team. Seeking to minimise regulatory burden when transposing should be a key consideration during negotiations.
2. EU Directive adopted at Council.	Begin to fill in transposition project plan and transposition table with lawyers.
3. EU Directive published on the Official Journal of the European Union (OJEU)	Finalise the transposition project plan (and transposition table if you intend to include one) with lawyers, reporting against each of the Guiding Principles for transposing EU legislation.
4. Reducing Regulation Committee (RRC) to review transposition project plan – two weeks post publication in OJEU	Send transposition plan to the RRC, plus relevant domestic Cabinet Committee and Secretaries of State for any other affected government departments.
5. Begin drafting Consultation document	This will need to reflect responses to the transposition project plan and include an Impact Assessment (IA) and updated transposition table (if you intend to include it).
6. Cabinet Committee clearance: Pre-Consultation	Send consultation document, IA, Regulatory Policy Committee (RPC) opinion, and transposition table to the RRC, plus relevant domestic Cabinet Committee and Secretaries of State for any affected government departments.
7. Minister to consider consultation representations	Advise Minister on responses to the consultation and revise draft plans for implementation as necessary.
8. Finalise documents for transposition	Complete IA, RPC opinion, transposition table (if you intend to include one) with lawyers, reporting against each of the Guiding Principles for EU legislation.
9. Cabinet Committee clearance: Final clearance	Minister may need to seek collective agreement from the RRC, plus relevant domestic Cabinet Committee and Secretaries of State for any other affected government departments.
10. Cabinet Committee granted on successful completion of the write round (if previous step included)	Updates required to the draft documents for transposition, based on Ministerial representations/ agreement, will be summarised in the round-up clearance letter.
11. Lay regulations before Parliament	Follow departmental procedure for laying regulations.
12. Notify the European Commission of implementation	Liaise with your EU coordinator if necessary.
13. Publish guidance	This should be at least 12 weeks before the implementation date.
14. Legislation takes legal effect	
15. Statutory duty for Ministerial review – five years post-legislation	Departments should coordinate this with and feed into European Commission reviews wherever possible.

Clearly this is a complex and involved process that can span a minimum of five years if all goes well. In that time and through this process, countless documents are created – be they minutes of meetings in the earliest stages, project plans, the texts of Select Committee consultations or the opinion of Parliament after having regulations laid before it – not all of which are available to the public. Thus from the outset the researcher, I discovered, is beset by two problems. First, the sheer amount of information available on a given area is daunting. And second, it is nigh on impossible to find a clear paper trail from point 1, Pre-transposition, to point 14, Legislation, taking legal effect. There are simply too many steps, too many possibilities for misplacement and omission.

How then can an accurate measure of the current state of UK law and its compliance with EU measures be made? Outside of a very lucky direct reference that I shall explore later, the answer I found was: by implication.

I began by comparing the text of each Decision and the date of its enactment with those of relevant pieces of UK legislation. If the Act or Acts came out prior to the Decision, I surmised that while it could certainly have been updated to better reflect the later publication, it would not have been created as a result of it. If it or they were promulgated after the Decision, however, I could infer more strongly that they were responsive: the reaction of the UK Parliament to the need to ensure full compliance with the EU's pronouncements. This methodology will be explored further as I discuss my findings in the coming sections.

The sample of Framework Decisions

Council Framework Decision 2004/68/JHA – the first incidence of a recurring problem

The Decision on child pornography has twelve articles, eight of which were to be transposed into national law. These are: Article 2, on offences concerning sexual exploitation of children; Article 3, offences concerning child pornography; Article 4, on instigation, aiding, abetting and attempt; Article 5, concerning penalties and aggravating circumstances; Article 6, on the liability of legal persons; Article 7, relating to sanctions on legal persons; Article 8, on jurisdiction and prosecution; and Article 9, concerning the protection of and assistance to victims.

I could say with certainty that the UK has transposed this Decision.

I can do so because, quoting the Commission's conclusions in COM/2007/0716 final, 'the UK satisfactorily responded to the Framework Decision requirements.'[17] Finding the evidence that led to this conclusion, however – updates to the law, that can be directly traced by the Decision by name – proved to be very difficult. So much so in fact that I found myself, for the first time, using the comparative method I mentioned above in order to draw what conclusions I could.

17 http://eurlex.europa.eu/smartapi/cgi/sga_doc?smartapi!celexplus!prod!DocNumber&lg=en&type_doc=COMfinal&an_doc=2007&nu_doc=716 (accessed 30/09/2013).

The Decision was published on 22 December 2003, and its mandatory completion date was 20 January 2006. In the UK, there are three pieces of legislation that concern the aspects of the law on child pornography contained within these Articles: the Sexual Offences Act 2003 (SOA); the Protection of Children Act 1978 (PCA); and the Criminal Justice Act 1988 (CJA). The SOA, sections 9–15 and 47–50 of which match Article 2 of the Decision closely, received the Royal Assent on 20 November 2003, a month prior to it coming into effect. Including the full text of all of these sections for analysis' sake would be inappropriate here, but the Article itself and sections 47 and 48 are reproduced below as examples. They state respectively:

> Article 2:
> Each Member State shall take the necessary measures to ensure that the following intentional conduct is punishable: (a) coercing a child into prostitution or into participating in pornographic performances, or profiting from or otherwise exploiting a child for such purposes; (b) recruiting a child into prostitution or into participating in pornographic performances; (c) engaging in sexual activities with a child, where (i) use is made of coercion, force or threats; (ii) money or other forms of remuneration or consideration is given as payment in exchange for the child engaging in sexual activities; or (iii) abuse is made of a recognised position of trust, authority or influence over the child.
>
> The SOA:
>
> 47(1) A person (A) commits an offence if — (a) he intentionally obtains for himself the sexual services of another person (B), (b) before obtaining those services, he has made or promised payment for those services to B or a third person, or knows that another person has made or promised such a payment, and (c) either — (i) B is under 18, and A does not reasonably believe that B is 18 or over, or (ii) B is under 13.
> 48(1) A person (A) commits an offence if — (a) he intentionally causes or incites another person (B) to become a prostitute, or to be involved in pornography, in any part of the world, and (b) either — (i) B is under 18, and A does not reasonably believe that B is 18 or over, or (ii) B is under 13.

As these extracts clearly show, there is parity here between the Decision and national law, and the same is evidenced when comparing relevant Decision articles with the PCA and the CJA. Sections 1 and 3 of the former, which came into force in 1978, correspond with Articles 3, 6 and 7 closely, as section 160 of the latter, enacted in 1988, does with Article 3. Respectively, the sections state:

> PCA:
> 1(1) It is an offence for a person — (a) to take, or permit to be taken or to make, any indecent photograph or pseudo-photograph of a child . . .; or (b)

> to distribute or show such indecent photographs or pseudo-photographs; or (c) to have in his possession such indecent photographs or pseudo-photographs, with a view to their being distributed or shown by himself or others; or (d) to publish or cause to be published any advertisement likely to be understood as conveying that the advertiser distributes or shows such indecent photographs or pseudo-photographs, or intends to do so.
>
> PCA:
> 3(1) Where a body corporate is guilty of an offence under this Act and it is proved that the offence occurred with the consent or connivance of, or was attributable to any neglect on the part of, any director, manager, secretary or other officer of the body, or any person who was purporting to act in any such capacity he, as well as the body corporate, shall be deemed to be guilty of that offence and shall be liable to be proceeded against and punished accordingly.
>
> CJA:
> 160(1) it is an offence for a person to have any indecent photograph or pseudo-photograph of a child . . . in his possession.

A final example of prior national legislation matching the Decision is the Accessories and Abettors Act 1861. Section 8 relates to the content of Article 4, and states:

> Whosoever shall aid, abet, counsel, or procure the commission of any indictable offence, whether the same be an offence at common law or by virtue of any Act passed or to be passed, shall be liable to be tried, indicted, and punished as a principal offender.

Despite all of the above-mentioned instances of similarity, I could find no evidence that they were anything more than coincidence: the UK law was the same in effect and did not require any amendment. The PCA and the CJA were enacted years prior to the Decision being published, and while the SOA was very close in time to the appearance of the Decision, there is no direct evidence of the passage of the UK provision being motivated by an awareness of the imminent appearance of the EU measure, despite the note in a Parliamentary Research paper entitled 'How much legislation comes from Europe?'[18]

Council Framework Decision 2002/946/JHA – a rare find

Framework Decision 2002/946/JHA aims to strengthen the penalties for activities supporting irregular entry into, transit through or to, and residence in, the

18 Research Paper 10/62, *How Much Legislation Comes from Europe?* House of Commons Library, 2012, 45.

UK. It has eleven articles, six of which were to be transposed into UK law by 5 December 2004. Two statutes in particular relate to this Decision: the Immigration Act of 1971, and the Nationality, Immigration and Asylum Act of 2002. The former, specifically section 25, relates to Article 1, on penalties, and was clearly enacted before the Decision, while the 2002 Asylum Act appeared concomitantly, and in part was a response to the Decision. Note the following statement from the Select Committee on Delegated Powers and Regulatory Reform:

> Council Framework Decision 2002/946/JHA on the strengthening of the penal framework to prevent the facilitation of unauthorised entry, transit and residence (which section 143 of the 2002 Act was enacted to implement)'[19]

This proved a rare find of paper trail evidence. For none of the other Decisions could I find something so clearly linking national law with a European antecedent; if such written links exist, they are not easily traceable. It is still a case, however, of taking the Select Committee's word for the outcome. On the face of it, it is a definite statement, but no citation exists within the text of this opinion – there appear to be no other direct references to any link between the Act and the Decision.

Council Framework Decision 2001/413/JHA – lateness?

The Framework Decision on fraud with no cash means of payment was adopted in 2001, and was to be fully transposed into UK law by 2 June 2003. Within this two-year period, nine of its fifteen Articles were to be incorporated. These were: Article 2, offences related to payment instruments; Article 3, offences related to computers; Article 4, offences related to specifically adapted devices; Article 5, participation, instigation and attempt; Article 6, penalties; Article 7, liability of legal persons; Article 8, sanctions applied to legal persons; Article 9, jurisdiction; and Article 10, extradition and prosecution. There are four relevant statutes: the Theft Act 1968; the Forgery and Counterfeiting Act 1981; the Computer Misuse Act of 1990; and finally the Fraud Act of 2006.

Applying the date test to these instruments shows, much as it did with the child pornography Decision, a clear division between those which came prior to the Decision and that which did not. Only the Fraud Act appeared after the Decision. Sections 6(1) and 7(1) of the Act include reference to issues within the scope of Article 4, the text of which states:

> Each Member State shall take the necessary measures to ensure that the following conduct is established as a criminal offence when committed

19 Select Committee on Delegated Powers and Regulatory Reform, *Twelfth Report*, February 2004, para. 3.

> intentionally: the fraudulent making, receiving, obtaining, sale or transfer to another person or possession of: — instruments, articles, computer programmes and any other means peculiarly adapted for the commission of any of the offences described under Article 2(b); — computer programmes the purpose of which is the commission of any of the offences described under Article 3.

By comparison, sections 6(1) and 7(1) read:

> 6(1) A person is guilty of an offence if he has in his possession or under his control any article for use in the course of or in connection with any fraud.
>
> 7(1) A person is guilty of an offence if he makes, adapts, supplies or offers to supply any article — (a) knowing that it is designed or adapted for use in the course of or in connection with fraud, or, (b) intending it to be used to commit, or assist in the commission of, fraud.

There is a similarity of wording but no further evidence of a direct transposition. Furthermore, if indeed this part of the Fraud Act was a direct response to the Decision, it was a late one.

Council Framework Decision 2004/757/JHA – going through changes?

There are two main statutes which deal with drug trafficking in the UK – the Misuse of Drugs Act 1971 and the Customs and Excise Management Act 1979, and this legislation may be seen to correspond with the requirements of the Framework Decision on drug trafficking. The following seven provisions were to be transposed: Article 2, crimes linked to trafficking in drugs and precursors; Article 3, incitement, aiding and abetting and attempt; Article 4, penalties; Article 5, particular circumstances; Article 6, liability of legal persons; Article 7, sanctions for legal persons; and Article 8, jurisdiction and prosecution. For the purposes of comparison, Article 2 of the Decision and sections 3 and 4 of the Misuse of Drugs Act are reproduced below:

> Article 2:
> Each Member State shall take the necessary measures to ensure that the following intentional conduct when committed without right is punishable: (a) the production, manufacture, extraction, preparation, offering, offering for sale, distribution, sale, delivery on any terms whatsoever, brokerage, dispatch, dispatch in transit, transport, importation or exportation of drugs; (b) the cultivation of the opium poppy, coca bush or cannabis plant; (c) the possession or purchase of drugs with a view to conducting one of the activities listed in (a) and/or (b); (d) the manufacture, transport or distribution of precursors, knowing that they are to be used in or for the illicit production or manufacture of drugs.

> Section 3(1):
> Subject to subsection (2) below — (a) the importation of a controlled drug; and (b) the exportation of a controlled drug, are hereby prohibited.
>
> Section 4(1):
> Subject to any regulations under section 7 of this Act for the time being in force, it shall not be lawful for a person — (a) to produce a controlled drug; or (b) to supply or offer to supply a controlled drug to another. (2) Subject to section 28 of this Act, it is an offence for a person — (a) to produce a controlled drug in contravention of subsection (1) above; or (b) to be concerned in the production of such a drug in contravention of that subsection by another. (3) Subject to section 28 of this Act, it is an offence for a person — (a) to supply or offer to supply a controlled drug to another in contravention of subsection (1) above; or (b) to be concerned in the supplying of such a drug to another in contravention of that subsection; or (c) to be concerned in the making to another in contravention of that subsection of an offer to supply such a drug.

This area of law is perhaps that with the least amount of relevant, recent amendment that could be directly attributed to the Decision. Both of the Acts that concern this matter are over thirty years old, and while both have been updated to better represent the current state of the drugs problem in the UK – wider definitions of certain types of drug and drug paraphernalia, and changes in the class of certain drugs (class A being the most dangerous and therefore most heavily penalised, class B less so, and class C less so again) – there was no traceable link between these changes and the Decision on drug trafficking.

Council Framework Decision 2001/500/JHA – a second lucky find, or a work of inference?

Framework Decision 2001/500/JHA is unique amongst those I researched, for two reasons. First, unlike the others, which, as a rule, have roughly two years between their implementation and completion dates, it had six; a reflection perhaps of a foreseen need for time from Member States to adjust their laws. And second, rather than detailing changes to be made to national legislation in its Articles, the Decision was concerned with ensuring that Member States had complied with a much earlier European obligation – the 1990 Council of Europe Convention on Laundering, Search, Seizure and Confiscation of the Proceeds of Crime. Article 6 of this Convention was especially important, and is reproduced (in part) below:

> Article 6(1):
> Each Party shall adopt such legislative and other measures as may be necessary to establish as offences under its domestic law, when committed intentionally:

a. the conversion or transfer of property, knowing that such property is proceeds, for the purpose of concealing or disguising the illicit origin of the property or of assisting any person who is involved in the commission of the predicate offence to evade the legal consequences of his actions;
b. the concealment or disguise of the true nature, source, location, disposition, movement, rights with respect to, or ownership of, property, knowing that such property is proceeds, and, subject to its constitutional principles and the basic concepts of its legal system;
c. the acquisition, possession or use of property, knowing, at the time of receipt, that such property was proceeds;
d. participation in, association or conspiracy to commit, attempts to commit and aiding, abetting, facilitating and counselling the commission of any of the offences established in accordance with this article.

In the UK, the Proceeds of Crime Act 2002 is the piece of legislation that most clearly covers the contents of the Convention – the implementation of which was the topic of the Decision. Sections 327, 328 and 329 appear to match subsections a, b and c of the Article almost exactly.

> Section 327(1):
> A person commits an offence if he — (a) conceals criminal property; (b) disguises criminal property; (c) converts criminal property; (d) transfers criminal property.
>
> Section 328(1):
> A person commits an offence if he enters into or becomes concerned in an arrangement which he knows or suspects facilitates (by whatever means) the acquisition, retention, use or control of criminal property by or on behalf of another person.
>
> Section 329(1):
> A person commits an offence if he — (a) acquires criminal property; (b) uses criminal property; (c) has possession of criminal property.

Whether this parity can be directly attributed to the Decision, however, is up for debate. According to the research paper 'How much legislation comes from Europe?',[20] noted above, the Act was indeed a response to a European obligation, but as was the case with the Sexual Offences Act 2003, the Decision itself is not named as the catalyst for the response.

20 Research Paper 10/62, note 18 above.

Conclusions

Considering a proclivity towards opting out of certain policies and measures,[21] a largely Eurosceptic national popular press, the promise of the present government to hold a referendum on EU membership, and the strident rhetoric of UKIP and speakers like Hannan in the European Parliament and Farage more locally, it is fair to say that the UK has a reputation for being an obstinately sceptical and unwilling member of the EU. Indeed, such an impression might lead observers to expect a record of reluctant and obstructive implementation and enforcement of EU obligations. But this snapshot study and report on implementation in the criminal law field, while revealing a problematical transparency, would suggest otherwise. The case of each of the measures studied reveals a straightforward and unfussy compliance. Each measure, either through new legislation or via existing compliant law, has been incorporated into national law, and this leads to some reflection on the gap between public posturing and the actual engagement with legal obligations.

Failure to transpose directives (or similar measures such as Framework Decisions), or inadequate transposition, is a frequent cause of complaint and formal action by the Commission against Member States,[22] yet the politically maverick UK appears to have a good record in this area of compliance with EU obligations. A glance at the case list under Article 258 of the TFEU and its predecessor provisions[23] will reveal that Britain appears less frequently in the list of defending Member States than many other countries. Indeed, in this respect the UK even appears in the light of a model citizen. In the words of a lawyer in the UK Treasury Solicitor's Department, commenting in 2009, the 'UK has a very strong record . . . according to the most recent figures available, for 2007, the UK was the only member state to see more infractions dismissed than declared', and in relation to Article 228 proceedings to impose a financial penalty on defaulting states, 'so far the UK has not been subject to such an action, and has in fact intervened in support of the Commission's enforcement.'[24] This would suggest that, whatever the nature of the political noise, in practice the UK has relatively few issues and problems regarding transposition and compliance, and even further, is very quiet and discreet about the process of transposition by not leaving much of an obvious paper trail as to how it is achieved.

One reflection on such an outcome is that it is not as contradictory as might first appear to be the case. On the one hand, it may be politically expedient in

21 At least at the legislative level of implementation. 'Ground level' implementation (via prosecution, trial and sentencing) is another matter, which proved to lie beyond the scope of the existing research, and is a much more problematical subject for research – see comments by Harding, in Chapter 8 of this volume.

22 Craig, P. and de Burca, G. (2011), *EU Law: Text, Cases and Materials*, (5th edition), Oxford: Oxford University Press, 423.

23 Most immediately, ex-Article 226 TEC.

24 Timothy Jones, 'How the UK adopts EU laws', BBC, Q & A, 21 July 2009. Article 228 TEC is now Article 260 of the TFEU.

addressing a largely Eurosceptic electorate and public opinion to make Eurosceptic noise in governance. But it may be equally expedient, in the 'real' business of governance and in relating to EU partner States and institutions, to be efficiently but quietly compliant. Certainly the internal attitude of government is to transpose EU measures as efficiently and cost-effectively as possible. This is the tone of the Government's own *Transposition Guidance* document.[25] This pragmatic and business-like approach is evident in a number of places in the *Guidance*, for instance at paragraphs 2.9 and 2.10:

> When considering how to transpose an EU Directive, you should therefore: Start from the position that the UK should not go beyond (its) minimum requirements.
>
> Government policy is that you should not to go beyond the minimum requirements of European Directives, unless there are exceptional circumstances, justified by a cost-benefit analysis and consultation with stakeholders.[26]

A similarly pragmatic and minimalist approach is evident in the apparent practice of accepting without much comment the existing provision in national law which already provides for what is laid down in the European instrument ('if it is not broken, it does not need to be fixed or talked about').

In short, it may be fair to say that the UK has a minimal but positive engagement policy when implementing EU legislation. This may arise from an instinctive reaction, to ward off European intrusion as much as possible. Or, it could be a canny political move to forestall Eurosceptic concerns. Or, it could be simple Anglo-Saxon pragmatism. Or, it could be a mixture of all of these things. I would hazard a guess that it is more of the second and third of these than the first.

Part of the explanation for this is likely to be historical. On entry into the European Community in the early 1970s, the UK was well developed and well prepared in legislative terms. As such, less work was needed to bring national law into line with the European position, and in this sense a kind of passive compliance that requires little to nothing from the Member State is natural and easy.[27] And naturally enough it only becomes a matter for debate when active steps and legislative change are required for purposes of transposition. But in such instances, the UK seems to have its position and ground well prepared.

There is an interesting example in relation to another Framework Decision, that relating to organised crime.[28] In pre-legislative discussion of the scope of this measure, the UK was unwilling to leave out the concept of conspiracy, and

25 H. M. Government (2013), note 16 above.

26 *Ibid.*

27 This goes some way to explaining why there are relatively few new additions to the statute book in response to the Framework Decisions discussed above. Much of what these measures required, as was the case with the Decision on drug trafficking, had been law in the UK for decades.

28 Council Framework Decision 2008/841/JHA, on the fight against organised crime, OJ 2008, L300/42.

so argued for its inclusion prior to agreeing to the passage of the decision.[29] The Commission ultimately agreed to include conspiracy, but – along with France and Italy – made it quite clear in an annotation that it was uncomfortable with having to do so:

> The Commission considers that the Framework Decision on the fight against organised crime fails to achieve the objective sought by the Commission in relation to Joint Action 98/733/JHA on making it a criminal offence to participate in a criminal organisation in the Member States of the European Union, and in relation to the United Nations Convention Against Transnational Organised Crime . . . to which the Community has been a party since 29 April 2004. The Framework Decision does not achieve the minimum degree of approximation of acts of directing and participating in a criminal organisation on the basis of a single concept of such an organisation, as proposed by the Commission and as already in Framework Decision 2002/475/JHA on the fight against terrorism. . . . The Commission is therefore obliged to note that the Framework Decision does not achieve the objective approximation of legislation on the fight against organised crime as provided for in the Hague Programme.[30]

By negotiating away the aspect of the decision that would require a reform of a key element of criminal liability, it could be said that the UK, as well as displaying its preference for not fixing things that are not broken, anticipated and forestalled Eurosceptic concerns by being seen to be standing up to the Commission. This may be interpreted as a political strategy of 'seeming obstinacy': on the one hand, a resistance to active changes in national law, and on the other, when compliance can occur quite easily, to do so without fanfare or bother.

29 See further the discussion by Banach-Gutierrez and Harding, Chapter 4 in this collection.
30 Mitsilegas, V. (2009), *EU Criminal Law*, Oxford and Portland, OR: Hart Publishing, 97.

Index